T0366484

RACISM AND SEXUAL OPPRESSION
IN ANGLO-AMERICA

RACISM
AND
SEXUAL
OPPRESSION
IN
ANGLO-
AMERICA

A GENEALOGY

LADELLE MCWHORTER

Indiana University Press
Bloomington and Indianapolis

This book is a publication of

Indiana University Press
601 North Morton Street
Bloomington, IN 474043797 USA

http://iupress.indiana.edu

Telephone orders 800-842-6796
Fax orders   812-855-7931
Orders by e-mail iuporder@indiana.edu

The paper used in this publication meets the minimum requirements of American National Standard for Information Sciences—Permanence of Paper for Printed Library Materials, ANSI Z39.48–1984.

Manufactured in the United States of America

Library of Congress Cataloging-in-Publication Data

McWhorter, Ladelle, date–
    Racism and sexual oppression in Anglo-America : a genealogy / Ladelle McWhorter.
        p.   cm.
    Includes bibliographical references and index.
    ISBN 978-0-253-35296-5 (cloth : alk. paper) —
ISBN 978-0-253-22063-9 (paper : alk. paper)
    1. Minorities—Civil rights—United States—History. 2. African Americans—Civil rights—History. 3. Gays—Civil rights—United States—History. 4. Racism—United States—History. 5. Homophobia—United States—History. 6. Whites—United States—Attitudes—History. 7. Eugenics—United States—History. 8. Abnormalities, Human—Political aspects—United States—History. 9. United States—Race relations. 10. United States—Social conditions—1865–1918. I. Title.
    E184.A1M357   2009
    305.800973—dc22
                                        2008048274

1 2 3 4 5   14 13 12 11 10 09

CONTENTS

ACKNOWLEDGMENTS

The research for this book was made possible in part by four grants, three from the University of Richmond (faculty research grants in 1998 and 2006 and an enhanced sabbatical grant in 2006–2007) and one from the Center for Lesbian and Gay Studies at the City University of New York, the Heller-Bernard Fellowship, awarded in 2006. I am extremely grateful for this financial support.

I am also extremely grateful for the collegial generosity of Dr. Todd May, Lemon Professor of Philosophy at Clemson University, and Dr. Ellen T. Armour, Carpenter Professor of Feminist Theology at Vanderbilt University. Both read entire drafts and some redrafts of this manuscript at various stages of development and offered extensive and invaluable criticism. Without their help and friendship over the years, this would have been a very different and much inferior piece of work, and I would be a much inferior philosopher.

Dr. Eduardo Mendieta, Associate Professor of Philosophy at Stony Brook University, supplied me with many important references and copies of papers at crucial junctures, read and critiqued the entire manuscript near the final stage of writing, and offered much-needed (and much-appreciated) encouragement, as well as good advice. Dr. Davonya Havis, Associate Professor of Philosophy (then at Virginia Union University, now at Canisius College) read several chapters of the work in progress and engaged me in wide-ranging philosophical conversation over many lunches and cups of coffee throughout my sabbatical year, thus helping me stay sane and relatively focused in the midst of what has been at times an almost overwhelming project. Both have my deepest gratitude.

I would also like to thank my editors at Indiana University Press, Dee Mortensen and Laura MacLeod, without whom this book could not exist, and an anonymous reviewer for the press, who offered extensive and helpful criticism as well as encouragement and enthusiasm for this project.

Finally, I would like to thank Carol Anderson, who as my line dance teacher was merely footnoted in *Bodies and Pleasures* but now, as my life partner, deserves to be featured here prominently. Carol patiently read (or in some cases patiently listened to me read aloud) every draft of every chapter of this manuscript; offered advice and suggestions for intelligibility, clarity, and tone; and never doubted that this at times strange and unwieldy book would get finished and make sense, even on days when I very much did. More than anyone, she has shared with me the pain and joy of this work over the past eight years. Words can't express how grateful to her I am for that.

RACISM AND SEXUAL OPPRESSION
IN ANGLO-AMERICA

TWO GREAT DANGERS

In the early morning hours of Monday, October 12, 1998, a twenty-one-year-old university student named Matthew Shepard died in an intensive care unit in Fort Collins, Colorado, six days after having been kidnapped, pistol-whipped, bound to a fence post, and abandoned in the freezing darkness a few miles outside Laramie, Wyoming. His murderers, Russell Henderson and Aaron McKinney, both also twenty-one years old, had encountered Shepard on the evening of October 6 at the Fireside Bar, a popular student hangout in Laramie. The two locals struck up a conversation with Shepard, whom they knew to be gay, by posing as homosexual themselves. They eventually convinced him to follow them outside to McKinney's pickup truck so they could go someplace more private to continue their conversation. Once their intended victim agreed to the plan and the three drove away from the bar, however, McKinney revealed their real intention, which was to humiliate Shepard because of his homosexuality and in the process to beat and rob him. McKinney prefaced the assault by announcing, "Guess what? We're not gay. You're going to get jacked. It's gay awareness week."[1]

The beating began inside the truck while en route. Once outside of town, McKinney and Henderson pushed Shepard out of the truck at gunpoint and then tied him to a split rail fence. For some time they continued to kick him and beat him with the butt of a stolen .357 magnum. He suffered a total of eighteen blows to the head, some of them hard enough to crush portions of his skull, severe bruising from repeated kicks to the groin, and numerous blows to the limbs and body. At some point early on, McKinney considered forcing Shepard to strip naked, but in the end he only took his size seven black leather shoes, which police later found in the truck bed. The two men also took Shepard's wallet and spent the rest of that night enjoying their booty: twenty dollars cash.

Late the next afternoon a young cyclist discovered Shepard, still tied to the fence with arms outstretched like a scarecrow and covered with blood. He was alive, but barely breathing. The cyclist immediately contacted the county sheriff's office, and a deputy was dispatched to the scene. Because of Shepard's unusually small stature—five-foot-two, 105 pounds—the sheriff's deputy at first reported that she was giving emergency first aid to a critically injured thirteen-year-old boy. Only later did authorities identify Shepard as an adult. His head and face were so disfigured that family members summoned to the hospital to confirm his identity could hardly recognize him.

Like most queer Americans and many non-queer ones as well, I followed the grim news regarding Shepard's condition and prognosis closely, day by day, for nearly a week. Every few hours, Rulon Stacey, head of Poudre Valley Health Systems, issued updates to the press. Stacey reported that because of severe damage to the brain stem, which controls heartbeat and breathing among other vital functions, doctors were unable to regulate Shepard's body temperature, which fluctuated from 98 to 106 degrees. His condition deteriorated steadily. It was clear to me by the final day that, given the extent of his injuries, his death was a blessing, if anything can be said to be a blessing in the aftermath of such outrageous cruelty.

I was on sabbatical that October, holed up alone in a little farmhouse in the Appalachian Mountains fifteen miles east of State College, Pennsylvania, polishing a manuscript on the work of Michel Foucault to be published the following year and wondering what I should write about next. My only interaction with other human beings through that long, sad autumn day was via email, but I was attached to the Penn State University LGBT listserv, so there was a *lot* of email. Most of the postings were from gay undergraduates expressing a newfound fear of walking alone at night or striking up a conversation with a stranger. Although I could not tell from their user names, I guessed that those who seemed most profoundly shaken were male, white, and very young. The rest of us had and have such fears, of course, but it didn't take Shepard's murder to instill them in us.

My own feelings on that day were just a grim heaviness, sorrow for a young man and a family and circle of friends whom I had never met, and an old familiar anger that manifested itself mainly in the repeated phrase, "How many times? How many times does this have to happen?" After all, what was done to Matthew Shepard, gruesome as it was, was nothing especially remarkable. It was certainly not the first time somebody had killed a queer, and it would not by any stretch of the imagination be the last.[2]

In fact, the Anti-Violence Project of New York estimates that on average about fifty Americans are murdered every year because their assailants believe they are homosexual or judge their behavior or appearance to be in violation of gender norms. About 60 percent of those murders are characterized by what the AVP terms "forensic overkill," meaning brutality far beyond what was necessary to end the victim's life (Brandt 1999, 4). Excessive brutality is a hallmark of hate crimes; such crimes are not just perpetrated against particular individuals the attackers want dead but against an entire group of people they want eradicated. If the AVP's estimate is even close to accurate, it is likely that by mid-life every nonheterosexual person has heard about scores, if not hundreds, of fatal and near-fatal attacks, many of which involved severe brutality and torture.[3] As far as I could see, the only remarkable aspect of the Shepard case was the fact that the media publicized it so energetically.

But I had little hope that media involvement, even if it persisted, would be sufficient to convince the public that assaults on and threats against homosexuals are important enough to do something about. First, the very fact that the Shepard murder got so much attention made it seem that deadly violence against gay men, lesbians, and transgendered people is extremely rare in our society. As Jean Baudrillard famously observed about Watergate, scandals often work to conceal the scandalous nature of everyday life. Singling out the Shepard murder for exclusive coverage actually worked to obscure the dozens of similar murders and thousands of nonlethal assaults against queer people in the United States in the same year. And with those other acts of violence eclipsed, it could be easy for many people to decide that there really is no problem, no general climate of homophobia, no reason for queer people to be afraid or to demand civic protection and support. And second, even before Shepard was dead, some people were insisting that Shepard himself, not his attackers and not our homophobic society, was responsible for his injuries. According to Bill McKinney and Kristin Price (Aaron McKinney's father and girlfriend), McKinney and Henderson crushed Shepard's skull and genitals and left him for dead only because he made a pass at one of them, not because they harbored any hatred toward homosexuals. Other commentators stopped short of accusing Shepard of sexual predation but did maintain that through carelessness and indiscretion he was responsible for his fate.[4] "He shouldn't have been so open about his sexuality. He shouldn't have been willing to leave a bar with strangers. He shouldn't have touched Aaron McKinney. People who do things like that deserve what they get." How many times do we have to hear people blame the victims of murder, queer-bashing, or rape? "She was asking for it." "He brought it on himself." "What do you expect?"

What indeed?

In the thirty-six hours or so following Shepard's death, a few Penn State students managed to put together plans for a candlelight vigil and announce the particulars on the listserv. That Tuesday evening, October 13, I got myself together, drove into town in the spitting rain, parked my car on Beaver Avenue, and walked a couple of blocks to the designated meeting place on West College. By 7:30 a small group had gathered at the Allen Street bus stop outside the old university gate. There were about thirty people in all. Most of them, like most of the population of State College, Pennsylvania, were white and very young. To my eye they all looked pale, scared, and vulnerable. One very enterprising young woman somehow got the crowd's attention and tried to say a few words appropriate to the occasion, but it was hard to hear her over the roar of buses and the blare of car horns. There was no microphone. Then a young man spoke, passionately but equally inaudibly. The rain came down a little harder. I looked around at those assembled. It was a miserable gathering, pathetic, hardly a show of community and strength in the face of adversity. Very soon people ran out of things to say or got tired of shouting over the traffic. The young woman who had opened the proceedings felt the need for some sort of closure, so she sang a show tune that was meant to be uplifting; but despite her beautiful voice, it didn't seem to do the job. The group fell silent.

Then somebody said, "Sing 'We Shall Overcome.'"

"I don't know the words," she said. A rippled murmur spread through the crowd. "Does anybody know the words to 'We Shall Overcome'? Can somebody start it?"

I was a bit taken aback; I don't remember a time *before* I knew the words to "We Shall Overcome." Its lyrics and melody were impressed upon my infant brain long before I could read, right along with "Jesus Loves Me" and "Rock-a-Bye Baby." In my childhood in the 1960s the rolling tones of "We Shall Overcome" were practically one with the atmosphere. During those few long moments standing there on West College Avenue in the relentless rain, the words of that song ran like rushing water through my head: "We'll walk hand in hand. . . . We are not afraid." They came to me with the clarity and beauty and power of Mahalia Jackson's voice, reverberating across thirty-five years of my life. I looked at two round-faced lesbians clasping hands in front of me, a pale tint of fear on their nineteen-year-old cheeks. Those words in that context, in the shadow of Matthew Shepard's horrific murder, meant as much to me as they ever had in any other place at any other time. I suddenly felt very old. Was it possible that nobody in that gathering besides me knew that song?

I don't have a good voice, but I can carry a tune, especially when I have license to choose my own key. I could have started the song, and then maybe through their unified voices, for just a few minutes, that frightened, wet, dejected little knot of people would have become something like a community united and supporting each other in a time of crisis. It is, after all, a very powerful song.

I could have. But I didn't. The moment passed. The gathering disintegrated without closure. Each one of us wandered away, carrying with us, not a sense that despite the violence and injustice all around us life can go on and love and respect do still exist—which is, I suppose what the candlelight shining in the darkness at such vigils is intended to instill in us—but rather with that sense of futility and hopelessness that drizzle and senseless death inspire.

As I drove through the profound rural darkness back to the solitude of my rented farmhouse with tears running down my cheeks, I asked myself: Why did I not do it? Why did I not do the one thing that might have salvaged that pitiful event? It wasn't modesty. In a crowd of strangers who would never see me again, I certainly wasn't too shy. But I could not bring myself to do it. I could not because, regardless of all the similarities between the death of Matthew Shepard and the death of, say, Emmett Till, I could not bring myself to take a song that to me meant hope in the face of white racism and use it to express hope in the face of heterosexist violence. I could not assimilate the two—the two forms of oppression, the two resistance movements, the two hopes. Trying to do so felt dangerous and wrong.

There were similarities, though, not only in the oppressions and the movements but even some very striking similarities in those two horrific murders, in spite of the differences that forty-three years inevitably make in human life in general and the obviously important difference in the race of the two victims. In the years since I stood on that street corner and did not sing, I have pondered those similarities at some length.

I don't remember the Till murder, which happened a few years before I was born. But contemporary accounts, like the news stories about Matthew Shepard, are vivid. In August of 1955, fourteen-year-old Emmett Louis Till, known to his family as Bobo, traveled from his home in Chicago down to the Mississippi Delta to spend some time with his uncle and aunt, Mose and Elizabeth Wright, and his country cousins. Four days after his arrival, on Wednesday evening, August 24, Till and several of his teenaged relatives drove into Money, Mississippi, and joined about a dozen other black teenagers who were chatting and playing checkers on the porch of the white-owned general store.[5] By most accounts, young Till was eager to impress his cousins and their friends. He bragged that back home he had a white girlfriend, a classmate whose picture he showed the other boys. They were skeptical. According to Till's cousin Curtis Jones, "one of the local boys" dared Till to prove himself: "Hey, there's a white girl in that store there. I bet you won't go in there and talk to her."[6] With his adolescent peers looking on, Till took the dare. He went inside the store where Carolyn Bryant, the twenty-one-year-old wife of the absent store owner Roy Bryant, was minding the counter.

Exactly what happened inside the store is a matter of dispute. According to Carolyn Bryant in her testimony at her husband's trial, Till asked for two pennies' worth of bubble gum. Then, when she handed it to him, he took her hand, squeezed it, and asked her for a date. She jerked away and tried to exit between the two front counters, but Till stepped forward and addressed her a second time.[7]

It is likely that Till was not as fresh as Bryant depicted him in court, but he did say or do something that upset her enough to cause her to leave the cash register unattended and head for a pistol she knew was concealed outside in her sister-in-law's car. Realizing that things had gone much too far, one of Till's cousins grabbed him and ushered him quickly toward the pickup truck. As Bryant fumbled with the pistol, Till, apparently still intent on impressing his young peers and insensitive to the danger he was placing all of them in, let out his now-famous wolf whistle, and the teens drove out of town.

Three nights later, Roy Bryant and his half brother J. W. "Big" Milam drove to the Wright home and demanded that Mose Wright relinquish his nephew. Mrs. Wright offered the men money to leave the boy alone, but they refused it and told her to go back to bed. They roused Till and ordered him to get dressed. When the boy failed to address Milam as "sir," Milam threatened to shoot him. In the darkness it was not clear to the occupants of the house exactly how many people were outside, but Mose Wright testified in court that one other man, probably "a colored man," was on the porch and that he heard a lighter voice, possibly a woman's voice, outside in the yard just before Bryant and Milam threw Till in the back of their pickup truck and drove away.[8]

Wright said later that he did not believe the men planned to kill Till, just discipline him; and indeed, after their trial was over Bryant and Milam told reporter William Bradford Huie that their original intention was only to scare the boy.[9] Milam, as an overseer on his brother's farm, prided himself on his ability to supervise and command the obedience of black men. It seems likely that he believed he could break Till and make the city boy behave like the field hands that answered to him at the farm.[10]

Milam and Bryant described to Huie how their plans changed through the course of the night. At first they drove around looking for a particular bluff that Milam knew. Once there, they intended to whip Till with Milam's army-issue .45 caliber pistol and then make him believe they were going to throw him in the river. In the moonless night, however, they couldn't find the place. Finally, so they told Huie, they gave up, drove back to Milam's house, and pistol-whipped Till in the tool shed.[11] The hundred-and-sixty-pound Till didn't scare easily, however. Milam said the boy bragged to him and Bryant about his sexual exploits with white women and showed them the picture of his white girlfriend. At that point they decided to kill him. They put him back in the bed of Milam's truck, picked up an old gin fan behind their brother's store in Itta Bena, and headed for the river. Around daybreak on Sunday, August 28, they stopped at the banks of the Tallahatchie and ordered Till to unload the fan and take off all his clothes. Milam asked him again whether he thought he was as good as a white man and whether he really had had sexual encounters with white women. Naked and at gunpoint, the boy didn't flinch and replied to both questions in the affirmative, whereupon Milam shot him through the head. He and Bryant then barb-wired Till's lifeless body to the gin fan and threw it into the Tallahatchie. Huie quotes Milam: "I didn't intend to kill the nigger when we went and got him—just whip him and chase him back up there [to Chicago]. But what the hell! He showed me the white gal's picture! Bragged o' what he'd done to her! I counted pictures o' three white gals in his pocketbook before I burned it. What else could I do? No use lettin' him get no bigger!"

What really happened between the time when Milam and Bryant abducted Till from the Wright home and when they threw his body in the Tallahatchie is still very much in dispute. A great deal of evidence suggests that the beating occurred not in Milam's tool shed but in his brother Leslie's barn in Sunflower County. If Till actually died at the barn, the trial should have been held in Sunflower County, which might have made a difference in the outcome. There is good reason to believe that law enforcement officials in Tallahatchie County manipulated the trial and suppressed evidence, actions they might not have had the power to take elsewhere but that may have been necessary to secure the not-guilty verdict and perhaps also to protect accomplices. So there is some reason to think that, in order to shield those who had obstructed justice on their behalf, Milam and Bryant lied to Huie about where the murder occurred. However, it is also possible that even if Till was tortured in Sunflower County he did not die there. Witnesses at Leslie Milam's farm said they saw a body removed from the barn that morning and placed in Milam's pickup. A tarp was thrown over the body. But according to at least one witness, there was movement under the tarp.[12] It is conceivable, then, that even though Milam and Bryant omitted the beating in the Sunflower County barn from their story to Huie, they still told the truth about where the fatal bullet was fired. It is even possible that Till was conscious enough to respond to Milam's questions at that point and that, knowing he was about to die, he refused to give Bryant and Milam the satisfaction they would have obtained if he had debased himself and denied his manhood.

Although some of the facts are in dispute, there are numerous echoes of the Till killing in Matthew Shepard's murder. In both cases two young men took it upon themselves to teach another young man a lesson; their apparent intent was to discipline and punish, to terrorize, and thereby to force submission. Both pairs of men employed the same means—late night abduction and pistol-whipping. Both victims were from out of town, arguably unfamiliar with the finer points of local mores, whereas the assailants were natives to the region where the murders occurred. Both cases received unprecedented media attention. Both victims' mothers actively promoted public awareness of the pervasive bigotry and systematic injustice of which their sons' brutal murders were emblematic. But the greatest similarity is that both Matthew Shepard and Emmett Till refused to hide or apologize for their sexuality; on the contrary, they affirmed and asserted it publicly. How important are these parallels? What do they indicate?

"It's not the same; it's not the same," a Binghamton University graduate student had said repeatedly to me and a white friend over lunch five years before Matthew Shepard was killed. In the aftermath of the 1993 March on Washington, we were discussing the fact that gay and lesbian activists often draw on the symbols and rhetoric of the black civil rights movement of the 1950s and 1960s. The Binghamton student was African American and gay, and he was insistent that white gay and lesbian people, like my friend and me, must be ever mindful of the differences between antiblack racism and heterosexism. Even when there are parallels, he said, the differences are still enormous, and it is a mistake as well as an insult to all African Americans ever to forget them. I took his point very seriously. Even though I have since learned that "We Shall Overcome" was sung by American labor unionists of all races long before the Montgomery Bus Boycott or the Greensboro lunch counter sit-ins, I still take his point very seriously. In part because of that conversation in the spring of 1993, I didn't sing on that autumn evening in 1998.

I didn't sing because I believed it was important for Matthew Shepard to remain Matthew Shepard and Emmett Till to remain Emmett Till, two separate individuals whose living and dying are different events in human history. I believed it was important to remember the differences between black and queer struggles, subcultures, and experiences of oppression.[13] I believed it was important to insist on the details that distinguish the networks of power that shape the histories of those struggles, subcultures, and oppressions. I still believe those things.

But I wanted to sing that night. I wanted to sing that song. I wanted to feel the power of the kind of solidarity and hope that song can evoke and to experience its infusion into that frightened and beleaguered little group. Did I do the right thing in refusing the temptation to call upon the memory and power of African American movements for justice and freedom in an effort to further the rights and interests, or at least comfort the fearful souls of nonheterosexual people? Years have passed. I'm still not sure.

I do know that laxity about differences between social movements, histories, and bigotries is dangerous. Significant details get erased. Genealogies get distorted, their power to enable resistance gets diminished, and their resources for creative change get locked away. When we conflate all gestures of resistance, when all of history gets reduced to a tale of all us good guys versus all them bad guys, everybody loses, because we all lose ourselves. The differences are what we have to hold onto; the differences are the source of possibility and strength. Like my lunch companion from Binghamton that afternoon so many years ago, we must insist on these all-important differences.

We—we philosophers and theorists, and our students and readers —can and often do talk about all this in the abstract. We cite great thinkers like Luce Irigaray or Gilles Deleuze or Jacques Derrida. But in countless moments like that one at the bus stop on West College Avenue in 1998, a person acts this way or that way. And those countless little acts shape the world. I made a world-shaping decision that night. Did I make the right one? What should I have done? What should one do?

My dilemma was, and is, this: There are not one but two great dangers. On the one hand there is the danger of identification, homogenization, and consequent erasure. By seeing all oppressions as the same, we can lose sight of the particular reality of our own situation as well as alienate potential allies for whom the differences are crucial. It was at least in part my acute awareness of this danger that stopped me from singing that night. But there is an other hand: There is also the danger of isolation, impotence, and collapse. If we maintain radical distinctions between political events, we may fail to see important overarching patterns and as a result miss opportunities to form and consolidate alliances that might counter the networks of power that oppress so many of us. We can speak of this philosophically as a question of the value of Sameness versus the value of Difference. Metaphorically, we can speak of the twin dangers of Scylla or Charybdis. But when it comes down to action, *ethically and politically,* how do we negotiate this passage?

For longer than I can remember, I have believed the greater danger was Sameness, the reduction of ultimately dissimilar things, people, and histories to one; that is probably why I am a poststructuralist thinker rather than a Hegelian dialectician or a Platonist. Not only have I witnessed the erasure of significant concerns when theorists and activists assimilated heterogeneous events and individuals to one analysis and program (for example, the virtual erasure of hetero-sexism and women's oppression in much Marxist analysis of class struggle), but I have also been impressed with the power of analyses that point out historical differences (for example, Michel Foucault's genealogy of sexuality) and thus offer renewed hope that the future, too, can be different from the present state of things.

But there is that other danger. And it is that other danger that caused and still causes me to question my decision not to sing on that October night. It is that other danger that has pressed me to explore the similarities between racist and heterosexist violence over the last several years, to see whether, despite all the differences in experience and effect, it might not be the case that somehow these things are joined together, part of the same matrix of power, employing the same means, serving the same aims, shaping the same lives. It is that other danger and that other set of possibilities that have moved me to write this book, despite the risks such an enquiry inevitably runs.

When I began this work in 1998, I believed that I was going to write a book about the ways in which racism and racist violence in the United States have influenced the development of sexuality, taking sexuality to be a *dispositif,* as Michel Foucault maintains in his *History of Sexuality, Volume 1* (that is, taking sexuality to be a network of power and knowledge that generates sexual identities and sexual subjects). I imagined that I would offer a description of race as a similar sort of *dispositif* or network of power and knowledge, one that produces racial identities and racial subjects, and that I would show how these two analogous networks of power intersect, and in many ways reinforce and at some specifiable times determine, each other's configurations and functions. I thought I would take the tools Foucault develops in his genealogical research and apply them to an area he did not explore in any depth. I did not want to write another book about Foucault but to write a Foucaultian analysis, a genealogy of race to place alongside his (and my own) genealogies of sexual normalization.

Looking back at that set of ambitions and hopes, I am embarrassed at how little I actually knew in 1998. Although I certainly was aware of Foucault's scattered comments about race in the fifth part of *The History of Sexuality*, I was unfamiliar with his far more systematic and extended investigation of race in his 1976 lectures at the Collège de France. I was utterly ignorant of vast reaches of U.S. and British colonial history that are crucial for understanding anything about race in this society in the present day. And I knew virtually nothing about the international eugenics movement, let alone its roots in the United States—despite the fact that I had lived and worked for six years in Kirksville, Missouri, where hospital and university buildings bear the family name of Harry Laughlin, director of the U.S. Eugenic Records Office from 1914 to 1939, and where Laughlin's papers are housed.[14] As I did the genealogical work on race and racism that informs chapters 2 through 6 of this volume, my vision of what this book would be underwent extensive and for a while virtually perpetual transformation.

The only aspect of the project that did not change throughout those years was my conviction that racism in twentieth-century Anglo-America had to be understood in light of Foucault's work on normalization. The white race, I knew, was and is viewed by most people—white or not and consciously or not—as the normal race, and all other races were and are viewed as deviant with respect to it. Racism plays out, then, as a crusade against deviance, against the threat posed by abnormality or pathology. And at times in U.S. history—particularly in the last third of the twentieth century and the first decade of the twenty-first—the institutions that further that crusade have been able to persist in their allegedly healthful pursuits without even avowing that their targets are races. I believed that if I could show that this was so, then I should also be able to show how heterosexism connects with racism. After all, the *dispositif de sexualité* is heteronormative. Like racism, heterosexism plays out as a crusade against deviance, against the threat posed by abnormality or pathology. So, I reasoned, two such similarly structured systems of normalization, coexisting in time and space, must inevitably share similar techniques for the production of normalized subjectivities and disciplined bodies. It was impossible that the two systems would *not* coalesce at important points. It was a matter of finding those points and articulating them.

I had Foucault's genealogy of sexuality before me, and I had explored it in depth in numerous seminars and articles and in *Bodies and Pleasures,* my 1999 book. If the development of race followed a trajectory similar to the one Foucault traces for sexuality in *The History of Sexuality, Volume 1,* I thought, it must have undergone a major transformation and expansion in the late nineteenth century with the emergence of what Foucault there calls "biopower," the confluence of disciplinary normalization and population management in vast networks of production and social control. Biopower transcends and to some extent negates sovereign power (power as traditionally conceived) and the discourses that rely and elaborate upon it. Its aim is to produce and intensify and direct vital forces rather than to limit and coerce what already exists. It was easy to see that race would be a useful tool in biopolitical practices, a tool for dividing and regulating populations and for frightening (or enticing) individuals into disciplinary conformity. But there was an important difference between race and sexuality with regard to the emergence of biopower: Foucault had shown (to my satisfaction at least) that sexuality—as a concept, a basis for personal identity, a region of scientific investigation—simply did not exist much prior to the nineteenth century. But clearly, race did. In the United States before the end of the eighteenth century and even earlier in the Anglo-American colonies, there were white people and black people and red and even a few yellow people, people who understood themselves and others to be members of races and to be essentially different from one another because of their racial identities. Race, unlike sexuality, could not have been an invention of biopower, even if it had been appropriated and reshaped in the nineteenth century to become biopower's tool.

So what *was* race, historically speaking? Where had it come from? How did it become available for biopolitical transformation and use? And when this appropriation and reshaping occurred, what relationships were created between race and sexuality? How did those relationships evolve as the biopolitical structures, institutions, and discourses that fostered and connected them evolved? I began my inquiry with the nineteenth century, but I soon found I had to go back further. How far back only became apparent to me when I read Foucault's 1976 lectures, *"Society Must Be Defended,"* where he traces what he calls "race war discourse" back to the Puritans in early seventeenth-century England.

Although I was interested in racism and heterosexism in the United States, I found Foucault's study of race war discourse and racism in Europe extremely suggestive. Race first meant lineage or tradition, Foucault notes, not physical appearance. But then, somehow, it had changed to become a biological phenomenon. I believed that by tracing how that change in meaning had occurred I might discover the mechanisms I was looking for and the ways in which sexuality and race had become linked and had begun to operate in similar, if not in exactly the same, ways. The material I gathered along these lines forms the substance of chapters 2 and 3 and then in turn the basis for chapter 4, where I investigate nineteenth- and early twentieth-century discourses of sexual predation, and for chapter 5, where I examine eugenics, the effort to improve the human race through selective breeding and the scientific management of sexualized populations. That work led me to the material that forms chapter 6, where I sketch out how the U.S. eugenics movement reformed itself in the aftermath of Nazism to become the pro-family movement, a movement that is still in evidence today and very much at the forefront of antifeminist and antigay politics, although it seldom avows its eugenic history and racial investments.

Through this process I came to see that my initial assumptions were not quite on the mark. Race was not merely analogous to sexuality as a *dispositif;* in fact, the two are utterly inseparable. It is simply impossible to understand racism in the United States without some understanding of how sexuality functions to normalize individuals and regulate populations. It is impossible to understand sexism or heterosexism in the United States without some understanding of how race functions to humanize and dehumanize individuals and to produce and reproduce populations. But race and sexuality are not merely mutually influential. They are historically codependent and mutually determinative. Approaching them separately therefore insures that we will miss their most important features.[15] Yet that is just what most people do—even some of the most sophisticated and thoughtful of theorists. Most feminists don't see racism as a crucial aspect of sexism (even though they may well believe racism is wrong and should be opposed[16]); likewise, most gay men, lesbians, and many transgender activists don't see racism as a crucial aspect of heterosexism and gender oppression; and most people of color, as well as most white antiracists, don't see sexism or heterosexism as crucial aspects of racism.[17] The result is that even the most dedicated, persistent, and well-intentioned activists not only fail to bring about the changes they seek but in many instances actually help perpetuate the very oppression and injustice they devote themselves to fighting.

I must make it clear that am *not* asserting that sex and race and sexual orientation "intersect," a claim that feminist theorists have been making for several years now. The metaphor of intersection does not begin to capture the complexity of the power relations brought to light here. Intersectional analyses tend to focus analytic attention primarily on identities rather than on institutions, discourses, and disciplinary regimes; but even when they do venture beyond accounts of identity construction, they still implicitly assume that racism, sexism, and heterosexism could and do operate sometimes in isolation from one another. My contention here is that in the twentieth century they do not.

Nor am I making the sweeping metaphysical assertion that we cannot end one form of injustice or oppression without ending them all. This is not a book about injustice or oppression in general; it is a book about racism and heterosexism in the United States. My claims are therefore historically specific: First, race and sexuality are essential organizing forces within specifiable, historically constituted networks of power, networks to which Foucault attached the name *biopower*; biopower would be impossible without them. Second, just as biopower requires race and sexuality, race and sexuality require biopower. They could not function apart from it, nor could they function apart from each other. And third, we will never understand how either race or sexuality operates, much less organize successfully to end the oppressive conditions and relationships that they underwrite, unless we examine them together.

As my project evolved through eight years of research, this book's purpose came to be to show what the world looks like when our customary assumptions of separateness are left aside, and racism, sexism, and heterosexism are approached and analyzed simultaneously. The picture that emerges is startling in both its familiarity and its lack thereof. I offer it in the hope that a different way of seeing might afford different ways of resisting, critiquing, and challenging the oppressions and injustices that plague us.

ONE

RACISM, RACE, RACE WAR

IN SEARCH OF
CONCEPTUAL CLARITY

The question I found myself confronting so painfully that October night and pondering so long after—the question of whether I (or for that matter anybody) should ever draw on the practical, symbolic, rhetorical, emotional, and moral resources of the black civil rights movement in efforts to foster queer community, protest anti-queer violence and discrimination, and demand respect for the rights and sensibilities of nonheterosexual and gender-transgressive people—was a relatively new one in the late 1990s. Not many years before, most gay men and lesbians had understood their movements as a more or less natural extension of the civil rights movements of the mid-twentieth century, and veterans of the black civil rights movement seldom challenged that belief.

In the 1980s a number of prominent African American leaders embraced gay rights as a subset of civil rights and began to speak out on behalf of gay men and lesbians. These leaders included Harold Washington in Chicago, David Dinkins in New York City, Marion Barry in Washington, D.C., Tom Bradley in Los Angeles, and, in Atlanta, Maynard Jackson, Andrew Young, and John Lewis. At the same time, there were a number of gay and lesbian African American activists—Mel Boozer, Gil Gerald, A. Billy Jones, Angela Bowen, Barbara Smith, and many others—who worked hard to build and nurture cooperation between the gay movement (as it was then called) and the black civil rights movement. In 1983, when Washington congressional delegate Walter Fauntroy declared gay rights about as important as "penguin rights" and refused to include gay issues in plans for the commemoration of the twentieth anniversary of the 1963 March on Washington, these leaders and others, including Coretta Scott King and Jesse Jackson, were quick to denounce his antigay stance and offer strong support for gay rights. Mrs. King called for an amendment of the 1964 Civil Rights Act to include sexual orientation. Rev. Jesse Jackson not only included gays and lesbians in his Rainbow Coalition but was outspoken in support of gay rights throughout his 1988 presidential campaign.[1]

Inside gay and lesbian communities and organizations, the relationship between whites and people of color was not necessarily so warm or respectful. Most white gay men and lesbians were not nearly as committed to ending racism as activists of color, straight and gay, were committed to ending heterosexism; in fact, some whites were quite entrenched in their racist animosity even toward fellow gay men and lesbians. When Urvashi Vaid became the first person of color ever to head a mainstream gay and lesbian organization—the Washington-based National Gay and Lesbian Task Force—in 1989, she faced tremendous obstacles, including that "simply pointing out the racial dynamics of a situation" provoked denunciations from white lesbians and gay men. One white male donor, who objected to her as both a radical and a woman, referred to her as "practically a nigger" (Vaid 1995, 274). Nevertheless, Vaid and others continued to press the movement to deal with its racism (as well as its sexism; it should be remembered that including lesbians in mainstream gay organizations had been controversial into the 1980s). Despite opposition from members who saw race as a "nongay issue," NGLTF lobbied for the Civil Rights Restoration Act of 1991 (Vaid 1995, 283), and it and other mainstream gay and lesbian organizations insisted that the steering committee for the 1993 March on Washington be 50 percent people of color and that all delegations be gender-balanced (Vaid 1995, 278). Meanwhile, with case loads changing in demographic composition, many gay-run AIDS organizations, such as Gay Men's Health Crisis, had to educate their staffs, dismantle racist assumptions, and refocus their efforts to serve a clientele that was no longer almost exclusively white and male (Vaid 1995, 298). Inside the gay movement there were serious tensions, but things were changing . . . slowly.[2]

Outside the movement through the 1980s and into the 1990s, the whites most often voicing opinions on homosexuality were members of the religious right, while white Americans in general seemed to be becoming more conservative on social issues. White politicians, noting that the grassroots influence and potential campaign contributions of the radical right far outweighed what gay and lesbian activists could muster, either courted the right openly or simply avoided such issues altogether. Judging by public discourse through the early 1990s, then, it seemed that whites were much more antigay than were people of color, particularly African Americans. In February of 1993 a *New York Times*/CBS News poll found that 53 percent of blacks but only 37 percent of whites felt that "homosexuality should be considered an acceptable lifestyle." In April of 1993, a Gallup Poll found that 65 percent of whites said gays should stay closeted, while only 29 percent of blacks did; 61 percent of blacks favored lifting the ban on gays in the military, compared with only 42 percent of whites; and 85 percent of blacks thought gays should have equal job opportunities and protections, while only 79 percent of whites thought so.[3] Thus the widespread perception that people of color—or at least African Americans—were more liberal than whites was founded on empirical as well as anecdotal evidence. White gay men and lesbians might not be fighting racism in huge numbers, but straight African Americans seemed like solid allies in the fight against heterosexism. In such a climate, erroneous as the assumptions that generated it may have been, white gay men and lesbians didn't hesitate to draw on the strategies, symbols, and rhetoric of the black civil rights movement both for inspiration and for organizing techniques. The Cracker Barrel protests are a case in point.

Nonviolent Queer Disobedience

In January of 1991, William Bridges, a vice president with Cracker Barrel Old Country Stores (a Tennessee-based chain of, at that time, ninety-eight "family restaurants" across the southeastern United States) issued a memorandum stating that the corporation would no longer hire or retain people "whose sexual preferences fail to demonstrate normal heterosexual values which have been the foundation of families in our society" (Kilborn 1992). Local store managers were instructed to fire all homosexual employees, effective immediately. Many did so. The company never divulged the total number of people it fired in ensuing weeks, but at least eleven made their terminations public. The first was George Wylie Petty, a waiter at a Tifton, Georgia, Cracker Barrel store. Petty's dismissal made the local news, but apparently he did not think the job—which paid only $2.13 per hour plus tips (Poole 1999)—was worth fighting to keep. He relocated to Florida "partly out of fear of harassment" (Morris 1991). Others with less mobility and more to lose stayed to fight the company's policy and expose its executives' bigotry. Several eventually described their experiences to a reporter for the *New York Times:*

> Samuel E. Hare, 25, had worked his way up at an outlet in Charlotte, N.C., to the point where he was training new workers and was in line for promotion to management. "I went in to look at my schedule for the next week," he said, "and I wasn't on it. I went in to see the general manager. 'Obviously there's a mistake,' he said. He said, 'Come in tomorrow, we'll put you on.' I went in and the district manager was there. They took me into an office. The general manager said, 'We have a new policy. Cracker Barrel no longer employs homosexuals. Are you gay?' I said yes. I never deny being gay. That's like denying yourself. He said, 'If you're gay, you're fired.' I asked for a pink slip with a reason. I've never gotten one."
>
> George Frisbee, 26, was training new workers as well, at a Cracker Barrel in Tallahassee, Fla. He said he had an argument with a waitress about his homosexuality. "She said I was going to burn in hell," he said. "I said, 'I don't have to listen to this.'" On his next day off, Mr. Frisbee said, the general manager asked him to come in. The manager and another manager were waiting in the parking lot. "One of them said, 'It has recently come to my attention that you are a homosexual, and since it is against our policy to hire them, we're going to have to terminate you,'" Mr. Frisbee said, adding: "There's absolutely no legal recourse. What they did is perfectly legal." (Kilborn 1992)

Frisbee was correct; there was and is no law at the federal level (and no state law in most states) that prohibits job discrimination on the basis of sexual orientation.

With no grounds to fight for their jobs in court, the only avenue open to this group of former employees was to bring direct pressure to bear on the company either through moral suasion or by compromising its ability to do business. Cheryl Summerville, fired after nearly four years from her position as cook at a restaurant in Douglasville, Georgia, took the issue to Queer Nation-Atlanta, which began pressing company officials for a meeting and demanding reinstatement and restitution for the ex-employees.[4]

In the public eye and under some pressure from its stockholders,[5] Cracker Barrel rescinded its policy on February 22, less than two months after it was issued, but no restitution was offered and officials stated that "in the future, we will deal with any disruption in our units . . . on a store-by-store basis" (Wagner 1991). Aggrieved employees and activists did not view that apparent concession as a victory. On the contrary, Queer Nation-Atlanta co-chair Lynn Cothren declared, "What that last sentence basically says is they're going to now discriminate against gays and lesbians on a store-by-store basis instead of on a corporate level. This new policy is just as much of an insult" (Wagner 1991). Rebuffed in its plea for a face-to-face meeting with company officials, Queer Nation began increasing its pressure on Cracker Barrel with a series of store pickets and sit-ins designed to bring public attention to the company's conduct and set the stage for a boycott that would lower profits and scare investors.[6] Over the course of the next year, more than a dozen protests were held in the Atlanta area alone, resulting in at least twenty-eight arrests, including Summerville, Cothren, and DeKalb County Commissioner Jacqueline Scott (Shepard 1992a). Queer Nation didn't exactly fill the jails as Martin Luther King and his followers had often managed to do, but with their nonviolent direct action approach, which was quite familiar and recognizable to Atlanta residents, they did manage to get media attention and sway public opinion.

Tactics were not the only thing Queer Nation appropriated from King's Southern Christian Leadership Conference, however. In case the similarities between the black civil rights movement and the Cracker Barrel protests were lost on some of their media audience, Queer Nation imported a few symbols and even made some direct comparisons. At a protest in Lithonia, Georgia, Queer Nation-Atlanta was joined by members of the National Organization for Women, two state representatives, and U.S. Representative Barney Frank (Democrat, Massachusetts). A veteran of the black civil rights movement, Frank was one of about a thousand white college students recruited and trained by the Student Nonviolent Coordinating Committee to work in Mississippi during "Freedom Summer," 1964

(McAdam 1988, 216). He was in Atlanta that Sunday because the next day he would serve as co-marshal of the city's annual Martin Luther King Day parade. His presence at the Cracker Barrel protest linked it symbolically but solidly with the movement that he would be honored the next day for risking his life to serve twenty-seven years before. State representative Nan Orrock (Democrat-Atlanta) made the link explicit in her speech to the crowd of 450 when she referred to Cheryl Summerville, the former cook who refused to accept Cracker Barrel's antigay employment policy, as "the Rosa Parks of this movement" (Shepard 1992b).

The Cracker Barrel protest movement's similarities to the boycotts and sit-ins of the 1950s and 60s was not merely superficial, a matter of symbol and rhetoric only. As was duly noted in the *Atlanta Journal and Constitution* at the time, Queer Nation-Atlanta co-chair Lynn Cothren was "an employee of the [Martin Luther] King Center [for Nonviolent Social Change] . . . trained in non-violent civil disobedience tactics" (Morris 1991). Hired in 1982, Cothren by that time had been working for the King Center for nearly ten years. Six years later, recalling the protests in an interview with the *Washington Blade,* Cothren emphasized Coretta Scott King's and the King Center's firm support for Queer Nation's efforts and acknowledged that "the campaign was organized to follow Dr. King's teachings on nonviolent social change" (K. Wright 1997, 30). The parallels were conscious, deliberate, and philosophically and historically informed.

Although the protests started in Atlanta under Cothren's and Queer Nation-Atlanta's leadership, they quickly spread across the eastern half of the country. At least three sit-ins sponsored by Queer Nation-St. Louis were held at a Cracker Barrel in Caseyville, Illinois, where at least five people were arrested and charged with criminal trespass, lewdness (because of graphic designs on their t-shirts), and disorderly conduct (shouting at employees to change the store's policy). There were similar protests in Florida, South Carolina, Tennessee, Michigan, and Virginia.[7] In addition to staging pickets, store sit-ins, and boycotts, Queer Nation members began buying Cracker Barrel stock, eventually amassing a total of ninety shares, each valued at about forty dollars. While $3600-worth of stock was not much in a rapidly expanding company with yearly sales of over $300 million, each share was a ticket to the annual stockholders meeting, where Cothren and five other members of Queer Nation staged what amounted to another sit-in and exhorted major stockholders and company officials to change their policies.

These efforts to transform policies and practices at Cracker Barrel were characterized in the press again and again as civil rights protests in the tradition of the Rev. Dr. Martin Luther King, and activists repeatedly linked their concerns to the fight against racism. "It's an issue of civil rights for everyone," Summerville proclaimed at a June 9, 1991, protest in Union City, Georgia (Hinmon 1991). Lili Baxter of the Fellowship of Reconciliation (an organization deeply involved in the King-era movement from its beginning in 1955) compared the ongoing effort to alter company policy to the civil rights struggles of nearly four decades before. Civil disobedience is a slow process, Baxter noted, but speed is not the measure of the potential for success: "The Montgomery bus boycott took more than a year. But the buses were desegregated" (Shepard 1992c).

Despite all these analogies, echoes, citations, and belabored parallels, a search of the popular press throughout 1991 and 1992 does not turn up cadres of black religious leaders or black columnists and editors denouncing Lynn Cothren and Cheryl Summerville in rallies and newspapers around the country as cultural plagiarists, political hijackers, pimps, or threats to black civil rights—accusations that would be hurled at white gay, lesbian, and transgender activists repeatedly through the coming years. While no doubt many blacks were uneasy with some of the borrowing, the comparisons, and the occasional overlap in personnel, very few voiced such concern publicly. Then suddenly (seemingly at least) everything changed.

A Decade of Growing Animosity and Distrust

On the morning of the 1993 March on Washington, the *New York Times* published a letter to the editor from Rev. Dennis G. Kuby that read in part: "It is a misappropriation for members of the gay leadership to identify the April 25 march on Washington with the Rev. Dr. Martin Luther King Jr.'s 1963 mobilization. Gays are not subject to water hoses or police dogs, denied access to lunch counters or prevented from voting. . . . The 1963 march on Washington symbolized a legitimate moral claim against historical wrongs that prevented blacks from voting, a right to an education and securing public accommodations and employment" (Kuby 1993). Unlike African Americans, Kuby suggested, gay men and lesbians, *qua* homosexual, are not

subject to gross mistreatment, crippling and sometimes lethal violence, or systematic discrimination, at least not in the same ways that
African Americans were fifty years ago. Thus, despite the analogies
many gay and lesbian activists like to draw—and did draw explicitly
in some speeches and chants at the 1993 march—gay political protests are nothing like black political protests and should not be billed
as such.[8]

A lot of people seconded Rev. Kuby. Through the next decade
his sentiments were echoed with increasing frequency and volume,
and media coverage of what some white gays and lesbians began
to call "black homophobia" intensified.[9] A year before Matthew
Shepard's murder, one particularly loud voice of denunciation was
that of Alveda King, a niece of the martyred civil rights activist.[10]
When gay and lesbian activists began working to secure legal protection against discrimination in California and to stave off a ballot measure in Maine whose passage would repeal legal protections already
in place, Alveda King launched a speaking tour and a series of rallies
designed to counter their efforts. On August 19, 1997, at a rally at
the capitol building in Sacramento, King insisted that her uncle would
never have supported any law prohibiting discrimination on the basis
of sexual orientation and that, furthermore, there was no legitimate
comparison to be made between the King-era civil rights movement
and the gay rights movement. "To equate homosexuality with race is
to give a death sentence to civil rights," she said. "No one is enslaving
homosexuals, or making them sit in the back of the bus." For gay and
lesbian activists to invoke the mid-twentieth-century black civil rights
movement's rhetoric or symbols in support of their cause was wholly
inappropriate and profoundly offensive, King maintained, for in fact
it was homosexuals themselves, not laws and policies discriminating
against them, that were the real threat to our society. "In California,
injustice is being done to family values," King declared ("One in
Every Family," 1997).

The Los Angeles Chapter of the Southern Christian Leadership
Conference immediately countered King's remarks. "The Martin
Luther King Jr. who founded the Southern Christian Leadership
Conference would not have been in league with any group whose
agenda was to exclude any segment of society that has suffered from
oppression and discrimination," said Executive Director Genethia
Hudley-Hayes at a press conference on August 20. Joined in her state-

ment by representatives from the Los Angeles NAACP Legal Defense and Education Fund, the MultiCultural Collaborative, and the National Black Lesbian and Gay Leadership Forum, Hudley-Hayes continued: "Gays and Lesbians qualify unquestionably in our minds as an oppressed group" (M. G. Smith 1997, 20). In fact, the NAACP already had a long history of support for gay and lesbian rights that included an endorsement of the 1993 March on Washington (Gates 1999, 25).

But King and her supporters were undeterred. She repeated her assertions on September 5 during a rally at the Team Disney corporate headquarters, where she also reiterated her earlier call for a boycott of gay-friendly Disney's theme parks and products, and again a couple of weeks later at a demonstration sponsored by a right-wing group called Concerned Women for America: "People can legally do what they want in their own bedrooms,[11] but don't expect us and our children to approve of, promote, or elevate sexual preference to a civil rights status" (Johnson 1997, R. Smith 1997). At a September 18 press conference, flanked by members of the Baptist Ministers Conference of Southern California and the Brotherhood Organization of a New Destiny, King stated: "I'm outraged that sexual preference and sexual conduct are being equated with skin color. . . . By inserting this behavior into civil rights law, the meaning of true civil rights is destroyed."[12]

King and her organization "King for America" had officially joined forces with Pat Robertson's Christian Coalition in Baltimore the previous May at an event called the Racial Reconciliation Congress, which the Christian Coalition had sponsored in an attempt to enlist African American support for its ultra-conservative social agenda.[13] In January of 1998, she held an interview with Robertson, followed by calls to a half-dozen radio talk shows, and accepted an invitation from Rush Limbaugh, an ultra-right-wing talk show host, to appear on his program to discuss her uncle's moral and political legacy (Foskett 1998). King then took her crusade to Maine. At a rally in February of 1998, she knelt on the capitol steps in Portland to pray that homosexuals "turn from their wicked ways." "God hates racism," she told the crowd of anti-gay demonstrators. "And God hates homosexuality" (Solomon 1999, 59). God himself was not a registered voter in the state of Maine, but a majority of those who were apparently agreed with King's take on the issue. The referendum passed. On

February 10, 1998, all citizens of Maine lost their legal protection against discrimination on the basis of sexual orientation.[14]

Declarations like King's were commonplace by the turn of the century. Whereas ten years before many white gay men and lesbians believed that straight African Americans were their "natural" allies, by the end of the 1990s many believed that straight blacks—at least the majority who were Christian or members of the Nation of Islam—were far more homophobic than straight whites. Whatever trust and openness might once have existed at the grassroots level was fast eroding.

Tensions escalated immeasurably in 2003, when same-sex couples began demanding marriage licenses and staging demonstrations and sit-ins at state license bureaus around the country, often singing "We Shall Overcome" and invoking names like Rosa Parks and Martin Luther King in statements to the press.[15] Although the NAACP offered unwavering support for full equality under the law, including marriage licensure for same-sex couples, more and more prominent African Americans felt called upon to take a negative public stand. By March of 2004, an online story headline at ABC News had become typical: "Are Gay Rights Civil Rights?" (Osunsami 2004). Temple University professor and author Clarence James said no, asserting: "The homosexual movement has nothing to do with civil rights. The civil rights movement was about a positive freedom, which is a freedom to rise to the highest levels of our capabilities. The homosexual movement is part of the sexual revolution. It is about negative freedom and the freedom from moral restraint" (Ly and Harris 2004).

The fact that the Massachusetts Supreme Court cited the *Brown v. Board of Education* decision as a precedent when it ruled that same-sex marriages had to be licensed under the state constitution outraged many black Christians. The three largest Boston-area black ministerial associations united to hold press conferences in front of the statehouse and issue press releases denouncing gay marriage. "I am offended that they're comparing this to civil rights," one minister, Rev. Jeffrey Brown, told reporters (DePasquale 2004). Views expressed in Boston were echoed around the country. In Atlanta more than two dozens black ministers issued a joint statement, which said in part, "To equate a lifestyle choice to racism demeans the work of the entire civil rights movement" (Niess 2004). In Chicago at a press conference held by African American Baptist ministers, Rev. Gregory

Daniels went so far as to proclaim, "If the KKK opposes gay marriage, I would ride with them."[16]

Ministers were not the only African Americans eager to register their offense at any equation of queer activism with the black civil rights movement. In a series of feature articles, Tennessee's *Jackson Sun* printed similar statements from a number of local residents. Fifty-eight-year-old Jackson native Mattie Burney said, "You can't compare it to what happened in the 1960s because it was a race issue. They weren't given a choice (due to skin color), whereas gays can walk into a place and not say they are gay." Louis and Sonia Reddick concurred—"There are no similarities whatsoever"—as did Richard Thomas, who insisted, "It's two separate issues entirely" (Booher 2004a). And echoing Alveda King, Shirlene Mercer disputed Coretta King's frequently reiterated claim that, had he lived, Dr. King himself would have supported the gay rights movement,[17] saying, "I never heard Dr. King make any statements affecting gay rights" (Booher 2004b). The *Baltimore Sun* carried several letters to the editor taking issue with the comparison between gay rights and black civil rights. One reader wrote, "The struggle of a people to be accepted for who they are is just not the same as the effort by a people to be justified in what they do" (Megary 2004). Boston Bishop Gilbert Thompson's statement to ABC News reporter Steve Osunsami seemed to sum up the sentiment: "I resent the fact that homosexuals are trying to piggy back on the civil rights struggles of the '60s." He went on to say, "I was born black. I was born male. Homosexuals are not born, they're made. They don't qualify" (Osunsami 2004).

In the midst of that controversy (by then as much an implicit attack on liberal black leadership as a dispute between black Christians and white gay and lesbian activists), with a U.S. Senate subcommittee preparing for hearings on a constitutional amendment to ban same-sex marriage, Rev. Jesse Jackson weighed in on the subject. Although Jackson had earlier expressed solid support for gay and lesbian civil rights, he backed away from his previous stands, reminding a Harvard University audience gathered to celebrate the fiftieth anniversary of the landmark Supreme Court decision in *Brown v. Board of Education* that gays were never enslaved or "called three-fifths human in the Constitution" and that, unlike African Americans, gays have always had the right to vote.[18] At no point in history, Jackson thus implied, will the situation of nonheterosexual Americans ever be enough like the situation of African Americans fifty years ago to justify appropriation and use of their rhetoric or tactics.

What had been a painful dilemma in 1998 was by 2003 a political minefield. Any suggestion that struggle for LGBT civil rights was in any way similar to the struggle for civil rights for African Americans was apt to provoke widespread hostility and accusations of antiblack racism. Even referring to LGBT political activity as an effort to win "civil" rights sometimes led to charges that LGBT activists were jeopardizing the few rights blacks had managed to secure. Civil rights was billed as a zero-sum game, and people who didn't fit the heterosexual or gender norms were routinely deemed less deserving than straight African Americans of the few rights there were to go around. I knew that much of the animosity that African American heterosexuals supposedly felt toward gay men, lesbians, and transgendered people was an artifact of the media driven by radical right wing ideologues and campaign strategists, but I also knew that some of the sentiment was real and was growing stronger. Jesse Jackson's turn-around was a clear indication of a grassroots swing to the right.

Racism against the Abnormal

In late 2003, in the midst of this rapidly intensifying public debate, a new volume of Michel Foucault's lectures at the Collège de France appeared in English translation (an exciting event in the small world of North American Foucault scholarship). It was entitled, simply, *Abnormal*.[19] The eleven lectures, which Foucault gave in weekly installments from January through March of 1975, explored the emergence of the concept of abnormality and the abnormal individual within forensic psychology. The epistemic domain of abnormality, Foucault argued in lecture three, was charted in forensic discourses on the basis of three figures: (1) the individual who acts against his or her own rational self-interest by breaking the social contract, (2) the wayward individual in need of correction, and (3) the masturbator. These three figures taken together marked out the territory, so to speak, and then coalesced through nineteenth-century discourses to give rise to the figure of the moral monster, the sexual predator, and eventually the psychopath.[20] The story he tells through these lectures culminates in an extremely provocative claim about the relationship between abnormality and racism.

In early nineteenth-century forensic psychology, Foucault tells us, criminal conduct was held to be contrary to human nature. Human nature was rational and self-interested, which is why representative government was possible: people upheld the law because it was in their long-term self-interest to do so. Those who broke the law for immediate gains were insufficiently rational, and those who broke the law in ways that offered them no advantage even in the short run were clearly irrational. As a violation of nature, criminality, even in its less horrific manifestations, was often linked with cannibalism and sexual perversion, supposedly the most extreme of acts against rational human nature (Foucault 2003a, 101–102).

Criminal irrationality might erupt in any variety of manifestations. Indeed, some people's irrationality might not be manifest in any way except in one terrible, unprecedented atrocity, such as in the case of the well-fed peasant woman who killed her daughter and ate her leg boiled with cabbage (Foucault 2003a, 102, 110). Obviously the existence of these moral and intellectual monsters was cause for tremendous concern. These criminals had to be identified and dealt with *before* they did any harm—a job the judicial system, with its focus on punishing past actions, was not equipped to do. But psychiatrists (who had invented this concept of criminality in the first place and were eager to extend their authority more deeply into the domain of jurisprudence) had a theory: these eruptions of unpredicted atrocity were instances of monomania, a highly focused form of insanity that had no symptoms other than the crimes to which it gave rise. Identification of monomania was extremely difficult; psychiatric expertise was required. Therefore, by 1839 French law recognized psychiatry as an important medical discipline and began officially calling upon it to discern not merely present mental competence (moral responsibility for an offense committed and competence to stand trial) but degrees of potential—that is, future—danger (2003a, 141).

Soon, however, psychiatrists began to reconceive mental illness; it was not primarily delirium—false belief or faulty cognition—but disturbance of the will. A person might see that an act was against his or her rational self-interest, yet still feel compelled to commit it. In other words, even a perfectly rational person might be insane. This new theory enabled psychiatrists to claim a much larger forensic domain, one including cases in which perpetrators carefully planned their crimes and alibis. This change had broad implications, for no matter how reasonable an individual might appear, if his or her behavior seemed aberrant, mental illness might well lurk in the background, and criminal acts might be the eventual result (Foucault 2003a, 159). Monomaniacal monsters were not real exceptions after all, then, for all compulsive people (people with disorders of volition) were more or less dangerous to society and in need of psychiatric supervision to keep their urges under control. Nonconformity was not mere eccentricity; very often it was symptomatic of disease. Further changes in French law made anyone who appeared to be a threat to public order subject to compulsory hospitalization.

This new policy of hospitalizing all threats to the public meant that families lost control over the fate of their wayward and unconventional members. Families were not allowed to harbor and protect such people; their oversight was now the prerogative of the state through the agency of the psychiatrist. Sometimes, of course, the state deemed aberrant individuals harmless and refused to hospitalize them even when their families wanted relief from responsibility for them. In such cases, families did have some recourse; they could pay psychiatrists to examine the individual and determine whether, although the person might not be a public danger, he or she was or might become a private danger within the household. If a psychiatrist determined that any such danger to the family existed, individuals could be hospitalized against their will. Thus did psychiatrists become deeply entangled in private family matters along with their deepening involvement with the law and the state.

This set of laws, public policies, and clinical theories and practices enabled a new intersection between psychiatry and organic medicine, which showed itself most clearly first of all in discussions of epilepsy (Foucault 2003a, 161). With the diagnosis of epilepsy (and later hysterical epilepsy), psychiatry identified a physiological condition that had both behavioral and psychic manifestations. Theoretical speculations about and practical interventions in cases of epilepsy operated as normalizing disciplines in two ways—that is, psychiatrists could impose their theories upon and regulate the lives of individuals on the basis of two distinct kinds of norms: norms of conduct and norms of organic functioning. Psychiatrists could identify individuals as abnormal in both registers simultaneously, giving a formidable medical basis for their judgments and clinical practices. Psychiatry was thus able to become "a technology of abnormality" (2003a, 163). It identified persons who it supposed could not be assimilated into the life of the community, and then it went to work to capture those individuals, discipline them, and thereby defend society from the threat they posed. In the process, the public became sensitized to newly recognized dangers: monomaniacs at first, then epileptics, hysterics, eccentrics, and nonconformists of all kinds. Such people—abnormal people—were not only problems for those whose intimate lives they shared but were threats to the general public and rightfully subject to surveillance and constraints imposed through psychiatry and other means by or on behalf of society as a whole.

French medicine and psychiatry influenced physicians in the United States tremendously throughout the nineteenth century.[21] French theories were taught in American medical schools, and any medical student who could afford to do so spent at least a year studying in Paris. In the course of their studies, whether at home or abroad, virtually all American medical students were exposed to the theories underlying the developing disciplines of psychiatry and criminology. In the 1860s, when degeneracy theory came to the fore in France and spread throughout Europe,[22] it quickly found its way into medical journals and medical practice in the United States as well. By the late nineteenth century, psychiatrists on both continents maintained that criminals and the mentally ill were "degenerates"—that is, persons whose life courses had veered off or fallen away from the normal path of human development as a result of either bad habits or bad heredity. Their condition was both mental and moral *and* physiological and heritable, and it was progressive in that it would likely worsen through the course of their lives and would likely be inherited in a more virulent form in their offspring in each successive generation.

Foucault does not discuss American medicine or psychiatry in *Abnormal,* but because French thought and practice was to so great an extent duplicated in the United States and because of my interest in understanding racism in light of Foucault's analysis of sexual normalization, I found a remark in the final lecture of the series especially striking. On March 19, 1975, Foucault made this rather dramatic, and in some contexts potentially inflammatory, assertion:

> With this notion of degeneration and these analyses of heredity, you can see how psychiatry could plug into, or rather give rise to, a racism that was very different in this period from what could be called traditional, historical racism, from

"ethnic racism." The racism that psychiatry gave birth to is racism against the abnormal, against individuals who, as carriers of a condition, stigmata, or any defect whatsoever, may more or less randomly transmit to their heirs the unpredictable consequences of the evil, or rather of the non-normal, that they carry within them. It is a racism, therefore, whose function is not so much the prejudice or defense of one group against another as the detection of all those within a group who may be the carriers of a danger to it. It is an internal racism that permits the screening of every individual within a given society. (Foucault 2003a, 316–17)

Once criminality and mental pathology became matters of deviant development and degenerate heredity in the late nineteenth century, psychiatry and related social scientific disciplines began to coincide with the racial disciplines that were emerging in full force at the time. Together, these discourses and the institutions that facilitated them created a new racism, the racism that would characterize the twentieth century in the United States. Foucault calls this "racism against the abnormal."

What Is Racism, Anyway?

In that final lecture in March of 1975, Foucault makes a choice very different from the one I made on the night after Matthew Shepard's death. He does not hesitate to draw on the history of oppression of nonwhite peoples to illuminate the suffering of nonheterosexual (and other "non-normal") people of all colors and ethnicities. And he goes even further. He chooses to *equate* racism and what, for lack of a better word, we usually call "heterosexism" or "homophobia" as well as other bigotries aimed at people considered deviant in many other ways.

However benign it may have been to state such an equation in 1975, by 2003 Foucault's claim was political dynamite. I heard my Binghamton lunch companion's voice in my head: It's not the same; it's not the same! What sense does it make to call prejudice and discrimination against those deemed abnormal *racism?* Isn't stretching the term to cover such disparate social phenomena a needless dilution of an important category of political critique? Worse still, isn't this just another example of a white person appropriating or colonizing critical territory that doesn't belong to him and that he has not done the work to cultivate? Doesn't this passage exemplify everything that critics of gay and lesbian and transgender political movements have been saying since 1993? And what was I, as a Foucault scholar and a queer, white, and antiracism activist, going to do in response?

In addition to trying to understand racism in relation to heter-onormativity and violence against gender transgressors and homo-sexuals, I needed to make sense of Foucault's comment. After all, my own hunches and hypotheses about the interrelationships of racism and heterosexism within regimes of biopower relied heavily upon Foucault's work. I believed that by using the tools he develops in his genealogical analyses of criminality, sexuality, illness, and abnormal-ity I would be able to show that racism is a biopolitical *dispositif* bound up with discourses of development and practices of disciplin-ary normalization that emerged in the nineteenth century. But I did *not* want to conflate racism with other forms of oppression. Was an analysis modeled on Foucault's in danger of ending with such a con-flation? Some serious exegesis was in order.

Foucault's use of the term *racism* in this passage seems to violate conventional definitions, so we might simply assume that he never meant for his assertion to be taken literally. Surely, he didn't really mean that homosexual people, for instance, are targets of racism. Instead of making a straightforward claim, we might conclude, he must have been engaging in overstatement calculated to provoke thought about how we typically conceptualize abnormality, or setting forth a metaphor designed to illuminate the situation of those deemed abnor-mal by way of allusion to the situation of racial minorities. Surely, what Foucault meant, we might be inclined to say, is that twentieth-century treatment of people whom our society has declared abnormal, sexually and otherwise, is *like* twentieth-century treatment of people whom our society has declared racially inferior. Allegedly abnormal people and allegedly racially inferior people occupy similarly subor-dinate positions in modern networks of power and knowledge.

But, as I knew very well, sweeping, undeveloped analogies are not among Foucault's standard tools of analysis. He rarely explicates any phenomenon by comparing it to, much less assimilating it to, something else; far more often he explicates one thing by *contrast-ing* it with something else, something generally taken to be very like if not identical with it. He surprises and provokes his readers by demonstrating differences where we thought there was homogeneity or continuity, not by showing us that things we thought were different from each other are in reality one and the same. To put it in more pedestrian language, Foucault is a splitter, not a lumper. That in itself is enough reason to think twice about assuming that what he is presenting in the eleventh lecture of *Abnormal* is a rash conflation or even just an analogy. So what other interpretative options are there?

The most obvious one, I realized, is that Foucault meant exactly what he said: the networks of power that make up what is aptly called racism in the twentieth century aim to eliminate, contain, manage, or exploit abnormality; and they operate in ways that very often threaten, harm, and oppress individuals who are classified as abnormal. Racism is a set of power relations that produce effects we call anti-Semitism and white supremacy. But racism is not identical with and exhausted by attitudes and actions that hurt people of color or Jews, as so many people suppose. It encompasses these phenomena, but it also exceeds them. It has a number of other effects as well.

Thus interpreted, Foucault's claim implies another: that within modern racist regimes of power, Jews and nonwhites—the usual objects of racist disdain and discrimination—are held to be abnormal in some respect, and it is in great part *because of* their alleged abnormality that they are despised, excluded, contained, managed, or exploited in ways that often threaten, harm, and oppress them. But the fundamental issue in all this is not religion or skin color per se; it is abnormality. Skin color and religious affiliation are taken as marks of abnormality alongside other kinds of somatic and behavioral marks—such as low IQ test scores, periodic epileptic seizures, unusual formation of the genitals, cross-gendered comportment, or same-sex coupling. The systems of oppression that so deeply and adversely affect Jews and people of color are substantially the same systems of oppression that so deeply and adversely affect people who are classified as, for example, disabled, intersexed, or transgendered. I could see that such a claim made historical sense, but I was still uncomfortable with this use of the term *racism*.

Even if modern racism ultimately could be thoroughly analyzed as a set of mechanisms that seek to dominate or eliminate abnormality (and that remained to be seen!), there are still big differences in the experiences, situations, and options of the very different sorts of people who are caught up in those mechanisms. The experiences of people who are labeled abnormal because they are, say, black versus people who are labeled abnormal because they are, say, transgendered are extremely different. So even if some of the theories, disciplines, and institutional forces are the same, why use the term *racism* to name all that? Wouldn't it make more sense to apply the term *racism* to the networks of power that negatively affect racial minorities only, and make up a different term for the general scheme of things?

Initially, I believed that Foucault's use of the term *racism* was ill-considered for just that reason. Whatever racism is, surely it has to have something to do with race; surely its main subjects and objects have to be identified as members of races, not just as people whose bodies or behaviors differ somehow from the norm. But in doing the work to be set forth in the coming pages, I eventually became convinced that it does make good historical, analytic, and in some contexts even politically strategic sense to use the term *racism* to name the much larger phenomenon and not just the part of it that applies directly to people of color or Jews. I know that is hard to believe without a lot of evidence; it was certainly hard for me to believe. But as the genealogy of modern racism offered in the next few chapters will show, Foucault's usage does not in the end really depart from the standard requirement that racism have something to do with race. Exclusion, oppression, hatred, and fear of abnormality as practiced and perpetuated in our society have everything to do with race, no matter which group of "abnormals" are the targets. Modern racism is about racial purification; it defines the abnormalities it identifies as racial impurities or as threats to racial purity. Modern racism is not really about nonwhites; modern racism is really all about white people. And once we fully understand *that*—and fully understand how *that* came to be, historically—our understanding of racism, sexuality, and the biopolitical regimes within which we live and know ourselves and each other will be dramatically and profoundly transformed.

This argument will be made at length in later chapters. For now, I only want to urge readers not to dismiss Foucault's apparently idio-syncratic use of the term *racism* without further consideration simply because it is, on its face, idiosyncratic. Even if Foucault is stretching or realigning the term, he isn't doing anything that scores of other race theorists and activists have not already done many times over during the last sixty years. If we throw out Foucault's claim just because he employs the term in a way different from his predecessors, we ought to throw out most of the writing on racism from 1950 forward.

According to the *Oxford English Dictionary*, the English word *racism* dates back only as far as 1936, when it appeared in a book by Lawrence Dennis entitled *The Coming American Fascism*.[23] The word's very first recorded appearance in any language was probably in the form of its German cognate a year or two earlier in an unpublished manuscript written by the famous homosexual rights advocate Magnus Hirschfeld.[24] *Racism* is therefore a very new word, much newer than most of the phenomena it purports to name. It arose and took hold in both English and German as a term of disapprobation when, in the words of British sociologist Robert Miles, "it became imperative for some academics and scientists, as well as political activists, to formulate a coherent rejection of the way in which the 'race' idea was utilised in Nazi Germany" (Miles 1989, 43). *Racism* was coined by opponents of Nazism to name the racial ideology of Nazism—in other words, to name something its coiners held to be a false theory, one distinct from other theories of race, that is, *theirs*.

Unlike *anti-Semitism,* which was introduced by Wilhelm Marr around 1879 to describe his own views (Wodak and Reisigl 1999, 177), *racism* was never a self-affirming term. Nor was it ever an epistemologically neutral term; the label *racist* was always intended to expose falsehood and to discredit the person to whom it was applied.[25] From the beginning, to call somebody a racist was to denounce that person as a purveyor of dangerous lies. In her influential 1940 book *Race: Science and Politics,* anthropologist Ruth Benedict described racism as a dogma in denial of science; anyone who could be characterized as a racist was automatically also characterized as either an ignoramus or a trenchant reactionary.[26] Shortly after World War II, UNESCO (the United Nations Educational, Scientific, and Cultural Organization) followed suit, characterizing racism as a willful misrepresentation of scientific knowledge. "Racism falsely claims that there is a scientific basis for arranging groups hierarchically in terms of psychological and cultural characteristics that are immutable and innate" (Miles 1989, 46). People who held to this theory or set of beliefs despite the scientific evidence against it were at best misinformed and at worst completely irrational. Persistent racism among the scientifically literate, among people who knew the scientific facts but still refused to draw nonracist conclusions, might even be a sign of mental illness.

Given these historical circumstances, it is really not surprising that most people deny being racist even while espousing views easily identified with white supremacy or anti-Semitism—sometimes in the course of the same sentence: "I'm no racist, but black people have a certain smell." Such declarations can be read this way: "I don't hold to a discredited theory; I'm in possession of a simple fact." And, if we define *racism* as it was defined in the 1930s and 40s, such a declaration makes as much sense as saying, "I'm no Christian, but miracles do occur." It is possible to reject a theory or a creed while accepting some of the propositions that support it or follow from it. The reason such declarations sound like nonsense today is that racism is no longer taken to be a theory; instead, most people understand it to be an attitude that expresses itself in propositions like "blacks have a certain smell." Given this more recent definition, the declaration "I'm not a racist, but blacks have a certain smell" is laughably illogical.

Early definitions and descriptions always cast racism as a set of theoretical propositions or beliefs. It was something both cognitive and conscious, not a range of behaviors or attitudes or institutional effects. Only a set of propositions could be racist in the adjectival sense, and the noun *racist* simply designated a person who espoused the theory of racism, just as the noun *creationist* designates a person who espouses the theory of creationism. And that was where application of the words as both noun and adjective stopped. Only beliefs and the people who held them could be called racist. Actions were not racist any more than actions are creationist, even though one's theoretical commitments might move one to act in certain ways. Personality structures and unconscious fantasies were not racist, although they might be hateful or phobic and thus dispose a person to believe in the theory of racism. And institutions could only be described as racist if they were devoted to application and dissemination of the theory of racism, such as might be said of the Ku Klux Klan. After the mid-twentieth century, however, the definitions of *racism* and *racist* underwent great and very rapid expansion.

Application of the term *racist* to institutions, their operations, and their effects, sometimes in spite of the intentions and desires of individuals within them, can be traced to activists Stokely Carmichael and Charles Hamilton, Robert Miles tells us. In *Black Power,* published in 1967, Carmichael and Hamilton write:

> What is racism? The word has represented daily reality to millions of black people for centuries, yet it is rarely defined—

perhaps just because that reality has been such a common-place. By "racism" we mean the predication of decisions and policies on considerations of race for the purpose of *subor-dinating* a racial group and maintaining control over that group. That has been the practice of this country toward the black man. . . .

Racism is both overt and covert. It takes two, closely related forms: individual whites acting against individual blacks, and acts by the total white community against the black community. We call these individual racism and insti-tutional racism. . . .

. . . When a black family moves into a home in a white neighborhood and is stoned, burned or routed out, they are victims of an overt act of individual racism which many people will condemn—at least in words. But it is institutional racism that keeps black people locked in dilapidated slum tenements, subject to the daily prey of exploitive slumlords, merchants, loan sharks and discriminatory real estate agents. (Carmichael and Hamilton 1967, 3–4)

They go on to quote Charles Silberman from *Crisis in Black and White:* "What we are discovering, in short, is that the United States—all of it, North as well as South, West as well as East—is a racist society in a sense and to a degree that we have refused so far to admit, much less face" (5).

Before the mid-twentieth century, it was not possible to assert that an entire country was racist no matter how much discrimination and exploitation it permitted or perpetuated. The word just didn't work that way. Only individual people, those who consciously espoused a certain set of propositions, could be called racists. Abstract entities like nation-states cannot espouse propositions. The fact is that theo-rists in the 1960s weren't actually discovering racism where nobody realized it existed before so much as they were redefining the term so that they could apply it in contexts where it could not have been applied before. They changed the way the word was used in both theoretical discourse and ordinary conversation, making it applicable to systems and networks of power that might operate without overt racist conviction or intention and to individual actions not obviously motivated by personal animosity or erroneous judgment. They altered the meaning of the concept.

And they were not the first to do so. By 1950 sociologists and psychologists were already suggesting that some sort of underlying personality structure or set of unconscious drives or fantasies disposes some individuals to believe in racism as a theory. Racism was the result of "race prejudice," an attitude or, as Harvard psychologist Gordon Allport famously defined it in 1954, "an antipathy based upon a faulty and inflexible generalization" (1954, 9). As that idea settled into public discourse, people began to conflate theoretical cause and effect and to refer to those deep, often unconscious aspects of personality and fantasy life not merely as causes of or motives for racist belief but as racism itself.

Thus the meaning of the word *racism* changed to include dispositions and personality traits. Once that happened, it became conceivable that a person might be a racist regardless of whether he or she had ever given the theory of racism any thought. A person need not have a conscious commitment to the tenets of racist theory to be a racist; even in the absence of belief in racist propositions—in fact, even in the presence of conscious rejection of racist theory—a person's gestures, feelings, and decisions could still be expressions of underlying, unconscious racism. This change in the meaning of the term prompted a lot of anxious soul-searching on the part of conscientious liberal white people who had thought up until that time that they were not racist at all. It may have resulted in some positive change in attitudes and behavior and interracial relationships, but it also created a lot of confusion, frustration, self-doubt, timidity, anger, and silent withdrawal from interracial dialogue.

Before World War II, it would have been nonsense to say that a person might harbor unconscious racism. Such a suggestion would have been analogous to saying that a person might harbor unconscious creationism. Creationism is a theory: one believes or disbelieves it; one does not harbor it unconsciously. In 1940 the same was true of racism. But by the last quarter of the twentieth century, if not earlier, the word *racism* did not function like the word *creationism* anymore. In fact, in liberal circles at least, it functioned a lot more like the word *alcoholism.*

As a white person, I have been told many times in many different contexts by many different people (most of them white) that I am necessarily and irremediably racist, regardless of my avowed convictions, and that my only honest option is to acknowledge that I am racist and then actively work to expose my racism and oppose it with deliberate antiracist efforts. Note the similarity to alcoholism. The alcoholic is told that she is by her very nature alcoholic, whether she consumes alcohol or not, and that her only honest, healthy option is to acknowledge her alcoholism and then actively work to expose the addictive aspects of her personality and oppose them at every turn. Racism, like alcoholism, is now held to be a condition of the personality or psyche that is so basic as to be ineradicable, a sort of enemy within that can never be vanquished but must be managed by means of strict self-discipline throughout one's entire life.

These expansions in definition have not gone uncontested. Many people object when institutions are deemed racist, contending instead that it is only some of the individuals within them, those holding to one or another racist theory, using the machinery of government or corporation to discriminate against those they view as inferior; it is these individuals who are properly held responsible for the effects that some theorists term "institutional racism." Some people even object to the idea that racism permeates the unconscious mental lives of people actively working against inequality and injustice. Racism is a conscious mental phenomenon, they say; people who believe in racial equality are simply not racists by virtue of that belief. In other words, there are still people who cling to the narrow, pre–World War II definition of *racism*.

Not infrequently, people who contest postwar semantic expansions and advocate restricting *racism* to its pre–World War II definition are viewed with suspicion by those who find the term analytically useful in application to institutions and personalities. "Neo-conservatives" just fear exposure as racists, say liberal and radical social critics; they just want an ideological cover under which to enjoy their skin privilege and conduct their racist business as usual. But advocates for a return to the 1930s definition think labeling nonconscious feelings or institutional effects racist is just a way to avoid grappling with the implications of messy empirical data. "Progressives" don't really want to analyze the political and economic realities; they just want to condemn "the system" and be done with it. All camps are extremely suspicious of each others' motives and utterly unwilling to take each others' concerns seriously. So the controversy intensifies, and consensus about the meaning of the term *racism* (let alone solutions to whatever problems it might name) recedes into the mists of improbability.

In sum, the word *racism* has become a political flashpoint loaded with connotation but lacking any stable referent at all—other than Nazism and its ideological spawn. It is a very powerful word, but without any stipulations regarding what it can and cannot name, it is not a very useful word in most analytic contexts. Should the term be limited to theories and conscious beliefs, or should it also include personalities, feelings, actions, life styles, practices, institutional structures, material distributions, procedural outcomes, and so forth? There is no agreement in sight. Moreover, even where subgroups of people do agree on what sorts of phenomena can reasonably be termed racist, there is still disagreement over what criteria should be used to determine the applicability of the term in individual cases. We might agree that racism can be an unconscious characteristic of a person's mental life and still disagree over which behaviors count as indications that a given person's mental life is aptly so characterized.

I don't mean to advocate or contest any of these definitions or applications of the words *racist* or *racism*. In the foregoing, I have aimed only to give some background to a conceptual controversy, not to participate in it. My goal has been to show that Michel Foucault is not the first person to suggest an altered or enlarged application of those terms. In fact, definitions and criteria for application of the words *racism* and *racist* have never enjoyed much stability in the seventy years of their existence. Charles Mills notes that "after decades of divergent use and sometimes abuse, the term [*racism*] has become so fuzzy and has acquired such a semantic penumbra of unwelcome associations that unless a formal definition is given, no clear reference can be readily attached to it" (1998, 99–100).[27] Sociologists Michael Omi and Howard Winant concur: "The distinct, and contested, meanings of racism which have been advanced over the past three decades have contributed to an overall crisis of meaning for the concept today" (1994, 70).[28]

Racism and Race

The question we should ask, then, is not: Is Foucault misusing the term *racism*? There are no set standards of correct usage. Instead, the questions we should ask are, first: *How* is Foucault using the term? and, second: Does his usage enrich or impoverish our understanding of the world? Does it augment or foster strategies that we find useful in our efforts to resist and alter networks of power that we find oppressive, or does it block those efforts or reinforce what we seek to dismantle? These questions can't be answered a priori. To ask them, therefore, is to commit ourselves to further consideration of Foucault's assertion that modern racism is racism against the abnormal.

It might still be objected, as I suggested above, that while innovation in usage is not ruled out in principle, any innovations introduced surely need to retain some connection to race. After all, what could *racism* possibly mean in the absence of race? In later chapters I will show that Foucault's account of racism does involve race as a central concept, even though not all the targets of racist practices are members of currently recognized racial minorities. But it should be remarked at the outset that the attempt to anchor racism by reference to race does not necessarily give racism any more conceptual stability than it has on its own. The ontological status of race, too, is a hotly contested issue; application of the term *race*, much like application of the term *racism*, is frequently disputed and always has been.

Here is a little taste of that long dispute over the definition of *race*. In the late eighteenth century, natural historians asserted that there are naturally given, distinct human types (which they called races for reasons to be examined in chapter 2), just as there are distinct types of dogs or horses. We may not have identified them all yet, they conceded, but distinct races are out there; it is just a matter of empirical investigation. One would think, however, that if these distinct human body types did exist in nature, anyone who turned a careful eye toward them would see pretty much the same set of divisions. Yet over the course of the eighteenth century, the number of supposedly naturally distinct races ranged from two all the way up to thirty-four; and in the nineteenth century, classification schemes became even more complicated. In 1860 French biologist Isadore Geoffroy Saint-Hilaire claimed to see four principal races and thirteen secondary races.[29] In 1865 T. H. Huxley proposed eleven races, but then in 1870 he changed his mind and proposed five principal and fourteen secondary races. In 1878 Paul Topinard said there are sixteen races, but in 1885 he revised his view with the claim that in fact there are nineteen. In 1899 Harvard sociologist William Ripley claimed that there are three distinct races in Europe alone—the Teutonic (or Nordic), the Celtic (or Alpine), and the Mediterranean.[30] Now, if distinct races really exist in nature, how could so many careful scientific observers of nature disagree so wildly on how many there are?

One reason for such wild disagreement was that the supposed experts could not agree on what bodily features should count as the marks of racial difference. Was it skin color? Was it hair texture, eye shape, skull shape, facial angle, cranial capacity, brain anatomy? For one reason or another, all of these measures proved unsatisfactory.[31] They failed to yield hard lines of demarcation between groups of people various scientists thought really did constitute distinct races— meaning that there were no such empirically evident morphological lines of demarcation. Nevertheless, racial classification had come to seem of the utmost scientific importance, so the work continued well into the twentieth century.[32]

Scientific definitions and criteria are confusing, but in practice nineteenth-century racial classification was positively bewildering. Anti-miscegenation laws and legally mandated racial segregation in many regions of the United States necessitated legal criteria for distinguishing one race from another. However, states were free to establish their own laws to govern the matter, and different states had different concerns. Some were worried exclusively about securing a distinction between Caucasians and Negroes and did not concern themselves at all with Native Americans or immigrants from Asia or Latin America, whereas others were eager to distinguish whites from Chinese or Mexicans.[33] These differing agendas led to different legal criteria for racial identification. Many states used a complex of skin color, hair texture, and eye shape as the primary means for distinguishing among races, but that left them with the problem of how to classify people of so-called "mixed" race. Most resorted to lineage, but without any interstate uniformity. For example, in Massachusetts as of 1810, a person who had at least six Caucasian great-grandparents (and thus conceivably one Negro grandparent and one mulatto parent) was Caucasian and so could marry a white person; in Michigan, however, a person needed to have at least seven Caucasian great-grandparents to be Caucasian. So there were people who were white in one state but black in another.

Looking to both appearance and lineage (and sometimes religion, language, and even place of residence), some states codified categories that did not exist at all in other states, such as "Creole" or "Indian" or "Colored."[34] Louisiana designated both Native and African Americans as "colored" but counted individuals with a minimum of seven white great-grandparents as white, at least for purposes of marriage. By contrast, in Virginia the terms *Negro* and *colored person* were synonymous, so Native Americans were not colored people.[35]

In some states, such as Tennessee, appearance was apparently irrelevant. Because admixtures of ancestry determined race and the relevant amounts varied under different state laws, a person could be Negro for purposes of marriage but Caucasian for purposes of voting. Thus, racial identity varied not only for people who might travel across state lines but even, in Tennessee at least, for a person staying in one place but desiring to exercise more than one legal right. In other states, however, appearance was everything, trumping lineage even where it was invoked in cases of "mixture." For example, in Ohio in 1859, a court ruled that even if a child qualified as white by having five (or more) Caucasian great-grandparents, if he or she looked like a Negro, he or she was a Negro and could not attend a white school. Hence it was possible for two children born of the same two parents to qualify as members of two different races under Ohio law.[36]

Supposedly all these laws were necessary because there were naturally existing distinct races of human being that had to be kept apart. But if there really were naturally distinct races, why did natural historians, biologists, sociologists, state legislatures, and judges not come up with roughly the same categories and criteria for identifying them?

In the twentieth century, after two hundred years of confusion and controversy, some people began to challenge the idea that races were natural kinds at all. In their 1936 book *We Europeans: A Survey of "Racial" Problems,* Julian Huxley and A. C. Haddon called for the concept of "race" to be dropped in favor of that of "ethnic group."[37] Shortly thereafter, in a famous speech entitled "The Concept of Race in the Human Species in the Light of Genetics," Ashley Montagu proclaimed that "the concept of race is nothing but a whited sepulcher, a conception which in the light of modern experimental genetics is utterly erroneous and meaningless" (Montagu 2000, 101). Such claims reverberate through race discourse today; one often hears it said these days that there is no scientific basis for the concept of race. Scientists like Frank Livingstone (1993, 133), Gordon Edlin (1990, 504), and Richard Lewontin (Lewontin et al. 1984, chap. 1), among many others, insist that genetics has shown that the term *race* has no natural referent. Instead of race, therefore, we should speak only of gene pools, populations, or clines. Yet whatever is meant by the terms, race and racial identities continue to be important aspects of contemporary life; race remains a standard category in education, public policy, marketing, and even in the nominally scientific discipline of medicine.[38]

Given the variation in the sense and reference of the term *race,* even if it is true that racism never appears in the absence of race, such a correlation by itself does not necessarily tell us anything about what racism is or what criteria to use in applying the term. To confuse matters further, there is evidence that racism *can* appear in the absence of race as a material target. Adolf Hitler—the indisputable epitome of racism in the modern world—may have held a view very close to that of Montagu and Livingstone. Herman Rauschning reports that in a conversation he had with Hitler prior to 1940, Hitler told him, "I know perfectly well, just as well as those tremendously clever intellectuals, that in the scientific sense there is no such thing as race" (in Brace 2005, 186). Hitler may not have believed that Jews constituted an ontologically real race, yet surely his actions regarding them were racist. The very term *racism* was invented to name his ideology.

My purpose in this section has not been to discredit the notion of race but only to show that the relationship between race and racism is complex and questionable, and thus to push aside facile objections to Foucault's terminology. I hope I have made it clear that Foucault's assertion cannot be dismissed as meaningless out of hand.

Normalization and Genealogical Counterattack

Frankly, though, when I first encountered Foucault's claim that modern racism is racism against the abnormal, I found it embarrassing. It seemed simplistic and trite—and thoroughly unworthy of a thinker as careful as Michel Foucault. However, the research that I did over the next several years convinced me that the statement makes a tremendous amount of sense. Yet appreciating the sense it makes requires understanding something about Foucault's genealogical method and his analysis of normalization.

Foucault's major study of normalization can be found in *Discipline and Punish: The Birth of the Prison,* which he finished in August of 1974 and which was published in February of 1975, just a month before he gave the final lecture of *Abnormal.* A central question there is: Why did imprisonment become the single form of punishment for virtually all types of crime? A crucial part of the answer lies, he thinks, in the development of disciplinary practices in other important social institutions. At the same time, for example, the lunatic asylum was becoming a machine for curing madness, hospitals were becoming machines for treating disease, and schools were becoming machines for generating learning (Foucault 1977, 165). And of course factories, where laboring bodies were collected and deployed, were machines in a very literal sense, producing skilled labor as well as commodities for sale. As these various "machines" were assembled and tuned, Foucault maintains, new techniques for subjugating bodies developed. Foucault calls them "disciplines." He writes, "The human body was entering a machinery of power that explores it, breaks it down and rearranges it. A 'political anatomy,' which was also a 'mechanics of power,' was being born; it defined how one may have a hold over others' bodies, not only so that they may do what one wishes, but so that they may operate as one wishes, with the techniques, the speed and the efficiency that one determines. Thus discipline produces subjected and practised bodies, 'docile' bodies" (1977, 138).

We should think of discipline as a kind of technology, Foucault says. It is not identical with the institutions in which it is found (1977, 28) but easily migrates across institutions and adapts to varying projects and goals. Disciplinary techniques—like all forms of power—operate on bodies. But whereas some techniques operate on bodies in an effort to make them *do* something—complete a certain amount of work, confess the truth, pledge allegiance to the flag, pay taxes—the normalizing techniques that arose in the nineteenth century operate on bodies to make them *function over time* in prescribed ways or at prescribed levels. Hence, from the perspective of normalizing discipline, no real distinction need be made between what we might like to think of as voluntary versus involuntary behavior; discipline conditions bodies' muscles and nerves as surely as it hones their perceptions and endows them with new cognitive or aesthetic skills. It works on bodies' instincts, habits, and reflexes as well as their tastes and beliefs. Thus these disciplines can easily combine techniques adapted from both religious practice and biological sciences and animal husbandry. Disciplines treat bodies, not as wholes but as sets of components that can be reconfigured for efficiency through various sorts of exercise (1977, 137). By means of graduated exercises, a body's components—and thus the body as a whole—may be developed in a specified way, its energies and growth channeled and cultivated, its developmental trajectories turned to desired goals. In effect, the bodies that we know and know ourselves as are constituted through these practices.[39]

Normalizing discipline involves three major types of technical instrument: hierarchical observation, normalizing judgment, and examination (all of which can be seen at work in the genealogy of racism to be traced in upcoming chapters). Hierarchical observation is the most intrusive. Because function rather than product is the focus of these interventions, disciplinary power cannot be effectively exercised only intermittently. There must be close attention to, and ongoing adjustment of, levels of functioning. Therefore, there must be constant or nearly constant surveillance. Initially, this may take the form of a superior watching a group of subordinates. But as systems grow, a problem arises: one person can't see everything simultaneously and unceasingly. As Foucault notes, this problem was solved in parish schools, for example, by selecting pupils to do very specific jobs of monitoring. Some pupils recorded absences or unauthorized movements; others noted behavior at chapel; others took down names of those who talked during periods of required silence; others had responsibility for counseling those who committed infractions. Good students were given the task of tutoring weak students and monitoring their academic progress. Monitoring of every aspect of each student's conduct and progress—of his functioning—was thus possible through a distribution of responsibility for oversight (1977, 175–76).[40] Foucault contends that these techniques of surveillance not only created an integrated system closely tied to the goals of the institution in which it operated but also constituted it as "a multiple, automatic and anonymous power" (1977, 176). Although surveillance was carried out by individuals, "its functioning is that of a network of relations from top to bottom, but also to a certain extent from bottom to top and laterally; this network 'holds' the whole together and traverses it in its entirety with effects of power that derive from one another: supervisors, perpetually supervised. The hierarchized surveillance of the disciplines is not possessed as a thing, or transferred as a property; it functions like a piece of machinery" (1977, 176–77). This dispersed surveillance retains the authority of hierarchy but combines it with the flexibility and agility of decentralization.

Ubiquitous surveillance identifies nonoptimal functioning, which in turn calls for adjustment. This is where normalizing judgment comes into play. To keep individuals functioning and progressing as they should, penalties for poor performance must be imposed and incentives for improvement offered. Assessments to determine distribution of penalties and privileges must be frequent. Thus, Foucault says, "at the heart of all disciplinary systems functions a small penal mechanism" (1977, 177). But these penalties and rewards are not distributed according to a binary formula of rule-keeping versus rule-breaking. "The whole indefinite domain of the non-conforming is punishable: the soldier commits an 'offence' whenever he does not reach the level required; a pupil's 'offence' is not only a minor infraction, but also an inability to carry out his tasks" (1977, 177–78). Disciplinary punishments often consist simply of additional repetitions of the same exercises in the effort to produce conformity to the behavioral or developmental—that is, the functional—norm. "Punishment" is essentially corrective. And it permits of many forms of quantitative innovation. This sort of system allows pupils to be judged against one another and ranked, and ranking then becomes part of the practice of normalizing judgment. To be ranked high is a reward in and of itself, whereas to be ranked low is shameful.

> In short, the art of punishing, in the regime of disciplinary power, is aimed neither at expiation, nor even precisely at repression. It brings five quite distinct operations into play: it refers individual actions to a whole that is at once a field of comparison, a space of differentiation and the principle of a rule to be followed. It differentiates individuals from one another, in terms of the following overall rule: that the rule be made to function as a minimal threshold, as an average to be respected or an optimum towards which one must move. It measures in quantitative terms and hierarchizes in terms of value the abilities, the level, the "nature" of individuals. It introduces, through this "value-giving" measure, the constraint of a conformity that must be achieved. Lastly, it traces the limit that will define difference in relation to all other differences, the external frontier of the abnormal (the "shameful" class of the École Militaire). The perpetual penalty that traverses all points and supervises every instant in the disciplinary institutions compares, differentiates, hierarchizes, homogenizes, excludes. In short, it *normalizes*. (1977, 182–83)[41]

What matters is not obedience but conformity. Bodies are to function in accord with an established norm, and they will be made to do so both by a ubiquitous force and by a ubiquitous enabling. Thus does discipline enhance the capacities and skills of bodies, while at the same time it renders them docile in the face of both authority and amorphous social expectation.

Examination, the third type of disciplinary technique Foucault identifies, is a ritualized combination of surveillance and normalizing judgment. He considers it separately because it produces the conditions for an expansion of normalizing disciplinary power through the acquisition of data and the creation of individual "cases." This data eventually enables disciplinary knowledges, what he at times calls the "psy disciplines" or, more generally, "the human sciences." Disciplinary knowledge is founded upon, and in turn produces, disciplinary power. In normalizing disciplines, knowledge and power are inextricably intertwined.

Foucault contrasts disciplinary power with what he sometimes calls juridical power, a contrast we will see exemplified in chapter 3 of this book in the respective proposals of Thomas Jefferson and Benjamin Rush for the treatment of freed slaves.[42] Juridical power, Foucault tells us, is concerned with law and obedience, not norm and conformity. It comes into play only when there is an infraction, whereas disciplinary power presses itself against the bodies whose functions it oversees virtually without interruption. According to purely juridical authorities, subjects are simply to remember the rules and follow them; norms of ongoing functioning are not at issue. When rules are broken, juridical punishment reestablishes an ideally static social order and reminds the offender (and others) of the law. Juridical power operates, then, on subjectivities as already constituted; it does not seek to reshape them in any way. Nor does it seek any knowledge of their interiority. What is to be known is the law and whether the law has been breached; what is to be seen is the authority of the lawgiver and the judge.

Our usual ways of thinking about power take the juridical as the model for all exercises and regimes of power. Power is thought of as negation, prohibition, limit, or repression; and it originates in the will of a sovereign lawgiver—be it a monarch or the rationally self-interested, naturally free individual of social contract theory. But Foucault found that way of thinking about power worse than unhelpful when he tried to understand how power works within institutions like the prison, the school, and the asylum. Psychiatric power, for example—which Foucault had studied extensively in the lecture series of 1973–74, now published as *Psychiatric Power*—doesn't operate on the model of sovereign/subject. The target of psychiatric power is not the juridical subject who must either obey the duly established law or suffer expulsion from the social body. It is the developing individual who must be directed, taught, and monitored in view of functional norms. Disciplinary power not only constrains this individual; it shapes him or her. "We must cease once and for all to describe the effects of power in negative terms: it 'excludes,' it 'represses,' it 'censors,' it 'abstracts,' it 'masks,' it 'conceals.' In fact, power produces; it produces reality; it produces the domains of objects and the ritual of truth. The individual and the knowledge that may be gained of him belong to this production" (1977, 194).

Normalizing power produces individuals as epistemic objects, as "case histories," as collections of measured deviations from given norms. It individuates its subjects by comparing them to one another and ranking them. It thus produces more or less normal subjects— individuals with certain life experiences, personal identities, self-concepts, emotional responses, bundles of habits and beliefs, and so forth. It also produces abnormal subjects, what Foucault refers to in *Psychiatric Power* as the "residual." Whatever classification system they use, disciplinary systems always confront this "external frontier of the abnormal" (1977, 183); they always "come up against those who cannot be classified, those who escape supervision, those who cannot enter the system of distribution, in short, the residual, the irreducible, the unclassifiable, the unassimilable" (2006, 53), which are in actuality products of the system of classification itself.

Foucault illustrates this last point with reference to military discipline. Until there was a standing army and military discipline, he notes, there were no deserters; "for the deserter was quite simply the future soldier, someone who left the army so that he could rejoin it if necessary, when he wanted to, or when he was taken by force. However, as soon as you have a disciplined army, that is to say people who join the army, make a career of it, follow a certain track, and are supervised from end to end, then the deserter is someone who escapes this system and is irreducible to it" (2006, 53).[43] Likewise, school discipline creates the residue of the feebleminded or mentally defective child. "The individual who cannot be reached by school discipline can only exist in relation to this discipline; someone who does not learn to read and write can only appear as a problem, as a limit, when the school adopts the disciplinary schema" (2006, 53). Foucault suggests that the mentally ill are those who are overdetermined in their residual existence, the residue of more than one or perhaps of all disciplinary systems in play.

But a disciplinary society will not tolerate any residue. Supplementary disciplines will emerge to deal with it. "Since there are feeble-minded, that is to say, individuals inaccessible to school discipline, schools for the feeble-minded will be created, and then schools for those who are inaccessible to schools for the feeble-minded." Disciplinary regimes will always produce their own "external frontier," a category of individuals who are defined by the fact that the discipline cannot assimilate them. But they will then extend themselves with new regimes designed precisely for that newly defined class. "In short, disciplinary power has this double property of being 'anomizing,' that is to say, always discarding certain individuals, bringing anomie, the irreducible, to light, and of always being normalizing, that is to say, inventing ever new recovery systems, always reestablishing the rule. What characterizes disciplinary systems is the never-ending work of the norm in the anomic" (2006, 54). This set of techniques, processes, and effects, taken together, make up what Foucault means by the term "normalization."[44] We live in a normalizing society, he contends, a society that insists on normality, all the while generating new forms of abnormality. We live in a society where abnormality is feared, where abnormal individuals are often considered sick and dangerous and legitimately subject to all sorts of constraints, and where normal people work very hard to avoid getting labeled abnormal because we all know what happens to those who do.

Much of Foucault's work through the middle of the 1970s was focused on delineating normalizing regimes in their operation. He clearly hoped that this work—histories of the present, as he sometimes characterized it—would compromise those regimes' hold over our daily lives and afford possibilities for creative disruptions. He called the technique he used to effect or enable those disruptions "genealogy."

Foucault's genealogical method of analysis and critique is especially effective in application to regimes of normalization, because showing how particular norms have emerged historically, shifted, and even sometimes disappeared entirely robs them of the basis for the claim to be natural, simply "given," or universal.[45] Genealogy traces and exposes the ways in which norms get established through political give and take, and sometimes through historical accident, and thereby reveals the networks of power that invest and deploy them.

Genealogical practice, as Foucault described it in his 1971 essay "Nietzsche, Genealogy, History," is always opposed to a search for definitive, unitary origins.[46] A genealogist never assumes that there was a moment when a particular phenomenon or concept arrived on the scene fully formed, remaining essentially unchanged in its descent to the present day. Instead, he or she assumes that existing phenomena and concepts are the offspring of multiple generations or iterations, involving irretrievable losses and frequent new combinations of characters and lineages. In seeking to understand a contemporary phenomenon, then, the genealogist looks for moments at which historically disparate elements aligned to delineate new objects of knowledge, fields of action, or ways of life and moments at which seemingly unitary objects, institutions, or systems fissured, allowing fragments of a previous unity to align with alien elements.

The lectures in *Abnormal* point to just such a set of events—the delineation of the field of abnormality within psychiatric and forensic theory and practice. Within this field there arose objects of knowledge—cases of monomania, masturbatory insanity, and hysterical epilepsy, for example—and ways of life, including the lives of career criminals and the lives of career psychiatrists. As we will see in chapters 3 and 4, this field of knowledge and practice, the field of abnormality, aligned with other political and scientific forces in the nineteenth century to enable another new phenomenon known as scientific racism.

Genealogy doesn't simply account for the emergence of things, however. It also typically destabilizes the very things it accounts for by showing how contingent they actually are. If monomania looks from a genealogical perspective like hardly more than a passing theoretical fashion—or, worse, a diagnostic category fabricated simply to leverage control over juridical resources—we may begin to suspect that psychiatric diagnoses of other sorts may also be contingent upon nonscientific or nonmedical concerns, and as a result, we may take them and the psychiatrists who wield them less seriously.[47] Thus, where power relations maintain themselves through claims to certainty and stasis, genealogy always has value as critique.

Foucault developed his genealogies of criminality, mental illness, and sexuality in part as critique, as a set of political tools to resist the power of institutionalized surveillance and punishment, regimes of medical and psychiatric treatment, and socially pervasive practices of sexual normativity. As he did so, however, he saw two important but potentially incompatible things. First, he saw that genealogy's critical edge depended upon its resistance to any sort of ultimate narrative unification; because it opposed itself to grand narratives and refused to found its own new epistemic field, it could not be easily co-opted by the master discourses it tended to undermine. But second, he saw that the stories he was telling about criminology, sexology, pedagogy, medicine, and the various "psy" sciences did tend to converge. As these disparate regimes and domains of power relations extended themselves and reinforced one another, they gradually formed a vast interconnected network. And thus a new "object" was coming into view, an emerging and shifting system of force relations and resistances that Foucault called "biopower." If "biopower" were to become the name of a new epistemic object, one that somehow accounted for the operations of disciplinary normalization in the disparate areas he had studied, genealogical practice could conceivably undermine itself and compromise its own effectiveness as critique.

Foucault's distress at this pass is evident in the opening paragraphs of his first lecture in the 1976 series. Over the past fifteen years, he says, we have seen that theories like Marxism or psychoanalysis—theories that purport to be "all-encompassing and global" (2003b, 6)—have in some ways hampered efforts to critique and alter social institutions that oppress people, even while they have offered a few useful tools. At the local political level, where people struggle, for example, against the authoritarianism of the medical professions or the domination of men over women or the degrading effects of imprisonment, global theories are helpful only when "the theoretical unity of their discourse is, so to speak, suspended, or at least cut up, ripped up, torn to shreds" (2003b, 6). It is local (as opposed to global) critiques that have brought about so much social change since 1960, and scholarship has made a difference when it has participated in these local critiques and reinforced them. The lesson to be learned is that scholarship is politically valuable because it can foster the emergence of "subjugated knowledges" that make critique possible by bringing forth "blocks of historical knowledges that were present in the functional and systematic ensembles, but which were masked" and by questioning the disqualification of knowledges that are supposedly insufficiently conceptual, naïve, historically inferior, or "below the required level of erudition or scientificity," such as "the knowledge of the psychiatrized, the patient, the nurse, the doctor, that is parallel to, marginal to, medical knowledge, the knowledge of the delinquent, what I would call, if you like, what people know" (2003b, 7). "I think it is the coupling together of the buried scholarly knowledge and knowledges that were disqualified by the hierarchy of erudition and sciences," Foucault said, "that actually gave the discursive critique of the last fifteen years its essential strength" (2003b, 8).

What this coupling engenders is an "historical knowledge of struggles. Both the specialized domain of scholarship and the disqualified knowledge [that lay] people have contained the memory of combats, the very memory that had until then been confined to the margins. And so we have the outline of what might be called a genealogy, or of multiple genealogical investigations. We have both a meticulous rediscovery of struggles and the raw memory of fights" (2003b, 8). Genealogy dislodges entrenched belief; it amounts to "an insurrection against the centralizing power-effects that are bound up with the institutionalization and workings of any scientific discourse organized in a society such as ours. . . . Genealogy has to fight the power-effects characteristic of any discourse that is regarded as scientific" (2003b, 9).

But in the face of "biopower"—vast, growing, and intensely interconnected networks of normalizing discourses and practices—was genealogy in all its anarchic insurrectionary glory really effective? First of all, were biopolitical regimes hampered or even interrupted by the criticisms launched? Foucault is pessimistic: "Look: ever since the very beginnings of antipsychiatry or of the genealogies of psychiatric institutions . . . has a single Marxist, psychoanalyst, or psychiatrist ever attempted to redo it in their own terms or demonstrated that these genealogies were wrong, badly elaborated, badly articulated, or ill-founded? The way things stand, the fragments of genealogy that have been done are in fact still there, surrounded by a wary silence" (2003b, 12). Foucault's work hadn't been discredited, but apparently it hadn't disturbed anybody much either. It hadn't provoked even the slightest defensive response.

Thus, January of 1976 was a time of reckoning regarding the political efficacy of genealogy. In that context, Foucault pointed

toward the second problem on the horizon, the potential for a reification of this new form of power that he had begun to discuss. "As
you know, and as I scarcely need point out," he said, "what is at stake
in all these genealogies is this: What is this power whose irruption,
force, impact, and absurdity have become palpably obvious over the
forty years?" (2003b, 12). Taken together, these genealogical fragments sketched out an epistemic field, an historically emergent form
of power. Was there some way to understand these mechanisms and
regimes of power and their interconnectedness and reciprocal rein-
forcements without positing a new epistemic object? "What is power?
Or rather—given that the question 'What is power?' is obviously
a theoretical question that would provide an answer to everything,
which is just what I don't want to do—the issue is to determine what
are, in their mechanisms, effects, their relations, the various power-
apparatuses that operate at various levels of society, in such very
different domains and with so many different extensions?" (2003b,
13). It was Foucault's pursuit of this question, and his effort to avoid
a reified answer in the form of a theory of power, that would lead him
to the issue of race.[48]

The Anti-Sovereign Discourse of Race War

Foucault's studies of psychiatry, medicine, sexuality, military discipline, carceral institutions, and related areas had shown not "the
brute fact of the domination of the one over the many, or of one
group over another, but [rather] the multiple forms of domination
that can be exercised in society; so, not the king in his central position, but subjects in their reciprocal relations; not sovereignty in its
one edifice, but the multiple subjugations that take place and function
within the social body" (2003b, 27). In light of these multiple forms
of domination, three aspects of traditional theories of power were
particularly troublesome: (1) the assumption that prior to the advent
of political power there already exists a subject endowed with natural
rights and abilities (the issue is how that natural subject can become
a political subject); (2) the assumption that prior to the advent of
political power there already exist other kinds of powers—capacities,
potentials, desires, natural relationships of domination, and so on, it
being the job of sovereignty to unite those powers into one political
system from which they will take their direction; and (3) the project
of demonstrating how a unified political system can claim legitimacy

prior to any given law and can serve as a basis for the function of positive law (2003b, 43–44).

This whole approach to phenomena of power was placed in question by Foucault's studies of patterns of domination and subjugation in institutional contexts like the nineteenth-century asylum and prison. Subjects were not merely absorbed into those systems of power and subordinated to them; they were shaped by them, and some forms of subjectivity emerged only within and were clearly entirely dependent upon them. Furthermore, disciplinary power didn't just seize upon capacities and potentials; it created them. And finally, the regimes Foucault investigated operated not so much according to law as according to shifting norms, and legitimacy was simply not at issue within them. To understand those power regimes requires that we ask, not by what right subjects may agree to being subjected in a political system, but "how actual relations of subjugation manufacture subjects." It requires that we not look for a central origin for the exercise of all powers but that we figure out "how the various operators of domination support one another, relate to one another . . . converge and reinforce one another in some cases, and negate or strive to annul one another in other cases." And it requires that we concern ourselves not with the legitimacy of these networks of relation but with "the technical instruments that guarantee that they function" (2003b, 45–46). Sticking to these issues may well enable us to avoid reifying the forces whose vectors we trace and thus to maintain "biopower" as a non-name, as a place-holder for a dynamic occurrence that cannot be objectified. The big question is how to carry out that plan: "How can we pursue our analysis of relations of domination? To what extent can a relationship of domination boil down to or be reduced to the notion of a relationship of force? . . . Is the power relationship basically a relationship of confrontation, a struggle to the death, or a war? If we look beneath peace, order, wealth, and authority, beneath the calm order of subordinations, beneath the State and State apparatuses, beneath the laws, and so on, will we hear and discover a sort of primitive and permanent war?" (2003b, 46–47).

If we did, we would not be the first. At the very same historical moment when modern states began to establish themselves as the guarantors of internal peace and to expel warfare to their margins and exteriors, where they placed it in the hands of institutionalized military apparatuses, there arose a critical counter-discourse in which war was taken to be the basis of social relations. Contrary to the social contract theorists, this discourse asserted that political power does not begin the moment war ends. States are born in conflict, battle, conquest. They impose their laws and institutions in order to secure their domination: "Peace itself is a coded war" (2003b, 51). The unifying action of the State is an act of violence against the multiple and disparate elements it encompasses. No one is or can be in a position of neutrality with regard to that ongoing act. We are all historically constituted as subjects of struggle within it, and the stories we tell about it are all necessarily politically charged. There is no neutral subjectivity, and there is no universal truth.

This anti-sovereign discourse of war begins, Foucault tells us, with the English Puritans in the 1630s. It critiques and dismantles the assertion of sovereignty in favor of an analysis of warring factions and decentralized struggles. It "cuts off the king's head" or "at least does without a sovereign and denounces him" (2003b, 59). Instead of focusing on the singularity of the sovereign, it focuses on the multiplicity of "races." Thus it begins as a counter-discourse over against the theories of political power that the modern era inherited from the medieval period and that it would redeploy in the form of classical liberalism. As Foucault shows, if we trace that transformation without a prior valorization of sovereignty, we get a history of "race war discourse" that can teach us a great deal about modern forms of power and resistance.

Race war discourse first emerges, according to Foucault, when various factions in English society, principally those more or less disempowered and humiliated by what they called the Norman government of James I, claimed that the Stuart monarchy was illegitimate. Oppressed by a king and court that had blood and religious ties to a foreign country and that conducted state affairs in a foreign language, a self-proclaimed Saxon underclass began to speak of themselves as an indigenous race over against a race of conquering aliens. The laws these aliens imposed were not a means to peace (as laws are allegedly supposed to be) but weapons of continued subjugation of the general populace, the rightful inhabitants and owners of the land. What underlay and pervaded all of seventeenth-century English society, according to these thinkers and rebels, was war—"basically, a race war" (2003b, 60)—one that allegedly had been going on since the Battle of Hastings in 1066.[49]

This discourse of race war was thus first of all a means of naming and underlining the presence of ongoing and egregious injustice, a pattern of domination not attributable to any one individual or law. It probably originated, but at any rate circulated, among the Puritans; then in somewhat altered form among the Parliamentarians; and yet again, in the demands of the Diggers and Levellers. In each incarnation, different though they sometimes were, race war discourse operated as a wedge for separating people from their sovereign, the better to lay hold of an alternative conception of the nation, not as the sovereign's property but as a kind of popular hereditary territory, a home. In short, race war discourse was invented by an oppressed group to consolidate its membership and harden them against their oppressors. It enabled the production of a counter-history that served to reify and rally a people for revolution.

Race and racism were not Foucault's primary focus in the 1976 lectures. Power was. "I was certainly not trying for one moment to trace the history of racism in the general and traditional sense of the term," he stated in response to a question posed to him just prior to the fifth lecture. "I do not want to trace the history of what it might have meant, in the West, to have an awareness of belonging to a race, or of the history of the rites and mechanisms that were used to try to exclude, disqualify, or physically destroy a race. I was—and in my own view, I am—trying to look at the emergence in the West of a certain analysis (a critical, historical, and political analysis) of the State, its institutions and its power mechanisms. . . . That, and not racism, is my basic problem" (2003b, 88). But by the end of his investigation, which culminates in a characterization of biopower in the final lecture on March 17, the two—racism and biopower—coincide to a striking degree. "The specificity of modern racism, or what gives it its specificity, is not bound up with mentalities, ideologies, or the lies of power. It is bound up with the technique of power, with the technology of power," he asserts. "We are dealing with a mechanism that allows biopower to work. . . . The juxtaposition of—or the way biopower functions through—the old sovereign power of life and death implies the workings, the introduction and activation, of racism" (2003b, 258).[50] Biopower can't function without racism, and modern racism takes shape within the forces of biopolitical function and expansion. *"Society Must Be Defended"* traces and analyzes race war discourse as it was transformed from a tool of the underclass to a tool of the bourgeoisie and as it was finally absorbed by the nation-state and translated into biological categories—with some horrific and catastrophic results.[51]

The differences between seventeenth-century race war discourse and modern racism are numerous, huge, and fairly obvious. In early race war discourse, there is no presumption of an essential morphological manifestation of racial difference—Normans look pretty much like Saxons. *Race* refers to lineage, or what we might call cultural heritage; the differences at issue are not differences of embodiment. As Foucault puts it, "Although this discourse speaks of races, and although the term 'race' appears at a very early stage, it is quite obvious that the word 'race' itself is not joined to a stable biological meaning" (2003b, 77). Race is a matter of language, tradition, and custom, not a matter of bodily differences and similarities. Second, race war discourse includes no comprehensive typology of racial kinds (such as the ones that begin to emerge in the work of eighteenth-century natural historians), only the posited opponents in this particular race war. Whereas modern racist discourse in Europe and the United States identifies all the earth's peoples as members of one or another of a definite (usually very small) set of races, race war discourse is unconcerned about peoples not involved in the immediate political conflict and makes no assertions at all about them. There are Normans and there are Saxons, and that is all that matters. Certainly, there are other races—hundreds or even thousands, perhaps—but exactly how many and exactly how they differ from each other is utterly irrelevant to this discourse. Third, in race war discourse there is no ahistorical moral, intellectual, or biological hierarchy of races: the bad thing about Normans is not that they are essentially intellectually or morally inferior to Saxons, but that they are here among us, planting their fiefs upon Saxon land; that they have humiliated Saxons as individuals and as a people, treated them unjustly, diminished the value and quality of Saxon lives, and robbed them of their rightful status. The animosity that self-proclaimed Saxons felt toward so-called Normans in 1630 was therefore very unlike the animosity of whites toward blacks in Selma in 1965. Seventeenth-century race war discourse, even at its ugliest and bloodiest, was far removed from modern racism.

So how did this discourse get "re-worked" to give rise to modern racism with its insistence on biological difference, comprehensive classification, and racial hierarchies? What elements of this early version of race war discourse gave rise to the racist discourses of the nineteenth century? What fell away and why? How does a discourse that begins as a way of affirming and strengthening an underclass become a discourse that affirms and strengthens a ruling class?

My answers to the first and second questions will occupy a great deal of space in coming chapters, but Foucault answers the third question himself very straightforwardly. Race war discourse did not belong exclusively to the underclasses even in the seventeenth century, he tells us, at least not for very long. This "is a discourse that has a great ability to circulate, a great aptitude for metamorphosis, or a sort of strategic polyvalence" (2003b, 76). Race war discourse is a powerful way of dividing "us" from "them," whoever us and them may be. Eduardo Mendieta has noted that, as Foucault analyzes it in these lectures, race is "a mechanism of power that proceeds or is guided by a logic that is executed in twos. The logic of race is a logic of a bifurcated social body" (Mendieta 2000, 12). Once set in motion, the dividing practice that is race war discourse becomes available for just about anybody to employ for setting one group against another. A hundred years after its English birth, for instance, Boulainvilliers appropriated race war discourse as a tool for shoring up the power of the French nobility over against Louis XIV's bureaucrats. The French nobility in the eighteenth century were the descents of the Germanic Franks, he claimed, whereas the king's administrators, the Church-trained Latin-speaking clerks, were the descendants of the Gauls. France was not one nation united under a sovereign; it was a territory in which two races were locked together in a long and obscure struggle. Boulainvilliers looked forward to a day when the aristocratic Franks would take back control of France from the Gaulish bureaucrats and the king they fortified and would reinstate themselves as the rightful rulers.

But once again, in this eighteenth century version of race war discourse the races in question are not morphologically distinct. They speak different languages and have different lineages and traditions (if we can believe Boulainvilliers), but these differences are cultural, not biological. It would be another hundred years and more before the word *race* would come to name anything like a biologically distinct human group. With that innovation came the movement most historians now call *scientific racism*, the immediate predecessor, Foucault tells us, to the state racism of the Nazi regime—and, we might add, to the racism that expressed itself in the United States in Jim Crow segregation, lynching, and acts of terrorism such as the bombing of Birmingham's Sixteenth Street Baptist Church. The story of how these changes occurred is not only interesting in and of itself but also, I believe, offers us an important perspective on contemporary struggles and brings to light some possibilities within them that we might not see from any other angle. After all, it is a story about how race became a form of embodiment perpetuated by sexual reproduction and of how some forms of embodiment as well as some forms of sexuality came to be viewed as mortal dangers to modern society.

Although I take my lead from Foucault's genealogical sketch in *"Society Must Be Defended,"* in the genealogy that unfolds in the chapters that follow I not only build upon Foucault's work but I also tinker with his dates, geography, and terminology. After all, I am interested in modern racism in the United States, and Foucault focuses exclusively on western Europe (in fact, exclusively on England and France), so at the very least I have to make some adjustments in my genealogical account to bring the story to this side of the Atlantic. In doing so, however, I have found that some other adjustments and refinements are necessary as well. One crucial adjustment is that, in my story, race becomes a matter of morphology—physical appearance—several decades before it becomes a matter of biology. The change in the meaning of the term *race* from lineage to embodiment occurs in the mid-eighteenth century in the United States, I argue, and I suspect that a similar transformation is just beginning in France and in German-speaking countries at about the same time. It seems to occur somewhat later in England, probably by three or four decades, and thus there the transformation from lineage to morphology coincides with the absorption of race as a concept into the biological sciences. But whenever this change occurred in European countries, here in the United States, race's shift in definition from heritage to physical appearance occurred *before* there was a discipline called biology. Only later, perhaps as much as fifty years later, did morphological race become biological race. Chapter 2 tells the story of this transformation from lineage to morphology, while chapter 3 tells the story of the transformation from morphology to biology.

In the process of separating morphological from biological race, my narrative also upsets Foucault's chronology regarding the development of state racism. He says scientific or biological racism enabled state racism, and it is certainly true that Nazism, for example, would have been inconceivable without biological discourses of race. However, Nazi Germany's was not the first government to make race a central part of its public policy or its governing strategy. It is entirely possible that the first government to do so was not that of a nation-state at all but that of a colony, England's Virginia Colony in the early eighteenth century, and that the first nation to do so was the United States of America in 1787. Relying heavily on the work of several prominent U.S. historians (including, among others, Edmund Morgan, Theodore Allen, and Anthony Parent), I will argue that Virginia's colonial government was the principal mechanism by which race was transformed from a concept of lineage to a concept of morphology and that morphological race played a central role in the colony's administration. Furthermore, the practices and policies that enabled this transformation continued after the American Revolution, so it could well be said that the United States is the birthplace of state racism, with Virginia as its cradle.

I do not think that either of these changes—the chronological separation of the transformations from lineage to morphology and then to biology, and the chronological reversal of the appearance of biological and state racism—in any way undermines Foucault's genealogical work. I view my changes to his story as refinements and supplementations, not challenges. My goal is to come to an understanding of the twentieth-century biopolitical phenomenon that is modern racism. What follows in the next two chapters, then, is an attempt to sketch modern racism's ancestry in somewhat more detail than Foucault offers in *"Society Must Be Defended"* so that we can move on in later chapters to an examination of racism against the abnormal.

TWO

A GENEALOGY OF MODERN
RACISM, PART 1
THE WHITE MAN COMETH

As Foucault suggests, not only in race war discourse but in seventeenth-century English more generally (as in German and French), the word *race* referred to heritage or tradition.[1] Regardless of how they looked, individuals belonged to a race if they grew up in its traditions, spoke its language, and practiced its religion. Membership had nothing to do with biological inevitability or essence. In the seventeenth century there was not, and never yet had been, any assumption that races were physically distinct natural kinds. This chapter tells the story of how that changed, of how race became a fact not about a person's ancestry and cultural practices but about his or her visible corporeality.

My contention here is that the white race was the very first race to be morphologically defined—as distinct from races such as the Saxon and the Norman that were defined by lineage and tradition—and that it came into existence through the course of the eighteenth century in the tobacco colonies of Anglo-America. Whiteness as a racial classification did not exist in the seventeenth century.[2] But it did exist in Virginia by 1723; by that date it was recognized in law and was in use in attempts to establish political and economic solidarity across differences that would themselves have been understood as racial divides in times past—differences of language, religious conviction, and national origin. It also ennobled those fundamentally expedient conjunctions by lending them an air of natural inevitability. By the end of the eighteenth century, people deemed white supposedly had a natural affinity for one another and a natural disinclination toward all those who were not deemed white; morphology was a unifying force more powerful than any cultural (or even familial) bond.[3] Almost all by itself, seemingly, morphology could create a nation out of people who had virtually nothing else in common.

British settlers arrived at Jamestown in 1607 and at Plymouth, by way of the Netherlands, in 1620. In those days *race* was still a new word in the English language, having been used to distinguish human groups only since about 1580, and race war discourse was still in its earliest formative stages. Most of the very first European inhabitants of what would soon be Anglo-America had probably never heard of race war, even though its principal theorists and disseminators were their Anglo-Saxon counterparts back home in the motherland. But their ignorance was fairly short-lived.

Plenty of English rebels and religious dissenters found their way to the "New World" after race war discourse became current in England. Thousands came over the next few decades—some as capitalists, most as indentured servants. A few even came as colonial officials. During Cromwell's rule in the 1650s, Puritan factions held some power in a number of American colonial governments, including those of Virginia and Maryland.[4] Undoubtedly, many of these men and women were familiar with race war discourse—most importantly as an interpretation of the political situation in England, the struggle between the Saxons and the Normans, but in some cases also in its more general strategic usefulness as a means of establishing and maintaining political distinctions.

After the Restoration of the Stuart monarchy in 1660, Charles II sent boatloads of Cromwellians into bond-servitude in the Virginia colony. In 1663, a number of these men helped foment what Theodore Allen calls "the largest, most widespread insurrectionary plot of bond-laborers" in North American history (Allen 1997, 152). The plot was initiated at Gloucester, where John Gunter, William Bell, and other laborers organized fellow tobacco workers—indentured servants, transported felons, and possibly some slaves (Parent 2003, 142)—into military companies prepared to seize arms and munitions and march from plantation to plantation killing opponents on their way to the colonial governor's mansion. Once there, if Governor William Berkeley refused their petition for freedom, they planned to depose him and "make and wholy submit and distroy the State of this Country of Vir'g" (Parent 2003, 143). The plot was betrayed to authorities before it could get seriously underway. Governor Berkeley sent his forces to ambush and capture the rebels. However, a counter-betrayal warned them of the danger, and most escaped into the Great Dismal Swamp at what is now the easternmost edge of the Virginia/North Carolina state line. Of those caught only four were hanged, leaving the rest to fight again another day (Allen 1997, 152). Hoping to avoid the trouble that might result from English rebels influencing colonial workers, Virginia's colonial government banned importation of convicted felons in 1670. Nevertheless, since Anglo-America was a handy repository for all manner of malcontents as well as official royal enemies, it is quite likely that a great many of the "settlers" (most of them chattel bond-laborers) in Virginia and elsewhere were well acquainted with the dissenter rhetoric of race war between the Saxons and the Norman usurpers and quite likely understood their sojourn and situation in North America to be a direct result of the ongoing English race war.

Beyond giving a voice to seething resentment toward the Stuart king who bound and exiled his enemies to the mosquito-ridden marsh-lands of the Chesapeake, however, race war discourse might have had little application in colonial territories like Maryland, Virginia, and the Carolinas. Who, after all, was being subdued and dispossessed there? Clearly not the Saxons, many of whom were there only because they had already been dispossessed and subdued elsewhere. On these shores it was first of all indigenous peoples who were placed under laws that operated more like weapons against them than like noble instruments of peace; not only were they being driven from their farmland and hunting grounds, but they were being captured by the thousands and sold into slavery in the European sugar colonies of the Caribbean.

The Puritan discourse of race war does not seem especially appli-cable, except possibly in reverse, to the situation on the western side of the Atlantic,[5] so it is not surprising that it does not seem to have given rise in any direct way to the racial discourses that eventually came to characterize the incipient United States of America. Benjamin Franklin's and Thomas Jefferson's racial discourses are not that of seventeenth-century dissenter race war; the concept of race itself had undergone significant change by their time, and they write from within a very different political milieu.[6] Nevertheless, we must not underes-timate the influence of race war discourse on the seventeenth-century Anglo-American colonial elite, the class of men U.S. historians call the "great planters." Although they would not have adopted the details of race war discourse as it was articulated in England to understand their own situation in colonial Virginia, Maryland, and elsewhere, they no doubt understood the value of the concept of race as a tool for dividing a population into opposing factions.[7] Furthermore, as the republican ideas of the English Commonwealth period filtered into eighteenth century scholarship and political analysis, elements of the old race war discourse, significantly reworked, did influence men like Jefferson, not only in their attitudes toward English authority but also in their attitudes toward American native peoples and toward their slaves. This point will be explored in some detail at the end of this chapter.

In order for modern versions of racism to establish themselves, the meaning of the term *race* had to shift away from lineage and language and toward morphology. Foucault sees this process beginning in the early nineteenth century, correlated in part with "nationalist movements in Europe and with nationalities' struggles against the great State apparatuses (essentially the Russian and the Austrian)" and with colonization (Foucault 2003b, 60). My narrative will locate its beginning somewhat earlier, but it will substantiate Foucault's claim that the process was driven by politico-economic considerations. The process was also fed by the classical scientific effort to tabulate natural entities—literally, to produce a comprehensive table of natural kinds—which we see in the work of Linnaeus, Buffon, Blumenbach, Voltaire, Herder, Kant, Cuvier, and countless others.[8] Both of these forces, which I would argue, *contra* Bernard Boxill, are inextricably intertwined, will be explored in this chapter.[9] Foucault does not offer any explanation of how the practices of natural historians, colonial administrators, or nationalist politicos conspired to construct morphological conceptions of race; he only notes that they did so. But recent work by a number of U.S. historians provides suggestive fragments of a story of the emergence of morphological race in North America.

The White Man Cometh

The first Africans arrived in Anglo North America in 1619. According to planter John Rolfe, they came to the Jamestown Colony aboard a Dutch man-of-war that had been trading along the Virginia coast (Blaustein and Zangrando 1991, 4). There were about twenty of them, all male, at least some having Christian names. Labor being in short supply in the colony, the Virginia Company's governor, George Yeardley, acting in his official company capacity, purchased the Africans from the Dutch. Thus, according to popular perceptions, did morphologically defined racial slavery begin in Anglo-America. Such a view is utterly anachronistic, however. The Africans were not purchased because they were dark-skinned people (*Negros,* as the Spanish termed it); they were purchased because they were laborers. If the Dutch had had Slavs or Irishmen or Swedes for sale that day, the same deal would have been struck. The Africans were considered to be of a different race from the Englishmen, but that was not because their skin was dark; it was because they were descended from different ancestors, spoke a different language, and practiced a different religion and different customs. The same would have been true of twenty Slavs, Irishmen, or Swedes. Neither slavery as it had developed by the end of the seventeenth century, nor racism as we understand the term, existed in England or in any of her colonies in 1619.[10]

What did exist in abundance in 1619 and increasingly in the next several years was horrific exploitation of all laborers, regardless of color, religion, language, or geographic origin. The death rate was very high; most laborers died within three years of arrival, long before their terms of indenture were up, so in effect their servitude was life-long. Discipline and punishment were brutal as masters attempted to get heavy labor out of debilitated workers who received no wages and had little hope of living to see better days. Masters bought and sold their English servants freely and sometimes gambled them away. As historian Edmund Morgan puts it, "Virginians dealt in servants the way Englishmen dealt in land or chattels" (Morgan 1975, 128). Buying and selling human beings was already something of a British scandal before the Africans arrived in 1619. And it just got worse. By 1625 Captain Thomas Weston refused to transport indentured servants to Virginia on his ship because "servants were sold heere upp and downe like horses, and therfore he held it not lawfull to carie any" (Morgan 1975, 129). In practice, Virginia planters were already slave owners in the 1620s, but most of their chattels were other Englishmen.

Technically speaking, of course, indentured servants were not slaves, although their living and working conditions were virtually the same as conditions would be for slaves a few decades later. The difference was that their contracts did not state that they served for life. Instead, they worked for some specified length of time, usually seven years. If they survived their term of indenture (many did not) and managed to hang onto their indenture papers and convince their "employer" to go with them to a court to have the term of contract officially terminated (this did not happen automatically),[11] then they were entitled to a form of compensation known as freedom dues. In Maryland, freedom dues included seed corn, tools, and a certain number of acres to start a new plantation. In Virginia, acreage was not given, only corn and clothing, but wages were high enough before mid-century for many freedmen to save money and then rent or purchase their own land (Parent 2003, 36). As the years wore on, however, enough indentured servants survived to acquire land and set up their own plantations that there was a glut of tobacco on the market. For that reason and others, prices fell. It became clear to the large landholders that this situation could not continue. Freedom dues had to be avoided; there was no room for more producers, and plenty of need for more labor. Upward mobility had to cease.

British law clearly forbade lifelong chattel servitude. It was true that men could be bought and sold, made to work for free, confined against their will, and beaten almost to death by those who possessed them, but they could not be made by law to suffer all these things for their entire lives. (Things were slightly different for women; as wives women *could* be bought outright, forced to work for free, and confined and beaten *for their entire lives*. Why were wives not considered slaves? British law prohibited husbands from reselling them after the initial purchase, so unlike slaves, wives did not have any exchange value and hence could not count as wealth.) Eager to eliminate class mobility, colonial planters found many creative ways to get around British law and to extract a lifetime of labor from their servants despite official prohibition. Theodore Allen puts the number of European men, women, and children brought to Virginia and Maryland alone between 1607 and 1682 at 92,000.[12] Of that number, he asserts, more than 75 percent—that is, more than 73,000—were made to be, in fact if not in law, lifelong chattel slaves (Allen 1997, 122).

They did not take to it kindly, any more than their African and Native American counterparts did. Allen documents hundreds of incidents of resistance and rebellion among laborers of all classifications during the colonial period. The entire colonial labor force was extremely unruly and, furthermore, quite apt to act with solidarity across what we now perceive as racial lines. European, African, and Native American bond-laborers often escaped together, sometimes seeking asylum in nearby Native American communities where they were welcomed. Many chose to fight rather than run, however, and groups of militant laborers—groups that we would now see as racially mixed—menaced planters throughout the seventeenth century, cooperating with each other apparently without racial discord.

How could planters bring such a large and volatile labor force under their control? And how could they prevent the planting class from expanding as former bond-laborers claimed title to fertile land? One way was to stop importing so many European bond-laborers (whose rights were recognized and sometimes upheld by European governments) and to find another source of chattel labor.[13] Native Americans were not optimal slave material, because their knowledge of the land and kinship ties with neighboring groups made successful escape a constant possibility.[14] If they were to be enslaved, it was best to ship them off the continent to the islands as soon as possible. But Africans, strangers in the New World without knowledge of the land or Old World governments to protect their rights, could be used indefinitely, and no freedom dues ever paid. As the life expectancy of immigrants of all descriptions lengthened, wealthier planters began to find it worth twice the cost of an indentured servant to buy a slave for life. Furthermore, slaves' value could be easily calculated on the market and thus could be reckoned into the value of a planter's total holdings; slaves were a form of wealth apart from the wealth generated by the labor they performed (Martinot 2003, 50).

As early as the 1640s, Virginians recognized that some men held property in slaves who had been acquired either through "wartime" capture of Native Americans or purchase from foreign traders (Morgan 1975, 297). But it was not until 1661 that the Virginia General Assembly took action to enslave individuals who began their lives in the Virginia Colony as free persons. In that year, the Assembly decreed that enslavement for life could be imposed by the courts as a form of punishment on Negro, but not European, law-breakers (Gossett 1997, 30).[15] Then, in September of 1664, the Maryland General Assembly proclaimed that "all Negroes and other slaves already within the province, and all Negroes and other slaves to be hereafter imported into the province, shall serve *durante vita*," for their entire lives (Blaustein and Zangrando 1991, 9). In the same act, Maryland imposed lifelong servitude upon children born of enslaved fathers, even if their mothers were not Negroes and not slaves, and imposed chattel servitude upon non-Negro women who married Negro slaves for the duration of their husbands' lives. In 1670, the Virginia General Assembly followed Maryland's lead in declaring that "all servants not being christians" who were brought to the colony by sea were to serve for life (Gossett 1997, 30). Since the only non-Christians arriving in Virginia by sea were from Africa, and very few Africans were arriving by any other mode of transport, this declaration meant that virtually all black laborers imported after 1670 would automatically be enslaved rather than indentured.[16] In 1676 and again in 1679, the General Assembly gave landowners who engaged in warfare with Native Americans the right to hold captives as servants for life, in effect issuing "a slave-hunting license" to the small planters in the western part of the colony (Morgan 1975, 328). And in 1682 the Assembly made all non-Christian servants slaves for life, thus placing Native Americans in the same category as Africans (Morgan 1975, 329). As a result, by 1676, the only laborers in Virginia who were not lifelong slaves were light-skinned.[17]

North American slavery was not at first, however, a racist institution (although obviously it was an unjust and oppressive one). As Eric Williams (among others) has argued, "Slavery was not born of racism: rather, racism was the consequence of slavery" (Williams 1944, 7). The initial and overriding motivation for African enslavement was neither sadism nor prejudice; it was profit. Wealthy and powerful Anglo-Americans did not institute the enslavement of Africans because they hated Africans or thought they were inferior but because they knew doing so was a way to increase their wealth and power and because by 1670 nothing substantial stood in their way.[18] Cultural and morphological differences were exploited to reinforce the institution once its political and economic benefits to planters were clear.

If planters were able to exploit these "racial" differences, we might suppose that there must already have been ambient antiblack sentiment among the general populace. But there is a lot of evidence to indicate that antiblack racism was not characteristic of bond laborers in Anglo-America in the seventeenth century. Edmund Morgan writes: "There are hints that the two despised groups initially saw each other as sharing the same predicament. It was common, for example, for servants and slaves to run away together, steal hogs together, get drunk together. It was not uncommon for them to make love together. In Bacon's Rebellion one of the last groups to surrender was a mixed band of eighty Negroes and twenty English servants" (Morgan 1975, 327). In fact, "there is more than a little evidence that Virginians during these years were ready to think of Negroes as members or potential members of the community on the same terms as other men and to demand of them the same standards of behavior. Black and white men and women serving the same master worked, ate, and slept together, and together shared in escapades, escapes, and punishments. In 1649 William Watts, a white man, and Mary, a Negro servant, were required to do penance for fornication, like any other unmarried couple, by standing in the church at Elizabeth River with the customary white sheet and white wand; and in 1654 the churchwardens of the upper parish in Northampton presented both a white couple and a Negro couple for fornication" (Morgan 1975, 155–56). As these examples show, not only was there sexual attraction and affection across racial lines, but clergy and parishioners seemed to have believed in moral equality and mutual accountability.

Sexual relationships between women of European descent and men of African descent were common enough that in 1691 the Virginia General Assembly—having passed a law previously that gave children the civil status of their mother rather than their father— imposed punishment on any European-American woman who gave birth to a mulatto child. Apparently the great planters feared that free mulattos—individuals whose fathers, grandparents, and perhaps half-siblings might be living in perpetual bondage—could become a large enough class of people that they might eventually pose a threat to social stability. The offending woman was to be fined fifteen pounds sterling or, if she could not pay (which was likely), be placed in bondage for five years beyond her term of indenture, and her child was to be held in bondage by the parish churchwardens until the age of thirty. The act also prohibited marriage between individuals of European and African descent, the penalty for which was banishment from the colony forever. Before 1691 interracial marriage was fairly common, as evidenced by the fact that prohibition in positive law was deemed necessary. Half of the African American planters on Virginia's Eastern Shore had wives of European descent in the mid-seventeenth century (Parent 2003, 116). Even after the act was passed, many

Virginians resented it and resisted, including George Ivie, a member of a distinguished family who petitioned for repeal of the law in 1699, and John and Sarah Slayden Bunch, who in 1705 petitioned to force their minister to publish their marriage banns (Parent 2003, 117).

What the planters exploited to reinforce the institution of African slavery through the last third of the seventeenth century and the first decades of the eighteenth was not preexisting racism; it was literally the differences among laborers in physical appearance, religion, and language. They played on those differences to create antagonisms that eventually became antiblack racism. Wealthy landholders incited antiblack racism, historians such as Edmund Morgan and Theodore Allen argue, by destroying solidarity between laborers of European descent and laborers of African descent and then by persuading European Americans to accept and eventually help enforce African Americans' enslavement.

This was no easy feat if for no other reason than that laborers knew that the lifelong enslavement of any group ran counter to the economic interests of them all.[19] And there *were* other reasons, including religious beliefs, friendships, and family ties. Without the divisions of racial antipathy, however, colonial laborers presented a formidable managerial challenge to their overlords. To meet that challenge, the governments of the tobacco colonies deliberately drove a legal and psychological wedge between laborers of African and European descent, and the various state governments continued this policy after their establishment along with the independent United States of America. This was done systematically through the late seventeenth and early eighteenth centuries, not so much by degrading chattel slaves (which would have been difficult, considering how degraded they already were), but rather mainly by lowering the legal status of free laborers of African descent and elevating that of free laborers of European descent.[20] By creating inequality in their labor force where it had not existed before, the great landowners incited interpersonal conflict and gave laborers of European descent a much larger stake in the status quo.

This is how, according to Allen, the so-called white race was created—the first race in human history ever to be defined purely morphologically. The white race was established as a legal and economic category in colonial and then in U.S. law and policy as a way of co-opting the European-American portion of the labor force (which of course by this point included a great many non-Englishmen, making the nationalist category ineffective for this purpose) so that enslavement of a subset of the total labor force—the African American portion—could proceed unhampered. We can take Allen's argument a step further and assert that the invention of the white race was, in effect, the invention of morphological race itself, a conception of race that was almost completely detached from both language and geographical origin, one that relied almost entirely on bodily marks as the essence of racial membership.

However much eighteenth-century European anthropologists, geographers, philosophers, and anatomists wanted to classify and debate the number and divisions between the races of "mankind," in practice morphological race is an Anglo-American invention, worked out in the give-and-take of material interests and legal and political institutions on the North American continent. We could even view these theoretical debates in Europe and elsewhere as anxious attempts to make systematic (and thus give the appearance of rationality to) what existed only in very imprecise and chaotic practice. The debates about classification were in part debates about which bodily marks should count as marks of racial distinction, an issue that was never settled in colonial law and obviously persisted long after the American Revolution as a nagging problem in U.S. law and policy. Where morphological race was concerned, scientific theory followed and attempted to explain, justify, and refine practice; it did not precipitate it.[21]

When they revised the Virginia Code in 1705, the Virginia General Assembly streamlined and systematized a number of laws enacted over the past forty-five years since the Restoration of Charles II and established a number of new laws that changed the civil status of free African Americans, differentiating them civilly in many ways for the first time from free European Americans. Their right to self-defense was limited; they were prohibited from congregating; they lost the right to vote in colonial elections. In addition to these changes, however, Allen emphasizes the method by which the new acts were promulgated. The General Assembly "took special pains to be sure that the people they ruled were propagandized in the moral and legal *ethos* of white-supremacism" (Allen 1997, 251), pains they persisted in taking with the enactment of more such laws over the next two decades. Allen describes the new rules in detail: "For consciousness-raising purposes (to prevent 'pretense of ignorance'), the laws mandated that parish clerks or churchwardens, once each spring and fall at the close of Sunday service, should read ('publish') these laws in full to the congregants. Sheriffs were ordered to have the same done at the courthouse door at the June or July term of court" (Allen 1997, 251). It should be remembered that church attendance in colonial Virginia was mandatory. Thus, three times a year every Virginian, regardless of race, had to listen to these statutes publicly recited. Clearly, the General Assembly believed these new laws were different enough from past practice and general sensibility that they might be forgotten or ignored unless they were pounded into people's memories. Allen continues: "If we presume, in the absence of any contrary record, that this mandate was followed, we must conclude that the general public was regularly and systematically subjected to official white-supremacist agitation. It was to be drummed into the minds of the people that, for the first time, no free African-American was to dare to lift his or her hand against a 'Christian, not being a negro, mulatto or Indian' (3:459)" (1997, 251).

I interrupt this passage, which I will continue to quote below, to point out that in 1705 Virginians did not as yet refer simply to "white people"; they resorted to a religious category—"Christian"—and a list of disjuncts—not negro, not mulatto, not Indian. The word *white* used as a racial category had already appeared in the Anglo-American colonies. It had existed in limited usage since about 1680 as a loose synonym for Christian, English, and free (Jordan 1968, 91), but apparently it was not widely enough understood to provide the clarity of meaning for which the General Assembly here was clearly striving. *White* does appear in Virginia law as a racial category by 1723, however—within eighteen years of its glaring absence in the slave code of 1705—as Allen's list reveals when he continues:

> It was to be drummed into the heads of the people that African-American freeholders were no longer to be allowed to vote (4:133–34); that the provision of a previous enactment (3:87 [1691]) was being reinforced against the mating of English and Negroes as producing "abominable mixture" and "spurious issue" (3:453–4); that, as provided in the 1723 law for preventing freedom plots by African-American bond-laborers, "any white person . . . found in the company with any [illegally congregated] slaves" was to be fined "(along with free African-Americans or Indians so offending) with a

fine of fifteen shillings," or to "receive, on his, or her, or their bare backs, for every such offense, twenty lashes well laid on." (4:129) (1997, 251)

All of this was to be reiterated season after season, year after year, in public, to captive audiences of laborers. Allen contends that if Americans of European descent already considered African Americans their inferiors, discriminated against them, refused to associate with them, and ignored their interests and needs, no such policy of public recitation would have been necessary, nor would many of the laws recited. The point was to produce racial division where little or none existed and to do so in order to divide the labor force and thus allay elite fears of a general uprising and a destabilization of the colonial economy.

The general laboring population was not the only group who had to be taught the lessons of morphological racism by colonial governmental officials. In 1723, after the Virginia General Assembly drastically curtailed basic civil rights for free blacks,[22] British Attorney General Richard West launched an inquiry. Denying any freeholder the right to vote in any colonial election on the basis of skin color was a clear departure from English law and from previous colonial statutes. West wrote, "I cannot see why one freeman should be used worse than another, merely upon account of his complexion" (Allen 1997, 241). In response, colonial governor William Gooch explained that free Negroes and Mulattos tended to be sympathetic to slaves, many having previously been slaves themselves. Therefore the governor thought it wise to affix to them "a perpetual Brand . . . by excluding them from that great Privilege of a Freeman" (Jordan 1968, 127). The "brand" was not a punishment for crimes committed; it was a label and a status "affixed" in order to neutralize and disempower, as well as to humiliate and degrade. William Gooch was no racist in the modern sense; he did not believe blacks were inferior to whites in virtue or intellect; in fact, he thought they were formidable adversaries with moral principals, material interests, affective relationships, and a stubborn love of liberty. He did not think they deserved to be degraded in law as a reflection of some natural state of degradation; he simply wanted to squelch labor unrest and reduce the risk of slave rebellions. Race hatred was not the fundamental motive for new racial distinctions in law. The basic motive was strategic: the easiest way to contain people who, because of their personal affiliations and histories, could not be supposed to support the current exploitive but quite profitable organization of colonial labor was to create law that marked them permanently as an underclass and distanced them physically and emotionally from other laborers who might otherwise share their interests.

Over time, these alterations of legal status had a psychological as well as a material effect, and it is easy to imagine how. In 1680 the General Assembly "prescribed thirty lashes on the bare back 'if any negroe or other slave shall presume to lift up his hand in opposition against any christian'" (Morgan 1975, 331). This measure was a particularly effective way of setting laborers at odds with each other along morphological racial lines in that it allowed servants to bully slaves without fear of retaliation, thus placing them psychologically on a par with masters. No longer could African Americans take up a weapon against or even strike a European American, no matter what the European American had done first. And everybody knew this, because the local magistrate or judge or the parish priest recited the law three times a year, every year. Placed in a position of almost absolute power over others, regardless of those others' racial differences and even if there are none, a fairly hefty percentage of people will take pleasure in exercising their "right" to harass and intimidate. Indeed, seventeenth- and eighteenth-century clergymen and social commentators pointed out that this was one of the moral problems with the institution of slavery; near-absolute power over another person had a corrupting influence over the power wielder, leading to cruelty and excess.

The General Assembly, slaveholders all, were simply extending one aspect of their own status to all European Americans, an aspect whose psychological effects they knew quite well. It would not have taken very long for African Americans to learn that it was imprudent to drink or gamble or engage in any kind of sporting competition or debate with men who could assault them with impunity at the slightest provocation and who could not be met with equal force on pain of legal punishment. The social life that binds people together was no longer possible once the right to self-defense was rescinded. It became necessary for free African Americans to distrust European Americans as much as enslaved ones undoubtedly did, and to use their free status to withdraw from "white" company—which not only made multiracial labor uprising less likely but made *any* form of alliance, including friendship and community, less likely. Gooch's plan—based on a practice already half a century old by Gooch's time—was brilliant.[23]

The Question of Race in Natural History

Colonial governments thus deliberately established morphological race as a civil concept that was contrary to tradition and legal precedent. Over the course of the eighteenth century, race, now a form of embodiment, became a form of subjectivity—of citizenship, of social status, and finally of personal identity. By Thomas Jefferson's day, race was no longer a matter of lineage or culture but was first and foremost a matter of morphology—skin color, hair texture, facial structure, and so on—along with the internal physiology that was thought to attend such variations, including increased or decreased capacity for rational thought. What had once been a political scheme had become, within sixty years, a kind of common sense. Law and policy in the new United States would thus be based on the assumption that racial subjectivity is real, that members of nonwhite races are incapable of exercising the responsibilities of full citizenship in a free republic, and that lifelong servitude is appropriate for some races and inappropriate for others.

This happened first of all as a matter of economic and political expediency and then as a matter of psychological and social consolidation of power and status, not as a result of innovations in scientific theory. Colonial planters sought to enhance their wealth by legalizing their right to as much land, chattel, and labor as possible. To hold onto that wealth, they gradually divided their workforce into two classes, slaves and free laborers. Individuals were slaves if circumstances enabled planters to force their service for life; individuals were term-servants if circumstances forced planters to recognize their rights as free persons at the end of a designated period of years. Over time, planters found it much easier to enslave Africans than to enslave either Europeans or Native Americans, so a great many Africans ended up enslaved, and eventually slavery came to be understood as a condition peculiar to people of African descent. In the beginning, however, there was no reason—either in the concept of "slave" or in British history or culture—to assume that all the slaves in Anglo-America would be dark-skinned. Once it became evident that the best source of laborers who could not successfully contest their enslaved status was the continent of Africa, however, the easiest way to mark off that class of people who were to be enslaved was by reference to their physical appearance. Most often the law and its fashioners were not required to give precise descriptions of physical difference or state a reason for making these distinctions, although when called upon to do the latter, officials such as Governor Gooch at times quite honestly cited political and economic expediency, not inherent difference, as the reason.

Indeed, in the late seventeenth century it would have been hard to refer to Africans as a distinct and unitary race, given the meaning of the word at the time. *Race* still referred to lineage. Therefore, just as there were many different "Indian" races—Powhatans, Monacans, and so on—and there were many different "white" races—Saxons, Normans, Franks, for example—there were, as planters who shopped for skilled African labor well knew, a number of dark-skinned races too. For example, the Igbo were especially valued in Virginia because of their skill in growing tobacco in their own country around the Niger delta, while planters in South Carolina and Georgia would pay higher prices for captives from Sierra Leone because of their knowledge of rice cultivation. Planters were well aware that Africans did not always speak or understand each other's languages, and they saw this as both a drawback and an advantage in labor management. As long as *race* meant "lineage" and "heritage," as long as its meaning was tied to religion and tongue, it had to have been obvious to European slave traders and to the Anglo-American gentry that there were a great many African races. Lumping together all Negroes and treating them as a separate class of people from everybody else who inhabited Anglo-America could not have been done on the basis of their status as a race until either (1) that class of people came to seem homogeneous in heritage and lineage, or (2) the concept of race underwent a significant change in meaning. Since the slave trade was not abolished in North America until 1808, more than a century after Virginia's colonial government began setting separate rules for whites and Negroes, by no stretch of the imagination could blacks have been seen as a culturally or linguistically homogeneous group during that hundred-year period. What made them one race rather than a large collection of races by the beginning of the nineteenth century was not an acquired homogeneity but rather a shift in the meaning of the word *race*.

We know from the history recounted thus far that there was plenty of material motivation among Anglo-America's elite to establish some kind of bond between themselves and the free laboring class made up largely of European immigrants, a bond that would reduce the likelihood of a labor uprising. They wanted to diminish overt class differences among European-Americans in order to maintain themselves as members of what was, in fact, a fairly exclusive ruling class. This was part and parcel of their effort to alienate enslaved laborers from the protection of the law and from the affection and concern of free laborers. When discursive realignments began to occur that made the concept of race available for application to their political circumstances, they rapidly took advantage of the situation.

Those realignments occurred in part as a result of the development of the discipline of natural history, which began in England with John Ray's publication of *The Wisdom of God Manifested in the Works of Creation* in 1691. Natural history was all about the identification and classification of natural beings, all of which, according to Ray and his colleagues, spoke of the glory and wisdom of their Creator. It was the Swedish naturalist Carolus Linnaeus whose work would dominate the discipline, however. In his *Systema Naturae*, first published in 1735 and revised repeatedly until his death in 1778, Linnaeus set out the system of classification of beings (by kingdom, phylum, class, order, family, genera, and species) that is the model for the system of classification still in use in biology today. Like Ray, Linnaeus was concerned to help the Christian reader along "the straight road to knowledge of his Creator's majesty, all wisdom, omnipotence, omniscience, and mercy, without which knowledge he cannot enjoy to the full those benefits for which he has been created by God" (Banton 1987, 46). To that end, he would arrange all created beings in a table so that each type could be known precisely by its degree of similarity to and difference from all other types of created beings. Knowledge of this vast system of identities and differences was knowledge of God's design and of one's own place within it.

Whereas nowadays we tend to think of these groupings of class, family, or genera as having something to do with the evolution of species and consequent genetic relationships among them, in Linnaeus's system the means of classification was purely structural—or, we might say, purely morphological. He examined the form, placement, number, and relative size of the generative organs of each type of being and then arranged them on a table where degree of distance indicated degree of difference. He assumed that for each degree of difference, a type of being existed, even if no such being had yet been discovered.

In other words, he assumed that nature is continuous, without gaps. And he believed that God had created all these types of beings simultaneously, just as they appeared in the eighteenth century. In other words, species have real essences that are immutable.

Obviously, individuals within a species may vary in appearance a great deal, especially if our only criterion of sameness is the structure of the generative parts. The same type of flowering plant may include individuals with very different leaf shapes, flower colors, stem lengths, and susceptibility to frost. Those differences do not indicate separate species as long as the stamens and pistols are the same in form, number, placement, and size and as long as cross-breeding produces fertile offspring. These different-looking plants of the same species are just variations, and variations within a species are not at all uncommon. Just as camellia bushes may be of different sizes and colors and may flower under somewhat different environmental conditions,[24] human beings may vary in size and color and adaptation to different climates and latitudes. In the 1758 edition of *Systema Naturae,* Linnaeus notes four varieties of the species *Homo sapiens,* Americanus, Europaeus, Asiaticus, and Africanus. He does not arrange these human varieties in any kind of hierarchy. They are simply variants, just like camellia bushes with red, pink, white, or yellow blooms.

Linnaeus acknowledged that his system of classification was artificial, meaning that it reflected his own choice to arrange beings according to the structure of the generative organs. It would have been possible to choose a different structure as the point of comparison—the organs of ingestion, for example. He hoped, however, that eventually, regardless of which structure was chosen for comparison, careful observation would yield a table of identities and differences that would mirror the relationships among species as they exist in nature. Other natural historians employing his procedure chose other starting points. But their aims were the same: to create a table of differences that would establish the identities of species, one that would reflect the real order that exists in the natural world.

Foucault points out that the fundamental principle operative in the discourse of natural history is that nature never leaps; nature is continuous and gapless from one being or type of being to the next (Foucault 1970, 147). But of course experience does not reveal this continuity directly. In our experience, nature's continuity is broken up and blurred—broken up because we can see spaces on our table of differences where there should be species we have not yet actually come across, and blurred because in terrestrial space, creatures of different types are all mixed up with one another (Foucault 1970, 148). These two disparities between our table and nature as it presents itself are both the result of the same set of factors. The space in which natural beings show themselves is not homogeneous. For example, there are differences of climate and elevation, and sometimes there are cataclysms such as volcanoes and earthquakes. The space of nature is subject to change over time, and these upheavals disperse beings that would otherwise lie near one another as they do in tables of identities and differences. Thus, the self-presentation of natural beings is subject to the vicissitudes of time and its impact on space, but they are not in themselves temporal beings, not yet evolving beings as they will become in nineteenth century biology. Linnaeus's classification of human varieties accounts for differences in morphology by way of differences in geographical space, and this way of accounting for what will later be called racial differences remained in ascendancy throughout the eighteenth century.

Linnaeus himself does not use the term *race,* however, and he is clearly talking about varieties, as distinct from races, when he writes about the four types of human being. *Homo sapiens,* all having similarly structured generative organs, and inter-fertile despite their other morphological differences, are one single species descended from one single set of ancestors. Any morphological varieties that might occur are generated by differences in climate, on Linnaeus's view, not by divergences in lineage. By contrast, race was a matter of lineage, tradition, custom, and language, not climate. Therefore, the morphological differences we might perceive among peoples in different parts of the world were not racial differences.

But the word *race* was already undergoing a definitional change, at least outside of scientific circles, even in Linnaeus's time. It had already been used interchangeably with the word *variety* in a popular 1684 travelogue written by François Bernier,[25] and it is easy enough to imagine why. Since Europeans believed that all human beings sprang from the original pair in the Garden of Eden, human presence across the planet could only be explained by migration, which they knew would have been a relatively slow process undertaken by travelers on foot. People who ended up in far-flung regions of the globe would be members of the same extended families, and they would intermarry.

Thus, they would start out as races in the old sense—as people with a common heritage different from others—and they would compound that difference over time morphologically by adapting to a climate different from the one their ancestors came from and the ones their distant cousins were busy adapting to. Their lineage would be written into their bodies.

Natural historians writing in Latin would not register this popular conflation, but natural historians writing in vulgar languages could and did. We see this conflation, which amounts to a process of redefinition, in the work of Immanuel Kant.[26] Like Linnaeus and like most natural historians in the eighteenth century, Kant believed that human variation was a result of adaptation to variations in climate. But climate alone was not a sufficient explanation of morphological variation, he believed, because it did not explain why those variations did not disappear when people moved to different climates. How did a person's ancestors' adaptations to a given climate result in heritable differences impervious to changes in climate? Why did white people stay white even if they moved to Asia? Why did black people stay black even if they moved to Europe? And why did their children inherit morphological variations that were unsuited to the climate they were born to?

Kant believed that the potential for morphological differentiation must have existed from the beginning of humankind. There were, he posited, four "germs" in the bodies of the original human beings, each one a set of potentials for changes in skin color, hair texture, facial structure, temperament, and other features. As migration occurred, environmental factors activated one or another of these "germs," which then manifested itself in a specific set of physical traits. Once the traits were fully manifest, the other three "germs," or morphological potentials, were lost. The result was that these changes became permanent in the lineage. Black people would never become white, Kant argued; the potential for whiteness was lost to them, even though it had been present in their ancestors. Nor would whites ever become black or yellow or red.[27] More importantly, the children of black people would never be white, because the potential for whiteness was lost to them as well, just as the potential for blackness was lost to the children of white people. Variation was not only a matter of adaptation to climate, then; it was also a matter of physical lineage. Morphological variation was, in short, racial. In Kant's work we see the melding of race understood as lineage with variation understood as morphology. The two concepts are becoming one.

In Kant's first essay on the subject of human morphological variation (published in 1775 and updated in 1777), he opined, "I believe that we only need to assume four races in order to be able to derive all of the enduring distinctions immediately recognizable within the human genus. They are: (1) the white race; (2) the Negro race; (3) the Hun race (Mongol or Kalmuck); and (4) the Hindu or Hindustani race" (Kant 2000, 11). Kant changes his mind about which groups should appear on this list over the next decade,[28] but, architectonically inclined as he is, in an essay published in 1785 and then forever after, he sticks with the number four. He writes, "We can assume four class differences in human beings with respect to skin color. We know with certainty no more heritable differences of skin color than these: the whites, the yellow Indians, the Negroes, and the copper-colored red Americans."[29] Despite his waffling on the status of Native Americans and Huns, the main point stands: Kant is interested in delineating and understanding a physical phenomenon, not a phenomenon that is primarily cultural or linguistic. Kant is not shy about correlating other phenomena with these physical differences—for example, he insists that dark-skinned people are lazy and dangerous, and red-skinned people are stupid—but he downplays language, tradition, and custom as he formulates his theory of human variation. Yet because he emphasizes heredity over climate, he calls these variants *races*.

Johann Gottfried von Herder objected to Kant's conflation of morphology and race. In his *Ideas on the Philosophy of History of Humankind,* first published in 1784, Herder voiced his concerns about those who "have thought it fit to employ the term *race* for four or five divisions, according to the regions of origin or complexion. I see no reason for employing this term. Race refers to a difference of origin, which in this case either does not exist or which comprises in each of these regions or complexions the most diverse 'races'" (Banton 1987, 52). In the third edition of his book, published in 1828, he repeated his reservations and elaborated:

> Some have for example ventured to call four or five divisions among humans, which were originally constructed according to regions or even according to colors, *races;* I see no reason for this name. Race derives from a difference in ancestry that

either does not occur here or that includes the most diverse races within each of these regions in each of these colors. For each people is a people: it has its national culture and its language; the zone in which each of them is placed has sometimes put its stamp, sometimes only a thin veil, on each of them, but it has not destroyed the original ancestral core construction of the nation. (Herder 2000, 26)

Herder acknowledges that families or tribes—that is, races—that migrated to different geographical regions eventually developed a particular set of morphological characteristics in response to their new climate—their new zone "put its stamp" on them—but their existence as a race is a separate issue from those morphological marks. Similarly, peoples unrelated to each other who migrate to the same geographical region will eventually develop a particular set of morphological characteristics in response to their new climate, but that fact alone will not unite them into one race. To suggest otherwise is to use language irresponsibly, Herder contended. Kant was not swayed, however, and insisted that his use of the term *race* made good scientific sense.

By the time of the Kant/Herder controversy in Germany, most Anglo-American statesmen and jurists, as well as most Anglo-American physicians, scholars, and clergymen, were already using the term *race* as Kant used it, as a conflation of lineage and morphology.[30] By far the most popular way of accounting for human morphological variation was by reference to climate, but like Kant, American natural historians had taken note of the fact that the children of black people are black and the children of white people are white even if they are born in a region of the world where the indigenous people are red or tawny. While Kant was working on his "germ" theory of human morphological difference, Samuel Stanhope Smith, professor of moral philosophy at the College of New Jersey (later Princeton University) and president of the college from 1795 until his retirement in 1812, tackled this very same issue. Unlike Kant, however, he did not assert that morphological variation, once established, was set for all subsequent generations of a given lineage.

At the 1787 meetings of the American Philosophical Society, Smith gave a talk that he published under the title *An Essay on the Causes of the Variety in Complexion and Figure in the Human Species.* In it he argued that morphological differences are the result of differing environments. Facial bones contract toward the nose in cold winds. Human skin darkens in the heat, the gases released through the skin in hot climates curl the hair, and so forth. Unlike Kant, however, Smith did not believe that these adaptations were fixed either for the lineage or for the individual him- or herself. Careful observation showed that in fact Europeans transplanted to North America were darkening, and Africans were lightening to more closely resemble the tawny natives. Residents of southern New Jersey were darker than residents of Pennsylvania, and residents of Maryland and Virginia were darker still. Furthermore, among the poorer white people of the Carolinas and Georgia, there are many "whose complexion is but a few shades lighter than that of the aboriginal Iroquois, or Cherokees" (S. Smith 1965, 43–44). Of course, this process of darkening in the New World was typically slow; it would likely be several more generations before European Americans would be as dark as the aboriginal peoples. But it was evident to Smith that epidermal adaptation to the new environment was taking place.

In a few exceptional cases, in fact, the process was swift. Smith made much of the case of Henry Moss, an African American born into slavery in Virginia who moved north after the Revolution and gradually turned white (S. Smith 1965, 58). At first white blotches appeared on his body. Then, after several years, the blotches grew into each other until Moss was entirely white. He attracted a great deal of learned attention and was placed on exhibit in Philadelphia in 1796 as a "curiosity of science" (Gossett 1997, 40). Smith took this case to be good evidence that a similar process would occur with all blacks who moved to colder climates, and he bolstered this with the repeated assertion that house slaves—who did not suffer as much exposure to sun, heat, or the noxious fumes of rotting matter in forests and wetlands as did those who worked out of doors—often had softer, lighter, more European features and hair texture than field slaves.[31]

The outcome of this process, whether swift or slow, would not be uniform gradation in color from north to south, however, since the elevation of the land, soil conditions, degree of forestation, proximity to salt water, and many other factors had their effects on air temperature and thus on body chemistry and morphology as well (S. Smith 1965, 24–26). Climate is a complex phenomenon, Smith cautioned, and should be expected to produce complex effects.

But, we might ask, if Smith believed that human variation was a matter of climate alone and not also a matter of inheritance, why use the term *race* for the phenomenon he studied? The answer lies in Smith's effort to incorporate the resistance to environmental determinism that was characteristic of his roots in the Scottish Enlightenment. Smith insisted that bodies are affected by the "state of society," meaning the organization of the economy, government, religion, and technology, as well as by "habits of living," the particular routine activities and experiences that make up an individual's life. Smith treats of these together, "because their effects are frequently so blended, that it is difficult, in many cases, precisely to discriminate them, and to assign each its proper head" (S. Smith 1965, 93). This category of forces includes diet and clothing, type of lodging, the type of work people do, their forms of government and worship, and even the degree to which they engage in artistic and intellectual pursuits. Every thought entertained, he asserted, leaves a trace on the visage (1965, 122).

Whereas we might think of culture as by definition nonheritable, for Smith the exact opposite is the case. Culture affects morphology in heritable ways just as surely as, and perhaps more permanently than, climate does. As these traces of thoughts and experiences etch themselves deeply into the bodies of a people, gradually what Smith calls their "constitution" will be altered. While accidental features acquired in the course of a lifetime—wounds, scars, blemishes, amputations, and other peculiarities—are not passed from parent to child, the constitution as a sort of malleable material substrate is inherited (S. Smith 1965, 126). Once these culturally induced alterations become constitutional, they tend to mark a people from generation to generation. Thus they become racial characteristics, although they are always subject to change when a people's circumstances change.

The environmental causes of variation are so complex, Smith believed, that it would be a waste of time to try to classify all the resultant varieties of human being. The important thing is to realize that all human groups are ultimately akin and that therefore the same moral rules apply to all of us. This last point was Smith's major concern; he begins and ends the 1810 edition of his essay with it, concluding:

> No general principles of conduct, or religion, or even civil policy, could be derived from natures originally and essentially different from one another, and, afterwards, in the perpetual

changes of the world, infinitely mixed and compounded. The
principles and rules which a philosopher might derive from the
study of his own nature, could not be applied with certainty
to regulate the conduct of other men, and other nations, who
might be of totally different species; or sprung from a very
dissimilar composition of species. The terms which one man
would frame to express the ideas and emotions of his own
mind must convey to another a meaning as different as the
organization of their respective natures. But when the whole
human race is known to compose only one species, this confusion and uncertainty is removed, and the science of human
nature, in all its relations, becomes susceptible of system. The
principles of morals rest on sure and immutable foundations.
(S. Smith 1965, 149)

Ultimately, all human beings have the same lineage, Smith insists,
and that is what truly matters, morally speaking, even if variations
of experience in the lineages of subgroups over time has led to differences in tradition, language, temperament, and morphology. Thus,
despite his firm conviction that skin color and other "racial" features
were not fixed, his understanding of race as environmentally produced morphological variation places Samuel Stanhope Smith at least
as close as, if not closer than, Immanuel Kant to the more modern
usage of the term *race*. Race is a matter of morphology.

Race as Morphology: Thomas Jefferson
and the Threat of Race War

Although Smith disagreed vehemently with the racial opinions of
his contemporary Thomas Jefferson, the two men's use of the term
race is virtually identical. For Jefferson, too, race is primarily a matter
of morphology, not lineage.

Jefferson is not often discussed in essays devoted to the history of
the concept of race, because he did not contribute anything original
to the discussion and his views on the matter appear to be a jumble
of inconsistencies.[32] He believed all the shortcomings he identified in
Native Americans were environmental in origin and would be corrected with education, but when he found some of the very same
characteristics in African Americans, he held them to be innate and
irremediable. He supported marriage between Native Americans and
whites but believed that marriage between whites and blacks would

engender mixed-race weaklings and so had to be prohibited no matter what the cost. He thought blacks and whites could never coexist peacefully and so proposed ending the importation of African slaves and shipping all African Americans "back" to Africa.[33] Meanwhile, as we now know from DNA testing, he was busy fathering "mixed-race" children with his slave Sally Hemings.

Jefferson is extremely important in this discussion, however, despite his lack of originality and his apparent lapses of logic. He was in a position to have much more influence on the development of racial discourse in the United States than did even very prominent educators and scholars such as Samuel Stanhope Smith. And he certainly had more influence on racial institutions and practices than almost any of his contemporaries. In Jefferson the two strands of racial discourse—the material concerns of the slaveholder and the intellectual concerns of the natural historian—fuse. Most importantly, though, it is in Jefferson's writings where we see not only the transition from race understood as lineage to race understood as morphology, just as we see in Smith's work, but we also witness a transposition of the old Puritan anti-sovereign race war discourse into the discursive machinery of the sovereign state.

In 1781, in his capacity as governor of the newly established state of Virginia, Thomas Jefferson responded to a set of queries placed before him by the French legate in Philadelphia. He revised his answers in 1782 and turned them over to be published privately in France in 1785. Two years later, in 1787, the document now known as *Notes on the State of Virginia* was published and sold in the United States. The book can be read straightforwardly as a report on Virginia's land, natural resources, and economic potential, and it certainly is that. In it we learn about the navigability of Virginia's rivers, the number of limestone caverns in the state, its annual rainfall, and where its copper and iron mines are located. But the book is much more than a compendium of facts and figures. Jefferson was an avid reader, steeped in the writings of natural historians—including, of course, the works of the prominent French theorist George Louis Leclerc, Comte de Buffon—and he was acutely sensitive to what he took to be Buffon's insulting assessment of Virginia's climate, flora and fauna, and human population. The French legate's queries provided Jefferson with an occasion for contesting Buffon's assertions point by point. Read thusly, as an assault on Buffon,[34] the *Notes* can help make sense of some of Jefferson's more glaring inconsistencies on the issue of race.

Like most natural historians in the eighteenth century, Buffon believed that variations in any species are a function of climate: changes in climate inevitably cause changes in species morphology. Species vary morphologically when dispersed subgroups adapt to different environments; once a subgroup is fully adapted to a particular climate, Buffon maintained, cross-breeding with other subgroups is detrimental because the offspring, likely bearing some morphological characteristics of each parent, will not be fully suited to the climate of origin of either one of them. Furthermore, Buffon thought, a hot, wet climate tends to be hard on most species and generally has the effect of rendering them smaller and weaker.

Jefferson was not particularly upset by these theoretical claims.[35] What he objected to was that Buffon offered as an example of the latter point the "fact" that the hot, moist climate of North America had produced species that were small and weak.[36] This was bad enough when applied to animals such as deer, beaver, fish, and game birds, and Jefferson was at pains to prove that in fact Virginia's species were just as big and fat as Europe's (Jefferson 1944, 78–87).[37] Worse, however, Buffon did not confine his observations to plants, fish, birds, and quadrupeds. He also insisted that the indigenous peoples of North America were smaller and weaker than Europeans because their climate stunted them and sapped them of vitality. Jefferson quotes Buffon's remarks at length:

> Although the savage of the new world is almost of the same height as the man of our world, that is not sufficient to make him an exception to the general rule of the diminution of human nature in this whole continent; the savage is weak and small in his reproductive organs; he has neither hair nor beard, and no passion for his female. Although lighter than the European, because he is more accustomed to running, he is nevertheless much less strong physically; he is also much less sensitive, and yet more fearful and cowardly; he has no vivacity, no spiritual activity; his physical activity is less a voluntary movement than a compulsion to act caused by necessity; take away his hunger and thirst and you destroy thereby the active principle of all his movements; he will remain stupidly still, standing or lying for whole days at a time. One need not seek

further for the cause of the scattered life of the savages and
their antipathy for society; the most precious spark of nature
has been refused them; they are lacking in ardor for their
female, and consequently, in love for their fellow-beings; not
knowing this most vital and tender attachment, their other
feelings of this nature are cold and sluggish; their love for
their parents and children is weak; with them, therefore, the
most intimate society of all, that of the immediate family, has
only the weakest ties; relationships between families have no
ties at all; as a result, no unity, no republic, no social state.
Their practice of love dictates their ethical morale; their heart
is frozen, their society and authority harsh. They look upon
their women only as maids-of-all-work or as pack animals
on whom they carelessly unload the burdens of the hunt, and
force them, without pity or recognition to do work which is
often beyond their strength; they have few children; they give
them little care; this is all the result of their original defect;
they are indifferent because they are weak, and that indifference towards sex is the initial blemish which wilts nature,
prevents it from blooming, and by destroying the seeds of life,
cuts off the roots of society. By refusing him the power of sex,
nature has mistreated and humbled him more than any of the
animals. (Jefferson 1944, 88)

Commentators make much of the fact that Jefferson goes to bat here
for (male) Native Americans. They actually do have beards and nor-
mal-sized penises, he contends. They are not impotent. They love their
families. It is true that they have fewer children, but that is because the
women must attend the men in their hunting and war parties when
"child-bearing becomes extremely inconvenient for them," so they
have learned to use herbs to induce abortion and infertility (Jefferson
1944, 90). Buffon is just wrong; Native Americans are not lacking
in vitality at all. Whatever defects they exhibit are the result of lack
of education and the periods of scarcity inevitable in a subsistence
economy. If they were to be fully assimilated into Anglo-American
culture, these defects would disappear.

But Jefferson's refutation of Buffon's description of Native
Americans is not so much praise for indigenous peoples as it is a
defense of the climate itself. Yes, we might read him as saying, climate
does shape its inhabitants, but this climate's effects are not detrimen-

tal. And the reason he makes this argument is not to assert the vitality of Native Americans (who may or may not ever actually be absorbed into the Anglo-American economy and finally get some schooling and enough to eat); it is to assure his readers of the continued vitality of transplanted Europeans. Since Jefferson is not contesting Buffon's basic premise—that climate shapes morphology and causes variation —he absolutely must show that *this* climate will not stunt species originally adapted to the climate of Europe—whether those species be sheep, hogs, or human beings.

In effect, Jefferson is arguing that people indigenous to the North American climate are *almost* white people—they may even have migrated from Europe originally, he suggests (Jefferson 1944, 119)—and they could *be* white people (again) if they were to acquire white people's technology and work habits. The two "races" could be blended into one without any loss of vigor. Jefferson never contests Buffon's theoretical premise that cross-breeding variants adapted to different climates results in weak offspring; instead, he minimizes the climatologically induced differences between Europeans and Native Americans. In fact, his willingness to embrace the prospect of marriage between whites and indigenous peoples could be seen as an indication that he believes Buffon's premise is correct. Noisy acceptance of intermarriage is a rhetorical flourish here that builds on precisely that premise. In effect, Jefferson is saying: "I am so sure that the North American climate has not made the natives appreciably different from Europeans that I would even be willing for our people to intermarry with them; we are so alike that the offspring would not be weak."

But African Americans are another matter entirely, because they were shaped by an entirely different climate. Any cross between Africans and whites would undoubtedly result in feeble offspring ill-suited to life in North America or, for that matter, anywhere else. Intermarriage between blacks and whites must be prohibited, and the punishments for white women who bear mixed-race children must be stiff enough to deter any interracial sexual liaison.[38]

Jefferson makes absolutely no effort to attribute any of the characteristics he finds objectionable in Africans to a simple lack of education or unfamiliarity with European technology. Instead, he repeats every derogatory cliché current among slave owners in his time. Blacks are ugly, which means that black men will lust after white women instead of black women, just as the African "Oran ootan" disdains the ugly female of his species and lusts after the black woman. Blacks "secrete less by the kidneys and more by the glands of the skin, which gives them a very strong and disagreeable odour." They sometimes appear to be brave and adventurous, but that is only because they are impulsive and all but incapable of forethought. It is true that they are more, rather than less, sexually ardent than whites, but their ardor is purely sensual and not mixed with the sort of affection that makes for strong family and social ties. They are unreflective, lazy, and poor in imagination (Jefferson 1944, 145). And they will always be this way, regardless of the effects of the North American climate and exposure to European or Anglo-American culture. African Americans are not white people and never can be.

Here Jefferson appears to be about as far away as he could possibly get both from Smith's view that races are entirely fluid and from his own view that minor changes in the living conditions of Native Americans will rid them of the detrimental marks of racial difference. But I would argue (1) that he is not as far away as it might first appear, and (2) that here again, as in his descriptions of Native Americans, Jefferson overstates his position for the sake of political expedience.

First, neither Smith nor Jefferson ever accepted a doctrine of climatologic determinism. Both men were far too influenced by the thinkers of the Scottish Enlightenment to believe that what we might now call culture had no role to play in shaping human habits, morals, and lifestyles. Smith incorporated that idea into his theory by insisting that tradition and social practices shape morphology in heritable ways by affecting a human being's constitution. Undoubtedly Jefferson held a similar view. Not just the African climate but African culture shaped the constitutions of Africans, and it did so in ways that will prevent them and their descendents from ever taking advantage of the aspects of European society that will raise the Native Americans out of savagery. Africa made them slow-moving and lazy. It diminished their intellectual and artistic capacities. It rendered them lustful but unloving. Once so constituted, even if they are malleable in many respects, they will not change in response to education. People who are stupid, thoughtless, indolent, and uncaring simply are not amenable to education and economic advancement. Given that such is the constitution of African Americans, they (unlike the European immigrants) will succumb to the hot, moist environment that has thus far kept the Native Americans in their savage state, and the defects it induces in them will simply augment those that the climate of Africa has already produced. In sum, therefore, while Jefferson's assessments of the abilities and potential of Native Americans and African Americans are very different, his underlying assumptions about race are not necessarily logically inconsistent and are not appreciably different from the views expressed by his contemporaries, including Samuel Stanhope Smith. Race is a morphological variation attributable to a combination of climate, culture, and lineage.

Jefferson's assessment of the political ramifications of the "fact" that there were basically two (not three) races coexisting in the United States brings us back to Foucault and race war discourse. Once race became morphology, and blacks and whites were defined as two distinct races, it was almost inevitable that anyone as steeped as Jefferson was in the political writings of seventeenth-century Puritans and their Whig successors would see the situation in the United States through the lens of race war discourse. Consider, for example, his 1774 "Summary View of the Rights of British America," wherein he asserts that the king of England has no right to dispose of Virginia's land. He writes:

> In the earlier ages of the Saxon settlement, feudal holdings were certainly altogether unknown, and very few, if any, had been introduced at the time of the Norman conquests. Our Saxon ancestors held their lands, as they did their personal property, in absolute dominion, disincumbered with any superior, answering nearly to the nature of those possessions which the feudalist[s] term Allodial. William the Norman first introduced that system generally. The lands which had belonged to those who fell in the battle of Hastings, and in the subsequent insurrections of his reign, formed a considerable proportion of the lands of the whole kingdom. These he granted out, subject to feudal duties, as did he also those of a great number of his new subjects, who, by persuasions or threats, were induced to surrender them for that purpose. But still, much was left in the hands of his Saxon subjects, held of no superior, and not subject to feudal conditions. These, therefore, by express laws, enacted to render uniform the system of military defence, were made liable to the same military duties as if they had been feuds; and the Norman lawyers soon found means to saddle them, also, with the other feudal burthens. But still they had

not been surrendered to the King, they were not derived from his grant, and therefore they were not holden of him. A general principle was introduced, that "all lands in England were held either mediately or immediately of the Crown"; but this was borrowed from those holdings which were truly feudal, and only applied to others for the purposes of illustration. Feudal holdings were, therefore, but exceptions out of the Saxon laws of possession, under which all lands were held in absolute right. These, therefore, still form the basis of groundwork of the Common law, to prevail wheresoever the exceptions have not taken place. America was not conquered by William the Norman, nor its lands surrendered to him or any of his successors. (Jefferson 1944, 16–17)

Jefferson here asserts that he is a Saxon and that the Virginia colony is a Saxon colony with land rights governed by Saxon, not Norman, law.[39] He understands Virginia's political struggles as a continuation of the race war that began in 1066.

One lesson Jefferson undoubtedly extracted from the Whiggish versions of British history that he studied so diligently was that two races cannot occupy the same land. When there are two races, there is, inevitably, race war. This belief, I would contend, not an offended humanism, is what lies most fundamentally beneath Jefferson's obsession with ending the African slave trade and abolishing American slavery.

Jefferson pushed for abolition of slavery even before independence. Along with other elite Virginia planters, he petitioned King George III to end the importation of Africans to the Anglo-American colonies, a petition the king ignored. He protested the king's refusal in the 1774 "Summary" (Jefferson 1944, 14), and in a paragraph omitted from the final version of the Declaration of Independence, he accused the king of cruelty against human nature, "violating its most sacred rights of life and liberty in persons of a distant people who never offended him, captivating and carrying them into slavery in another hemisphere, or to incur miserable death in their transportation thither" (Parent 2003, 173). After independence he continued to press for an end both to the slave trade and to slavery itself.[40]

But if Jefferson was so adamantly opposed to slavery, why did he continue to hold slaves? And if he was such a defender of humanity and equality, why did he insist that all emancipated slaves be banished from the state of Virginia and advocate removing all African

Americans from North America? Jefferson answers the latter question himself in *Notes on the State of Virginia:* "Deep rooted prejudices entertained by the whites; ten thousand recollections, by the blacks, of the injuries they have sustained; new provocations; the real distinctions which nature has made; and many other circumstances will divide us into parties, and produce convulsions, which will probably never end but in the extermination of the one or the other race" (Jefferson 1944, 144–45). In short, we cannot live together without race war.

Meanwhile, as long as there are blacks here among us, we had better keep them enslaved, for if emancipation is not coupled with exportation, the problem is not only unresolved but is actually exacerbated.[41] Whether enslaved or free, blacks posed a constant threat to the stability of the new nation just as the Saxons posed a constant threat to Norman government. Fundamentally, this was not an issue of morality or justice; exportation was not even a course dictated by a specifically antiblack sentiment. It was an issue of race per se, now morphologically defined to be sure, but still conceived as the source of inevitable conflict and war. That is why, as his plans for exiling blacks to Africa stalled, Jefferson again and again expressed a sense of impending doom.[42] The blacks could not be contained forever. They would rise up. The result would be horrific bloodshed, and the hard-won country would be lost. In 1797 Jefferson wrote: "If something is not done, and done soon, we shall be the murderers of our own children" (Jordan 1974, 169). While readers over the years usually have interpreted this passage to mean that present inaction will result in future deaths, now that we know that five of Jefferson's children were members of the "opposite race," one cannot help but believe that Jefferson imagined and dreaded this horrible prospect as a literal possibility. Jefferson was deeply influenced by the Saxon discourse of race war. But he moved farther away than even his contemporary Samuel Stanhope Smith from the concept of race as a matter of lineage. That the children he fathered with Sally Hemings were of his lineage, he knew full well, but they were not of his race. They would be on the other side once the war began.

From Morphology to Biology: Foucault's "First Transcription"

Foucault describes what he calls a "transcription" (Foucault 2003b, 60) of the concept of race from early race war discourses—where proponents of the discourse were an out-group protesting governmental oppression—to biological discourses propounded by an elite intent on using the machinery of government and science to manage and at times eliminate the groups it despised and feared. In that process, which he says stretches from the early seventeenth to the mid-nineteenth centuries, the concept of race changed from one of lineage to one of physicality, and this change set the stage for race to function as a strategic deployment in biopolitical normalization and population control in the twentieth century. In my narrative of the ancestry of modern racism, I have separated the bare physicality of race—morphological race—from the physiological account of race that appeared in the nineteenth century. This chapter has focused almost exclusively on the seventeenth and eighteenth centuries; only in the next chapter will I take up the story as it unfolds in the nineteenth century. I insist here upon this separation because I believe things occurred somewhat differently in the United States than they did in Europe, especially in England; and more importantly, because dividing my discussion of the "transcription" into two phases makes clearer the ways in which the concept of the abnormal comes into play in racial discourses, a crucial point for the larger project of coming to an understanding of Foucault's claim in the eleventh lecture of *Abnormal* that modern racism is racism against the abnormal.

Chapter 3 will take up the second half of what Foucault calls "the first transcription," the biologization of morphological race and its subsequent role as a mark of development—or the failure or arrest thereof. Once race becomes a function of development, it becomes a temporal phenomenon that can be characterized by normality, deviance, or pathology. It is this race—developmentally conditioned, biological race—that is the object of modern racism, whose birth will be described in chapter 4.

THREE

A GENEALOGY OF MODERN RACISM, PART 2

FROM BLACK LEPERS TO IDIOT CHILDREN

In his experiment to determine whether or how far power might be thought on the model of warfare, Foucault puts forth some fragments of a genealogy of modern racism from about 1630 to the outbreak of World War II. In chapter 2 I elaborated on the first half of that genealogy with my examination of race from 1630 to the last years of the eighteenth century, by which time—at least in Kant's Prussia and Jefferson's United States—race was a morphological phenomenon, a matter of physical structure and appearance, not a matter of lineage as it had been in previous centuries. By that time race was a fact, first and foremost, about human bodies. But it was not, strictly speaking, a biological fact. Biological race—and biological racism—could not come into existence before the science of biology itself came into existence, bringing with it its concepts of function and development, and that did not occur until the turn of the nineteenth century. Race's transformation and absorption into biological theory and its deployment in biopolitical regimes then occurred slowly over the next several decades.

The word *biology* was coined in 1802 to name what contemporaries perceived as a genuinely new science.[1] Unlike its predecessor, natural history, which focused on the visible structure of natural beings, biology (the science of life) focused on processes. Foucault indicates this distinction by pointing out that within the framework of biology a human being (like all other living things) is primarily "a being possessing *functions*—receiving stimuli . . . reacting to them, adapting himself, evolving, submitting to the demands of an environment, coming to terms with the modifications it imposes, seeking to erase imbalances, acting in accordance with regularities, having, in short, conditions of existence and the possibility of finding average *norms* of adjustment which permit him to perform his functions" (Foucault 1970, 357). Biological science transformed human bodies, in effect: entities that were before conceived as structural assemblages, as extremely complex self-replicating machines, were reconceived as shifting manifestations of temporal processes, functional organisms. In the course of that transformation, race too underwent a fundamental change. In the late eighteenth century, race was a structural aspect of bodies: differently raced bodies had differently shaped and colored parts. In the nineteenth century, however, race came to be a matter of function, not structure per se: differently raced bodies *behaved* differently. Over the course of their lives, differently raced bodies could be expected to grow, learn, mature, and decline at different rates and thus to exhibit different material manifestations.

Foucault contends that this shift toward conceiving of living bodies as inherently temporal entities begins in the early nineteenth century with Cuvier, a somewhat controversial claim among historians of science. It is Jean-Baptiste Lamarck after all, not Georges Cuvier, who is generally credited with the founding of biological science and the introduction of historicity into the natural world. It was Lamarck, not Cuvier, who insisted that species are mutable and that fossils are the remains of the ancestors of beings presently alive, a theory that came to be called the Development Hypothesis.[2] To many historians, Lamarck's work clearly prefigures the evolutionism of the second half of the nineteenth century, while Cuvier's belongs among the relics of the era of static classification.[3]

However, what is crucially important for biological science, Foucault contends, is not the hypothesis of species mutability but the notion that life is essentially temporal. Cuvier insisted that organs can be understood only in relation to the work they do; their configuration is functional, not simply structurally elegant—and most certainly not the result of structural variation on a divine theme, as his arch-adversary Etienne Geoffroy Saint-Hilaire seemed to believe—and thus they can only be understood as they occur through time. To be sure, Cuvier did insist on the fixity of species over against Geoffroy's willingness to consider the possibility that new species can emerge from alterations in those already in existence (Appel 1987, 131), and in that respect he seems further away than Geoffroy and Lamarck from the evolutionary theory that would arise in the last third of the century. But Cuvier's conception of temporal functioning is a much more radical departure from the assumptions of natural history than Lamarck's seemingly proto-evolutionary theory is, Foucault argues. It is true that Lamarck believed in the transformation of species, but he conceived of it "only upon the basis of ontological continuity, which was that of Classical natural history. He presupposed a progressive gradation, an unbroken process of improvement, an uninterrupted continuum of beings which could form themselves upon one another" (Foucault 1970, 275). For Lamarck the universe of living beings was really still just a vast array of structural identities and differences; the array as a whole was dynamic, but the relationships among beings that constituted it was as static as it had been for Linnaeus.

What was really necessary for the transition from natural history to biology and eventually to biological evolution was the idea that beings are to be identified not through their placement on a grid of continuously differentiated structure but rather through events internal to organisms, namely, through the functions that produce and sustain those structures: the universe of beings is not a table-like grid of discrete identities but a discontinuous collection of interactive functions. The same functions—respiration, for example—can be performed by differently structured organs (gills versus lungs, for example). We must look inside organisms to find their affinities with one another. When we do so, we will see resemblances in *effect* without resemblances in *appearance*. We will learn that functions produce and sustain structure; structure is secondary. In the wake of Cuvier, biologists reconceived *Homo sapiens* and living beings generally as organisms with functioning systems—digestive, respiratory, reproductive, circulatory, and so forth—rather than as sets of structures—skeletal, digital, genital—as the natural historians had done. Although Cuvier did not see all the ramifications of his own claims, the classical table of identities and differences is simply shattered in his thought, whereas in Lamarck's work the table remains intact even as the organisms progress en masse toward higher states.

Cuvier's work thus sets the conceptual stage for organisms to exist in conflict or even in some cases to be unable to coexist, Foucault maintains. Darwin's theory of natural selection would have been impossible had Cuvier and others not jettisoned the notion that nature is a continuous, harmonious set of relationships and begun to look for the "conditions of life," the means by which each type of organism sustains itself in interaction with its environment, including other organisms. "Around the living being, or rather through it and by means of the filtering action of its surface," Foucault writes, "there is in effect [according to Cuvier] 'a continual circulation from the outside to the inside, and from the inside to the outside, constantly maintained and yet fixed within certain limits. Thus, living bodies should be considered as kinds of furnaces into which dead substances are successively introduced in order to be combined together in various ways.'"[4] This dynamism, not the lock-step "development" envisioned by Lamarck, gave rise to the science of life as we know it.

> The discontinuity of living forms made it possible to conceive of a great temporal current for which the continuity of structures and characters, despite the superficial analogies, could not provide a basis. With spatial discontinuity, the breaking up of the great table, and the fragmentation of the surface upon which all natural beings had taken their ordered places, it became possible to replace natural history with a "history" of nature. It is true that the Classical space, as we have seen, did not exclude the possibility of development, but that development did no more than provide a means of traversing the discreetly preordained table of possible variations. The breaking up of that space made it possible to reveal a history proper to life itself: that of its maintenance in its conditions of existence. (Foucault 1970, 275)

Cuvier's work bequeathed to the world the science of functional and developmental norms. Organic systems fluctuate within delineable patterns of functioning, patterns that can be studied, quantified, and graphically plotted to yield statistical norms. Organisms begin life in a certain form, add mass at a certain rate, manifest new behaviors at certain stages, reproduce at a certain developmental point, show predictable signs of aging, and eventually decline in functioning and die. All these changes taken collectively—and, more specifically, the processes by which they occur—are what we call life. That is the object of biological investigation and knowledge. Historicity has thus entered into the living body; change, dynamism, *development* are the essence of the organism.[5]

Morphological race, as a phenomenon of bodily structure, was still closely allied with the discourses of natural history and their emphasis on the spatial relationships among organs or parts. But the concept of race would change with the emergence of biological thinking, and very quickly. By the 1850s, the absorption of race into biological discourse, and its attendant recasting as a phenomenon of function and development, was complete not only in scientific circles but in popular culture, at least in the United States. Races deemed inferior were characterized as retarded, as primitives or lifelong children constitutionally incapable of adult self-discipline or full participation as citizens in a democratic society, a developmental incapacity that was held to be physiological and inevitably heritable.[6]

It was this shift from the morphological to the physiologically developmental, furthermore, along with the rise of secular disciplinary practice, that allowed the concept of race to migrate from regimes of power that were fundamentally deductive (regimes of juridical or sovereign power) to regimes that were fundamentally normalizing and biopolitical. Once integrated into biological discourse, race could be deployed in institutions and practices where it could be fused with the new concept of developmental sexuality and exploited as an instrument in the management of populations and the intensification of productive forces. This chapter presents a sketch of how that transition occurred. But following Foucault's injunction to pay attention to exercises of power in their eventfulness, we will not focus our attention first so much on biological theory as on political events and institutions in the United States at the turn of the nineteenth century.

By 1800 a large number of Americans believed that slavery posed a serious problem for their young country. It offended the religious beliefs of many—including Quakers, Unitarians, Baptists, Presbyterians, and several other groups. Many believed the existence of the institution corrupted the morals of citizens who held slaves or grew up with them, because it fostered conduct that resembled tyranny in individuals who needed to develop the values and behaviors appropriate to civic life in a republic of equals. Additionally, the security risks in parts of the country where slaves formed a large portion of the population could not be denied; bloody rebellion was an ever-present possibility. And, finally, slave labor was just not as profitable for most planters as it once had been; at times owners found that housing, clothing, and feeding an ever-increasing number of slaves, some of whom were too elderly or disabled to work at all, was a financial burden not sufficiently offset by the savings in wages. (This would change dramatically with widespread use of the cotton gin.) These factors contributed to the decision to abolish the slave trade in 1808. But abolition of slavery itself was a sticky matter. Some planters—particularly in rice-growing regions of the coastal South—still did find slavery quite profitable, and they opposed abolition with all their might. But even planters in the tobacco states, who might have happily divested themselves of their responsibility for their slaves, were not willing simply to turn them loose into the local countryside as free human beings. What civic status would such people have? Unprepared for independence, what havoc might they wreak? How could they be kept under control?

By examining two divergent approaches to the issue of what to do with black people in America in 1800, we can see (1) how morphological race functioned in sovereign or deductive political discourses and practices, and (2) how disciplinary practices—the precursors to normalizing biopolitical practices of surveillance, ranking, and examination—were already beginning to change the concept of race from pure morphology to something more like functional or developmental difference. Thomas Jefferson's plan to deport African Americans to colonies in Africa exemplifies a deductive approach, while his friend Benjamin Rush's plan to establish domestic training colonies to prepare blacks for U.S. citizenship offers a glimpse into the future of race as a biological category and an element in networks of biopolitical normalization.

Deduction or Discipline: Thomas Jefferson versus Benjamin Rush

Again and again from 1779 until his death in 1826, Thomas Jefferson urged his fellow Americans to abolish slavery and make plans to remove all black people from U.S. soil as quickly as possible.[7] Otherwise, he feared, in a generation or two blacks would begin to think of themselves, not as enslaved Africans or children of Africans, but as *Americans,* who were, as such, entitled to land and liberty.[8] The result would be a fight to the death between two morphologically distinct races—race war—which might well destroy the newly sovereign nation.

At the turn of the nineteenth century, African Americans were not a segment of the population that might simply be rounded up and driven out, as would be done with the Cherokees in 1838, for the vast majority were the legally acquired property of U.S. citizens.[9] Given the classical liberal principles upon which the new country was founded, Jefferson could not advocate seizing property of any sort without compensating its owners, so he insisted that the U.S. government should purchase slaves from their masters, emancipate them, and then deport the entire black population to Africa or the West Indies. Jefferson reckoned the total cost (purchase and transport) at about $900 million—an enormous sum of money—and he calculated that the removal to a suitable colony overseas would take about twenty-five years. The project was admittedly a massive and costly undertaking, but Jefferson had no doubt that it was absolutely essential for national security.

Even aside from the huge amount of money needed—a major obstacle in itself—Jefferson foresaw a serious logistical problem: in twenty-five years' time the black population would likely double, doubling in turn the cost of purchase and the length of time necessary for deportation. Thus, despite all efforts, the financial and logistical problems would still exist twenty-five years hence, at which time the threat would have become even worse. To make the undertaking feasible, Jefferson proposed that the government buy infant slaves only, because they cost a mere $25.50 each. Adolescents and adults would live in the United States as slaves until their deaths; only their offspring would be purchased for colonization. Children could remain with their mothers until old enough to work—presumably six or seven years, although Jefferson does not specify—at which time the federal government would take them, train them for their role in establishing and maintaining a colony, and deport them as soon as possible. This would reduce the government's financial outlay considerably and prevent an increase in population meanwhile.[10] Although this plan would break up families and thus cause maternal suffering (he does not acknowledge any potential suffering on the part of the children, fathers, or other relatives), Jefferson believed it was necessary to create a racially homogeneous nation on North American soil in order to forestall a politically and economically devastating race war.

Jefferson was (among other important roles during this time) president of the United States; in other words, he was a chief executive officer acting on behalf of a sovereign nation in the name of what we might call homeland security. The machinery of republican government that we citizens of the United States of America call our own was both the object of concern that motivated this plan and the technology whereby it was to be accomplished. That the president of the United States proposed to tear hundreds of thousands of young children from their parents' arms, systematically and definitively, as an inexpensive means of ethnic cleansing—and he saw nothing wrong with this course of action, either morally or legally[11]—is a fact well worth pondering in all its subtleties and ramifications. For our relatively limited purposes here, however—coming to an understanding of how morphological race was transformed into an instrument of biopower—it is important to see that Jefferson's plan grew out of a regime of power different from the ones that developed later on in nineteenth century, one we might characterize, following Foucault's analytics of power in *The History of Sexuality, Volume 1,* as "sovereign," "deductive," or "juridical." The purpose of law and government was to establish order and maintain it, not by changing those subject to it by guiding their development through normalizing regimes, but simply by eliminating disobedience and squelching challenge. Anything that posed a threat to order was to be met with overwhelming force and, in one way or another, totally negated. Jefferson's solution to the United States' racial problem was calculated simply to eliminate what he perceived as a threat, namely, the possibility that blacks might rise up and challenge the legal and political apparatus that enslaved them. The course that he advocated was literally one of deduction rather than death (the sovereign solution Foucault discusses most extensively in *Discipline and Punish* and the fifth section of *The History of Sexuality, Volume One*), but deportation or exile is the civic equivalent of a sentence of death. Jefferson proposed literally to deduct a couple of million human bodies from the total sum of bodies on U.S. soil.[12] He could not imagine any way to handle a threat to national security other than simply to remove it. He could not think in what Foucault calls biopolitical terms; he could not imagine power employing resistances and challenges and breaches of law to develop new resources for self-enhancement. He could not imagine a politics of normalization. But such a thing was not far out on the horizon.

Jefferson's plan is usefully considered in contrast to what is sometimes called the "internal colonization" proposal of his friend and fellow signatory of the Declaration of Independence, Dr. Benjamin Rush. Like his comrade Jefferson, Rush was a committed and outspoken patriot, risking his life and career for the revolutionary cause on many occasions. He had a strong republican vision, an endearing but seemingly uncontrollable propensity to write inflammatory letters to newspaper editors, and a lot of plain old physical courage. But Rush was not cut out for a career in government, so he dedicated most of his life not to politics but to the practice of medicine. In addition to his many pamphlets and his service as physician general in the revolutionary army, Rush is remembered for his heroic (though tragically ill-conceived) effort to combat the yellow fever epidemic of 1793 (in which at least 10 percent of the population of Philadelphia perished)[13] and for his thirty years as chief physician of Pennsylvania Hospital's lunatic ward, which earned him the title "the Father of American Psychiatry."[14] Rush and Jefferson disagreed at times, but they were good friends and frequent correspondents from the 1770s until Rush's death in 1813.

As a devout Presbyterian (educated at Edinburgh), Rush was adamantly opposed to slavery on moral and religious grounds. He joined the Pennsylvania Abolition Society when it formed in 1794 and worked tirelessly to further its agenda through the last two decades of his life. Unlike Jefferson, Rush did believe that a biracial population could live together in peace. After all, in Philadelphia, he lived and worked alongside free blacks.[15] He therefore advocated abolition of slavery by whatever means necessary, beginning with the immediate cessation of the slave trade.[16] He favored voluntary manumission as a result of moral suasion directed toward slaveholders, but he also supported high taxes on slave importation and boycotts of products made by slave labor.[17] Where morality failed, he believed, self-interest might prevail in effecting mass emancipation.

The question was what to do with African Americans once they were free. Generations of illiterate slaves were not well prepared for self-governance, Rush believed. What was most needed was education, preferably Christian education, to prepare freed people for citizenship in a nation of equals. But peaceful assimilation into the general population would be much easier, he reasoned, if racial differences could be minimized or erased, and his medical experience led him to believe that elimination of racial difference was a real possibility.

Whereas Jefferson and Samuel Stanhope Smith believed that all racial features were a direct result of the natural impact of variant

climates on generic human bodies, Rush believed that the African
climate had played only an indirect role in the production of African
racial features. Black was not the normal color of any human being's
skin, he insisted in an address before the American Philosophical
Society in 1797, even of skin long exposed to sun and high tempera-
tures; on the contrary, black skin had to be a symptom of pathology. The climate of Africa created the conditions under which skin
diseases were likely to take hold. Over time leprosy developed there
and became widespread, darkening the skin, curling the hair, flatten-
ing the noses, and swelling the lips of most inhabitants of the African
continent. This form of leprosy is heritable, he explained, much as
consumption and madness are heritable. In fact, inheritance had
become the disease's primary means of self-perpetuation; it had long
since entered a relatively noncontagious state, so that casual contact
with victims did not result in transmission. Rush cautioned, however,
that prolonged intimate contact could still communicate the disease.
At least two white women who had married black men developed
the condition, a fact that made marriage between African Americans
and persons of other races medically inadvisable. If the disease could
be contained and its sufferers treated, however, it could probably be
eradicated. Then black people could be white people—that is, thin-
lipped, straight-haired, light-skinned people with protruding noses.
Morphology could be remade.

Rush believed, as did most of his well-educated contemporaries,
that living bodies were basically complex machines. Disease was a
malfunction of the machine. Accordingly, the physician was a kind
of mechanic. Sick or damaged bodies could be reconfigured through
careful use of treatments and disciplinary regimes. Rush emphatically
disagreed with people who held that there is a life force seated in the
human body, as many normalizing disciplinarians soon would.[18] Life,
he said, was the result of certain arrangements of matter responding
to stimuli. God endows matter with the possibility of coming to life
by giving it a certain arrangement (a structure) that is predisposed to
respond to stimuli. Then God sends the stimuli, which are necessary
not only to spark life but also to sustain it. Life does not inhere in
the body but exists only in complex relationships among the body's
structure, environmental stimuli, and the benevolent actions of an
Almighty God: "Admit of a principle of life in the human body, and
we open a door for the restoration of the old Epicurean or atheistical

philosophy, which supposed the world to be governed by a principle called nature, and which was believed to be inherent in every kind of matter. The doctrine I have taught, cuts the sinews of this error, for by rendering the *continuance* of animal life, no less than its commencement, the effect of the constant operation of divine power and goodness, it leads us to believe that the whole creation is supported in the same manner" (Rush 1947, 179). The mechanical body only operates when set in motion by an external force. Only then does it come to life or is it sustained in its life.

In human bodies, according to Rush, life consists of sensibility, motion, and thought. Thus the mind, too, is part of the machine and is brought to life and sustained in the same way as the heart and limbs. The physician must treat the mind just as he must treat the body. Psychiatry was thus no different from any other medical specialty and could not be separated from any other subfield of medicine in general practice.

All diseases, both physical and mental, were the result of either too much or too little vascular tension, Rush maintained. The pulse rate of a sick person was a key indicator of the degree and direction of imbalance.[19] Leprosy resulted from too little vascular tension, as indicated by a relatively slow or weak pulse. Treatment consisted in various strategies for quickening the heart rate. Rush advocated bleeding and purging as means to cleanse African Americans of leprosy. Fear raises the pulse rate as well and therefore might be useful in treating black leprosy, although Rush did not specify any particular method for inducing it (Rush 1799, 296). Furthermore, there is great curative power in vigorous activity, especially heavy physical labor, so he prescribed farm labor as one possible remedy of the black leprosy in his 1797 address.

Three years before presenting these ideas to the American Philosophical Society, Rush had proposed to donate 5,200 acres of land in Bedford County, Pennsylvania, to the Pennsylvania Abolition Society for the establishment of an all-black farming colony to be called Benezet; the land was finally transferred a decade later in 1804 (Rush 1951, 755–56). Ronald Takaki has suggested that Benezet was intended as a facility for quarantine (a leper colony, to be exact) (Takaki 2000, 31). He believes Rush meant to isolate blacks as vectors of contagion. But that scenario seems improbable. Rush showed no hesitation in mingling with blacks himself or allowing his wife and children to do so. He seemed quite sure that the disease was spread only through habitual sexual contact or heredity, making absolute quarantine unnecessary. However, since he did believe that heavy labor was good medicine for leprosy, he must have thought that an all-black farming community would afford a unique opportunity to make observations and comparisons among different therapeutic regimes and to keep careful records of the results. The "internal colony" of Benezet (and others for which Benezet might have served as a prototype) may very well have been intended as a clinical staging site for experimentation and treatment. At the very least, Rush envisioned such colonies as disciplinary mechanisms to train freedmen to take their places in a republican society.

Like so many American patriots of his generation, Benjamin Rush wanted to make self-governing republicans out of shopkeepers and common laborers, not to mention black slaves and rising generations of middle-class white children. But moral exhortation was not the only way to effect such transformations. Because the mind is part of the body-machine complex, Rush maintained, the moral faculty is deeply influenced by physical causes. Physical causes—such as extreme hunger, fever, adverse climate, and distilled spirits—can debilitate the moral faculty and lead to vice, he pointed out; but physical causes may also invigorate the moral faculty and lead to virtue. Physical disciplinary regimes could therefore be very effective in re-tooling former British subjects to function as self-governing Americans. Proper and regular diet, labor and exercise, and measured use of solitude, pain, music, fermented liquors, aromas, and sociality were all important tools for the creation of virtuous republicans. Rush even held out the possibility that certain drugs might prove valuable in this effort (Rush 1947, 181–207). He sums up his view in a striking passage in an essay entitled "Of the Mode of Education Proper in a Republic," where he writes: "I consider it possible to convert men into republican machines. This must be done, if we expect them to perform their parts properly, in the great machine of the government of the state" (1947, 92).

Rush's optimism about the possibility of biracial coexistence was clearly founded on his unwavering faith in possibilities and techniques of mechanical disciplinary regimes. Throughout his life, he was involved in efforts to build and strengthen the institutions that he believed would transform generic human bodies into free and virtuous citizens. He helped to found Dickinson College and Franklin College (later Franklin and Marshall). He advocated free education for African Americans and for the poor of all races. He campaigned against the use of corporal punishment in schools in favor of a system of reward and punishment (which was to consist primarily of enforced solitude for wrongdoers) and was adamant that capital punishment must be abolished in the new nation in favor of penitent confinement and disciplined labor. At the Pennsylvania Hospital he initiated and set the standards for the practice of psychiatry in the United States. Rush's influence on all the major types of public institutions in the nineteenth century—from the institutions of government and the military to pedagogy, medicine, and psychiatry—are inestimable.

Rush's leprosy theory was not taken up by his contemporaries or students, and his preferred treatments for so many diseases—copious bloodletting and vigorous gastrointestinal purging—were questioned even in his own lifetime.[20] His medicalization of racial difference and in particular his pathologization of African American racial features, however, prefigure the race theory of the late nineteenth century and its preoccupation with contagion, degeneracy, and hereditary disease. Furthermore, his application of the disciplinary techniques of longitudinal record-keeping, patient surveillance, and strictly regimented physical discipline—which he developed during his service as physician general of the U.S. military during the American Revolutionary War, in his efforts to quell the yellow fever epidemic in Philadelphia in 1793, and in his work at the Pennsylvania Hospital—paved the way for the normalizing disciplinary techniques used in the U.S. military, the nation's institutions of public health, and the practice of psychiatry throughout the nineteenth century.

Before the middle of the nineteenth century, racial characteristics would be understood as manifestations of vital processes and on the axis of pathology and health. And once race came to be so understood, it would fit easily into the institutionalized disciplinary regimes that Rush's work had helped to establish and that, by the end of the nineteenth century, would coalesce into the broad networks of normalization that define so much of the world that we live in today. Rush and Jefferson are a study in contrast, not just because Rush is an optimist and Jefferson a pessimist about the future of race relations, but because Rush is at the forefront of the development of a new kind of power/knowledge network, while Jefferson's thought remains completely confined within eighteenth-century discourses of sovereignty. Thomas Jefferson may be a national hero, but Benjamin Rush is truly our biopolitical forefather.

Race as Developmental Failure: Biology and Ethnology in the Nineteenth Century

Rush's theory that blackness was a form of leprosy never caught on, but within thirty years after his death, his belief that racial difference was best understood as a manifestation of physiological processes rather than a matter of static structure was commonplace. As the discipline of biology took hold of scientific imaginations and institutions in the Western world, morphology in all its manifestations, whether normal or pathological, was believed to be a transient product of functions. Process, not structure, became primary. Therefore, what ultimately distinguished one race from another—and, significantly, what made one race more valuable or venerable than another in the minds of most Europeans and North Americans—were the complex developmental processes underlying and giving rise to each race's characteristic morphological and behavioral traits. In the nineteenth century, morphology was no longer race itself but a set of markers indicating race—which in some cases only highly trained specialists were able to discern.

So many factors and forces contributed to this shift in the concept of race that it is impossible to explore them all here. We will have to content ourselves with a quick look at only three confluent sets of events: (1) the rise of comparative anthropology and the theory of polygeny (the theory of separate racial creations) between 1790 and 1850, (2) the growing strength of the idea that ontogeny recapitulates phylogeny during the same period, and (3) the emergence in the 1830s of a strong and vocal abolition movement in the United States that compelled proponents of slavery to formulate, for the first time, a coherent justification for their practices.

Comparative Anthropology and Polygenism

In 1799 Louis François Jauffret founded the Société des Observateurs de l'Homme, the world's first anthropological society. Its members, naturalists and physicians, literary figures and explorers, pledged themselves to observe various human groups—or races, as Cuvier termed them in the "instructive note" he prepared for members in 1800 (Stocking 1968, 19)—and, based upon these observations, to classify them according to their customs, languages, and anatomy. The Société called for a study of the effects of climate on body form in different parts of France, compilation of a dictionary of all known languages, establishment of a museum of comparative ethnography, and a host of equally ambitious projects that were never realized because the association collapsed for political reasons in 1804. But the group was able to mount one expedition; in 1800 Société members sailed to Africa, Tasmania, and New Holland (Australia) on a voyage that, despite setbacks and failures, did yield considerable scientific rewards.

Prior to the expedition, mentioned above, Cuvier wrote out detailed instructions, including specifications for the procurement and preservation of human remains. George Stocking recounts these directives as follows:

> Of the various skeletal remains, the most important was the skull. Unfortunately, skulls were not easy to procure. Cuvier suggested therefore that when the voyagers witnessed or took part in a battle involving savages, they must not fail to "visit the places where the dead are deposited." When they were able—"in any manner whatever"—to obtain a body, they should "carefully note all that relates to the individual from whom the cadaver came." Then the skeleton must be properly prepared: "To boil the bones in a solution of soda or of caustic potash and rid them of their flesh is a matter of several hours." Once prepared, the bones of each skeleton were to be put in bags, labeled, and sent to Europe, where they might be reassembled. It would be desirable also to bring back some skulls with the flesh still intact. One had only to soak them in a solution of corrosive sublimate, set them out to dry, and they would become as hard as wood, their facial forms preserved without attracting insects. True, the sailors might think this barbarous, "but in an expedition which has as its end the advancement of science, it is necessary for the leaders to allow themselves to be governed only by reason." (Stocking 1968, 30)

Such "specimens" would play a crucial role in anthropological theorizing for years to come.[21]

The young medical student and zoologist in charge of carrying out these instructions was François Péron, who had been greatly influenced in his thinking about the peoples of Africa, Tasmania, and Australia by the work of Jean Jacques Rousseau. Péron believed that the Tasmanians were the closest of all known human groups to "noble savagery," Rousseau's term for the state of existence of Europeans before modern civilization softened and corrupted them. He was eager to determine the degree to which all the other groups approached either the savagery of the Tasmanians or the civilization of the French. Over the course of his short career—he died in 1810 at age thirty-five of the tuberculosis that he contracted on the voyage— Péron was to lose his youthful enthusiasm for savagery and come to see the Tasmanians not as noble but as "degraded" (Stocking 1968, 37). The aspect of Péron's project that did endure was his belief that races of human beings could be ranked according to their degree of civility and that civility was somehow connected with anatomy. That view was widespread by the time of Péron's death.

Many of the participants in the expedition were extremely influential in the subsequent development of anthropological race theory. Probably in 1801, but certainly from 1802 to 1804, Jauffret drew on the expedition's observations to give a course at the Louvre entitled "D'Histoire naturelle de l'Homme." Other members of the Société put the data gathered to good use as well, as did closely associated nonmembers, including Julien Joseph Virey, who published *Histoire naturelle des Genre Humain* in 1801, where he argued that races were actually separate species. Virey's scientific version of polygenism, though rejected vociferously by Cuvier, would play a key role in proslavery rhetoric in the United States from the 1830s forward.

Whether they believed that human beings constituted one species or many, however, French naturalists in the early nineteenth century were sure that African, Australian, and Tasmanian races were anatomically quite different from Europeans. They measured and described various parts of innumerable bodies with the goal of identifying the precise set of physical characteristics that delineated each race and distinguished them from one another. As Cuvier's instructions indicate, by far the most copiously measured body part was the head. Blumenbach, the father of anthropology, had undertaken extensive study of the cranium as a means of differentiating and classifying human types in the late eighteenth century. French naturalists were merely following his lead, as would ethnologists in the United

States in ensuing years. Very quickly, measurements of the head came to be seen as indicators of brain size and therefore of reasoning capacity. Races with big heads were clearly superior in rationality and thus capable of far more technological and civil innovation than races with small heads. Northern European males were, without a doubt, the biggest-headed people in the whole wide world.

Ontogeny Recapitulates Phylogeny

During the same decade in which the Société de l'Observateurs des l'Homme was formed, early scientific versions of recapitulation theory were emerging. In 1793 anatomist Carl Friedrich Kielmeyer suggested that there is a parallelism between the stages of structural development in the mammalian fetus and the structure of various living organisms or "lower" animals.[22] Shortly thereafter, Kielmeyer's colleague Johann von Autenrieth gave the first sustained argument for recapitulation theory in morphology in 1797, holding that "completed forms of lower animals are merely stages in the ontogeny of higher forms" (Gould 1977, 126). The hierarchical chain of living beings is recapitulated in the ontogeny of the individual, in other words. Autenrieth ended his discussion by suggesting that blacks must be considered lower on the scale of being than whites, because they bear "certain traits which seem, in the adult African, to be less changed from the embryonic condition than in the adult European."[23] Autenrieth's assertion announces the beginning of a transition from race as pure morphology—bodily structure and appearance—to race as a category and an indicator of biological development, a transition that would enable the development of scientific racism over the next several decades.

German embryology and French anatomy converged in the 1820s. Geoffroy drew on Kielmeyer to develop his recapitulation theory, which was elaborated by his disciple Etienne Sèrres, who also took up and greatly extended Johann von Meckel's theory of arrests in development (Appel 1987, 126). Geoffroy and Sèrres began applying the theory of arrests in development to their studies of "monsters" in 1821. Any kind of "deformity" earned an individual the appellation of "monster." (Geoffroy's son Isidore would coin the name "teratology" for this new discipline.) In contrast to eighteenth-century thinkers like Benjamin Rush, they hypothesized that there is a developmental force in all living beings. In monsters, this force is either too weak or too strong. If too strong, the affected organ replicates its own normal form (as when a child is born with six toes on each foot). If too weak, the organ affected fails to develop beyond the stage at which it resembles a homologous organ in a lower species. This latter would be an example of an arrest in development, and in many cases it would cause spontaneous abortion and death of the fetus. In instances where it was not fatal, however, Sèrres believed it might be possible to restart the developmental process and cure the individual of deformity.

At first Sèrres spoke only of arrests in the development of individual organs, but by 1824 he was speaking of stages of development in entire bodies and claiming that lower animals are in effect embryos of higher animals. By 1832 he held that the entire human fetus passes through fish, reptile, and bird stages on its way to recognizable human form (Appel 1987, 124). Human beings are what they are because they surpass all other animals developmentally. Not absolute difference but relative degree of development distinguishes one species from another. From there it was a short step to the idea that degree of development distinguishes one race from another; racial difference, too, could be reduced to developmental degree. Sèrres asserted that African males were less advanced from the fetal state than European males as evidenced by the shorter distance between their penises and their navels (Gilman 1983, 41; Gould 1981, 40).

Sèrres' recapitulation theory, although certainly controversial, was extremely influential, through both his many publications and his teaching. As chief physician at Paris's prestigious Hôpital de la Pitié, which attracted medical students from all over the world, he trained hundreds of medical scientists. Thus it came about that Autenrieth's early suggestion that racial difference might amount to a difference in the degree of anatomical development fit right into the mainstream of French and German biological thinking by the 1830s.

Anthropologists, building on the ideas of the anatomists, pointed out that notable anatomical differences between races were paralleled by notable differences in the degree to which the various races were civilized. One explanation for that parallel could be derived from racial differences in the size of the cranium, which indicated corresponding racial differences in the size of the brain. Races appeared to be more or less capable of civilization, depending on how large their brains were. The smaller the brain, the less civilized the human being.

With recapitulation theory as a scientific background, ethnologists had no trouble conceiving of morphological race as a result of arrests in biological development, and racial difference as a mark of relative success or failure in a biological march toward social and moral as well as physical perfection.

Proslavery Responses to the U.S. Abolition Movement

Meanwhile, back in the United States, politicians and intellectuals were still preoccupied with the question of how to avert race war. Jefferson's idea of sending all the African Americans overseas still sounded good to many people; in 1817 the American Colonization Society was founded and began to raise private funds for the project, but progress was slow. In 1832 President Andrew Jackson vetoed a bill that would have allocated federal money for the effort, probably largely because, despite the fact that only free blacks were being enlisted as colonists, slaveholders—who were by this time reaping enormous profits in a booming world cotton market[24]—saw the deportation movement as an implicit threat to their labor pool.

Some saw it differently. Far from posing a threat to the institution of slavery, William Lloyd Garrison declared in 1832 that colonization was actually a proslavery plot to rid the country of free blacks who might take up arms to liberate their bonded brethren. The next year, in 1833, the American Antislavery Society was founded under his leadership, and by 1835 it was inundating Congress with petitions to put an end to the hateful practice of enslaving fellow human beings. This onslaught forced slavery's supporters to articulate a rationale for their favored institution and to argue not only for its economic expedience but also for its civic and moral value. They quickly gathered up the available fragments of argumentation and bundled them into a shaky justification for racial slavery.

The reigning theory of racial difference in the United States was still that of Samuel Stanhope Smith. Race was a product of environment and could change with environment. If Negroes were "degraded" in mind and body, it was because of circumstances that could be altered. According to historian George Fredrickson, "open assertions of *permanent* inferiority were exceedingly rare" before 1830 (1971, 43). Even the colonizationists, eager to rid the country of black bodies, believed African Americans were capable of rising to the challenge of establishing and maintaining a new nation-state on the continent of their ancestors. In the proper climate and with a good dose of Anglo-American technical and moral education, a black civilization might well flourish. Fredrickson notes, "One can go through much of the literature of the [colonization] movement from 1817 to the late 1830s without finding a single clear and unambiguous assertion of the Negro's inherent and unalterable inferiority to whites" (1971, 12). Some people were pessimistic about blacks' potential, as Jefferson was, but belief in immutable biological inferiority was far from commonplace.[25]

As long as most people thought African Americans were capable of rising above the condition of slavish dependence (however difficult that process might be), defending slavery was an uphill battle. What was needed was a strong case for black incapacity, based not on external circumstances or the interaction between corporality and environment but on something inherent in black bodies, something that would not change regardless of changes in civil status or geographical location. That something was readily available in the biological theories circulating in Europe by 1830, and American intellectuals were in a good position to draw on them—and to put them in the hands of proslavery politicians and the general public.

Stuart Gilman (1983, 27) has argued that historians have paid insufficient attention to the role that clinical medicine played in the development of scientific racism in the nineteenth century, and indeed attention to the ways in which European race theory was disseminated in the United States does lead one to conclude that the institutions as well as the practice of clinical medicine played an extremely important part. Paris was the center of medical research and education in the West by the early 1820s, attracting more than two hundred medical students from the United States in the 1830s alone (Horsman 1987, 43).[26] The Hôpital de la Pitié, one of the three most renowned hospitals in France and housing one of only two public dissecting schools, was a primary destination for many of them. The chief physician at La Pitié throughout the 1820s and 1830s was none other than Geoffroy's disciple, recapitulation theorist and teratologist Etienne Sèrres.[27] American medical students at La Pitié and La Charité lived and breathed French and German theories of biological development in those years. None left Paris without exposure—most likely quite extensive—to the reigning theories of embryological recapitulation and its retardation or full cessation through arrests in development, and with them the notion that human races represent different stages of development. Popularization of the idea that racial difference was a difference in degree of biological development, as a result, was largely the work of prominent American physicians in close contact with European physicians, anatomists, and ethnologists. Samuel George Morton is a prime example.

Born into a wealthy Philadelphia family in 1799, Morton received the best medical education to be had in the United States. He took his first medical degree in 1820 under Philip Syng Physick at the University of Pennsylvania, at that time the premiere medical school in the country. But he was not satisfied with his American education and so took a second degree from the University of Edinburgh in 1823. Realizing that Edinburgh was no longer the leader in medical education in Europe, however (as it had been in Benjamin Rush's day), Morton took a year (1821–22) to study clinical medicine in Paris. He returned to Pennsylvania in 1824, where he established a lucrative medical practice (Brace 2005, 80). Although his primary professional commitment was always to medicine (by 1830 he was teaching in the medical department at Pennsylvania College), his scientific interests were very broad. From the earliest days of his career, he was a member of the Academy of Natural Sciences in Philadelphia, which he served as an officer for many years. He made major contributions in a number of scientific fields, including pharmacology, paleontology, zoology, and geology, quickly developing an international reputation. His work brought him into close touch with scientists all over Europe, and he enjoyed tremendous professional respect throughout the scientific world.

In 1830, while preparing a series of anthropology lectures, Morton found that he was unable to locate skull specimens to illustrate Blumenbach's five varieties of human beings. He set out to remedy that situation by assembling a private collection of skulls from around the globe. By the time he deposited the collection in the Academy of Natural Sciences in the late 1840s, he had about seven hundred human skulls and another seven hundred skulls of other animals. Over the course of his studies, Morton devised at least a dozen types of cranial measurement for comparing these skulls. He had samples from more than forty locations in North and South America alone, which he used in his most famous work *Crania Americana,* published in 1839.

Morton based his classification of skulls on Blumenbach's typology —Caucasian, Mongolian, Ethiopian, American, and Malay—but unlike Blumenbach, who believed these varieties shaded into one another,[28] Morton believed they were radically distinct, and his measurements bore out this hypothesis. Furthermore, he believed that external factors like climate were not the source of the differences; instead, the differences were inherent and unalterable. Native Americans simply did not have the cranial capacity of Europeans, which explains why they had not developed the technologies or forms of government that Europeans had developed and why they never would. With the help of British Egyptologist George Gliddon, Morton acquired a number of African skulls in the 1830s and 40s and in 1844 published a sequel to his earlier work, this one called *Crania Aegyptiaca*. In it he presented what he viewed as proof that the ancient Egyptians were Caucasian rather than Negro, thus casting doubt on one of the major pieces of evidence abolitionists used to argue that, despite their current condition, African Americans were capable of civility and independence.[29]

Some have argued that Morton, as a consummate scientist and a Northerner, could not have set out to distort data. The falsities that clearly exist—and apparently there are many[30]—must have been pure errors of one sort or another, for what interest could a man like Morton have had in bolstering the institution of slavery? Of course such an assumption overlooks the class interests that elites can share even when they do not share the same cultural milieu as well as the possibility that even a well-educated person can be mistaken about what his or her interests actually are. But whatever Samuel Morton may have believed, it is clear that he did have a political agenda. He deliberately inserted his anthropological work into the slavery debate on the side of slaveholders. In 1843 Morton directed Gliddon to deliver a copy of *Crania Aegyptiaca* to Secretary of State John C. Calhoun (Fredrickson 1971, 77), perhaps the most prominent spokesmen for slavery in the decades before the Civil War. The following May, while Calhoun was negotiating over the question of whether Texas would be annexed to the union as a slave state, Gliddon met with him in Washington. Gliddon and his collaborator Josiah Nott later described this fateful meeting:

> Mr. Calhoun declared that he could not foresee what course the negotiation might take, but wished to be forearmed for any emergency. He was convinced that the true difficulties of the subject could not be fully comprehended without first considering the radical difference of humanity's races, which

he intended to discuss, should he be driven to the necessity. Knowing that Mr. Gliddon had paid attention to the subject of African ethnology; and that, from his long residence in Egypt, he had enjoyed unusual advantages for its investigation, Mr. Calhoun had summoned him for the purpose of ascertaining what were the best sources of information in this country. Mr. Gliddon, after laying before the Secretary what he conceived to be the true state of the case, referred him for further information to several scientific gentlemen, and more particularly to DR. MORTON, of Philadelphia. A correspondence ensued between Mr. Calhoun and Dr. Morton on the subject, and the Doctor presented to him copies of the *Crania Americana* and *Aegyptiaca*, together with minor works, all of which Mr. Calhoun studied with no less pleasure than profit. He soon perceived that the conclusions which he had long before drawn from history, and from his personal observations in America, on the Anglo-Saxon, Celtic, Teutonic, French, Spanish, Negro, and Indian races, were entirely corroborated by the plain teachings of modern science. (Nott and Gliddon 1854, 51)

Ever since the abolition movement had become a serious political force in the mid-1830s, Calhoun had been constructing new arguments to support the institution of slavery. As South Carolina's senator, he had asserted on the Senate floor in 1837 that subordination and economic exploitation of the masses was a necessary condition for advanced civilization, which he took to be an obvious good. But, he said, subordination naturally created potentially destabilizing resentment and resistance. Therefore slavery was the ideal arrangement. Unlike other means of subordination, which were only partial, slavery's subordination was complete; it suppressed resistance utterly and so gave society much more stability than it otherwise would have.[31] Abolitionists were not swayed by this argument. They held that slavery was an absolute evil, regardless of its economic and cultural benefits to the ruling class. Calhoun needed another angle. Morton gave it to him.

Morton's skull measurements clearly showed that Mongolians, Malays, Ethiopians, and (Native) Americans have smaller brains than Caucasians (and Caucasian females have smaller brains than Caucasian males); hence, the level of intelligence in these races (and in the female sex of all races) must be relatively low. Nothing could change that fact. No amount of education or training would turn the descendants of Africans into self-disciplined republicans capable of participation as citizens in a free society. Calhoun made political capital of Morton's scientific claims. If left to their own devices, he argued, African Americans would simply return to a state of savagery or barbarism. Of course, savagery and barbarism were bad ways for anybody to live, including savages and barbarians. At least as slaves, intellectually inferior blacks had the benefit of exposure to civility and enjoyed some of the material advantages of a technologically advanced society.

Calhoun reinforced his argument for annexation of Texas as a slave state with data from the 1840 census, which showed that in states where slavery had been abolished, blacks fell into poverty, immorality, and disease. "For example, the census showed that 1 out of 96 blacks in the free states was deaf, mute, blind, or insane, while the ratio in the slave states was 1 in 672. In Massachusetts, where slavery had been abolished sixty years earlier, and where 'the greatest zeal' on behalf of black people existed, their condition was 'amongst the most wretched,' with 1 out of 13 'either deaf and dumb, blind, idiot, insane or in prison'" (Bartlett 1993, 311). Slavery was beneficial not only to elite Southern planters, he maintained, but also to the slaves themselves! Of course, Calhoun knew by 1844 that the 1840 census was seriously flawed. The House of Representatives had already passed a resolution directing him to review it in light of charges made by Edward Jarvis and George Tucker that it was full of errors.[32] But he seems to have believed that, whether the figures were exact or not, slavery was the only thing standing between African Americans and total degradation and thus the only thing standing between his beloved South Carolina and descent into chaos. Morton's work placed a respectable scientific foundation beneath that belief.

In this relationship between John C. Calhoun, the statesman, and Samuel George Morton, the scientist, we see the confluence of forces creating the conditions within which race was transformed from a morphological to a biological concept in popular discourse. From the 1840s forward, race would no longer be simply a matter of physical appearance; instead, it would become a matter of organic function and physiological development. The visible marks of morphological race would become signs of developmental progress or, alternatively, degeneration or arrest. Racial inferiority would become a matter of measurable deviation from established developmental norms.

Morton himself tended toward the view that the five races of humanity were in fact five distinct species, a view that became very popular in the United States in the 1840s. Blacks and Native Americans were bestial; as such, they had to be either exterminated or subdued. The kindest choice, surely, was domestication under the protection of white male authorities. Against their opponents, who would deport blacks to a future of hopeless savagery in Africa or set them free to roam the American countryside without supervision and proper care, defenders of slavery thus took the moral high ground.

The problem with this polygenous line of argument, though, was that most scientists, following Buffon, held species to be distinguishable only on the basis of an inability to cross-breed and produce fertile offspring. In most cases species cannot cross-breed at all; frogs cannot have sex with hogs, for example. But where the edges of species are more blurred—the distinction between asses and horses is a classic example—the deciding factor is whether the progeny of a cross-union can reproduce. Mules, as we know, are sterile; so asses and horses are separate species, despite an occasional case of mutual attraction. If the five races of humanity were to be considered five different species under the existing definition, Morton knew, it would have to be shown that their offspring were infertile, and that just did not seem to be true. Mulattoes abounded, and they seemed perfectly capable of making more mulattoes. What was a polygenist to do?[33]

Another Philadelphia-trained American physician, Josiah Nott of Mobile, Alabama, came to Morton's aid.[34] Dr. Nott was a native of South Carolina, a lifelong slaveholder, and a family friend of John C. Calhoun. Like Morton, he had the best medical education available in the Western Hemisphere at the time, including a residency in Philadelphia under Philip Syng Physick in 1827–29 and a year in Paris at the Hôpital de la Pitié in 1835–36 under Etienne Sèrres and Pierre-Charles-Alexandré Louis. Subsequently, he enjoyed a lucrative medical practice among Mobile's elite (which meant that he also treated their slaves). In 1843 Nott published an article in the *American Journal of Medical Sciences* entitled "The Mulatto—Hybrid—probable extermination of the two races if the Whites and

Blacks are allowed to intermarry" in which he argued that mulattoes are ultimately infertile. Many of them cannot reproduce at all,
he claimed, although sometimes they do conceive. Mulatto women
are delicate; they suffer from many reproductive disorders that may
result in spontaneous abortion and are poor nurses for their weak
babies. The few children who do survive infancy are almost always
chronically diseased and short-lived, and those who survive to sexual
maturity are even less fertile than their parents. Within two or three
generations, mulatto lines are always extinct. "What," Nott asks,
"could we expect in breeding from a faulty stock—a stock which has
been produced by a violation of nature's laws, but that they should
become more degenerate in each successive generation?" (Nott 1843,
255). Although all of his evidence was anecdotal and gleaned from
a mere handful of sources, Nott averred that it was reasonable to
conclude that Anglo-Saxons and Africans are distinct species and
to suspect that Caucasians in general and both Africans and Native
Americans were separately created lines. Upon reading the article,
Morton contacted Nott and thanked him for his scientific efforts.
The two became correspondents, and Nott visited Morton frequently
on his trips to Philadelphia. Their scientific exchange eventually led
Morton to declare his commitment to polygenism.

Nott's ideas were increasingly influential through the 1840s
(Horsman 1987, 101). Asked to address the Louisiana General
Assembly in 1848 on the biological inferiority of the Negro (a subject Nott referred to as "niggerology"), Nott obliged with a lecture
in which he not only maintained his view that blacks were a separate
species but also declared that the original stock of white people was
Germanic and that the Celts—by which he meant both the Bretons
and the Irish—were an inferior, only quasi-white race that would
soon fade away with the advance of Anglo-Saxon civilization.[35] Nott
arranged to have this lecture published in 1849 by a New York firm,
thereby gaining a broader audience. The next year he contributed a
paper to the meetings of the American Society for the Advancement
of Science in which he argued that, since Jews' stereotypic features
are the same the world over regardless of climate or environmental
condition, racial biology is destiny.

Through Morton, Nott began corresponding with George
Gliddon. They too became friends and eventually partners in producing what many historians now see as the most comprehensive
work of what has come to be known as the American School of

Ethnology. Their book *Types of Mankind,* which included essays by Morton and Swedish émigré botanist Louis Agassiz, was published in 1854. It argued that racial types are fixed, that Caucasians are a separate species from other races, and that racially mixed blood-lines are doomed to extinction.[36] It pushed the point that civilization and morality are matters of biological development exclusively and are beyond the reach of social and educational interventions. The book enjoyed immense popularity despite its length and cost.[37] It was reissued ten times before the end of the nineteenth century and was quoted extensively in both scientific and lay contexts throughout North America and Europe. Through it, among other means, these four men completely overturned the older environmental theories of thinkers like Samuel Stanhope Smith and created a respectable intel-lectual foundation for the biological determinism and scientific racism of the nineteenth and twentieth centuries.

We might be tempted to think that a theory of fixed types runs counter to the fundamental tenets of biology as a science of living function and of the body as a manifestation of temporal processes, but in fact the two sets of ideas were not in conflict at all, as Foucault's discussion of Cuvier's fixism in *The Order of Things* suggests. A given body is a manifestation of a developmental process. That process might be basically the same for all living beings, as Geoffroy and Sèrres would have it, with differentiation of species or races within species occurring as a difference in developmental rate. (If one could slow development considerably or stop it at a given point, the "human" fetus would effectively be a reptile or a bird.) Or the process might differ qualitatively as well as quantitatively in each species, making resemblances in structure across species merely coincidental, as Cuvier believed. But either way, creation seen as a whole was a developmental hierarchy. There were not only different kinds of living beings; there were advanced beings and arrested beings, more and less developed beings, higher and lower beings. Difference in morphology always indicated a difference in degree of development, which in turn always indicated a difference in value. And in the final analysis that meant that inferior races were inferior because they were less well developed. Members of those races, therefore, were aptly compared to "lower" animals and to the prehistoric ancestors and the contemporary chil-dren of superior races. And they were best treated accordingly, as children or savages.[38]

Bestial savages and nineteenth-century white children did not form a homogeneous category for the purposes of moral judgment and action, however. And thus "the South's fundamental conception of itself as a slaveholding society was unstable," George Fredrickson maintains. "In the intellectual context of the time, the notion of the slave as dependent or child implied one kind of social order; the view that he was essentially subhuman suggested another" (Fredrickson 1971, 58). On the one hand, if slaves were human beings arrested in development at the stage of childhood, slaveholders had a paternal duty to care for their charges and to serve as their moral guides. Such an image lent enslaved blacks an aura of moral innocence to match their presumed stupidity. On the other hand, if slaves were brutes whose natural savagery had to be held in check by strict discipline and exhausted by hard labor, slaveholders were obliged to take what-ever steps were required to guarantee the security of the local white population while squeezing a profit out of the morally and physically dangerous element they found it necessary to employ. On the one hand, the plantation was a large and permanent family and a loving one when properly managed. On the other hand, the plantation was a hard-nosed capitalist venture involving all sorts of risks and trade-offs, and violence was an integral part of its functioning. These two very different scenarios, along with their divergent implications, were both products of application of the same biological concept—namely, that of life as development—to the field of racial difference.[39] Both were perfectly plausible, given the science of the day; neither could be refuted and dispatched, and each found sympathetic ears among factions of political activists of all stripes. But they led to very differ-ent sets of conclusions about morality and justice.

In sum, two divergent images of blacks—as dependent children in need of fatherly guidance and support, and as murderous sav-ages barely held in check by whip and chain—arose and coexisted in proslavery rhetoric from the late 1830s onward. Both images would continue to circulate long after the abolition of slavery in debates over African American participation in government and mainstream social life and would play important roles in the creation of the complex laws and social norms that came to be known as Jim Crow segrega-tion. For a while, their obvious incompatibility created friction among the groups that espoused them. But over time there came a reconcili-ation of these two images of "inferior races." It arrived by way of a revision, not in the concept of race, but in the concept of childhood.

By the end of the nineteenth century, children were no longer the innocent dependents they had once been; instead, they were the ontogenic recapitulation of their own savage ancestors.

Idiocy and the Criminalization of Childhood

In 1821 the Massachusetts Assembly appointed Josiah Quincy chair of a committee directed to write a report on poverty and organized relief throughout the commonwealth. Quincy's committee immediately went to work investigating local strategies, questioning local officials, amassing statistical data from surveys and polls of citizens, reviewing county and municipality financial records, and soliciting opinions from experts in Europe. In 1824 New York established a similar committee under the leadership of John Yates that undertook to do the same assessment of that state's poor citizens and relief programs. At the time Quincy and Yates did their studies, only a few of the larger cities in the United States had any sort of shelter for housing the poor at public expense. In most areas the poor lived in their own homes or with relatives or friends and were given direct aid in the form of food or fuel or medical care when need became dire. Parishes, counties, and municipalities handled these cases as they saw fit. But the Quincy and Yates reports, along with the reformist sentiments and interests that had spawned them, very shortly changed everything.

Reformers maintained that by gathering the poor together under a single roof, a poorhouse or almshouse, assistance could be provided much more effectively and inexpensively than under the existing and rather haphazard system of "outdoor relief." Their arguments prevailed. By 1840, Massachusetts had 180 almshouses valued at $926,000 on 17,000 acres of land. In other words, in less than twenty years, state and local governments were heavily invested in institutionalized public assistance. The pattern was repeated in New York. By 1835 fifty-one of the state's fifty-five counties had an almshouse. By 1850 the number of people living in such facilities across the nation approached 10,000 (Rothman 1971, 183). In 1827 Pennsylvania went so far as to abolish all public assistance other than that given inside almshouses; people who wanted aid had to go live in a poorhouse whether they had another place to live or not. The city of Chicago took the same approach, banning "outdoor relief" in 1848. Even in rural areas, almshouses were maintained in the belief that "indoor relief" was the best way to handle poverty, even though much of the time there was no one to live in them. Somehow it had become common sense that people without a clearly defined productive role to play in society should be segregated in special institutions.[40]

In theory, the almshouses of the Jacksonian period bore little resemblance to the few poorhouses that had existed in the eighteenth century. As historian David Rothman puts it, "The new almshouse would insist upon order, discipline, and an exacting routine" (1971, 188). Its purpose was not only to meet the material needs of the poor but to reform them by breaking them of their bad habits and intemperance and instilling a respect for order and authority. The new almshouse would "rescue" the poor from the temptations that besieged them in the outside world and discipline them to resist temptation when they returned to the community. Inmates would be classified and separated by sex, age, health, and history and inserted into a strict schedule of activities through the day, emphasizing work for those young and strong enough to do any.[41] They would be kept under close surveillance by guards with the authority to coerce them into following the regime. They would sleep in cells, eat together at long tables on a precise schedule, and wear prescribed clothing.

> An early morning bell would waken the inmates, another would signal the time for breakfast. Residents were to proceed immediately, but not in formation, to the dining hall, take their assigned seats, and finish their meal in the prescribed time; those guilty of wasting or pilfering food would be punished by a decrease in rations or, at the superintendent's discretion, solitary confinement. After breakfast they were to enter workshops, and again the threat of reducing provisions and solitary confinement hung over anyone who might be slothful or sloppy in his labor. No one could leave the institution without the manager's permission; no one could come to visit without his formal approval. Those almshouse residents who faithfully obeyed the regulations would be allowed to remain with friends for a few days once every two months. Habitual violators would suffer curtailed rations or confinement and repeated offenses would bring still more severe punishments. The essence of the institution was obedience to its rules. (Rothman 1971, 191)

It is difficult to imagine how, under these disciplinary conditions, a family might stay together or an able-bodied adult might re-establish him- or herself as an independent member of the community. Like all normalizing institutions, the almshouse tended to individualize its occupants, disregarding their affiliations with each other or with relatives and friends outside; it also tended to decrease their access to gainful employment even while purporting to instill a positive work ethic and marketable skills. Little wonder that its inmate populations quickly increased.

As early as 1833, the Boston House of Industry was so crowded that inmates slept seven to a cell; nine officials supervised an inmate population 623. There was no operative system of classification; people were more or less thrown together regardless of sex, age, disease, or ability. Most residents sat idle day in and day out, left to their own devices without any official surveillance whatsoever, much less discipline or training. Similar problems were noted in other institutions over the next fifteen years. By 1857 a state investigation revealed that

> almost all of New York's almshouses were "badly constructed, ill arranged, ill warmed, and ill ventilated." The able-bodied paupers were not at work, and classification was nowhere to be found. Old and respectable army veterans lounged about with the most degenerate characters; even the sexes were not separated, so that illicit relations and illegitimate births occurred regularly. Despite all these faults, supervisors and trustees rarely visited the institutions. "As receptacles for adult paupers," the investigators told the legislature, "the committee do not hesitate to record their deliberate opinion that the great mass of the poor houses ... are most disgraceful memorials of the public charity. Common domestic animals are usually more humanely provided for than the paupers in some of these institutions." (Rothman 1971, 198)

The almshouse was supposed to be a disciplinary institution that would not only remove paupers from public view but would redeem and remake them into productive citizens. Reality was falling far short of the dream.

The dream, however, was still intact. During this same period, the mania for institutionalization had produced penitentiaries, reformatories, and lunatic asylums as well as almshouses. These facilities were coming under fire for some of the same reasons—overcrowding, failure of inmate classification, insufficient order in daily routines—

but virtually no one wanted to return to a system of "outdoor relief." Institutionalization was here to stay. In fact, it was about to proliferate in response to the very problems it had generated—its own "residue," as Foucault terms it in *Psychiatric Power*. What was needed, officials decided, was a diversification of institutional types. It was time to get people out of the almshouses who did not belong there and put them into a new set of disciplinary institutions designed to deal with a newly identified set of physical and moral shortcomings.

At the same time, as Foucault points out, the concept of madness was undergoing a dramatic realignment that would have substantial effects on a variety of related concepts, would bring several new concepts and practical possibilities into play, and would result in the expulsion of some classes of inmates from lunatic asylums. Eighteenth-century psychiatrists had believed that madness was fundamentally an error in judgment or a refusal of truth; the lunatic insists that he is Jesus Christ or Louis XVI and will not countenance any claim to the contrary. Recovery amounts to relinquishment of fondly held falsehoods. The very height of madness, however, was thought to be characterized not by audacious assertions of untruths but rather by the silent detachment of what psychiatrists then called "idiocy," a condition in which a person refuses assent not just to some truths but to all of them (Foucault 2006, 205). Eighteenth-century physicians assumed that despite the absence of outward symptoms of delirium, the idiot lived in a sort of dream-world that precluded meaningful contact with reality and thus precluded learning.

Jean-Etienne Esquirol, however, rejected the idea that madness was refusal of truth, seeing it instead as an organic pathology, and by 1817 he was classifying idiots as a separate group altogether. "Idiocy is not a disease," he insisted, "but a condition in which the intellectual faculties are never manifested, or have never been sufficiently developed." Jacques Etienne Belhomme took a very similar position in 1824, writing that "idiocy is . . . a constitutional condition in which the intellectual functions have never developed" (Foucault 2006, 205). These statements about the nature of idiocy mark a radical departure from the past. As Foucault puts it, "Idiocy is not defined therefore with reference to truth or error, or with reference to the ability or inability to control oneself, or with reference to the intensity of the delirium, but with reference to development" (2006, 206). Idiocy was an outcome of a natural process of maturation gone awry.

Still somewhat influenced by the structural thinking of the previous century, both Esquirol and Belhomme thought of development or the lack of it as a static quality of an organ or being; something was either developed, or it was not. In idiots, the organs of cognition were not developed, so idiots were not ill, like lunatics, but rather were deformed, like monsters. Clearly, idiots did not belong in lunatic asylums. They were not sick and would not respond to medical treatment. But they could not simply be transferred to already overcrowded and compromised almshouses or reformatories either. What to do with them?

An answer was brewing in the mind and work of Esquirol's young student Edouard Seguin. Drawing on advances in biology—such as the work of Etienne Sèrres at the Hôpital de la Pitié through the 1820s—Seguin had a much more nuanced understanding of the notion of development. Sèrres's efforts in the new science of teratology involved the concept of arrests in development, the idea that developmental processes can be interrupted by trauma and simply halted. Idiots, Seguin insisted, did not *lack* development, as Esquirol would have it; rather, their development was arrested. And that meant there was hope that the process could be restarted. What was needed was the right kind of stimulation.

In 1840 Seguin was promoted to the position of head teacher of idiot children at Salpêtrière. There he devised a training system that he called physiological education.[42] It had three parts. First was muscular education, which consisted of physical exercises and gymnastics to stimulate and strengthen the body and increase its level of activity and interaction with the environment. Second was education of the senses, which consisted of a graduated set of exercises designed to stimulate the idiot child's interest and curiosity so that his or her activity might begin to be directed and willful. Seguin started with the sense of touch, presenting the child with objects of unusual or surprising texture or elasticity, for example. The point was not simply to give the child a tactile experience, but to stimulate him or her to think about the experience of the object. Seguin followed this principle through education of the other senses as well. The third part of Seguin's program was moral treatment, which he adapted from Pinel and Esquirol, and which we might call socialization or training in social interaction and public conduct. Seguin was adamant that idiots should not be excluded from normal social relationships; he insisted on taking his advanced idiots to museums, public parks, and church services, where they could mingle with those not so designated. True freedom—true humanity—he believed, could only be experienced and lived as a member of a community in relation to others, so it required the self-discipline to present oneself in society with civility and consideration (Trent 1994, 52).

Seguin had some remarkable success with his idiots, but not with his superiors at Salpêtrière. He soon found himself without a job. Over the next few years he established a small private school for idiots in Paris and published his theories widely, always including detailed descriptions of his techniques. His work impressed a generation of social reformers in Britain and the United States, which, after the death of his wife, paved the way for his immigration to the United States in 1850.[43]

These changes in the theory of madness and idiocy, which enabled Seguin's innovations in pedagogical practice, occurred during a period when French law regarding institutionalization was changing, and French institutions, consequently, were changing as well. As mentioned in chapter 1, in 1838 the French parliament enacted a law making madness per se, not familial request, grounds for commitment to an asylum. Only a medical assessment could certify cases of madness, but such cases demanded immediate confinement whether the next of kin wanted to relinquish the lunatic to the state or not. "The mad individual now emerges as a social adversary," Foucault writes, "as a danger for society, and no longer as someone who may jeopardize the rights, wealth, and privileges of a family. The mechanism of the 1838 law designates a social enemy" (2006, 96). Psychiatric power joined with state power to dispossess the family of its control over its mad members and consolidate normalizing institutional authority.

But what about idiots? On the one hand, there was both the obvious theoretical reason and a less obvious economic incentive to exclude idiots from institutions. Following Esquirol and Belhomme, many psychiatrists no longer considered idiots to be mad. Furthermore, each *department* was required to pay for the upkeep of the asylum inmates they sent for incarceration, so local governmental officials were hesitant to commit individuals who did not pose a serious threat to the public (Foucault 2006, 220). But on the other hand, there were social and economic incentives for institutionalization. These idiots languishing at home were interfering with the productivity of the industrial labor force; parents could not leave their idiot children alone at home all day while they went off to work. Employers and public officials worried about the social and economic effects of families unable to support themselves and their idiotic members, or, alternatively, unsupervised idiots running loose while responsible relatives were shut inside factories (Foucault 2006, 213).

Increasingly, this set of problems was solved by widespread fraud. The law allowed for confinement of idiots if they were found to be dangerous to the community; an idiot who if left alone might commit arson, murder, or rape absolutely had to be institutionalized. Psychiatrists, eager to extend their influence, willingly agreed to certify idiots dangerous, whether they were or not, in order to relieve the family of responsibility, stabilize the labor force, and make themselves ever more indispensable to public safety. According to Foucault, "The doctors of the period from 1840 to 1860 say this clearly. They say: In order to get care for him we have to write false reports, to make the situation look worse than it is and depict the idiot or mental defective as someone who is dangerous" (2006, 220). Therefore, at the same time that Seguin was finding that idiots could be educated and socialized, law and public policy in France conspired to depict them as irreparably antisocial and dangerous. And at the same time that idiocy was being defined as something quite distinct to illness, French hospitals were opening wings for idiots, and they were being placed under physicians' care. The result was expansion of physicians' control and authority and, as Foucault puts it, "the gradual development of a whole medical literature that increasingly takes itself seriously, which will, if you like, stigmatize the mentally deficient and actually make him into someone who is dangerous" (2006, 220). By 1895, D. M. Bourneville insists that "a high proportion of criminals, inveterate drunks, and prostitutes are, in reality, imbeciles at birth" (Foucault 2006, 220).

A somewhat different but equally fateful set of institutional patterns was just beginning to emerge in the United States in the 1840s. In 1848, just two years before Seguin's arrival in the United States, some of his American admirers—Samuel Gridley Howe in Boston and Hervey Backus Wilbur in Barre, Massachusetts—opened schools for idiots and began to employ Seguin's pedagogical techniques. Like Seguin, they were convinced that idiocy was a matter of arrested development and could be remediated, at least to some extent, with methods that would compensate for the insufficiency of the natural developmental force. Idiots were not lunatics; they were children, and if not helped would remain children for the rest of their lives.

The first schools for idiots were very small and very labor-intensive. Superintendents like Howe and Wilbur worked directly with pupils alongside the teachers they hired and trained. Pupils usually lived in the same building and dined at the same table with the faculty and their families. But for financial reasons schools began to grow larger and to take pupils with more and more complicating disabilities. The effort expended upon each child diminished, and success stories declined in number. Institutions slid toward custodial care rather than education fairly rapidly. This trend was amplified by the move among officials in other kinds of institutions—lunatic asylums, reformatories, almshouses, and so forth—to rid themselves of the idiots in their care. As quickly as space in idiot asylums could be found, administrators in other institutions ejected inmates who could be classified as idiots and sent them to state-funded idiot schools.

This tendency, brought about mainly by economic considerations, was exacerbated by theoretical shifts and by some medical administrators' desire for status and political clout. In the first schools, educators served as chief administrators, aided by a medical supervisor. But as physicians took control of institutions away from pedagogues through the 1850s, a medical model began to replace Seguin's pedagogical model of treatment for idiots. Many specialists agreed with R. J. Patterson, medical superintendent of the Ohio Asylum, who wrote, "Idiocy, though not a disease, may be regarded as that condition, in which, from the effects of physical disease in fœtal or infantile life, or from defective organization of the nervous system, the intellectual and moral powers have never been developed, except in a slight degree. Idiocy, then, has a physical rather than a mental origin" (Trent 1994, 18). Medical treatment was likely to be necessary for many cases therefore, and idiot asylums needed to resemble hospitals more than schools.

There had always been some acknowledgement of idiocy as a pathological condition, of course. Early reformers, including Howe, believed that idiocy was a kind of physical degeneracy in a bloodline resulting from the sins and excesses of progenitors.

> The moral to be drawn from the existence of the individual
> idiot is this,—he, or his parents, have so far violated the natu-

ral laws, so far marred the beautiful organism of the body, that it is an unfit instrument for the manifestation of the powers of the soul. The moral to be drawn from the prevalent existence of idiocy in society is, that a very large class of persons ignore the conditions upon which alone health and reason are given to men, and consequently they sin in various ways; they overlook the hereditary transmission of certain morbid tendencies, or they pervert the natural appetites of the body into lusts of divers kinds,—the natural emotions of the mind into fearful passions,—and thus bring down the awful consequences of their own ignorance and sin upon the heads of their unoffending children.[44]

These sins included intemperance; idleness resulting in poverty or, alternatively, overwork driven by vain ambition; licentiousness; self-abuse; consanguinity (by which was usually meant marriage between cousins); and failed attempts at abortion. Sin broke down the parental constitution so that children were plagued with any number of diseases and disabilities. Some had tuberculosis; some were insane; some were alcoholics. And through the generations these maladies would be compounded as the bloodline spiraled downward to extinction. These poor idiots were the very embodiment of the theory of degeneration, often at its most extreme point. Their condition was a medical one, even if it was not classifiable as a disease.

The effort to minister to and educate idiots always involved the belief that idiocy's appearance bespoke a familial taint, even though superintendents in search of financial support from the wealthy parents of idiot children often downplayed degeneration theory in their sales pitches.[45] Except in the cases where masturbation was a seeming obsession and was thus a convenient explanation for their condition, idiots themselves usually were not held responsible. Most idiocy was congenital, so the infant victims of it were not themselves guilty of intemperance or licentiousness. However, no one doubted that virtually all idiot children would eventually begin to engage in these sins if they were not well-disciplined and would pass their degeneracy on to any children they might produce. In 1861, Connecticut superintendent Henry Knight characterized untrained idiots as "passionate, filthy, self-abusive, animal-like, gluttonous, given to irrational behavior, and intemperate" (Trent 1994, 17). Institutions were thus essential, not so much for the sake of the idiots themselves, but for the sake of the health and safety of the general public. As in France, in the United States idiots were increasingly perceived as a public threat.

In his 1858 book *The Mind Unveiled; or, A Brief History of Twenty-two Imbecile Children,* Isaac Newton Kerlin of the Pennsylvania asylum introduced a new concept, that of the "moral idiot." According to Kerlin, a moral idiot was the degenerate offspring of an intemperate or otherwise offending parent. His cognitive disability involved impairment of the moral faculty so that he "recognized no obligation to God nor man" (Kerlin 1858, 48). If not appropriately disciplined and trained, the moral idiot was likely to be a thief and a liar, an arsonist, and possibly even a murderer.

Kerlin's moral idiots were all male, but as the horrific possibilities of generations of murderous degenerates sank into the public consciousness, official attention began to focus more often on female idiots of reproductive age.[46] Females were believed to present a greater threat to public health than males because, while a defective male was not likely to attract the sexual interest of a normal female, a defective female could contrive to partner with normal males.[47] Feebleminded females thus were more likely to spread venereal disease and produce offspring even more degenerate than themselves, corrupting the bloodlines of normal male citizens in the process. Advocating institutions especially for feebleminded female offenders, Josephine Shaw Lowell thus addressed officials in Albany: "Even the weak State of Hawaii, in order to save its people from the contagion of a physical leprosy, has established an asylum for all who are tainted, on a separate island, to which all lepers of whatever rank are banished for life. Shall the state of New York suffer a moral leprosy to spread and taint her future generations, because she lacks the courage to set apart those who have inherited the deadly poison and who will hand it down to their children, even to the third and fourth generations?" (Lowell 1879, 199–200).

By 1884 Kerlin had replaced the concept of the moral idiot with that of the moral imbecile (Trent 1994, 88). The term "idiot" by then designated cases so low functioning as to be virtually incapable of great mischief, while the newer category of imbecile evolved to designate feebleminded children who were mobile, verbal, and hence capable of a certain amount of calculated violence and cunning. In fact, Kerlin went on to declare, it is possible for a person who has no cognitive impairment whatsoever to be morally impaired in this way; thus, there are some moral imbeciles who are not, cognitively speaking, imbeciles at all. But whether they have cognitive impairment or not, such children must be institutionalized. For their own good and the good of society—not to mention the financial and political enrichment of psychiatric superintendents—such children require lifelong custodial care. Kerlin saw the matter in evolutionary terms. "The moral sense being the latest and highest attribute of our rising humanity, it is the first and most to suffer from the law of reversion to lower type" (1889, 37).

By the end of the nineteenth century, feebleminded children and the adults they grew to be were not simply the victims of parental indiscretion and a financial burden to society; they were a social menace. Most of society's ills could be traced directly to the swelling numbers of adolescent and adult imbeciles in the world. If not segregated in institutions, imbeciles would practice prostitution and spread venereal disease, produce idiot children out of wedlock, swell the ranks of the poor and consumptive, steal, set fires, and engage in drunken rampages. In 1909 Walter Fernald summed up the problem: "Every imbecile, especially the higher-grade imbecile, is a potential criminal, needing only the proper environment and opportunity for the development and expression of his criminal tendencies. The unrecognized imbecile is a most dangerous element in the community. From a biological standpoint, the imbecile is an inferior human being" (Trent 1994, 161).

The reason for all this was fairly simple. Idiots and imbeciles were arrested in their development. They were stuck at a certain stage of childhood where the basic principles of morality are not grasped. Whatever caused this arrest in development, whether the sins of their mothers and fathers or some unavoidable accident in utero or at birth, the fact was that imbeciles were not to be trusted. Regardless of how capable some of them might at times appear, they could not handle civic responsibility or freedom any more than could the average eight-year-old child.

In this process, childhood itself was in effect criminalized. Normally developing children were said to recapitulate the stages of savagery and barbarism of their remotest ancestors, so that at a certain age every child is a savage and hence, by the standards of civilized society, a criminal. According to Cesare Lombroso (writing in 1876), criminals simply are modern-day savages; they are "atavisms" or "throwbacks" to past stages of human development. Just as fetuses in the womb recapitulate all the phases of evolution at an accelerated pace, children recapitulate all the phases of human development from savagery to civilization. And just as a fetus whose development is arrested at a certain point will exhibit the organic form of some prehuman ancestor, a child whose development is arrested at a certain point will remain a savage. Such a child, Lombroso believed, will be unable to adjust to civic life; as an adult he or she will be violent and antisocial. "One of the most important discoveries of my school is that in the child up to a certain age are manifested the saddest tendencies in the criminal man. The germs of delinquency and of criminality are found normally even in the first periods of human life" (Lombroso and Ferrero 1958 [1895], 53). Thus we end up with an equation: child = savage = criminal.[48]

Although most of Cesare Lombroso's works were not translated into English until the 1910s (Rafter 1997, 113), they were translated into French in the 1880s and widely read and discussed among the well-educated in the United States throughout the late nineteenth century. According to Eric Carlson, the first article on criminal anthropology published in the United States was written by William Noyes in 1888 and was "unalloyed Lombroso" (E. Carlson 1985, 135). The British sexologist Havelock Ellis did much to bring Lombroso's theories into the English-speaking world with his 1890 book *The Criminal,* which contained extensive and sympathetic discussion of Lombroso's research. By 1891, when Robert Fletcher gave his presidential address to the Anthropological Society of Washington, D.C., on the hereditary influence in the formation of the criminal character, it was clear that Lombroso had arrived in the United States (Rosen 2004, 7). And along with Lombroso's theory that criminals are living representatives of a primitive human past came his view that normal children pass through savage/criminal phases of development and simply are savages/criminals until they reach a level of maturity that supports moral restraint and the exercise of will over instinct. Thus, G. S. Morse, one of Lombroso's American followers, wrote in 1892 that "it is proved by voluminous evidence, easily accessible, that children are born criminals" (Gould 1977, 124–25).

In the first decade of the twentieth century, G. Stanley Hall, whom Stephen Jay Gould has called "America's most diligent and famous student of child development," held the view that children between the ages of eight and twelve are in effect mature savages (Gould 1977, 139, 141). That view persisted well into the twentieth century, with the famous child-care specialist Dr. Benjamin Spock reminding parents in 1968:

> Each child as he develops is retracing the whole history of mankind, physically and spiritually, step by step. A baby starts off in the womb as a single tiny cell, just the way the first living thing appeared in the ocean. Weeks later, as he lies in the amniotic fluid in the womb, he has gills like a fish. Towards the end of his first year of life, when he learns to clamber to his feet, he's celebrating that period millions of years ago when man's ancestors got up off all fours. . . . The child in the years after six gives up part of his dependence on his parents. He makes it his business to find out how to fit into the world outside his family. He takes seriously the rules of the game. He is probably re-living that stage of human history when our wild ancestors found it was better not to roam the forest in independent family groups but to form larger communities.[49]

Normal people pass through these stages of savagery and barbarism quickly and, given good guidance and parental restraint, without serious antisocial incident. But when a person's development is arrested— as is the case with people who are mentally impaired or who belong to races that, as a whole, are not as highly developed as the Anglo-Saxon, these stages of savagery are never completely overcome.

In 1910 Henry Goddard, a student of G. Stanley Hall, introduced a new classification of mental impairment based on intelligence testing. He called those who scored lowest, with an intellectual "age" of infancy to two years, idiots; those whose intellectual "age" was three to seven years, he called imbeciles. But he introduced a new word, *moron,* to designate a new category that had not been included in previous assessments of feeblemindedness. Morons were people with intellectual ages of eight to twelve years. They were perfectly capable of reading, writing, and doing arithmetic. They could attend school, hold jobs, and function in the community. The problem with morons, according to Goddard, was that they would never exhibit the refined judgment or moral sense of a fully formed adult. And thus they were terribly dangerous.

With the addition of morons, the ranks of the feebleminded theoretically doubled, to an estimated 2 percent of the total population (Trent 1994, 162). But they were to go higher still. In 1912 Goddard began testing new arrivals at Ellis Island and soon revealed astonishing data showing that between 40 and 50 percent of all incoming immigrants were feebleminded, many of them morons. Then he turned his attention to testing World War I army recruits—that is, mostly nonimmigrant males. Joining with Robert Yerkes, Lewis Terman, and others (and funded by the Committee on Provision for the Feeble-Minded) during the summer of 1917, Goddard helped to develop the Alpha and Beta IQ tests that Colonel Yerkes and those he supervised would administer to a total of 1.75 million young men. They found that 40 percent of the white men were feebleminded and an overwhelming number, 89 percent, of the African American men were mentally deficient by the standards of the test.[50]

Alarming and almost unbelievable. But in the end, it all stood to reason, did it not? Intelligence and morality were matters of development. The most highly developed people in the world were to be found in northwestern Europe, a subgroup of the Caucasian race known by 1899 as the Nordics.[51] The United States had been settled for the most part by people of that stock—primarily Anglo-Saxons. But throughout the nineteenth century a combination of forces had changed the population. There was, first of all, emancipation of the slaves and inclusion of African Americans among the citizenry. Additionally, there were waves of immigration of inferior white stock known as Alpines and Mediterraneans; among these were Catholics from Ireland and Italy, and Jews from Eastern Europe.[52] There was the cumulative effect of intemperance, feminism, and sexual indulgence on the Nordics themselves. And, finally, medical science and bleeding-heart sentimentality-made-public-policy had reversed the natural law of survival of the fittest and allowed weaklings of all races to live and reproduce. Of course the number of idiots and imbeciles was increasing! Compared to adult male Anglo-Saxons, most people in the world were idiots, imbeciles, and morons; and they were breeding like proverbial rabbits.

Having only recently become acquainted with the idea of biological progress through dissemination of Darwin's and Herbert Spencer's work, elites in the United States and Europe were terrified of losing their hold on it. The natural progress of evolution cannot be allowed to dissipate through degeneracy, dilution, and intermarriage with inferior races, they told each other. The downward spiral must be stopped. It was time for the great nations of the world to take control of their breeding populations in the interest of the future of civilization.

Race at the Turn of the Twentieth Century

By the end of the nineteenth century, through a complex combination of disparate forces, including both scientific theory and economic and political struggle, race was no longer merely a morphological category, a designation of physical appearance only loosely associated with heredity. Integrated into the science of biology—both pre- and post-Darwinian biology—racial difference was, essentially, developmental difference. Appearance was simply a manifestation of a developmental process. Members of "lower" races and sub-races bore the stigma of arrested development just as criminals and mentally deficient individuals did.[53] Such people were in effect children in quasi-adult bodies, stunted and marked in various physical ways by their biological incompletion and deficient in reason and restraint but with all the drives and desires of sexual maturity. Charles McCord, writing specifically about African Americans, summed up this line of thinking in 1914:

> The Negro race is a primitive race. The average Negro is a child in every essential element of character, exhibiting those characteristics that indicate a tendency to lawless impulse and weak inhibition. His childlike weakness and improvidence and his disposition to live only for the things of to-day tend to bring him to dependence in sickness and old age, or lead him into excesses and neglect of his body that bring him to an early death. As a criminal he is a creature of elemental passion and weak will: he sins more often merely because he is tempted than he does of set purpose. . . . As a child, also, is the Negro in his moral conceptions. He lacks the power of evaluation. He cannot realize the dignity of statute law nor feel his personal responsibility to the moral law. (McCord 1914, 108, 116)

Imbeciles, criminals, prostitutes, consumptives, Africans, Asians, Mexicans, Jews, Irishmen, masturbators, deaf-mutes, epileptics, psychopaths, and shiftless Appalachian paupers might look different from one another at a glance, but in effect they were all alike. They were all children out of control, throwbacks, savages, and degenerates. And they all posed a serious threat to the continued purity of highly evolved Nordic germ plasm.

This is scientific racism. As Foucault makes clear in *"Society Must Be Defended,"* this is a racism preoccupied not with attacking members of another race but with protecting the boundaries of *the* race, the only race that matters, the human race embodied in its "highest" representatives. This is by definition a racism espoused by elites, not ignorant "rednecks," who were in fact among its victims, first as targets of its purification programs and later as scapegoats for its excesses. It is a racism in some respects continuous with the practices of slavery and colonial conquest and exploitation of earlier centuries, but unthinkable in the absence of the biological sciences, clinical medicine, and institutional psychiatry that arose in the last half of the nineteenth century. It sought to intensify and augment and improve human intelligence, productivity, and mastery of nature; and its activities were heavily funded by some of the wealthiest corporate tycoons and philanthropists in the world as well as by millions of tax dollars at the federal, state, and local levels of government in most Western nation-states and especially in the United States and Germany. It was a racism that attempted to control and enhance every aspect of human reproduction and sexuality in order to direct the course and evolution of human life itself. In short, this was a racism characteristic of a regime of biopower.

FOUR

SCIENTIFIC RACISM AND THE THREAT OF SEXUAL PREDATION

On Sunday, March 7, 1965, John Lewis, Hosea Williams, Amelia Boynton Robinson, and nearly six hundred other civil rights marchers confronted the Dallas County, Alabama, Sheriff's Department and a contingent of Alabama state troopers on Selma's Edmund Pettus Bridge.[1] At issue was African Americans' right to vote and the fact that three weeks earlier a state trooper had shot and killed a young black man, Jimmie Lee Jackson, who had dared to demand legal protection to exercise that right.[2] A hundred and fifty deputies and troopers, some of whom were on horseback, attacked the unarmed assembly with canisters of C-4 tear gas, bull whips, and billy clubs. More than ninety marchers were treated at Good Samaritan Hospital and Burwell Infirmary for gashes, fractures, gas burns, and broken teeth. Seventeen were hospitalized, including Lewis, who suffered severe head wounds, and Robinson, who was nearly gassed to death. Two weeks after "Bloody Sunday," with their way cleared by an order from Federal District Court Judge Frank Johnson, several thousand marchers proceeded under the leadership of Rev. Dr. Martin Luther King from Selma to the state capitol at Montgomery to take their cause to the governor.[3] Before they reached their destination two more protesters lay dead, but 25,000 streamed onto the capitol grounds to confront the civil authorities.

The antiblack racism that John Lewis and Amelia Boynton Robinson and all the other marchers stared in the face on Bloody Sunday—racism official, armed, and mounted on horseback—was a direct descendent of the scientific racism that had taken shape a century earlier. Among the claims it made were these: (1) blacks must not have civil status equal to that of whites (specifically, they must not vote, serve on juries, or hold public office); (2) blacks must not attend school with or have social access to whites; (3) blacks must not hold positions of authority over whites in industry, business, or institutions of higher education; and (4) blacks must not be permitted to marry or engage in any form of sexual activity with whites. The reasons offered for these prohibitions rested on the race science of the nineteenth century, which included such propositions as these: (1) black bodies physically contaminate the spaces they occupy, smell bad, are messy and disorganized, and carry disease; (2) blacks are intellectually inferior to whites, have poor judgment, and lack foresight, which renders them irresponsible and impulsive; (3) blacks are lustful and devoid of self-control; and (4) one drop of black blood introduced into a white bloodline will corrupt that bloodline forever, killing or stunting offspring and potentially wiping out the line altogether.

In the early decades of the twentieth century, these propositions were regularly articulated in public, and not infrequently they found their way into law and public policy as well as the scholarly and popular presses. By 1965, after three decades of public contestation and scientific debate, they had begun to sound more like irrational assertions than like the objective conclusions of well-supported scientific arguments. But they had been just that: reasoned conclusions resting comfortably on an edifice of empirical data and generally accepted scientific theory. The racism we now know as "race prejudice" and "bigotry" was scientific racism minus its scientific warrant, clinging to the political and social world like the shells that locusts have left behind.

From the perspective of the marchers on the Edmund Pettus Bridge on Bloody Sunday, the powers they were confronting were enormous and terrifying. In fact, however, those brutal forces, formidable as they were, were but a meager remnant of the awesome constellation of power networks that had framed, enforced, and furthered those propositions in previous decades, a constellation that included scientific theories and data that not only justified but demanded white domination. This chapter will reconstruct that science and examine its role in shaping modern racist public policy and social practice. It will also tell the story of how the figure of the homosexual arose within those same racist scientific discourses and science-influenced social practices and will show the close kinship between the myths of the black rapist and the homosexual predator.

The Rising Tide of White World Supremacy

Sixty-five years before Bloody Sunday, at the turn of the twentieth century, the locusts were very much with us. The best science available informed those racist propositions and upheld them. Species evolve through environmental pressures and competition for mates and resources. Evolution proceeds as a result of the natural selection of adaptive traits passed from one generation to the next as unit characters like the ones Gregor Mendel identified in peas.[4] New species or, just short of that, distinct variations or races emerge when divergent lines of one species become separated and face differing environmental pressures.[5] If those divergent lines are forced back together in the same environment, natural selection will preserve one and bring about the subordination, decline, or extinction of the rest. In any species comprising more than one morphological variety, race war is, to put it simply, a natural inevitability. Turn-of-the-century biology had effectively elevated race war to the status of natural law. It might not be pretty, but it was a fact of life. And all educated people were called upon to put aside their sentiment and religious dogma and accept the truth.

Science thus portrayed racial conflict as an inevitable subplot in an evolutionary narrative. There had once been a time when the human species was undifferentiated, a time before races and thus before racial conflict. In the far distant, prehistoric past, all families of the human race were savages.[6] Incapable of deferring gratification and uninhibited by reason, men and women acted on impulse like beasts. They were violent and lusty; they knew no laws of person or property; they were motivated entirely by fear or by physical attraction. But one germ line, developing in the harsh reaches of northwestern Europe and facing environmental pressures more demanding than those to be met in virtually any other habitable region on earth, gradually became capable of resisting the lure of immediate pleasure and of enduring pain in order to gain some control over their environment and their future. To borrow Nietzsche's phrase, these "magnificent animals" gradually began to develop the capacity for memory and self-restraint. The need for hard thought enlarged their brains, and their enlarged brains enabled more hard thought. Reason, not impulse or desire, began to dominate their mental lives, and their coarse bodily features underwent subtle refinement. They began to cooperate and plan, and then to invent and organize. They developed rudimentary government, crafts, and forms of art. In short, they became *civilized*. Through succeeding generations they endured much and they hoped much, and thus they slowly became capable of conquering the world.[7]

This process was thoroughly biological. Civilized man was a civilized body, a product of naturally selected germ plasm. For longer than anyone could measure, the Nordic germ line, of which the Anglo-Saxon was a major subset, had developed through internecine struggle for survival against the odds and the elements. Only in the last few centuries had that struggle yielded a race so superior to its own ancestors (not to mention the other races on earth) as to be capable of advanced technology and representative government, the tools that enabled exploration, colonization, and world domination. But that day had finally come, many people believed; world domination was the clear biological destiny of that blue-eyed, blonde, fair-skinned race.

There were a few scientific skeptics, however—men who doubted that Anglo-Saxons could ever conquer the *entire* world for the simple reason that they had evolved in a cold, dry climate and were not viable outside of it. These nay-sayers opposed spending tax money on invasions and colonization in the tropics, often pointing to France's disastrous attempt to build a canal through the Isthmus of Panama. Having begun the project in 1880, the French halted it largely as a result of disease. Twenty-two thousand workers had died, most of malaria and yellow fever, leaving no one fit to work. Clearly, critics said, evolution made the hot, wet climate an obstacle that whites simply could not overcome.

Were the critics right? The issue was seriously debated in William Ripley's 1899 classic *The Races of Europe*. "There is no question of greater significance for European civilization than the one which concerns the possibility of its extension over that major part of the earth which is yet the home of barbarism or savagery," Ripley wrote.[8]

> The modern problem plainly stated is this: First, can a single generation of European emigrants live? and, secondly, living, can they perpetuate their kind in the equatorial regions of the earth? Finally, if able permanently so to sustain themselves, will they still be able to preserve their peculiar European civilization in these lands; or must they revert to the

barbarian stage of modern slavery—of a servile native population, which alone in those climates can work and live? An
area of fertile lands six times as great as that cultivated by the
people of Europe to-day stands waiting to absorb its surplus
population. But its point of saturation will obviously soon be
reached if traders and superintendents of native labour are
the only colonists who can live there. Moreover, the problem
of acclimatization has a great political importance; for if any
one of these European nations be possessed of a special physiological immunity in face of the perils of tropical colonization, the balance of power may be seriously shifted. (Ripley
1913, 560–61)[9]

Such a European race did exist, but not in Europe. It was Americans
who proved the skeptics wrong. In 1904 Dr. William Crawford
Gorgas of Mobile, Alabama, took over medical supervision of the
Canal Zone. Gorgas maintained that the mosquito, not the tropical
climate itself, was responsible for the spread of disease.[10] Ridiculed
and opposed by many, but backed by President Theodore Roosevelt,
Gorgas imposed sanitation measures that wiped out much of the mosquito population, enabling construction to progress to completion.
Thus Gorgas proved that an intellectually superior white race could
adapt to life anywhere on the planet. Science and technology could
make anything possible—science and technology developed by, and
for, the white race.[11]

Meanwhile, to add even more empirical weight to the claim that
white world domination was imminent, a great deal of evidence suggested that the darker races were dying out. Study after study confirmed that Native Americans were careening toward total extinction. They simply could not compete in the struggle for survival with
the hardier, more intelligent whites. They succumbed to disease and
alcohol in far greater numbers and at younger ages than white people
did, and their birthrate was low. Since they were prone to violence
and ill-suited to steady work, they had to be contained and harshly
supervised, leading to even more early deaths. "The Indian is on the
verge of extinction," proclaimed American statistician Frederick
Hoffman in 1892, "and the African will surely follow him, for every
race has suffered extinction wherever the Anglo-Saxon has permanently settled."[12]

In fact, Joseph Camp Kennedy had announced the prospective

extinction of the American Negro thirty years earlier, in his *Preliminary Report on the Eighth Census* published in 1862. Numerous subsequent studies had confirmed his claim, including the statistical analyses of the Ninth and Tenth Censuses, data gathered by the U.S. military, and several investigations undertaken by American insurance companies.[13] By Hoffman's time, the assumption was commonplace. According to historian John Haller, "The belief in the Negro's extinction became one of the most pervasive ideas in American medical and anthropological thought during the late nineteenth century" (Haller 1970, 155).

Hoffman's data were incomplete because, as he was the first to point out, only one southern state (Alabama) had a bureau of vital statistics in 1892, and of course the bulk of the black population was in the South. He had to rely on city documents and on death rather than birth records. Still, there could be no mistake about the eventual outcome. The interest to science lay in delineating the specific natural processes by which this extinction would occur, and Hoffman had some hypotheses. "There are *two* main causes of mortality among the adult negro which cannot but be of the most momentous influence upon the future generations," he observed; "these are venereal diseases and deaths from consumption. Any physician who has practiced among colored people will bear me out in my statement that at least three-fourths of the colored population are cursed with one kind or another of the many diseases classified as venereal. The gross immorality, early and excessive intercourse of the sexes, premature maternity, and general intemperance in eating and drinking of the colored people are the chief causes of their susceptibility to venereal diseases" (Hoffman 1892, 534). Evolving in warm, lush Africa, Negroes had never faced a hostile environment and thus had never developed the mental capacities that Northern Europeans had required just to survive, according to Hoffman. Their consequent deficiency in abstract reasoning ability rendered them unable to foresee the consequences of actions and thus unable to control their emotions and resist their physical impulses. They thus inevitably fell victim to syphilis and gonorrhea and the many other debilitating diseases caused or spread by sexual contact or over-indulgence. In addition, however, they lacked physical resistance to pathogens. Far more often than whites, they contracted tuberculosis and pneumonia; and far more often, they did not have the strength to recover. The Negro constitution is simply inferior, Hoffman concluded. "Aside from consumption, nearly all of the other fatal diseases will be found to be more fatal to the negro than to the white man" (Hoffman 1892, 535). Even malaria, to which Negroes had once been supposedly immune, was seen to be a statistically greater threat to blacks than to whites by the end of the nineteenth century.

But the biggest factor in the coming extinction of the Negro race was their "inferior womanhood." It is because of the weakness of their women that "the whole body politic of the colored race is undermined and finally doomed," said Hoffman (1892, 535). Young black women were found to die at an even higher rate than young black men. For the past twenty-three years in New Orleans, Baltimore, and Washington, Hoffman reported, black females had not only failed to increase at the same rate as females among whites, but in absolute numbers the population had declined. Black population gains in those cities were thus entirely male, a fact that would eventually render the race unsustainable. Additionally, those black women who did survive to conceive were less likely than white women to carry a pregnancy to term and deliver a living child. No other conclusion was possible: "What else but final extinction can be the future of the negro, thus presenting all the evidences of a vanishing race?" (Hoffman 1892, 541).

A decade later, however, Negroes had failed to vanish or even thin out to a noticeable degree. On the contrary, the Twelfth Census indicated a population gain of 18.1 percent, which was still far short of the increase seen in the population of whites (21.4%) but was about fifty percent higher than Hoffman's prediction. Was this an indication that white world domination was not biologically inevitable?

No, of course not, said Chicago physician Charles Bacon, taking up the question in 1903. The riddle could be solved by taking note of environmental factors. The degeneration that would ultimately destroy African American fecundity had yet to register in population statistics, Bacon believed, because it would not manifest itself in the first generation born after emancipation, but only in their progeny.

> If we admit that the physical condition of the race began first to decline in the time of the convulsions that succeeded the war, we must remember that the propagating element of the population for the first twenty or thirty years was born before the period of convulsion and change in the manner of living.

> Therefore the inheritance of the adult negro population of
> the last twenty years should not have been seriously affected.
> A degeneracy caused by a diseased inheritance would only
> begin to show in its full force now. If then to the unfavorable
> environment that has caused so much trouble in the last forty
> years we now add an increasingly bad heredity, we may expect
> to find a decline in fecundity which, added to the factor of a
> large mortality, will eventually interfere with the population
> increase and at last cause its decline. (Bacon 1903, 341–42)

The first generation of blacks born in freedom would have inherited
constitutions from their parents that were forged in slavery under the
supervision of whites. Slavery had been kind to the Africans, Bacon
explained, echoing John C. Calhoun. It lifted them out of vicious
savagery, fed and clothed them, and placed constraints upon their
impulses and desires, and thus it had allowed for "a gradual intellectual and moral advance. Only a single or a very few generations
removed from a savage or semi-savage state, they were learning by
association with the whites and by enforced routine some of the lessons of civilization that many races have acquired only by centuries
of experience." But with the abolition of slavery, that benign period
of tutelage came to an abrupt end, and blacks were thrown into a
state of "childish license and ignorant confusion." It wasn't their fault
really. "Self-control, perseverance, moral stamina, are qualities hardly
to be expected from a race so shortly removed from savagery and just
released from bondage" (Bacon 1903, 339). Freedmen were simply
inadequate to the task of providing for themselves and their children.
Given the limits imposed on them by their retarded racial evolution,
they did not have the intelligence to plan and save and put by. They
did not have the self-discipline to resist the tempting pleasures of the
moment. They fell into poverty and succumbed to vice. They crowded
into small living quarters where "modesty and decency, according to
the meaning of civilization, are impossible" (339). Sexual immorality
became rampant. And these conditions undermined their reproductive
vitality. "Under these unfavorable physical and moral conditions children are born with weakened or diseased bodies. They are neglected,
improperly fed and cared for" (339). From there, each generation
would fall lower into misery; there would be a downward spiral of
consumption and venereal disease, alcoholism, epilepsy, insanity, and
sexual perversion.

All the scientific experts agreed. Physiologically inferior to whites, African Americans would suffer tremendous setbacks in physical and mental health in the absence of close white supervision. Reports of these setbacks came in from all quarters. Dr. J. F. Miller, superintendent of the Eastern Hospital in Goldsboro, North Carolina (a hospital "for the accommodation of the colored insane"), reported that tuberculosis rates as well as rates of insanity were rising steeply in the black population. Both conditions were rare among blacks during slavery, Miller claimed.

> It is an undisputed fact, known to our Southern people that no race of men ever lived under better hygienic restraints or had governing their lives rules and regulations more conducive to physical health and mental repose. Their habits of life were regular, their food and clothing were substantial and sufficient, as a rule, and the edict of the master kept indoors at night and restrained them from promiscuous sexual indulgence and the baneful influences of the liquor saloon. (J. F. Miller 1896, 289)

But with emancipation, the Negro's natural intellectual inferiority made physical and moral degeneration inevitable: "Licentiousness left its slimy trail of sometimes ineradicable disease upon his physical being, and neglected bronchitis, pneumonia and pleurisy lent their helping hand toward lung degeneration" (J. F. Miller 1896, 290).

Insane asylums all over the country recorded a dramatic rise in their black populations.[14] The percentage of African Americans in the Alabama Insane Hospital (later Bryce State Mental Hospital in Tuscaloosa) rose from 3.2 in 1865, to 17.2 in 1880, to 22.9 in 1890. By 1900, 27.5 percent of the hospital's inmates were black, so the state constructed a second mental hospital at Mount Vernon exclusively for blacks (although a fair number remained at Tuscaloosa). In 1910, blacks accounted for 31.5 percent of the patients in the two hospitals, nearly ten times the percentage of less than fifty years before (Hughes 1992, 445). This sort of increase was typical. Furthermore, studies conducted in prisons in Alabama, New Jersey, New York, Pennsylvania, and Ohio showed a higher mortality rate among black prisoners than among whites. Since black and white prisoners supposedly lived under identical conditions, officials saw these statistics as confirmation that African Americans were simply constitutionally unhealthy compared to whites (J. Haller 1970, 157), and without strong constitutions themselves, they could not hope to pass down strong constitutions to their offspring.

Thus there was no doubt in any respected scientist's mind at the turn of the twentieth century that the white would prevail over the darker races. It was not a matter of personal or political desire; it was a matter of biological fact. Some were gleeful about that fact. Others were worried about it.[15] But none questioned it. The laws of nature had made it so, and the laws of nature had to be respected.[16] The white race, the bearers and bringers of civilization, had risen up at the biological forefront of the human race. One day, once the darker races declined and died away, the white race would be the only race. On that great day, the white race finally would be the human race, purged forever of its savage past. That was the inevitable evolutionary future, beautiful and sparkling and beckoning to every loyal Nordic son.

Evolution Must Be Defended

Or was it? Despite its biological superiority, the white race's hold on its constitutional gains was very fragile. Scientists noted two sets of reasons for this fragility. First, there were the difficulties of the process of evolutionary development itself; it sometimes took a heavy toll on even quite superior bodies. Second, there was the possibility that the evolutionary process could be interrupted: degenerative disease could be introduced into Anglo-Saxon bodies, and Anglo-Saxon blood lines could become contaminated with inferior germ plasm. Both phenomena posed a threat to humanity's Nordic future.

The first type of threat could be surmounted if the right steps were taken. It was a matter, first of all, of proper diagnosis. In 1869, neurologist George Beard began disseminating his theory that modern man (and of course only white men were truly modern in evolutionary terms) was apt to suffer from a condition he called "neurasthenia."[17] The primary causes of neurasthenia, according to Beard, were the telegraph, steam power, the periodical press, the burgeoning natural sciences, and women's intellectual activity. By speeding up the processes of ordinary life, modern civilization may overwhelm the individual with stimulation and overtax newly evolved central nervous systems. The results vary in different people, but they include diathesis (predisposition to disease), drug use, hay fever, neuralgia, dyspepsia, asthenopia (eye-strain, often with headache or dizziness), tooth decay, baldness, temperature sensitivity, diabetes, trance, difficulties during dentition as well as during puberty and menopause, insanity, various forms of sexual dysfunction, and a host of other conditions (Beard 1972a, vi–ix; 1972b, 14). The modern nervous system was a finely tuned system, Beard maintained, and thus it was more likely than a coarser, more primitive system to slip out of balance. This was especially true in the earliest phases of transition from a lower to a higher type, particularly the phase that the advanced classes in the United States had entered in the nineteenth century (hence Beard's claim that Americans were the first people in history to suffer from neurasthenia). Beard predicted that over the next fifty years the proportion of nervous disorders found in the U.S. population would fall, even though absolute numbers would rise, as more and more people were born with sufficiently developed nervous systems to take the strain (1972a, 293). "In this cruel process," Beard wrote, "thousands have perished—are perishing today; but from the midst of this confusion, conflict, and positive destruction a powerful and stable race has been slowly, almost imperceptibly, evolving" (1972a, 304).

Despite his optimism, however, Beard conceded that racial improvement was not inevitable. "It is a principle of evolution," he wrote, "that functions, when disturbed by disease, decline, decay, and disappear in the reverse order in which they develop" (1972b, 66).[18] If the current generation were to succumb to the degenerative effects of neurasthenia, it was possible that evolution would be arrested or even reversed. He advocated aggressive treatment—especially by means of a variety of forms of electric shock therapy, which he developed over the course of twenty years of medical practice—and warned of the grave dangers of neurasthenia misdiagnosed and untreated. Not all medical practitioners took Beard's theory seriously (although neurasthenia did quickly find its way into the mainstream of medical and psychiatric practice),[19] but virtually all did agree that even those at the forefront of evolution could slip back into savagery if assailed by degenerative disease, which might be brought on by a variety of "race poisons," including masturbation, syphilis, exposure to environmental contaminants such as lead or mercury, or the excessive use of alcohol.[20]

The second and much more worrisome set of threats to civilization arose in the interaction of the evolutionary avant-garde and their backward neighbors. Despite whites' biological superiority over other races, because the traits that insured civilization were recently acquired, they were less securely etched into the constitution. If superior people mated only with others equally superior, these recently acquired traits would be perpetuated. But it was possible for the traits to be lost—"swamped," as it was often put—by the more brutish traits of the lowly masses, be they the colored hordes or the inferior Celts, Slavs, or Mediterraneans.

Fortunately, according to many self-identified Nordic writers of the period, well-bred whites had a natural aversion to individuals of inferior races, particularly to blacks, and so would not choose to associate with them socially or sexually. But again, there were two problems. The first was that this aversion was not shared by nonwhites, whom many whites believed wanted both social and sexual access to white bodies whenever and wherever possible. The second was that many whites were not well-bred; some were of degenerate stock, but even among those who were not, women and children were vulnerable to seduction and corruption—women because females are less evolved than males and thus weaker of will and intellect, and children because, as they recapitulate the stages of savagery and barbarism in their development toward adulthood, they have a natural affinity with the lower races.[21]

Both of these problems surface constantly in the extensive late nineteenth and early twentieth-century literature on sexual predation, anxiety over which fills the pages of medical and forensic journals and monographs. Most people who have a basic knowledge of U.S. racial history are familiar with the late nineteenth-century myth of the black rapist, a savage sexual predator that simply did not exist in the antebellum period, despite the proximity of white and black bodies on Southern plantations and in the homes of the professional classes. The idea that black men wanted sexual possession of white women and would go to any length to get it was fabricated only in the political and economic aftermath of emancipation; it served as a rationalization for violence directed against black men who achieved some measure of material success. Less widely known, however, are the facts that at the same time the myth of the imbecilic rapist was also formulated, followed by the myth of the seductive moron, and that this period also saw extensive elaboration on the myth of the syphilitic whore. As I will discuss in upcoming pages, by the early twentieth century all of these predatory figures were popularly held to pose basically the same threat: corruption and displacement of superior germ plasm, and thus the end of civilization. All were seen as a grave danger to the biological supremacy of the Nordic race and its natural destiny, world domination. It was within that set of panic-driven sexual discourses that the homosexual was born and would take a place alongside the black savage, the menacing moron, and the disease-ridden prostitute as a biological threat to white male supremacy. Against all of these presumed sexual predators—these vectors of defect and abnormality—Nordic evolution would absolutely have to be defended.

Negroes and Women and Throwbacks—Oh, My!

Baltimore physician William Lee Howard discussed the threat to evolution through black-on-white rape and seduction in the journal *Medicine* in 1903, beginning with this assertion: "The truth is that the negro of to-day, untrammeled and free from control, is rapidly showing atavistic tendencies. He is returning to a state of savagery, and in his frequent attacks of sexual madness, his religious emotionalism, superstition, and indolence, is himself again—a savage" (Howard 1903, 423). Before the end of his second paragraph, Howard connects Lombroso's theory of criminal atavism, four decades of medical literature on the dramatic rise of mental illness among African Americans, and the burgeoning psychiatric discourse on the sexual menace of the feebleminded to his view that "biological differences between races of distinct ethnic origin result in psychologic and social differentiation impossible to harmonize" (1903, 423).

Ostensibly presenting an argument merely against admitting blacks to white universities, Howard launches into a graphic discussion of alleged anatomical difference designed to strike fear in the hearts of fragile Nordics everywhere: "To understand the ineradicable racial traits of the African [meaning their supposed ineducability] one must know the structural life and habits resulting from a certain biologic basis. We must penetrate beneath superficial ideas, throw aside prudish philosophy, and open our eyes to anatomical and psychical facts if we wish to render justice to civilization. Silence regarding sexual matters must give way to vocative statements, for it is by these unavoidable statements that we must be guided in dealing with the negro question" (1903, 424). In other words, prudery be damned; Howard would speak frankly about the true dangers of Negro sexuality. Readers of Foucault's *History of Sexuality* will recognize this as a version of the ubiquitous turn-of-the-century call for an end to silence on the issue of sexuality. The same call is made in George Beard's work. Medical literature of this period screams for the need to investigate and openly discuss all things sexual. However retrogressive Howard's racial discourse sounds these days, he was part of the progressive movement when it came to sexuality, as were many other scientific racists. What Foucault calls the *dispositif de sexualité* was an important means by which they gained leverage to remake society according to their racist vision.

It is a waste of time and money to try to educate Negroes, Howard insists, because the part of the African brain devoted to ethical decision making is extremely small compared to the part devoted to sexuality. "Sexual instinct—as emotion, idea, and impulse—is a function of the cerebral cortex. The sexual sphere of the cerebral cortex may be excited, in the sense of excitation of sexual concepts and impulses, by processes in the generative organs. Now as these organs in the Negro are enormously developed, as his whole life is devoted to matters appertaining to the worship of Priapus, it is to be expected that the sexual centers in the cortex are correspondingly enlarged" (Howard 1903, 425). He cites empirical studies showing that black men have enormous penises, sized to fit black women's vaginas, which are equally huge.[22] His argument runs like this: we know that black penises and vaginas are very large; therefore, a significant portion of the black brain must be devoted to sexual functions; therefore, there is less brain mass available for other functions, in particular for reasoning.

No doubt this argument was augmented contextually by the commonly accepted scientific view, based on Samuel Morton's work, that Negro brains were smaller than white brains to begin with. It was also lent plausibility by the extensive anthropological and medical literature on the enormous size of African women's clitorises and labia minora, including the so-called Hottentot apron. The standard text in gynecology in the nineteenth century (by H. Hildebrandt) linked the Hottentot apron with the enlarged clitorises supposedly typical of white lesbians. This connection between "primitives" and "degenerates" would be elaborated in subsequent studies of black as well as white lesbians into the 1940s.[23] We will return to this theme in chapter 6.

Given all this, we should not be surprised to learn that post-pubescent Negroes—of both sexes, since both sexes have these enormously developed generative organs—experience periods during which their cognitive centers are completely overwhelmed by the activity of the sexual centers of the cerebral cortex. Howard calls these periods episodes of "sexual madness" during which Negroes exhibit, among other organic disturbances, all the signs of lycanthropy, an organic insanity that is heritable (and is characterized, he explains, by delusions that one is a werewolf) (1903, 424). According to Howard, in Negroes lycanthropy is so common as to be a racial trait with widespread occurrence in both men and women. He concludes that, because no amount of educational training will alter brain structure, it is futile to send Negroes to college. In the course of making this main point, however, Howard articulates the scientific reasoning behind the claim that Negroes can never be trusted with institutional or corporate responsibility or authority over whites in any setting, a claim that would persist long after the supporting argument was forgotten.

Negroes are anatomically and physiologically prone to poor judgment and lack any reliable means of self-control, Howard warns. Their madness drives them to licentious behavior so intense and unbridled that it may often result in rape and, since they also have unusual susceptibilities to venereal disease, tuberculosis, and virtually all forms of insanity (susceptibilities believed heritable), rape may result in spread of their contagion to their unwilling sex partners (who may be defenseless white women) as well as into the next generation through their offspring (who may be even more highly dangerous mulattoes). Negroes must be contained, kept under surveillance, and placed in "quarantine" from all members of the white race (1903, 424). Through the first eight decades of the twentieth century, this idea would inform efforts to prevent public school desegregation and fuel the movement for private and home schooling for white children. Even as youngsters, blacks were assumed to be sexual predators who could not be trusted to sit in classrooms alongside the rising generation of the bearers of civilization.

Dr. Howard's diatribe was not published in some underground cultish tabloid. It is to be found, with many similar articles, in a respected medical journal. And there are no articles by other physicians or medical researchers disputing its evidence or contesting its conclusions. On the contrary, corroboration and augmentation abound, and from northern as well as southern sources. Consider this passage from an article by Drs. Hunter Mcguire and G. Frank Lydston, the latter of whom was a prominent American sexologist and a professor at the Chicago College of Physicians: "When all inhibitions of a high order have been removed by sexual excitement, I fail to see any difference from a physical standpoint between the sexual furor of the negro and that which prevails among the lower animals in certain instances and at certain periods . . . the *furor sexualis* in the negro resembles similar sexual attacks in the bull and elephant."[24] Lydston opposes lynching but advocates state-sponsored castration as a way to deal with Southern Negroes' propensity to rape:

> In my opinion there is but one logical method of dealing with the rapist, and that is total ablation of the sexual organs. The criminal is thereby not only incapacitated from a repetition of the crime, but put beyond the power of procreating his kind. A few "complete" eunuchs scattered throughout the South would really be the conservation of energy, so far as the repression of sexual crime is concerned. Executed, they would be forgotten; unsexed and free, they would be a constant warning and ever-present admonition to others of their race. (Lydston 1904, 424)

A progressive, Lydston would not limit castration to black rapists, however. "To be effectual, asexualization should be enforced against rapists of whatever color. Unjust discrimination against the blacks merely serves to defeat the purpose of the method. The double color standard of virtue has already worked great harm." Of course, he is quite sure that the percentage of blacks deserving asexualization would be far greater than the percentage of whites because of "hereditary influences descending from the negro's barbaric ancestors" and because "physical and moral degeneracy,—the latter involving chiefly the higher and more recently acquired attributes,—with a distinct tendency to reversion to type, is evident in the Southern negro" (Lydston 1904, 393, 394).

Black females were no less a threat to civilization than black males on the prevailing medical view. Although less likely to corrupt a white bloodline by sheer physical force, females too experienced these periods of sexual madness during which they tried to seduce callow white males and give them syphilis or any number of other degenerative diseases. Currently popular discussions of antiblack racism through history often focus on defamation of black male sexuality from Reconstruction forward rather than on campaigns against the sexuality of black women and girls. But as Howard's article suggests, the myth of the black rapist was only one face of a more general myth —that of the atavistic or degenerate sexual predator poised to destroy civilization—and that myth certainly included the myth of the seductive Jezebel.[25] Perhaps because campaigns against black female sexuality tended to blend into campaigns against female sexuality in general, they are sometimes not perceived as racial in nature. But I contend that they were and that, moreover, campaigns against female sexuality in general in this period were racial in nature, regardless of the race of their female targets. The overriding motivation and justification for such campaigns was the purification, preservation, and ultimate evolutionary triumph of the white race, whether the females to be controlled were classified as black, red, yellow, or white.

I pause here to acknowledge a possible objection: black women and girls were seldom lynched for their sexuality. Lynching, which reached an all-time high in 1892 with a total of 231 deaths reported (Frederickson 1971, 273), was all about black (male)-on-white (female) rape, or at least the fantasy thereof, so obviously whites at the turn of the twentieth century were far more upset about black male sexuality than about black female sexuality.[26] What sense, then, does it make to insist on a unitary analysis?

It is worth taking some time away from my main line of argument to respond to this question, because it grows out of what I strongly believe is a pernicious misinterpretation of the historical record. My answer is that it makes the same sense that Ida B. Wells, Walter White, and Angela Davis have made in their writings on lynching. "Of the 1,115 Negro men, women and children hanged, shot and roasted alive from January 1, 1882, to January 1, 1894, inclusive," wrote Wells, "only 348 of that number were charged with rape. Nearly 700 of these persons were lynched for any other reason which could be manufactured by a mob wishing to indulge in a lynching bee" (Wells 2002, 109). Citing a 1931 publication by the Southern Commission on the Study of Lynching, Davis notes that between 1889 and 1929 only 16.7 percent of lynching victims were accused of rape and 6.7 percent of attempted rape (Davis 1981, 189). Orlando Patterson has noted that, insofar as any wrongful act was alleged, "the single most important reason for lynching was murder and assault by Afro-Americans against Euro-American men" (Patterson 1998, 224).[27] But in many cases there was no effort to trump up a charge of wrongdoing of any kind. The victims had simply run afoul of wealthy or prominent white citizens by succeeding at business, attempting to vote, engaging in labor union activities, or threatening to sue a white man (Gossett 1997, 270); they were attacked because, intentionally or not, they were mounting a challenge to white supremacy. Lynching was a way "to get rid of Negroes who were acquiring wealth and property and thus keep the race terrorized and 'keep the nigger down.'"[28] Since most of those acquiring wealth and influence were adult males, adult males made up the greater share of lynching victims.[29]

This fact was no secret in communities where lynching occurred. White people didn't need the excuse of a rape charge to condemn a black man or woman who got "uppity." "Uppitiness" in and of itself was good enough to serve as the stated reason for killing an African American. Uppitiness was apt to be attributed to any black person who succeeded at business, bought land, or tried to cast a vote; all black political or material progress was perceived as a direct threat to white supremacy.[30] But uppitiness could also consist in nothing more than ordinary displays of intelligence or self-respect. As A. Philip Randolph noted, "Anything may occasion a community to burn a Negro. It might be a well-dressed Negro; a Negro who speaks good English or a Negro who talks back to a white man" (in Wintz 1996, 257).

Economic considerations played a major role in lynching, but economic calculation was not the sole driving force; white people were defending white power, white dominance, which by the late nineteenth century most whites held to be valuable in and of itself, far beyond financial measure.[31] The point here is that when white people—especially newspaper editors, sheriffs, attorneys, and legislators—claimed that white fears of black male sexuality drove the lynching craze, they were stating something they knew to be less than entirely true. But they articulated and perpetuated this claim because, to the degree that it was believed, it enabled federal, state, and local law enforcement officials to characterize the phenomenon of lynching not as murder but as a sort of rogue juridical form, a ritual of popular justice.

In point of fact, most nineteenth-century lynchings did not resemble nineteenth-century legal execution. Victims were seldom simply hanged, as criminals were. Most were tortured to death; many were repeatedly mutilated and burned, and their corpses desecrated. Often their clothes, and frequently their body parts (including genitalia, ears, eyeballs, fingers, bones, and internal organs), were distributed to onlookers or even auctioned off as souvenirs, and whatever remained afterward was put on public display.[32] The point of these horrific procedures was not punishment, at least not primarily. It was twofold: first, a direct challenge to white authority was simply eliminated (although that could have been accomplished with much less pomp and circumstance); and second, the entire black population was subjected to a lesson in discipline.[33] I would maintain, in fact, that this disciplinary purpose was the principal purpose. Lynching was intended to instill a crippling fear in every African American who might ever think of achieving something or of distinguishing him- or herself in any way. To stand out was to risk being picked off. The safest thing to do was to blend in, stay with the group, raise neither voice nor eyes, and never, ever assert oneself. Walter White of the NAACP reports that between 1882 and 1927 4,951 individuals were lynched (1969, 227). But millions of people were terrorized into humiliating conformity to a debased stereotype of underachievement and poverty.[34]

In sum, however much lynchers might have believed in the importance of their work, the statistics suggest that most of them knew it was not about protecting white women from rape; it was about maintaining a docile and exploitable underclass.[35] And however much they might have relished their work, they were very aware that it was far more than sadistic entertainment. It was a political act, an exercise of power that reinforced and was reinforced by a network of economic and political relations. Lynching was necessary to ensure that blacks (and immigrants from China, Mexico, Italy, and elsewhere, as well as white Americans who might be moved to raise a question or two)[36] understood that they were under constant surveillance by an entire populace, that they had better control themselves and their loved ones, that they had better be docile, had better keep their eyes to the ground and their noses to the grindstone. For at least sixty years, lynching was a crucial component of a set of disciplinary practices that trained racially identified bodies to conduct themselves in ways that white supremacists dictated. Lynching was biopolitical terrorism insofar as its target was not merely, or even mainly, the individual bodies that it subjected to torture and death but the entire racial populations to which they belonged.

The myth of the black rapist was not the primary motive for most lynchings, but it *was* law- and policymakers' primary justification for doing little or nothing to stop the practice. Whenever activists lobbied for legal change, the myth allowed a discursive shift away from white supremacist terrorism and toward the purported menace of uncontrolled black sexuality.[37] While anti-lynching activists advocated stiff penalties for law enforcement officials who failed to protect persons in their custody, aggressive prosecution of mob leaders, and compensation to victims' families, white journalists and lawmakers drew on the myth that lynching resulted from whites' fear of black male sexual aggression to call for more stringent law enforcement to keep black men in line and thus reassure white communities that the legal system could handle the "problem" without their extra-legal help.[38] Physicians' voices were prominent in these law and policy discussions. For example, E. F. Daniel of Austin, Texas, used the myth to bolster his call for new laws mandating castration of all sex offenders. Daniel wrote: "Rape, sodomy, beastiality [*sic*], pederasty, and habitual masturbation should be made crimes or misdemeanors, punishable by forfeiture of all rights, including that of procreation; in short, by castration, or castration *plus* other penalties, according to the gravity of the offense."[39] In response to such expert opinions as these, in the first decade of the new century both Nevada and Washington passed laws mandating castration for certain classes of criminals.[40]

It is important to see, then, that there are really two myths at work here in tandem. One is the myth of the black rapist, but the other is the *myth* of the myth of the black rapist, that is, the myth that white people lynched because they believed black men raped. It was very much in the interest of a white elite to perpetuate this second myth, the myth that lynching occurred because whites thought black men were sexual predators. That myth allowed governmental inaction against lynchers, which permitted the terrorism to continue, but it also allowed governmental *action* against blacks. It justified putting in place more law enforcement officials, more surveillance, and more extensive prison systems—mechanisms that facilitated governmental, social scientific, and medical management of all sectors of society, not just of blacks.[41] No matter how many times Ida B. Wells and Walter White and any number of other African American journalists and activists brought the empirical facts to the fore—that lynching was not primarily about white fear of black sexual predators—the old double myth was trotted out to protect the practice of lynching from legal intervention and generalized public disapproval and to camouflage the ongoing growth of what Foucault calls the carceral system. To hold onto that idea in the present day—the idea that lynching was about white fears of black male sexuality—is to participate in what was basically a political cover for sixty years of state-facilitated terrorism against the entire black population of the United States of America and for the institutionalization of that terrorism in the twentieth-century penal system.[42]

This is not to say that white people did not think black men were sexual predators. Of course they did, whether that belief was the primary motive for most lynchings or not. That idea increasingly took hold through the late nineteenth century, helped along significantly by the pronouncements of the medical profession, as seen in the quotations from Drs. Howard and Lydston. It became very widespread, and it continues to flourish today.[43] My only point in this excursus on the phenomenon of lynching is that we need to analyze the myth of the black rapist, not so much in the context of more-or-less institutionalized ritual murder, but in the context of other discourses of sexual predation that arose and gained force in the late nineteenth century, discourses that fed a whole series of movements to incarcerate, institutionalize, segregate, sterilize, and in some cases eliminate certain classes of people from American society. Racism was definitely at work in these movements. But it was not simply antiblack prejudice coupled with a neurotic Victorian preoccupation with sexual purity; it was scientific racism, racism focused, not first of all on the "lower" races, but on the future human race—the Nordic race and its evolutionary supremacy, reproductive potential, and self-proclaimed civil singularity.

The tenets of what we now call scientific racism made the notion that black men were sexual predators virtually inescapable. The black race's development was believed to have been arrested at a savage stage of evolution; their brains were largely given over to the generative functions; they lacked capacity for abstract reasoning and were deficient in will power; they were like (Nordic) children in their general lack of foresight and self-control. With strong sexual urges and no civilized sense of modesty, it was inevitable that black men would force themselves on others. But these tenets made equally inescapable the notion that black women were sexual predators, limited in the amount of physical force they could muster against an unwilling adult male perhaps, but just as much of a biological menace to those whom they did manage to overwhelm or seduce.[44] Black women and even barely pubescent girls were blamed for corrupting employers and for enticing the children they nursed into the debilitating habit of masturbation. They were routinely harassed by public health officials and police as alleged carriers of disease. They were assumed to be whores and prostitutes, regardless of their actual behavior or life style, insatiable bitches constantly in search of something to fill up those enormous vaginas, luring naïve white boys and young men with their primitive wiles in order to produce dangerously degenerate mulattos who might sneak across the color line and pass for white, there to wreak biological havoc for generations.

If we refuse to be fascinated by the violence of lynching and the rhetoric that surrounded it, we will note that not only Negroes of both sexes but all "mental defectives" were believed to be potential, if not already actual, sexual predators. People with "feeble minds" were by definition people who had little reasoning power and poor judgment, people who were at the mercy of their own passions and biological impulses, people with enormous sex drives and genitals to match. Lynching was primarily a political and economic phenomenon, as Ida B. Wells and others argued at its height. It was able to operate as it did—with the myth of the black rapist as an alibi—because of a larger political and sociological phenomenon taking place at the same time, namely, the rise of the myth of the atavistic sexual predator. In other words, politically and economically motivated lynching of black men was given cover by the link that nineteenth-century physicians and psychiatrists forged between unbridled sexuality and intellectual abnormality or deficiency. Forging that link required popular demonization of the mentally handicapped.

Intellectual Segregation: Protecting Civilization from the Menace of the Feebleminded

The atavistic sexual predator could come in any color, size, or shape. It could be black, white, red, yellow, or brown. It could be male or female or even some horrible mixture of the two. Intellectually weak, and thus governed by impulse rather than reason, all degenerates and throwbacks lacked moral inhibition and tended toward sexual excess.

At least since the 1820s, when European physicians first began to make studies of a class of people they called "cretins," mental deficiency had been linked with heightened sexual desire and stamina.[45] Today cretinism is understood to be a severe retardation of development that occurs as a result of a deficiency of iodine—hence, iodized table salt. Through most of the nineteenth century, however, European biologists believed cretinism was a hereditary condition, because cases were clustered in villages where many of the inhabitants were related. Cretins were not only severely mentally impaired but were physically retarded as well. In 1857, Morel described Marguerite Gros, age twenty-three, as follows: She "appears like a ten-year-old girl. She is not quite 977 mm tall and weighs about 20 kg. Noticeable is the lack of any sign of puberty and the retention of all her milk teeth. Her genitalia are no more developed than those of a seven or eight-year-old child. The pubis is totally hairless. The feeling of shame seems not yet to have been awakened."[46] In fact, Mademoiselle Gros not only submitted without embarrassment to a full physical examination but was known to everyone in her village as an avid masturbator—as, indeed, were most of the other cretins studied. Lack of sexual shame and a propensity to masturbate in full view of others was therefore assumed to be an aspect of the cretin's essential biological nature. Through the rest of the century, as the class of people considered feebleminded expanded beyond cretinism, the presumed tendency to sexual excess spread across various classifications of "defectives."

Cretins were tiny people who never reached sexual maturity. Their sexual excesses were merely unsightly or disgusting. But imbeciles (a class of defectives that emerged in the latter half of the nineteenth century) were another matter entirely. Full-sized, sexually mature, and sporting abnormally enlarged genitals,[47] they were thought to have the primitive urges of the prehistoric savage with little or no mitigating civility. Imbeciles, especially those classified as moral imbeciles, were natural criminals prone to indulge in acts of larceny, arson, murder—and, of course, rape.[48] Lurid accounts of child-rape and mutilation were fairly common, even if the crimes themselves were not. Psychiatrists in particular were eager to convince the general public that imbeciles posed a serious danger to the community and really should be locked up in asylums before their full savage potential was realized.

By the late 1870s, the main justification for committing children and adults to institutions for the feebleminded was not the training or welfare of the individual; it was the protection of society—both now and in the future. In 1878 the Newark Custodial Asylum for Feeble-minded Women was founded as a result of Josephine Shaw Lowell's exhortations and political lobbying. Her goal was not only to get dangerous imbeciles off the streets but also to prevent degenerates from having sex, both with so-called normal people and with each other. "What right have we to-day to allow men and women who are diseased and vicious to reproduce their kind, and bring into the world beings whose existence must be one long misery to themselves and others?" she demanded. It was the duty of the government and the taxpaying public to make sure these dangerous people were segregated for life from normal, healthy Americans (Lowell 1879, 193). Thirteen years later, Lowell's concerns were clearly shared by her entire profession. Speaking before the Association for Medical Officers of American Institutions for Idiotic and Feeble-minded Persons in 1891, A. E. Osborne accounted for the growth in institutions and institutional populations with a single sentence: "Society is organizing everywhere for self-protection" (Rafter 1997, 63). The myth of the evolutionarily backward or degenerate sexual predator in all its forms functioned as leverage when medical and psychiatric professionals, educators, and social reformers agitated for permanent institutionalization of the feebleminded at state expense and for flexible rather than fixed prison sentencing.

At the same time that racial segregation was being codified in many parts of the United States, intellectual segregation was taking place as well—and just as systematically. In both cases the segregation was supported in great part by the repeated, scientifically supported insistence that the people to be walled off or pushed back behind the color line were sexually dangerous. Until we place the myth of the black rapist in that context—that administrative, medical, and governmental context—we will not understand its power or its modes of operation and resilience. Violent campaigns against black male sexuality were not bizarre outbreaks of hysteria in the late nineteenth century; they were part of a massive effort to delineate and manage all human bodies, to direct and control human evolution itself, to hasten the day when evolution would finally purify the human race of defect and weakness and Anglo-Saxons would inherit the earth.

Over the next two decades, local, state, and federal governments took up the issue.[49] In 1914 the Virginia General Assembly commissioned the State Board of Charities and Corrections to study "Weak-Mindedness in the State of Virginia." Their report, issued in 1915, begins with the assertion that "the civilized nations of the earth are awakening to the menace of the feeble-minded, and there is now universal interest in the world-wide investigation of this problem" (*Mental Defectives*, 1915, 11). It recommends that all Virginians incapable of managing their own affairs be placed under state supervision on account of mental defect.[50] Marriage should be prohibited by law, and sterilization should be performed on all those from whom consent could be obtained. (It would be another decade before the state would waive the requirement of consent.) All mental defectives should be required to register with the State Board of Charities and Corrections, which would function as the agency in charge of supervising defectives in both public and private custody. If a mentally defective child remained in the care of parents, the parents would have to report to the agency on a regular basis and demonstrate compliance with state regulations to contain the threat to public health that such a child necessarily posed.

By the time the San Francisco Panama Pacific Exposition opened in 1915 (which was, in part, a celebration of the opening of the Panama Canal), the menace of the feebleminded was recognized as a national problem. The Exposition's Race Betterment exhibit explained the menace in graphic terms. The feebleminded were "spreading like cancerous growths" and "infecting the blood of whole communities" (Kline 1997, 15). Not only were they breeding among themselves and thus increasing the financial burden on the society that had to support them; they were also corrupting bloodlines that were otherwise untainted. Psychologist Lewis Terman wrote, "There is a growing conviction that society, in self-defense, will be driven to provide institutional care for every feeble-minded individual throughout the reproductive period."[51]

Feebleminded women in particular were seen as a serious problem all across the nation. In 1918 Terman and his colleague William Lucas portrayed female morons as a threat to national security. Passing for normal, they lurked around military bases and seduced unsuspecting soldiers who then contracted venereal disease.[52] That year Congress appropriated money through enactment of the Chamberlin-Kalen Bill to create a civilian quarantine and isolation fund to build twenty-seven new institutions for the feebleminded and to expand sixteen existing facilities. William Lee Howard's proposal of quarantine was becoming a reality, although not so much for African Americans in the throes of *furor sexualis* as for whites—most of them poor, ill-educated white females, whose alleged intellectual inferiority and attendant sexual promiscuity was blamed for the spread of syphilis and gonorrhea in the U.S. military. Over the next two years, thirty thousand women suspected of sexual activity around military bases were brought into official custody. Over half of them, more than fifteen thousand, were committed to custodial institutions for the rest of their reproductive lives.

In 1910 the category of the feebleminded expanded to include not only the idiot (a person with a mental age of less than two years on the Simon-Binet scale) and the imbecile (a person with a mental age of two to seven years) but also the moron, a person with a mental age of up to twelve years and thus one who could read, write, do arithmetic, and hold down a job. (It should be remembered that in 1910 it was very common for twelve-year-olds to hold down full-time jobs.) Additionally, the category included the moral imbecile, a person who might be cognitively normal but was immoral by conventional standards. All of these people, with the exception of idiots, were thought to pose a serious threat to normal people everywhere, who might at any time become their sexual prey. But morons and moral imbeciles were especially frightening and insidious. The Virginia commissioners wrote: "These people have none of the stigmata of the lower grade of mental deficients, and are not as easily recognized as the idiot and low-grade imbecile" (*Mental Defectives* 1915, 11). Like mulattoes who might pass as white, such people could pass as normal and thus enter into liaisons with normal people. Only an expert could distinguish them from the general population. Therefore the commission advocated mandatory intelligence testing in public schools, intellectual classification of all school children, and state supervised custody for any child discovered to be an imbecile or moron. This supervised custody would continue for life, because no amount of education or training would erase the defect. Once a child was labeled mentally defective, it did not matter what he or she might accomplish; the abnormality was still present. As Martin Barr, chief physician of the Pennsylvania Training School, put it, "To replace what has never been placed is impossible" (1913, 130).

The Virginia commissioners pulled no punches: "Many of the high-grade are sexual perverts and criminals" (*Mental Defectives* 1915, 12). "In the female you find a mind seven to ten years with a weak will in a body of an adult, 17 to 30 years of age, fully developed sexually, and once she goes wrong, passion-driven, she is difficult to control ever after. As with the female, so with the male, only the former constitute the greater menace." At one Virginia facility the medical superintendent had told the commissioners that such women "were the most difficult to control in the institution, and every one of them had had children—from one to three children each. At a leading institution the only building we saw with bars on the windows is the one in which mentally defective, sexually immoral women are confined" (*Mental Defectives* 1915, 12). Should such women get free and blend back into society, they would pose a major threat to the evolutionary supremacy of the white race.

Thus we see that by the early twentieth century, biological and social scientists, physicians, psychiatrists, and social reformers were calling for all these groups—inferior races as well as inferior whites—to be contained, monitored, and aggressively managed. How each group was to be managed differed in different disciplinary schemes. But in many cases the plans proposed would have affected all or most such groups in much the same ways. For example, had the call for lifelong institutionalization of all persons deemed mentally defective been realized, more than one out of every ten white Americans would have been incarcerated[53]—simply removed from society for their rest of their reproductive, if not their entire lives, their civil personhood erased along with their civil liberty, and their labor power placed in the hands of the state to offset the cost of their "maintenance." But people of color, too, would have been subject to this sort of incarceration, perhaps instead of imprisonment or mass ghettoization and impoverishment. Careful study of the population figures in the Virginia State Board of Charities and Corrections report of 1915 suggests that the category "feebleminded" included a huge percentage of the African American population. The research team tested inmates in prisons, almshouses, epileptic colonies, and insane asylums. Where the results are broken down by race, it is clear that they were identifying a 75 to 90 percent rate of feeblemindedness among African Americans already in state custody. Similar rates were found in other studies of African Americans outside state custody.[54] And this does not include any testing for moral imbecility without cognitive impairment. Thus, full implementation of plans like that presented to the Virginia General Assembly would likely have entailed sex-segregated incarceration from puberty to old age for at least three-quarters of the African American population of the United States. Although never presented as such, institutionalization of the feebleminded would have functioned, among other things, as a "solution" to the "problem" of the presence of blacks on American soil that Thomas Jefferson himself might have admired.[55]

Lynching as a public ritual enforcing white supremacy began to fade away in the 1930s, but that was not because white people ceased to fear black male sexuality; it was because community-organized, extra-legal violence, which had always been a bit of an embarrassment to public officials, had only been tolerated as long as there were no reliable alternatives.[56] Once managerial alternatives existed, lynching lost its social and political sanction and was either abandoned as a practice or driven underground.[57] The theories and data these various professional reformers produced thus rallied support for, justified, and then enlarged and perpetuated legal, institutional, and social arrangements that constituted those alternatives. They erected society's defense against evolutionary disruption and enabled the Nordic race to continue its march toward world domination. And they did so largely by focusing attention, not on race per se, but on what they viewed as excessive and deviant sexuality. Nevertheless, everyone at that time understood that they did so in the service of white supremacy. Only subsequently did that link become obscured.

From Masturbator to Homosexual: The Construction of the Sex Pervert

In our post-Freudian era it is all too easy to assume that sexuality was always a central issue in human societies and that racism was always and inevitably a product of sexual fantasy. The latter assumption is especially easy to make, given all this talk of enormous penises and huge, cavernous, engulfing vaginas dripping with syphilis. But what actually occurred, I believe, is something close to the reverse, namely, that sexuality as a unitary field of knowledge and a network of institutional power is to a great extent a creature of scientific racism—or, more conservatively, that sexuality's overwhelming significance and pervasive force in early twentieth-century Anglo-America is largely due to the ways in which the forces of scientific racism used it to fashion white supremacist strategies and management techniques.

I have already pointed out that scientific racists were prominent among those calling for an end to what came to be called Victorian sexual repression in the early part of the twentieth century. Scientific racists like Howard and Lydston insisted that sexuality be studied and publicly discussed; after all, the future of The Race was in the balance. Sexuality as the means of reproduction had to be safeguarded and nurtured. As the site where the forces of development were most likely to falter or go wrong, it also had to be diligently monitored. Most importantly, as the mechanism by which the forces of evolution would produce the future of humanity, sexuality had to be carefully and painstakingly shepherded and managed. Science would lead the way. Biologists, physicians, sexologists, and psychiatrists would discover sexuality's laws and norms. Forensic and psychiatric experts would develop techniques to contain deviance. But then these scientists and technicians, along with educators and religious leaders, would have to train each and every Nordic man, woman, boy, and girl to recognize signs of trouble in themselves and others and to instill in them the self-discipline necessary to stay within the parameters of healthy functioning.

Although Foucault does not tell precisely the story that I will develop here—in fact he seems to give sexuality chronological precedence over scientific racism[58]—his history of sexuality can help us understand how sexuality came into existence as a scientific phenomenon in the nineteenth century and thus how it became available for incorporation into scientific racist projects. In fact, he links them explicitly in the fifth part of *The History of Sexuality, Volume 1* (Foucault 1978, beginning on 137, but see especially 147–50). It will be worthwhile to backtrack somewhat and review that history in anticipation of the emergence of yet another sexual predator with over-sized genitals: the Homosexual.

Foucault asserts that sexuality as a unitary field of knowledge and experience did not exist in the seventeenth century. That is not to say that there were no orgasms or pregnancies, no courtship rituals or condemnations of carnal sins. Of course there were—and a lot else besides—all of which eventually became part of what we now think of and experience as sexuality. Foucault's point is that what now seems to be a unitary phenomenon at the center of human life and personal identity was then fragmentary and dispersed into a variety of separate domains, many of which were peripheral to most individuals' daily life, health, and well-being. People didn't think of themselves as fundamentally sexual beings, as beings with a sexual orientation and a sexual identity that established them in their very selfhood. Consequently, they didn't need to spend a lot of time trying to decipher the sexual meanings of their dreams, fears, jokes, or slips of the tongue. And when something went wrong in their relationships or emotional lives, they didn't presume that whatever was wrong necessarily had anything to do with their libido. By the end of the nineteenth century, however, people in the mainstream of modern culture in industrialized countries did think of themselves as fundamentally sexual beings. They did believe that the most mundane aspects of their feelings and behavior as well as their bodily health were deeply connected to their sexual natures, so they thought that when something went wrong for them, it probably did have something to do with their sexual desires or practices. They also thought that when something went wrong with other people—when they behaved in seemingly irrational or unusual ways, when they fell ill, when they expressed feelings different from the norm—something might be wrong with their sexuality. Sexuality had become an object of knowledge by the end of the nineteenth century, and a very precious object of knowledge at that. Knowing one's own sexuality and understanding the sexuality of others—especially abnormal others—had come to seem crucial to getting along in the world.

Foucault suggests that this change occurred both accidentally and on purpose. It was accidental in the sense that nobody set out to make the change and nobody envisioned the ultimate outcome. Various people were interested in this or that question or problem and were busy investigating or experimenting or theorizing or manipulating their little region of the social and intellectual world. But as their projects progressed and they shared their techniques and ideas, previously disparate domains of knowledge linked up, and networks of institutionalized practices assembled. This occurred on purpose in the sense that many people had an interest in, and made a conscious effort to establish, these links and cross-references and institutions. And as the networks grew, some people who might not have been so powerful before—psychiatrists, to pick just one example—became much more powerful. Such people did what they could, then, to protect and further the movements that were already underway. Thus did change occur. In 1750, no one was a sexual being; in 1950, everyone was. Without anyone ever having decided to make it so, sexuality had become a central feature of human life.

Foucault identifies four movements that gathered many scattered ideas, theories, practices, and interests and bundled them together in the eighteenth and nineteenth centuries—four movements that eventually coalesced to produce sexuality as a coherent domain. The first was what he calls the "hystericization of women's bodies." This occurred slowly, first through the medicalization of pregnancy and the pathologization of deviation in fetal development and maternal behavior, and then through the broadening out of the maternal function into the domestic space of the family and the elongated time of child rearing so that feminine un-health translated into familial instability, potential or actual. Whether pregnant or not, whether a mother (yet) or not, every (middle- and upper-class white) woman was subject to the vicissitudes and demands of her uterus and all the important aspects of human life to which it was connected. Her reproductive life—which turned out to be virtually her entire life—cried out for medical management. The second movement Foucault labels "the pedagogization of children's sex," by which he refers to efforts to prevent children from damaging their health and reproductive potential through precocious sensuality, and programs to educate children about reproduction and their eventual roles in it. One prominent aspect of this movement is the long war on masturbation, which in the nineteenth century became "the most important problem in medical science" (Gilman 1985, 40). The third movement, according to Foucault, was "the socialization of procreative behavior," the most obvious manifestations of which are the "family planning" and eugenics movements (to be discussed at length in chapter 5); and the fourth was "the psychiatrization of perverse pleasure" (Foucault 1978, 104–105), which began as a set of problems in forensic medicine. Initially these movements were disparate local efforts to address a multiplicity of perceived problems. Only by sharing techniques, vocabularies, resources, and insights over time did they finally coalesce into the great apparatus of power/knowledge that Foucault calls the *dispositif de sexualité.*

Foucault's sketch of this history in his *History of Sexuality, Volume 1,* has been filled in and elaborated by numerous authors over the last thirty years. There is no need to examine it in all its detail here. Instead, I simply want to suggest some of the ways in which these movements articulated with the discursive and institutional practices of scientific racism to give rise to the figure of the feebleminded or weak-willed sexual predator in all his/her guises: the black rapist (and erstwhile werewolf), the alluring syphilitic whore, the sex-crazed imbecile, the conniving female sexual invert poised to recruit, and the homosexual child molester. Scientific racism, with its intense fear of genetic corruption, created this figure; and in it—long after scientific racism's official demise and, indeed, throughout the twentieth century down to the present day—its racist preoccupations and presumptions live on.

The direct ancestor of the late nineteenth century's sexual predator was the early nineteenth century's masturbator. The masturbator—a man, woman, or child consumed by deviant desire and addicted to the practice to the point of death—made a rather sudden appearance in European history in the eighteenth century. Prior to that time masturbation was officially condemned as a sin because it made use of the generative organs to produce a sterile pleasure, but it was not thought to pose a medical threat. Then suddenly everything changed.

Sometime in the first decades of the eighteenth century—some scholars say 1700, others 1710, and still others 1715[59]—an anonymous treatise appeared in Holland and England entitled *Onania, or the Heinous Sin of Self-Pollution and All Its Frightful Consequences in both sexes, considered with Spiritual and Physical Advice to Those who have already Injur'd themselves by this abominable Practice.*[60] It purported to be a moral warning, but it insisted that the wages of this particular sin were not to be collected exclusively in the hereafter but were very much a part of this world. People who indulged in the sin of Onan[61] risked "cessation of growth, phimosis,[62] paraphimosis, strangurious,[63] priopism, fainting fits, epilepsy, impotence, and in woman, fluor albus,[64] hysteric fits, consumption, and barrenness" (Fishman 1982, 274). Luckily, there was a remedy for all of these complaints, which the pamphlet advertised.[65] Medicine could be purchased at specified London outlets for twelve shillings a bottle. Despite the high price, sales of both the remedy and the 88-page pamphlet were brisk.[66] This frankly frightening piece of entrepreneurialism was reprinted in English eighteen times over the next sixty years and was translated into French and German as well.[67]

Physicians did not take the tract's message seriously.[68] Masturbation was not a medical issue—let alone a medical emergency—until 1758, with the publication of *Onanism or Dissertation on the maladies produced by masturbation* by Swiss physician S. A. Tissot, who enlarged the list of masturbation's physiological effects, adding dyspepsia, blindness, vertigo, hearing and memory loss, headache, impotence, irregular heartbeat, rickets, and chronic conjunctivitis. In addition, it could produce nymphomania, especially in blondes, as well as a variety of structural changes in the genitals and even the entire body. Men would see a decrease in the size of the penis, Tissot held, while women would experience enlargement of the clitoris and labia minora and a reddening of the labia majora. Masturbation could also increase the size of hands and feet in both sexes and cause acne, clammy palms, stooped shoulders, pale and sallow complexion, dark circles around the eyes, and a slow, dragging gait. As if that were not enough, case studies revealed that masturbation was a major cause of insanity, and it produced a tendency to consumption that one could pass on to one's children.

Tissot's work was enormously influential.[69] His ideas found their way into medical diagnosis and practice across Europe and eventually in the United States. By 1812, Benjamin Rush held that masturbation was a factor in at least four of the cases of insanity that he treated in the Pennsylvania Hospital lunatic ward (Hare 1962, 4). But it was in the social reformist climate of the 1830s that the medical model of masturbation really took hold. Sterling Fishman writes:

> It was in this climate that one sees the campaign against childhood sexuality, especially masturbation, which had been conducted on a limited and individual basis in the eighteenth century, transformed into a crusade. A new sense of purpose infuses the writings of moralists and physicians on the subject. Their aim was no longer merely to save or cure individual souls, but to save "society." As a French physician wrote in mid-century: "In my opinion neither the plague, nor war, nor smallpox, nor a crowd of similar evils, have resulted more disastrously for humanity, than the habit of masturbation: it is the destroying element of civilized society." (Fishman 1982, 277)

As physicians came to see themselves and to be seen not just as private advisors but as guardians of public health, this crusade gathered strength and influence.[70]

Admission and discharge records for Charity Hospital of Louisiana in New Orleans show that the first patient to be admitted there for treatment for masturbation entered the hospital in 1848. Over an eighty-six-year period, many more patients were hospitalized for the disease, and at least two were reported to have died from it. The last admission for masturbation was recorded in 1933 (Engelhardt 1974, 238–39). If we take Charity Hospital's records as indicative of national trends, it would seem that at least by the 1840s masturbation was widely seen in the United States as an organic malady, or at least as a cause or symptom of organic disease, and that this perception persisted well into the twentieth century.

A disease requires a treatment. Prior to 1850, most cases of masturbation were treated with hydrotherapy, diet, and exercise. Some of the most famous dietary regimes involved foods manufactured especially to reduce the craving for sexual stimulation. In 1834, for example, Dr. Sylvester Graham introduced his food line, which included Graham crackers; and later in the century, the Kellogg brothers of Battle Creek, Michigan, introduced granola, shredded wheat, and cornflakes as masturbatory inhibitors. The introduction of sports and gymnastics into school curricula was part of this anti-masturbation movement, as was the founding of health clubs for adults. The Young Men's Christian Association eventually decided to provide gymnasiums for its members in part because intense physical activity was thought to reduce the appetite for "self-abuse."[71] After mid-century, however, medical treatments for masturbation became more invasive (or heroic, depending on one's point of view). Between 1850 and 1879, surgery was recommended more frequently than any other type of intervention (Fishman 1982, 277). Clitorectomy and circumcision were favored treatments, although castration was sometimes used in extreme cases.[72] In addition, physicians burned and blistered the areas of excitation, introduced needles into the prostate and bladder, and applied electrodes to both the exterior and the interior of the genitalia. Many also prescribed drugs, including camphor, potassium bromide,[73] and opium. And a wide range of devices were developed for preventing erection or contact between genitals and hands.[74] These included bands to constrict blood flow to the penis, small bands stitched into the open end of the foreskin to keep it from retracting, spiked metal rings that would inflict pain upon erection, straight jackets, mittens, and various types of bindings.

The best medicine was, of course, prevention. Physicians exhorted parents, educators, and clergy to stop masturbation before it started by keeping children busy, physically active, and under constant surveillance. In 1858 Samuel Gridley Howe, ever mindful that masturbation could result in total idiocy in either oneself or one's offspring, wrote, "It behooves every parent, especially those whose children (of either sex) are obliged to board and sleep with other children, whether in boarding schools, boarding houses, or elsewhere, to have a constant and watchful eye over them, with a view to this insidious and pernicious habit" (Howe 1972–, 31). Children's interaction with servants should be monitored lest they learn from their inferiors.[75] And, as age and understanding permit, they should be warned explicitly about masturbation's terrible effects.[76] As Foucault points out, virtually all of late eighteenth- and especially nineteenth-century pedagogy referred in one way or another to what we would now call childhood sexuality and to an institutionalized desire to manage children's bodies, emotional attachments, and pleasures. The architecture of dormitories, the protocols for gaining permission to use the toilet, the construction of toilets themselves, the cut of school uniforms, as well as the content of instruction bespoke a deep concern with the possibility that children might masturbate, alone or with others.

Foucault insists that this set of concerns is not best analyzed as sexual repression. For one thing, it was accompanied by a huge increase in the volume of discourse about genital pleasures, so it makes little sense to characterize the phenomenon as a kind of silencing. For another, the effect was not to decrease the incidence of masturbation, solitary or mutual, but rather to inform children about such practices and no doubt increase their curiosity; in other words, intensified discourse and ubiquitous nondiscursive references to these pleasurable possibilities served as temptations, or incitements, to use Foucault's term. Incitement warranted more intensified surveillance and control, so that within a few decades more or less permanent mechanisms were in place for monitoring and managing the lives of middle-class children and their families.

The Masturbator was the incarnation of management's failure. Addicted to the debilitating practice, he or she was sallow, weak, and exhausted, yet consumed with desire for ever more stimulation. Reason gave way to impulse; inhibitions were lost; madness ensued. This portrait was the one that physicians, educators, and public officials held up to patients, parents, teachers, and children as they placed ever-increasing demands for transparency, accessibility, and conformity on their shoulders. Terror at the thought of encountering the Masturbator, of becoming the Masturbator, or of allowing one's youthful charges to become the Masturbator drove people to accept all kinds of intrusions into their private lives and even into their bodies. That terror made possible an extensive and institutionalized network of surveillance and social control, and it served as the prototype of terrors to come.

Foucault's work shows the importance of looking at such phenomena from the outside, so to speak—that is, looking at their effects and the interests they produce rather than at their own internal rationales. Educators and physicians said they were attempting to eradicate masturbation, but even when their procedures had the opposite effect,[77] they did not change their strategies. Obviously, then, other interests and aims—such as making money and extending their spheres of influence—were at work. Nevertheless, and keeping in mind this crucial insight, we must pay some attention to what the anti-masturbation crusaders were saying about themselves, to their professional justifications for their actions, because without credible justifications, people simply would not have tolerated their intrusions and treatments. What contemporary acne sufferer would allow a physician to attach electrodes to his penis and eyelids and run a current through his body? Yet in the nineteenth century, people not only submitted to these procedures; they asked for them and paid for them. One condition of the extension of medical authority was that physicians be able to tell a good story about what they were doing to people.

Thus it was never enough simply to say that masturbation caused acne or blindness or insanity; there had to be a theory about why. Early theories had to do with depletion of semen. Since the time of the ancient Greeks, many people had believed that semen was condensed or rarefied blood, the counterpart to the menses. Tissot asserted that one ounce of semen was equivalent to forty ounces of blood, so obviously semen was a precious commodity, quite apart from its importance in reproduction. In fact it *was* blood, rarefied in the testicles and then pumped back into the body to stimulate production of muscle and hair. If, instead of returning to the body, it was evacuated in large quantities, inevitably the body would weaken.[78] It was prudent for males, therefore, to limit indulgence in orgasmic pleasures of any kind. Some physicians recommended sexual intercourse no more than once per month, thus further aligning ejaculation with menstruation. Others thought once every two weeks was about right. In young, healthy men, less cautious physicians were likely to accept ejaculation as often as once a week. This advice was given not primarily to insure healthy offspring or even to contain sexual intercourse within marriage.[79] It was primarily to protect the health and vigor of the man himself.

In the nineteenth century, however, physicians became much less convinced of semen's physiological value for the body that produced it. As the medicine of Benjamin Rush gave way to the medicine of George Beard, fluids and the stimuli and pressure they might exert on internal organs were discounted in relation to something much more rarefied, something called "nervous force." The damage supposedly done by masturbation shifted from depletion of the body's fluid resources to depletion of its dynamic vitality. According to Beard, "any injury that comes from this habit or from excessive sexual intercourse is due not so much to the loss of semen—which is a comparatively trifling matter—as to the *nervous excitement.*"[80] Sexual excitement convulsed the body and enervated it, a principle equally applicable to males and females. This energy loss might be offset by the energy produced in an encounter between two people, but masturbation, considered an essentially solitary act even when practiced in pairs or groups, did not allow for such compensation.[81]

By the 1870s, when Beard did most of his work, there was plenty of data to support the assertion that "there are cases of insanity, imbecility, and of death brought on by self-abuse and spermatorrhea" (Beard 1972b, 120). For example, in his annual report for 1848, the superintendent of the Massachusetts Lunatic Asylum noted that 32 percent of current admissions were a result of "self-pollution" (Duffy 2003). If that figure was representative, nearly a third of the lunatics in the United States were victims of masturbatory excess. As lunatic asylums filled and overflowed throughout the nineteenth century, fed by emancipated Negroes and ill-adjusted foreign immigrants, masturbation was seen to be a major, and very costly, social problem.

But the problem was not confined to the present. Over-stimulation of any organ, especially during its developmental phase, was thought to cause permanent damage.[82] When the organs in question played major roles in the reproductive process, there was a direct threat to reproductive potential. Dr. William Hammond, for one, was certain that masturbation in childhood and youth led inevitably to adult sexual impotence in both males and females. Masturbating males might become totally incapable of intromission, and masturbating females might become totally unwilling to permit it. In this way, the practice of masturbation posed a threat to the ability of a race to reproduce itself.

That was not the worst problem, however. According to the theory of organic degeneration that gained currency in the 1860s, the morbid somatic effects of masturbation were not confined to the present generation, and even limited indulgence could have a compounding effect. Robert Nye sums up the problem: "In the absence of some countervailing external force, the syndrome developed an autonomous hereditary momentum, exhibiting its advance in worsening behavior and physical signs. The weakened capacity for 'resistance' made the individual organism vulnerable to disease and hostile environments. The 'moral' effects expressed themselves as will pathologies, that is as a catastrophically reduced ability to resist 'impulsions' of instinct, the blandishments of sensual allure, the wine shop, or easy money" (Nye 1985, 59–60). White men and women who masturbated, it would seem, ran the risk of becoming just like newly emancipated Negroes, unable to see the consequences of their actions or resist the allure of sources of immediate gratification. Masturbators who managed to reproduce despite their debility would pass their weakness on to their progeny in ever more concentrated form, bringing forth children who were alcoholics or epileptics and grandchildren who were idiots or homicidal maniacs. Just as the bloodlines of Indians and Negroes were declining toward extinction, white bloodlines could be corrupted by masturbators and brought to a similar evolutionary end. Survival of the fittest meant survival of the strong-willed, and masturbation was both a symptom and a cause of weak will. As Lamarckian Social Darwinism swept over the intellectual landscape, masturbation was frequently seen as a serious threat to human evolution and the civilization it had produced.

Thus elevated to a the status of a threat to the continuation of the Race, a sensual pleasure that had little or nothing to do with procreation or physical health or heredity became a focal point for all kinds of therapeutic and pedagogical intervention. And those interventions were tolerated—in fact, demanded—by the educated public, because masturbation had been connected scientifically with concerns about health, procreation, and heredity through the emerging concept of "sexuality." Masturbation produced not just nervous excitation or debility but, precisely, a disturbed or corrupted sexuality. Thus it affected all aspects of that sexuality, including what we might call a person's gender (gait, gesture, vocal tone, dress, hobbies, career interests, and so on) and appearance and civility, as well as his or her sense of self, familial relationships, friendships, and ability to procreate.

Preventing masturbation among the better classes of white people was crucial if the human race was to survive. Thus the project of stopping it grew into the enormous task of managing upper- and middle-class childhood.[83] Educators and physicians and, increasingly, state officials of various sorts, called upon women to take on the burden of much of this work—under the supervision of professionals, of course. Motherhood was an increasingly demanding occupation, and women were increasingly viewed as almost hopelessly inadequate to the task. Women were too ignorant of sexuality themselves to be of much help raising sexualized children. Many of them were just too lazy to do the work of surveillance or too busy with their own selfish (oftentimes "feminist") pursuits to care for their children properly.[84] Mothers had to be disciplined, educated, and brought into line. And a tremendous amount of guilt had to be infused into the situation to keep them in the home watching over their charges as their opportunities for independence and self-possession multiplied. Over the course of the late nineteenth century especially, middle-class white women—the mothers of the Nordic race and humanity's future—were the subjects of unprecedented psychological and anatomical inquiry and the objects of both intense therapy and pervasive social restraint. They were exalted as the bearers of the white race and simultaneously vilified as the monsters that stunted and endangered it.[85]

The main problem with women, apart from their obvious intellectual inferiority to men, was their sexuality. Contrary to the clichés we so often hear about nineteenth-century conceptions of white womanhood, virtually no one believed that women of any race had no sex drive.[86] On the contrary, because women were not as intellectually advanced or evolved as men, they were more subject to passions and biological impulses than men were and less able to resist temptation through strength of will.[87] Voluptuous urges were an inevitable and, indeed, a fundamental aspect of women's physiological and emotional life. The important difference between males and females in this respect was that a female's desire was thought to be too inchoate and undirected to come to consciousness and underwrite goal-oriented sexual behavior until it was brought into focus by an external agent.[88] In the best of circumstances, that would be her husband, who would both concentrate her sexual ardor and act as the object of it.

The idea that women had sexual needs was so generally accepted as to operate explicitly in nineteenth-century American marriage law. As Matthew Lindsay points out, one major purpose of marriage was to "accommodate sexual indulgence" for both husbands and wives (Lindsay 1998, 548). Impotence was thus invariably grounds for annulment. In 1887 one jurist wrote, "If a party is permanently unfit for sexual intercourse, he or she is not competent to marry."[89] The issue was not procreation; barrenness and infertility were not grounds for dissolution of marriage. The issue was sensual satisfaction; judges assumed that women as well as men would be tempted to seek satisfaction elsewhere if they could not find it in the marriage bed. Annulments were granted to allow the unsatisfied spouse to marry someone else, someone who could fulfill his *or her* sensual needs.

Of course, there were always circumstances that fell short of the best. Females' voluptuous desires could be aroused and focused prematurely, prior to marriage. If that happened, few girls or young women would have the strength of character to resist. This is why unmarried Victorian females were thought to be either virgins or sluts. Girls who were exposed to lewd behavior at an early age—immigrant children, for example, living in crowded tenements, or Negro children living in crowded share-cropper shacks—would of course be aroused as soon as arousal was physically possible. Hence, they would become prostitutes.[90] But even little white girls of the middle and upper classes living in decent homes might become slutty, uncontrollable wenches if they fell under the wrong influences—if servant girls taught them to masturbate, for example, or if they had carnal contact with boys of a more primitive race, or (later in the century) if they rode a bicycle or operated a treadle sewing machine.[91] All women had a latent sexuality just under the surface, waiting to be called out and husbanded. Too often, that evocation occurred in such a way as to bring about the state of motherhood in one who was not under the control of a morally upright, responsible gentleman. Consequently, a great many mothers were, in one way or another and to some degree, lascivious sluts and insatiable whores—or at the very least preoccupied with their own desires and ill-prepared to be a responsible steward of Nordic germ plasm.

If inappropriately and prematurely stimulated, women masturbated incessantly and thus became ever more deeply depraved. Clitorectomy was often called for and sometimes performed.[92] But that didn't stop them from seducing innocent men and children and leaving wide swathes of disease and degeneracy in their wake. Whatever their race, whether young or old, rich or poor, women were scary people in the nineteenth century. The ones who did make it onto the pedestal were a small minority, and as precious as they were rare. And good men had quite a job to do to keep them up there, what with all those lustful, large-genitaled degenerates dancing around on the ground. Middle- and upper-class white men had to cultivate all their strengths and groom one another carefully in order to meet the challenge.

It was very important, therefore, for white men to be manly—virtuous, brave, and governed by reason. Those who faltered—the ones who slipped into sexual overindulgence, debilitated themselves through overwork, or otherwise overextended themselves and developed neurasthenia or some other degenerative disease—had to be put back on the right road as soon as possible, often with the help of physicians like William Hammond. If a young engineer spent too much time with his instruments and equations and as a result became impotent with his young wife (it was well known that abstract thought interfered with sexual potency, and mathematics was virtually always a dampening influence), Dr. Hammond would give him a quick treatment of electric shock and recommend that he take a long vacation. If a young minister found himself unable to consummate his marriage as a result of debilitation through nocturnal emissions, Dr. Hammond would prescribe a high-fat diet and bromides and give him a twice-weekly treatment of galvanic current through the urethra.[93] These cases were manageable. With the help of modern science and technology, masculine potency could be reclaimed and marital success secured. But some cases were more serious.

By the early twentieth century, many psychiatrists, following Emil Kraepelin, no longer believed that masturbation led directly to insanity.[94] The listlessness, pallor, and tendency to trancelike fixations previously thought to be symptomatic of masturbation and a precursor to masturbatory insanity were now believed to herald the adolescent onset of schizophrenia, regardless of whether the patient had ever masturbated or not. Masturbation still posed health risks, to be sure, and still jeopardized the evolution of the white race, but it did so largely within the province of neurology, as William Hammond's and George Beard's work exemplify, not psychiatry per se.[95] It could lead to a kind of madness, but only indirectly, and that was certainly not the worst thing about it.

Masturbation could undermine Nordic masculinity by producing a nervous exhaustion that rendered a man indifferent to the attractions of the opposite sex. Realizing he could not achieve erection in the presence of a female, the masturbator developed a dread of what would eventually be called "heterosexual encounters." Beard called it a "dread of intercourse" (Beard 1972b, 106). Meanwhile, masturbation inevitably heightened desires even as it diminished normal physical capacities. The masturbator required more stimulation to achieve satisfaction, and soon simple self-abuse would fail to gratify. He began to crave ever more perverse activities, and, in his "dread of intercourse," he turned to his own sex. Thus the masturbator eventually would become an insatiable effeminate pervert.[96]

In the worst cases, these perverts became delusional. They took on women's names and dress. Some even insisted that they really were women. This was monomania, a form of insanity that was incurable.[97] In less advanced cases, the pervert understood that he was perverted, although he might enjoy his perverse indulgences so much that he did not want to be cured. In fact, Beard believed most sex perverts fell into this category: "Cases of sexual perversion are very much more frequent than is supposed; but they are rarely studied by scientific men, and only in exceptional cases do they consult scientific men. This class of people do not wish to get well" (Beard 1972b, 101). Beard compares them to opium eaters on this point.

Masturbating women were subject to this same pattern of indifference, fear, and perversion. As James Kiernan writes, "The female masturbator of this type usually becomes excessively prudish, despises and hates the opposite sex, and frequently forms a furious attachment for another woman, to whom she unselfishly devotes herself" (Kiernan 1888, 172). Kiernan links this behavior to necrophilia and vampirism. But the outcome of masturbation was not simply uncontrollable perverse desire and self-debasement in ignoble practices. The effects in both sexes were constitutional, according to Beard: "The subjects of these excesses go through the stages of indifference and of fear, and complete the circle; the sex is perverted; they hate the opposite sex, and love their own; men become women, and women men, in their tastes, conduct, character, feelings, and behavior" (Beard 1972b, 106). Through masturbation, individuals virtually changed their sex. What greater threat could there be to Nordic masculinity?

Obviously, for men this was an evolutionary step backward, and thus it was a loss not only for the individual but also for the entire race in its journey toward world domination. We might imagine that for women, though, sexual "inversion" was an evolutionary step forward, since men were held to be higher on the evolutionary scale than women of any race. But not so. In fact, of course, these masturbating monsters did not actually rid themselves of their original anatomical sex before taking on the traits of the other; consequently, they merely blurred the lines between the sexes in their conduct and physiology and thus became a sort of hybrid or third sex. This blurring was itself degenerate, for sexual differentiation was widely believed to a product of advanced evolution. Krafft-Ebing asserts this as a matter of stage setting for his *Psychopathia Sexualis:* "The secondary sex characteristics differentiate the two sexes; they present the specific male and female types. The higher the anthropological development of the race, the stronger these contrasts between man and woman, and vice versa" (Krafft-Ebing 1965, 28).

Similar comments abound in biological, sexological, and medical literature. Savages were much less sexually differentiated than civilized Victorian ladies and gentlemen, the experts asserted. Native American females, for example, had coarse features and physical strength that approached the masculine. The same could be said of African females and American Negresses. Even in somewhat more advanced races—such as the Chinese and the Jew—sexual difference was less apparent than in the refined Nordic race.[98] Kiernan employed this common belief in his study of sexual perversion in 1888: "The original bi-sexuality of the ancestors of the race, shown in the rudimentary female organs of the male, could not fail to occasion functional, if not organic, reversions when mental or physical manifestations were interfered with by disease or congenital defect. The inhibitions on excessive action to accomplish a given purpose, which the race has acquired through centuries of evolution, being removed, the animal in man springs to the surface. Removal of these inhibitions produces, among other results, sexual perversions."[99] Once the patient's will-power or reason was compromised by masturbation or degenerative disease, "reversion" to the primordial bestial type would be the result. Female inverts, therefore—with their husky voices, educational ambitions, and incredibly enlarged clitorises—were just as evolutionarily retrograde as their mincing male counterparts, and in their lusty, predatory pursuit of weak-willed white woman-flesh, they were every bit as dangerous to the future of the Nordic race.[100]

The slide from masturbation to homosexuality seems bizarre from a twenty-first-century perspective.[101] However, that is partly because current definitions of masturbation are very narrow compared to the definitions operative in the nineteenth century. We think of masturbation as self-stimulation only, accomplished with the hand or perhaps with an object held in the hand. But consider this textbook definition of masturbation from 1896: "venereal orgasm by means of the hand, the tongue, or any kind of body by one's self or another person" (Gibson 1997, 116). The war on masturbation was not, in fact, confined to the "solitary sin"; it included attacks on what we would call mutual masturbation and oral sex.[102] By mid-twentieth-century standards, some nineteenth-century "masturbators" subject to these dramatic social and medical interventions were not actually masturbating; they were committing homosexual acts and would have been considered homosexuals.[103] By nineteenth-century definitions, however, they remained onanists, not inverts, until they graduated from mutual masturbation, fellatio, or cunnilingus to anal intercourse or tribadism, or when their appearances or manners were judged to be gender-transgressive.

There were two categories of inverts. First, there were those whose condition was a result of self-induced degeneracy through willful vice. These despicable individuals should be punished to the full extent of the law unless they had already passed into the stage of incurable monomania. However, increasingly influenced by the personal disclosures of inverts themselves, many nineteenth-century physicians began to believe there was a second group. George Beard, for example, held that "when the sexual debility becomes organized in families, then children may be born with this tendency" (Beard 1972b, 107). Similarly, Krafft-Ebing noted that some inversion appears to be congenital and that the degeneracy that produces sexual inversion is heritable (Krafft-Ebing 1965, 188). Studies of hermaphrodites demonstrated that male and female sex organs could sometimes be mixed together in a single body. We know that some people are born with the gonads of one sex but genitalia characteristic of the other, many physicians reasoned, so maybe some people are born with the gonads and genitalia of one sex but the brain and neurological system of the other. They may look like normal males or normal females, but neurologically they are hermaphrodites.[104]

Whether congenital or acquired, if degeneration was so far advanced that monomania had set in, lifelong confinement was the only course of action that made any sense. It wouldn't do to have monomaniacal sexual inverts running around loose, especially with a population of fragile white people in the throes of a difficult evolutionary advance that many were ill-prepared to negotiate. But it might not be fair to punish congenital inverts, many physicians and sexologists believed, because their actions were not truly voluntary. As James Kiernan put it, "There can be no legal responsibility where free determination of the will is impaired" (1892, 185). Congenital inverts were naturally weak of will, lacking in "nervous force," unable to resist the perverse urges that their degenerate condition aroused. Such individuals might undergo episodic periods of organically produced sexual furor during which they were entirely devoid of self control. (He does not say whether inverts ever believe themselves to be werewolves, but the similarity to Howard's 1903 description of the uneducable Negro is unmistakable.) The question was how to identify these individuals before they did any damage and eliminate the danger they posed without compromising the justice system by punishing people whose actions were totally involuntary. Thus began an entire neuropsychiatric industry—data collection and classification leading to establishment of signs and procedures by which forensic experts could recognize a genuine sex pervert when they saw one.

This was especially important because when the law took hold of sexual inverts without sound psychiatric advice, judges were apt to impose a fixed prison sentence and be done with the matter. At the end of the sentence, however, a congenital invert would still be a congenital invert. If released, he or she would simply "prey on society again." Psychiatrists had a better, more scientifically informed solution: Persons "mentally and sexually degenerate from the first, and therefore irresponsible, must be removed from society for life"

(Krafft-Ebing 1965, 335). They should not be stigmatized as criminal or subjected to punishment; they simply needed lifelong psychiatric care, and society needed protection from their morbid influence.

Neurologists and psychiatrists both in Europe and in the United States tended to agree on this point. Edward Mann, medical super-intendent of New York's Sunnyside Sanitarium for Diseases of the Nervous System, held that many cases of sexual inversion were congenital atavisms: "There is very often a true congenital moral deprivation with strong animal propensities, which makes a person practically insane from birth. . . . There is an entire perversion of the moral principle and there are no good or honest sentiments" (1892, 272). Mann's definition of insanity was more commodious than most, but his practical conclusion was the same: a penitentiary stint cannot reform these people. Even if they are not accused of any crime, Mann believed, sexual inverts must be institutionalized, because insane people belong in insane asylums, and all sexual inverts are insane. Sexual inversion is "an abnormal state, in which there is a morbid perversion of the natural feelings, affections, inclinations, habits, moral dispositions and natural impulses, without any remark-able disorder or defect of the intellect or knowing or reasoning facul-ties, and without delusions. It seems to be a reasoning monomania and sometimes an erotomania. The conduct is affected more than the conversation, but the patient is none the less insane" (Mann 1893, 271). Furthermore, these insane sex perverts should be institutional-ized because they can induce perversion in sane but weak-willed or immature individuals and will do so if given half a chance (1893, 274). G. Frank Lydston concurs: "All incurable victims should be permanently removed from our social system. They are sources of moral contagion and promoters of sexual crime to whom the right to remain in society should be denied" (1904, 421).

That is to say, sexual inverts recruit. As Krafft-Ebing noted, many inverts whose condition is acquired rather than congenital got the way they are, not merely by making depraved, self-indulgent choices (which they did, and for which we must condemn them), but also by becoming the prey of congenital inverts. As so many physicians of the time pointed out, middle- and upper-class white men, with their newly evolved and relatively weak hereditary traits for civil-ity and their highly refined, tightly integrated nervous systems, were very fragile creatures. In their high-stress positions as the captains of industry and the inventors of the future of mankind, they were really quite vulnerable. Especially in youth and young bachelorhood, they might succumb to the influences of hardened, manipulative inverts and engage in mutual or oral masturbation. Without intervention, the situation could escalate. They could lose their manhood and be lost to the Race. Perhaps even more frightening was the specter of the female invert preying upon the delicate flower of white womanhood, offering not only the attention and caresses her suitors or young husband might not have the time to provide but also dubious opportunities for excitement such as intellectual conversation, a college education, · or a serious role in a movement for political or social reform. Sexual inverts were sexual predators; for the sake of the future of the Race, they had to be stopped.

Although there were dissenters, many sexologists believed that white female inverts were particularly intelligent and cunning.[105] They had masculine brains, after all—not quite white male brains, but brains like those of males of lower races, the Chinese for instance.[106] Like male inverts, mental defectives, and savages, they also had heightened sex drives. "The sexual life of individuals thus organized manifests itself, as a rule, abnormally early, and thereafter with abnormal power" (Krafft-Ebing 1965, 223). Female inverts of all races were usually classified as either nymphomaniacs or erotomaniacs.[107] Either way, like all black men and women, they were sexually insatiable. When they found a white woman who was neurasthenic or suggestible, they would not hesitate to entice her into a sexual relationship that would drag her down the path on which their own primitive or degenerate natures had already set them.

A surprising number of white women were vulnerable to same-sex seduction, according to the experts. That they didn't often succumb had more to do with external circumstances than with their own potentials and inclinations. Krafft-Ebing believed that most white women who began life with a tendency toward inversion (at least those of the middle and upper classes) were saved from expression of it by the constraints of Victorian feminine education.

> I have through long experience gained the impression that inverted sexuality occurs in woman as frequently as in man. But the chaster education of the girl deprives the sexual instinct of its predominant character; seduction to mutual masturbation

is less frequent; the sexual instinct in the girl begins to develop only when she is, with the advent of puberty, introduced to the society of the other sex, and is thus naturally led primarily into hetero-sexual channels. All these circumstances work in her favour, often serve to correct abnormal inclinations and tastes, and force her into the ways of normal sexual inter-course. (Krafft-Ebing 1965, 262–63)

This fact explained the high frequency of frigidity in married women, he believed; frigid women were latent inverts, saved from degener-ate (but satisfying) sexual expression by the strictures of Victorian upbringing. All would be well unless such a lady came into contact with an irrepressible invert who appealed to her dark side. In that event, Krafft-Ebing warned, "we find situations analogous to those which have been described as existing in men afflicted with 'acquired' antipathic sexual instinct."[108] Including both supposedly congenital and supposedly acquired inversion, he provides a list of "possible sources from which homosexual love in woman may spring":

1. Constitutional hypersexuality impelling to automasturba-tion. This leads to neurasthenia and its evil consequences, to anaphrodisia in the normal sexual intercourse so long as *libido* remains active.

2. Hypersexuality also leads for want of something better to homosexual intercourse (inmates of prisons, daughters of the high classes of society who are guarded so very carefully in their relations with men, or are afraid of impregnation,—this latter group is very numerous). Frequently female servants are the seducers, or lady friends with perverse sexual inclinations, and lady teachers in seminaries.

3. Wives of impotent husbands who can only sexually excite, but not satisfy, woman, thus producing in her unsatisfied desire, recourse to masturbation, pollutions of a woman, neurasthe-nia, nausea for coitus, and ultimately disgust with the male sex in general.

4. Prostitutes of gross sensuality who, disgusted with the inter-course with perverse and impotent men by whom they are used for the performance of the most revolting sexual acts, seek compensation in the sympathetic embrace of persons of their own sex. These cases are of very frequent occurrence. (Krafft-Ebing 1965, 263)

In sum, then, girls who masturbate, girls who are sequestered from male attention, girls who are afraid to have sex for fear of pregnancy,

wives whose husbands are poor lovers, and women whose male partners force them to do disgusting things are likely to turn willingly
to any female invert in the vicinity. No wonder Victorian physicians
feared the lurking presence of the atavistic, Chinaman-brained white
female invert![109] Virtually every girl and woman they knew was a
latent case of inversion just waiting to happen!

With these strokes, by the last decade of the nineteenth century,
psychiatrists and neurologists painted the portrait of the homosexual
predator, both male and female. This person was degenerate, sexually
insatiable, in some descriptions insane and in some savagely atavistic,
but in all cases not governed by reason or moral principle, and able to
pass his or her condition to others through both heredity and entice-
ment analogous to infection. Obviously such a person was a threat
to the biological integrity of the Race and to the continued evolution
of Civilization. Equally obviously, the threat posed was basically the
same as that posed by the menacing imbecile and the savage Negro
in the throes of his or her periodic *furor sexualis*. What was at stake
was the purity of the Race and its fitness for survival. All these sexual
predators were vectors of genetic pollution, conduits of abnormality
and defect, pipelines for impurity. They all had to be neutralized.

Declaration of War against the Homosexual Predator

As many commentators have noted over the years, medical and
social scientific discourse does not equal popular perception. But there
is plenty of evidence to suggest that it was not long before this portrait of the newly christened Homosexual, male and female, found its
way into the popular imagination as a sexual predator and menace
to civilization alongside the Black Rapist and the Syphilitic Whore.
One of the first widely discussed cases was that of Alice Mitchell, who
murdered her lover Freda Ward in 1892. The front page of the *New
York Times* on January 26 carried the headline: "A Most Shocking
Crime/A Memphis Society Girl/Cuts a Former Friend's Throat" (Katz
1983, 223). Newspapers all over the country covered the story for the
next six months, throughout the investigation and trial. Mitchell and
Ward had been involved in a "lesbian love affair" and had planned
to elope, with Mitchell posing as a man. When Ward withdrew from
the relationship and returned her engagement ring, Mitchell resolved
to kill her. "I would rather she were dead than separated from me
living," Mitchell stated (Katz 1983, 224). In July 1892, Alice Mitchell
was declared incompetent to stand trial and was remanded to an

asylum. The defense had argued that she suffered from hereditary degeneration, despite her membership in a reputable Memphis family. "Mitchell represented an atavistic and primitive disposition that defied civilized behavior and that manifested itself in an innate propensity to lust, immorality, and criminality," historian Jennifer Terry writes. "The fact that she behaved like an uncivilized man was itself evidence of her lunacy" (Terry 1999, 86). This case brought female sexual inversion to the attention of thousands of newspaper readers across the United States and forged a link in their minds between homosexuality, homicidal mania, and regression to earlier stages of evolution—not to mention the ever-popular threat to white womanhood.[110] Other well-publicized events over the next twenty years would consolidate that link. The 1895 trial of Oscar Wilde received a tremendous amount of press coverage in the United States. Wilde was portrayed as decadent and degenerate as well as sexually inverted and was denounced as a privileged dandy who used his wealth and social position to purchase the favors of working-class boys. His effete effeminacy, like Alice Mitchell's atavistic virility, was constantly foregrounded.

Still, these sensational stories chronicled seemingly isolated events; sexual inverts, predatory and murderous though they may be, were surely very rare creatures. Most of the people who engaged in perverted sex acts were just ordinary low life—Negroes, immigrants, tramps, imbeciles, epileptics, the urban poor.[111] Some of them probably were congenital sexual inverts; the line between the two sexes was not very hard-and-fast among them to begin with. But the idea that sexual inverts might exist in large numbers among (and poised to prey upon) the better classes of white people was not something that occurred to the average white person who considered himself or herself a member of the better classes.

Peter Boag has argued that the homosexual predator, perceived as a pervasive social threat conceptually separate from the blanket threat of low-life vice and degeneracy, dates back to 1912 and the eruption of the Portland YMCA scandal. In that year a routine arrest led police to uncover an entire subculture of middle-class white homosexual men, involving not only dozens of upstanding citizens of Portland but also men in cities up and down the West Coast and inland as far as Walla Walla, Washington. It came to light that many of their contacts were made through the local YMCA and that many liaisons involved teenaged boys. Subsequent trials, covered by newspapers throughout the Pacific Northwest, introduced readers to the theories and vocabularies of Richard von Krafft-Ebing and Havelock Ellis. In the aftermath, there were loud calls for more and better sex education in colleges and public schools to make sure that white boys and young men understood the risks and were prepared to avoid these dangers.[112]

Similar subcultures were discovered in subsequent years. In 1918 more than thirty arrests were made in San Francisco, and further investigation would likely have produced more, except that it was called off when the names of several prominent men began to come up in interrogations (Loughery 1998, 5). In 1919 scandal broke out in the navy town of Newport, Rhode Island, implicating scores of servicemen as well as local residents. Trials stretched into 1920 and eventually resulted in hearings in the U.S. Senate (Loughery 1998, 11).

By the time Radclyffe Hall's *The Well of Loneliness* went on trial for obscenity in 1929, Americans—at least those living in larger cities—were well aware of the existence of homosexual subcultures and the people who populated them. Throughout the 1930s, "lurid and morbid stories of homosexuality filled the tabloid press and became common in cheap, popular fiction" (Terry 1999, 189). New York mayoral candidate Fiorello La Guardia promised to raise Depression-era property values by cleaning up the city; as mayor shortly thereafter, he authorized police crackdowns on everything that might be construed as homosexual, including cross-dressing and cabaret performances that included so-called "pansy acts." Hundreds of homosexual men and women were rounded up in raids on bars and clubs.[113]

In 1935 New York's Committee for the Study of Sex Variants was established. Its chair was Eugen Kahn, the leading U.S. authority on psychopathy. Members included psychologist Lewis Terman, psychiatrist Adolph Meyer, gynecologist Robert Latou Dickinson, and physical anthropologist Earnest Hooten.[114] The committee sponsored an extensive empirical study of homosexuality resulting in *Sex Variants: A Study of Homosexual Patterns,* a two-volume work written by psychiatrist George Henry. Among its conclusions were the following: "Society must protect itself by classifying sex variants as soon as it is possible to do so" (Henry 1941, 1025). Young people should be screened and their relationships carefully monitored so that sex variants are identified before they have a chance to influence anyone around them. Sex education should begin in infancy so that normal children are able to recognize and protect themselves against these people. "Artistic tastes, gentler manners, or other special characteristics on the part of a man or unusual self-assurance and aggressiveness on the part of a woman suggest sex variant tendencies" (1941, 1027). Children must be warned away from men with style and imagination and women with any potential for leadership. Sex variants are typically gender transgressive, the report emphasized. Masculinized females (many of whom have enlarged clitorises, which Dickinson took the trouble to examine closely and sketch for inclusion in the volume)[115] take an aggressive attitude toward society and are intolerant of the female role in marriage and childrearing. But gender transgression may not be readily apparent, Henry cautioned; feminized males may overcompensate by striving for virility through cruelty and tyranny or may engage in "aggressive conflict with society" (1941, 1024). In any case, these people are dangerous. They threaten the very foundation of Civilization.

Homosexual scandals and descriptions of lurid murders apparently involving homosexual lust abounded in the popular press from the late 1930s onward.[116] Experts such as Dr. David Henry Keller, interviewed in *Time* magazine, called for strong prophylactic measures: psychiatric study of every juvenile offender (apparently regardless of his or her crime), rapid trials, no bail or parole, no suspended sentences, creation of a "farm-hospital-prison" in every state where sex offenders could "be kept for life and forced to earn their own maintenance," and castration of all persons committed to such institutions ("Pedophilia" 1937, 44). Estelle Freedman notes that between 1937 and 1940, and again between 1949 and 1955, the *New York Times* published an average of forty articles per year on sex crimes; a number of prominent national magazines did so as well, brandishing headlines such as "Queer People," "Sex Psychopaths," and "Terror in Our Cities" (Freedman 1989, 205). Not all of these stories focused on homosexuality, but many did. And in any case, the lines between various forms of sexual psychopathy were very blurred, as the opening paragraph of a 1949 *Newsweek* article demonstrates: "The sex pervert, whether a homosexual, an exhibitionist, or even a dangerous sadist, is too often regarded merely as a 'queer' person who never hurts anyone but himself. Then the mangled form of some victim focuses public attention on the degenerate's work. And newspaper headlines flare for days over accounts and feature articles packed with sensational details of the most dastardly and horrifying of crimes."[117] Homosexuals were indistinguishable from any other sort of "queer," and horrific violence was an ever-present possibility.

As a result of this general education in sex criminology, by the mid-1950s homosexuality was virtually synonymous with sexual predation. And images of homosexuality changed little in the 1960s and 70s, despite the Stonewall Riots and Gay Liberation. The myth of the homosexual predator lurking in the shadows was still alive and well enough to fuel campaigns such as Anita Bryant's 1977 effort to repeal civil rights in Dade County, Florida, with the slogan "Save Our Children" and State Senator John Briggs's move to prohibit employment of gay and lesbian teachers in California public schools (Loughery 1998, chap. 21). In the 1980s, gay men were branded as the source of HIV, not simply its victims. In the 1990s, the possibility that the United States might allow openly gay men and women to serve in the military elicited widespread verbalization of fears that "normal" soldiers would then be subject to rape in showers and barracks. And despite years of social scientific studies showing that most children who are sexually abused are girls who suffer at the hands of men with intimate access to them in their own homes (e.g., fathers, step-fathers, uncles), American parents began the twenty-first century with the firm conviction that their children's worst enemies were lesbian feminists and homosexual priests.

Predators in Perspective

It is hardly necessary to assert that the most pervasive image of the homosexual in our culture is that of the sexual predator—the lurking, child-molesting, virgin-corrupting, disease-spreading pervert. We all live with that image even if we don't subscribe to it. We may have laughed when Matthew Shepard's murderers attempted to apply that label to their five-foot-two-inch, 105-pound victim, but we recognized the ploy, and we knew that many Americans would believe it. For many Americans believe that all homosexuals are sexual predators even if they are too small, weak, out-gunned, and out-numbered to protect themselves against their intended victims' outrage. Perhaps the only way to rid ourselves of this image's influence is to see it in the context of its history alongside the images of the imbecilic sex criminal, the black rapist, and the Jezebel or syphilitic, feebleminded whore.

Although these latter figures arose in disparate social, political, and professional contexts, they are remarkably similar. These creatures are, either continually or episodically, outside the governance of reason. Their affliction in every case is a matter of development—either faulty, arrested, or retrograde. They cannot be assimilated to society both because they cannot manage their own behavior well enough to function within its civil constraints and because they pose a biological threat to it in the form of contagion and corruption of germ plasm. The predatory homosexual, whether male or female, is their cousin, formed in the same lineage and carrying the same taints. For the sake of national security and the future of the human race and civilization as we know it—in other words, in the name of Anglo-Saxon world domination—all these people had to be segregated from the rest of the population. If they were outside our national boundaries, we had to close our borders to them. If they were already inside and we needed their labor, we either crowded them into ghettos or prisons or confined them in work camps and warehouses misnamed "asylums."

These mythic predatory figures were in fact all very much the same, even if the real flesh and blood faces and bodies that instantiated them varied in color, gender, and age. They were all the haunting presence of the savage ancestor, the bestial atavism, the throwback to an uncivilized past. They had no place in that bright and shining future that evolution promised. They would be surpassed, laid to rest, buried.

It was a racial dream inspired by three hundred years of technological innovation and imperialist conquest and suffused with a science that took development to be the foundation and meaning of life. As a racial dream, a dream that was to be made reality through the willpower and work of the dreamers, sexuality was its primary tool. Along with genocide, sexuality was the main medium through which populations, races, the Race could be shaped.

That science lost its status as truth in the 1930s, a story the next chapter will trace. But the dream lived on. So did the mechanisms and alliances that had been put in place during that great rush of Anglo-Saxon self-assurance: the carceral system and all its peripheral apparatus of surveillance, the sex-saturated nuclear family, a social welfare system that was all about the welfare of "society" and not at all about the welfare of the weak, the poor, or the disabled. By that time, three generations of Americans—of all descriptions—had been taught the tenets of white supremacy from the cradle. Their teachers had been scientists, physicians, scholars and educators, civic leaders, clergymen, even presidents. In the process, they had been taught that sexuality—procreation and heredity, public health, and child rearing and family life, as well as gender roles, bodily pleasures, and personal identity—lay at the base of all that they held or should hold dear and that the world as they knew it might come to an end if they or those around them were to deviate from prescribed sexual norms.

The science receded. But the husks and shells it left in place— the armor and weaponry it had constructed for itself to aid in its advance—remained, ready to be donned and wielded by anyone who could maneuver into position. Racism, even stripped of its scientific logic, still presented a formidable front, as John Lewis and Hosea Williams and Amelia Boynton Robinson well knew, standing on the Edmund Pettus Bridge in 1965. Scientifically grounded or not, it could still exercise a profound influence over all aspects of public and personal life. And it could still be deadly. The next two chapters show the ways in which its effects extended through the twentieth century and into the twenty-first in the lives of all Americans, but especially in the lives of those deemed abnormal.

FIVE

MANAGING EVOLUTION

RACE BETTERMENT, RACE
PURIFICATION, AND THE
AMERICAN EUGENICS MOVEMENT

Sexuality came into conceptual existence in nineteenth-century medicine as an essential source of vitality and a common seat of disease. A healthy sexuality made for a healthy body and a healthy mind; likewise, a diseased, defective, or arrested sexuality posed serious physical and mental problems and risks. Simultaneously, in nineteenth-century anthropology, sexuality appeared as the impetus for familial life and thus the ground of civil society, the biological force that brought people together and informed their emotional, moral, and civic relationships.[1] Rarified almost to the point of invisibility, yet constantly present and all-pervasive, sexuality was both indispensable for physiological and social order, and awesome in its destructive potential. As industrializing nation-states consolidated their power throughout the nineteenth century, not merely the birth rate or the infant mortality rate but the sexuality of their populations in all of its many manifestations became a central focus of administrative concern.

The issue was bodies—their strength, their productivity, their capacities, their circulation. For a nation-state to maintain and better its position vis-à-vis other nation-states politically and economically, the bodies of its people—its soldiers, its laborers, its mothers—had to be healthy, variously skilled, and mentally competent. Children had to be trained and educated. Workers had to be induced to follow rigid schedules and to conform their habits and desires as well as their muscles and nerves to the demands of increasingly sophisticated machines. Contagion had to be controlled. At the local level of institutions and practices, these projects were multiple and required creation of and experimentation with various disciplinary regimes—medical protocols, pedagogical techniques, systems of rewards and punishments, and so forth. At the national level of policy and planning, these projects often blended together and required statistical projections and management of populations. While physicians aimed to rid each patient of disease, public health officers aimed to maintain acceptable mortality and morbidity rates. While teachers aimed to teach every pupil to read, government statisticians and policy makers aimed to maintain an optimal degree of popular literacy. These levels constantly interacted: disciplinary strategies set the limits on policy options, while policies underwrote disciplinary strategies. New techniques changed the statistical landscape at times, and population shifts demanded new techniques. But certainly by the end of the nineteenth century, these differing levels and the technologies they developed and deployed were interlocked, forming a network of power that sought to manage the most basic functions of human life—a network that Foucault calls biopower.

But to what end? In most industrialized states, the answer was that the nation was an end in itself, to which the individual at times had to be subordinated. Still, one could ask why. What was the nation that it should demand and expect individual sacrifice? The nation could not simply be equated with the government that operated in a given territory. Nor could it be simply a set of institutionalized values, ideals, or principles. Of course it included those things—a nation needed a government and a territory and individuals through which to manifest itself. But to command patriotic loyalty, it had to transcend those things. It had to be much more than the sum of its evident parts. The nineteenth-century nation thus constructed itself as an organic entity of mythic proportion, a living tradition, a race. And the sciences of race—which by the end of the nineteenth century included evolutionary biology—lent solemn credibility to that myth.

The nation, the race, was a living thing that transcended the individuals who composed it at any given moment. But with the assimilation of evolutionary theory in the latter half of the nineteenth century, the nation became not only a living being but also an evolving being. And thus it transcended the individuals who composed it in yet another, and highly significant, way. While each individual was destined to express only the germ plasm with which he or she was endowed at conception, the nation was destined to supersede itself.

The individual man Moses would not live to see the Promised Land, but with discipline and perseverance, the Children of Israel could. Similarly, the current generation of individuals would not achieve evolutionary perfection, but with diligence and sacrifice, the nation could. The nation, not the individual, was the subject of the great epic narrative of evolution.

Of course, the nation in this sense—the living race—was always an abstraction at best. Nowhere was that more evident than in America. The United States was obviously not a nation, demographically speaking. England might claim to be English, with a smattering of Scots and Celts. Frenchmen might wax poetic about being French.[2] These terms meant something more than just citizenship or the geographical accident of birth. They meant tradition, character, lineage, blood. These were also abstractions, of course, but their longevity gave them plausibility. Undeniably, however, the United States was a mere conglomerate, an amalgam of "nations." It was a legal rather than an historic and organic entity, a government created by something like agreement or contract among several different sets of constituencies and imposed on many more. One's heart could swell when contemplating making a sacrifice for France or when called upon to do one's duty for England. But for the United States? There was no tradition stretching back through the ages, no singular heritage of language and custom; the United States was a creature of documents, not of blood. What was there to be loyal to? What was there to love? What was there to inspire self-sacrifice?

Many historians have written of the American desire for a distinct national identity in the nineteenth century. For some Americans this desire took the form of a drive to develop a distinctly American art or literature. For others it took the form of a drive to create an educational system with universities that would rival the best in France and Germany. But by 1900 many Americans, including soon-to-be-President Theodore Roosevelt, had turned to scientific racism to provide the United States with a sense of national identity. Scientific racism enabled a narrative of Anglo-Saxon territorial expansion that made the founding population racially continuous with a national past set in the northernmost regions of Europe. There *was* a nation, the Nordic nation. And the United States, including its institutions of government, was its creation, a civil society made possible through the mechanisms of biological inheritance and natural selection.[3] The others—the Cherokees, the Africans, the immigrants from Ireland, Poland, China, Italy, and so forth—were Americans in law only. They were part of the citizenry (or, at least, the population), but they were not part of the nation. Evolution dictated, however, that someday the citizenry and the nation would be identical. The Indians and the Negroes would be extinct. Immigrant labor would be minimal and too low-wage to enable immigrants to pay the poll tax and vote. Nordics would populate as well as own and administer the entire territory. The biological promise handed down by Darwin would be fulfilled.

Meanwhile, state officials and professional administrators of all sorts faced the difficult task of governing a conglomerate mass and shaping it into a nation-state that could compete successfully with the great nation-states of the world. The issue, once again, was bodies—distributing them across territory, extracting labor from them, limiting their consumption of resources or increasing their consumption of commodities, disciplining them for greater things. By the turn of the twentieth century, the primary means for managing bodies—both for survival and material success in the short run and for the sake of that glorious Anglo-Saxon future—was through their sexuality. This was so not only because it mattered a great deal which bodies reproduced and how often and because pursuit of genital pleasures brought bodies into close contact and thus spread disease, but also because sexuality was developmental. As a temporal, functional unfolding, sexuality could not only be regulated; it could be cultivated, intensified, and redirected. By means of sexuality, an Anglo-Saxon nation-state could be formed and strengthened—an Anglo-Saxon nation-state the likes of which had never been seen before, a national superpower that could dominate and impose Anglo-Saxon order and values upon the entire world. Sexuality was the invention, the technological apparatus, that would enable scientific racism to operationalize itself as the eugenics movement.

Development was the fundamental concept in virtually every human science of the day—biology, medicine, psychology, anthropology, sociology, criminology. Reality was development—patterns of change that could be measured, projected, and normed. Management of developmental processes involved elucidating these norms and then determining the means and extent to which normal curves could be altered to maximize whatever was identified as the good. Foucault

calls this way of thinking and approaching the world "normalization." At the level of population, normalization is a matter of enacting
policies to alter statistical norms—for example, mortality rates, crime
rates, migration rates. At the level of local institutions, normalization
is a matter of identifying abnormal individuals and then, to the extent
possible, disciplining abnormal bodies to approximate the existing
norms—for example, to exercise and eat so as to maintain a body
within established size parameters, to acquire a skill in a designated
amount of time, to enact a gender-appropriate self-presentation.[4] All
such undertakings rest on the notion that reality is developmental,
constantly changing but in predictable ways. Normalizing management amounts to harnessing developmental force and bending it in
the direction desired.

Sexuality was the name of a kind of natural force in the normalizing discourses of the late nineteenth and twentieth centuries, a very
powerful force animating much of human life and culture. As such,
it had an essential role to play in national unity and competitive success. It created familial bonds and community cohesion. It insured
generational continuity. These were natural processes. But with a little
ingenuity, natural forces could be harnessed; developmental processes
could be intensified or redirected to serve almost any human purpose.
People are motivated by sexual desire. The more intense the desire,
the greater their motivation. It was a matter of exciting desire in the
right contexts and attaching it to the proper objects—heterosexual
partners, sleek automobiles, the plunder and annexation of weaker
countries. People are also motivated by fear, and fear could be associated with sexuality in ways that would augment desire and focus it. It
was a matter of exciting fear and attaching it to the proper objects—
black rapists, lurking lesbians, flaccid penises, being thought queer—
thus creating a desire for protection and a willingness to purchase it in
exchange for money, privacy, independence, or freedom of movement.
The manipulation of a thoroughly sexualized social environment was
a highly effective and relatively inexpensive way of managing bodies
and populations.

As Foucault tells us, Victorian attention to sexuality was never
really about inhibition or enforced conformity, even though some of
the strategies employed were extremely repressive at times. Sexuality—
both normal and abnormal—was to be *used*. And to be used to its
full potential, it had to be well dispersed, intensified, and carefully

attended. This notion was nowhere more clearly expressed than in Dr. Mary Streichen Calderone's 1963 statement at the founding of the Sex Information and Education Council of the United States. "We must block our habit of considering sex as a 'problem' to be 'controlled,'" she said. "Emphasis must be on sex as a vital force to be utilized" (Moran 2000, 162). Abnormal bodies had a particularly important role to play in these projects. Not only were they the targets that kept many disciplinarians in lucrative business, but they were also the danger to which authorities pointed whenever they needed the docile cooperation of purportedly normal people—which of course was virtually all the time. This is how "sexual perversion" came to be seemingly so widespread and widely recognized at the turn of the century. It served, Foucault tells us, as both the target and the point of departure for organized exercises of power at every social level.

This was also how race, perceived now as a manifestation of evolutionary development (or its relative lack), came to be thoroughly sexualized. If sexuality lay at the foundation of the family, morality, and civil society, then the problem with inferior races—evident in their generally acknowledged failure to maintain stable family life, abide by clear standards of morality, and govern themselves—was a problem with their sexuality. Racial difference, thus, was sexual difference. The (highly idealized) Victorian middle-class white heterosexual male head of household was the norm. Whatever departed from that norm was obviously abnormal. That abnormality might be anatomical—and those huge vaginas, clitorises, and penises on Africans were testimony that it was—but more importantly, it was physiological, neurological, and psychological. With their unrefined nervous systems, the backward races could not experience true erotic connection as Anglo-Saxons could; they could only experience animal urges, drives, furors, and paroxysms. As Julius Carter puts it, citing in particular G. Frank Lydston and Havelock Ellis, "Book after book on sexuality includes passages or entire chapters explaining the development of the richly satisfying modern love union in contrast to the 'sensory and motor sluggishness,' erotic inadequacy, and emotional poverty of relationships among 'primitive' peoples. . . . The erotic inadequacy of savages was the result of their closeness to the animal realm. To Progressive-era sexologists, animality meant not passion, but rather simple, shallow desires, felt in seasonal cycles and unmixed with affection" (Carter 1997, 158). Compared to the Anglo-Saxon standard of evolutionary development, all sexuality among inferior races was primitive, animalistic, and (for duly evolving humans) abnormal. The fact that so much homosexual activity could be found among those races was just more confirmation of what was already known.[5]

Sexuality was crucial to the establishment of national identity and the progress of the nation-state not only because it was a means for adding bodies to the population and for cementing kinship and community ties but also because it was a means for redesigning the population both as individuals and as a whole. It was good to have a large citizenry; there was military and industrial strength in numbers. But it was much more important to have a loyal, energetic, healthy, skilled population willingly placing itself under constant administrative and corporate surveillance and control. The various new and developing technologies of sexuality made that possible, so the forces within the United States that aimed to Nordicize the body politic appropriated and adapted them. By the turn of the twentieth century, sexuality as a set of administrative mechanisms and concerns was thoroughly interpenetrated with racial discourses and practices in the United States. Race and sexuality had become both conceptually and practically inseparable.

By 1900 American public discourse was all about race—racial progress, race betterment, the improvement of the race. Social problems—poverty, drug abuse, public sanitation, infant mortality, perversion, disease—all were framed as problems besetting "the Race" in its ascent to evolutionary perfection. Many of the articles and speeches that have come down to us from that time, if read in isolation, appear to be referring to the progress or improvement of the *human* race, not the white race or the Anglo-Saxon or Nordic race alone. But to most educated self-identified white Americans at the turn of the twentieth century, the future—new and improved—human race *was* the white race. Biology decreed that the others just weren't going to make it. A better human race, a more highly evolved human race, simply was a whiter human race.[6]

Hence, government and professional policy decisions made in the name of race betterment implicitly (and quite often explicitly) aimed at reducing the proportion of nonwhite people in the general U.S. population and at reducing the proportion of white people with characteristics deemed "dysgenic," such as epilepsy, alcoholism, mental deficiency, lunacy, deafness, blindness, sexual inversion, criminality, pauperism, nomadism, and a host of other traits, including a disposition to tuberculosis, syphilis, and cancer. These decisions were not seen as antithetical to letting nature take it course; they were seen, precisely, *as* nature taking its course. The U.S. government was a creature of Anglo-Saxon germ plasm. By curtailing immigration from Asia and Southern and Eastern Europe; by upholding state and local segregation laws that effectively denied African Americans education, medical care, and opportunities for material advancement; by restricting and licensing marriage; by putting "inferior" people in sex-segregated custodial institutions for the entirety of their reproductive lives; by sterilizing tens of thousands of its own citizens; by refusing to institute realistic relief programs for the sick and needy and legal protection for victims and potential victims of hate violence; and by encouraging social disdain for the disabled, the dark-skinned, and the poor, the U.S. government was fulfilling its biological mandate. People who decried such things were just sentimental fools, throwbacks to a prescientific age.

This was the intellectual and political climate in which the American eugenics movement flourished. The story of that movement is an important chapter in the story of modern racism for at least two reasons. One is that the eugenics movement united various localized racist practices into a broad network of institutions that crucially affected the lives of literally millions of people world-wide.[7] It was scientific racism operationalized at a national and global level. The other is that reaction against some aspects of the eugenics movement gave us the term *racism* and initiated a continuing public discourse about racial prejudice and bigotry that, I will argue, actually worked to mask institutionalized mechanisms of sexualized, race-driven social control. The rest of this chapter consists of a look at both those aspects of modern racism's story.

Managing Evolution

Phase I: Immigration Restrictions and Marriage Regulations

The beginnings of the American eugenics movement might be said to lie in the 1890s, with the first organized efforts to restrict immigration for reasons of biological inferiority and population

control. In 1894 three members of the Harvard class of 1889—
Prescott F. Hall, Robert DeCourcy Ward, and Charles Warren—
founded the Immigration Restriction League.[8] Their goal was to pass
legislation to prevent immigration from countries they believed were
peopled by inferior racial stock.

At least one apparently race-based restriction on immigration
already existed by that time. Twelve years earlier, in 1882, Congress
had acted to prevent Chinese residents of the United States from
becoming naturalized citizens and had suspended Chinese immigration for ten years.[9] But support for these anti-Chinese actions was
motivated by economic rather than eugenic concerns.[10] Also largely
for economic reasons, Congress had passed a law requiring immigrants to pay a head tax of fifty cents when entering at any port, and
barring immigration of convicts, lunatics, idiots, and persons likely to
become public charges. In 1891 it added persons with loathsome or
contagious diseases, dependent persons, and polygamists to the list of
those to be excluded and established a Superintendent of Immigration
to oversee medical examinations at all ports and at the Canadian and
Mexican borders. The main purpose for all of these measures was to
reduce fiscal expenditure and to protect American labor (although
eugenic arguments were beginning to be heard). In 1892 the Chinese
Exclusion Act was extended for another ten years, as it would be
again after the turn of the century.

Unlike these earlier restrictions, however, those proposed by the
Immigration Restriction League were promoted on eugenic grounds.
The League sought to bar immigration of members of certain races
as a means to protect superior American racial stock—middle- and
upper-class northeasterners of alleged Anglo-Saxon heritage—from
dilution through social and sexual interaction with less-evolved and
less-civilized peoples. In other words, as they saw things, these inferior
peoples posed a biological threat to the American population and its
reproductive potential. They lobbied Senator Henry Cabot Lodge to
introduce a literacy test for all would-be immigrants as a way to limit
entry by race on the assumption that biologically inferior races had
lower literacy rates.[11] The bill passed in 1897, but President Cleveland
vetoed it. Eventually the League—which by 1904 included among
their membership A. Lawrence Lowell, president of Harvard; William
DeWitt Hyde, president of Bowdoin College; James T. Young, director
of the Wharton School; and David Starr Jordan, president of Stanford

University—would succeed not only in establishing a literacy requirement but in creating far more formidable obstacles to immigration
(Bruinius 2006, 262–63).

The League accomplished its goals in part by allying itself with
the American Breeders Association, founded in 1903. With a grant
from the Carnegie Institution, the ABA set up the Cold Spring
Harbor Station for Experimental Evolution in 1904, placing Charles
Davenport in charge (Rosen 2004, 34). In 1909 it established a
Committee on Eugenics with David Starr Jordan as chair and with
members Davenport, Alexander Graham Bell, Vernon Kellogg, Luther
Burbank, William Earnest Castle, Adolf Meyer, H. J. Webber, and
Friedrich Woods. Their purpose was threefold: to investigate, educate, and legislate. For investigation and educational purposes, they
established the Eugenics Record Office, headed by Harry Laughlin.
As to legislation, in their mission statement, they wrote, "Society must
protect itself; as it claims the right to deprive the murderer of his life
so also it may annihilate the hideous serpent of hopelessly vicious pro-
toplasm. Here is where appropriate legislation will aid in eugenics and
in creating a healthier, saner society in the future" (in E. A. Carlson
2001, 194). One of the committee's legislative concerns was immigration restriction. When it formed a subcommittee on immigration in
1911, it formalized its already close relationship with the Immigration
Restriction League by appointing League founder Prescott Hall to
membership.

Meanwhile, in 1907, President Roosevelt reached a "Gentlemen's
Agreement" with Japan to halt Japanese immigration to the United
States (Dowbiggin 1997, 120), and Congress established an Immigration Commission to study the impact of immigrants on U.S. society.
The congressional commission had nine members, a staff of 3,000
and a budget of a million dollars for two years of fieldwork. It took
up the League's call for a literacy requirement (which was enacted ten
years later). But the immigration restriction movement got its biggest
boost in 1910 when the U.S. Public Health Service invited psychologist Henry Goddard to Ellis Island to administer his new IQ test to
immigrants. After several months of testing, Goddard reported that,
by the measure of his version of Théodore Simon and Alfred Binet's
Intelligence Quotient Test, 40 percent of Jews arriving at the port
(mostly from Eastern Europe) were feebleminded.[12] In the midst of a
general public crusade against imbecilic sexual predators and criminal

morons, opponents of immigration were up in arms. Congressman
Albert Johnson of Washington, who had been elected in 1912 on
the strength of his promise to combat the evils of foreigners, began
pushing for a legal limit on the number of people who could enter
the country. In 1919 he succeeded in capping immigration at 355,000
people per year. Quotas were set by country, based on the U.S. population in the 1910 census. But Johnson wasn't finished. As chair of
the Congressional Committee on Immigration, he held hearings on
the matter in 1920 and 1921, bringing in Dr. Harry Laughlin, superintendent of the Eugenic Records Office at Cold Spring Harbor, as
an expert witness.[13] Laughlin testified that immigrants from Russia,
Poland, Italy, and neighboring countries were disproportionately
likely to become insane or ill and to be involved in criminal activity.
He also testified that morons—persons with IQ scores that placed
them in the mental age range of eight to twelve years—are especially
difficult to detect and very dangerous:

> We find that the moron girl is highly fertile sexually. She has
> not any sexual inhibitions, as a rule, and her fecundity is lim-
> ited only by the number of children and coming in contact
> with men; that is, physiological, not social, conditions limit
> the fertility of the average female moron that is not placed in
> an institution and protected.
>
> Now, a moron can slip through the immigration sieve, as
> it exists today, pretty easily. And the moron is really a greater
> menace to our civilization than the idiot. . . . A moron comes
> before the immigration board, passes the very elementary
> tests, and is admitted. (in Bruinius 2006, 258)

Obviously inferior blood was going to be introduced into the American
population unless the races harboring these fecund moron females
were barred from entry entirely.

Spurred by this and other sobering information, Congress
passed and President Coolidge signed the Johnson-Reed Immigration
Restriction Act of 1924, which capped immigration at 150,000 per
year and stated that "the annual quota of any nationality shall be 2%
of the number of foreign-born individuals of such nationality resident
in the continental United States as determined by the United States
census of 1890."[14] In light of Laughlin's racist warnings, the 1890
census was taken as the base standard because it did not reflect the

large number of Southern and Eastern European immigrants who had arrived in the meantime and would have been counted in the census of 1920 (E. A. Carlson 2001, 260). According to President Coolidge, immigration restriction was necessary because "America must be kept American."[15]

Many eugenicists wanted restrictions on marriage as well as on immigration in the hope that by barring some classes of people from marrying they would also prevent procreation. From the 1890s through the 1920s, state legislatures passed what Matthew Lindsay has termed "a momentous series of new laws that dramatically circumscribed who was eligible to participate in the institution of marriage" (1998, 542). Marriage had always been subject to some state regulation in the United States, but before the 1870s even simple licensure was nonexistent. Courts routinely upheld the marital rights of spouses who were joined by nothing more than an oral agreement with no witnesses present. New state laws in the 1870s and 80s required licenses, registration, and ceremonies with witnesses if marital rights were to be upheld in court. But with the exception of anti-miscegenation laws and bans on consanguinity, there were still few restrictions on who could enter into the marital state until 1895 when Connecticut banned marriage and cohabitation for "feeble-minded, imbecilic, and epileptic men and women under 45 years of age" (Lindsay 1998, 542). By 1914, more than half the states barred imbeciles, idiots, lunatics, and the feebleminded (Larson 1995, 22); and by 1929, nineteen barred those with venereal disease.

Even in states where prohibitions did not exist or were minimal, however, the entrance to matrimony was closed to some. In Chicago in 1912 the Very Reverend Walter Taylor Sumner of the Protestant Episcopal Cathedral of Saints Peter and Paul declared that he and his staff would no longer marry couples not certified by a physician as "normal physically and mentally" and having "neither an incurable nor communicable disease."[16] Within two months, two hundred Chicago area clergy endorsed the health certificate plan. Sumner stated, "We seek to protect the integrity, sanctity, and future health of the home by joining in matrimony only those who are fit to propagate a normal race" (Rosen 2004, 59). Ministers in New Jersey, New York, Pennsylvania, and Massachusetts followed suit. In 1913 Wisconsin passed a law requiring medical certification for marriage.[17] By 1929 nine other states had done so as well (Lindsay 1998, 542).

Of course, as Charles Davenport pointed out, the worst sort of people will have children anyway, marriage or no marriage: "The reproduction of the feebleminded will not be, to an important degree, diminished by laws forbidding the issuing to them of marriage licenses. Most of them have weak sex-control. If it is easy and cheap to get married, they may do so; otherwise, they will have children without getting married" (in Larson 1995, 97).

Restricting marriage licensing was practically futile except as a symbolic gesture and as a tool of public education. Effective eugenic regulation of procreation would require state-imposed "sex-control"— "sex-control" for those unfit to reproduce, that is. For those deemed eugenically superior, sex was to be strongly encouraged. If anything, fertility control was what had to be banned.[18] The American Breeders Association (renamed the American Genetics Association in 1912) and many other groups worked hard to educate the Nordic populace on the importance of selectively prolific breeding and to inculcate eugenic values in the young. By 1910, eugenics was a frequent topic in magazine articles, public lectures, and even church services. By 1914, forty-four American colleges and universities offered courses in eugenics, and by 1928 the number had increased to 376 and enrolled 20,000 students (Paul 1995, 10; Selden 1999, 49). Nineteen-fourteen also saw the First National Conference on Race Betterment, which was held in Battle Creek, Michigan. American Genetics Association president John Kellogg called for the creation of awards to promote eugenic practices. As a result, state fairs throughout the 1920s routinely held "Better Baby" and "Fitter Family" contests where human beings were judged in much the same way as their prized livestock.[19]

Eugenicists were very successful at getting their views into high school and college science textbooks, including the idea that intelligent, well-educated people should have at least four and, if possible, six children.[20] Between 1914 and 1948, 87 percent of science textbooks discussed eugenics and 70 percent recommended it as a practice (Selden 1999, chap. 4). One widely used 1941 textbook contains this passage:

> The feebleminded are breeding much faster than the *mentally* fit. To meet this situation, it is necessary to have some *physical* control, thus preventing this kind of person from breeding. Two methods, one *segregation* into separate institutions for males and females, and the other *sterilization* or prevention

of breeding are possible practices. A third is by practicing *eugenics,* by having those of good physical constitutions and *mental* ability marry and have children.[21]

The author of this passage, biologist George William Hunter, published ten such textbooks for high school students between 1914 and 1941, textbooks that were used in public schools well into the postwar period.

In addition to textbook authors, high-profile professional educators were deeply involved in the eugenics movement. Besides those already mentioned—A. Lawrence Lowell, William DeWitt Hyde, James T. Young, and David Starr Jordon—Charles W. Eliot, president of Harvard was very active. Along with Jordan, Eliot was on the 1928 Central Committee of the Race Betterment Conference, as well as in the Eugenics Society of America and the Eugenics Committee of the United States (Selden 1999, 95).[22] Clergymen also spread the eugenic gospel. In 1926 the American Eugenics Society began offering monetary prizes to ministers, priests, and rabbis who gave eugenics sermons. They advertised the contest in 180 religious newspapers and many secular ones as well. The sermon topic for 1926 was "Religion and Eugenics: Does the Church Have any Responsibility for Improving the Human Stock?" Only sermons actually preached before a congregation were eligible for entry; nearly three hundred were submitted (Bruinius 2006, 235). First prize was $500.[23]

State governments cooperated in the effort to educate the youthful bearers of Nordic germ plasm. Dr. W. A. Plecker, state registrar, used the occasion of passage of Virginia's 1924 Racial Integrity Act to publish a pamphlet that was distributed to school libraries across the Commonwealth along with the text of the new law. In it he wrote:

> As each young man and young woman is the prospective head of a new family each one should use his and her highest reasoning faculties, when selecting a life mate.
>
> See by careful investigation that you are not marrying into a family containing members who are hereditarily defective physically, mentally, or morally. Remember that the 200,000 feeble-minded persons in the United States furnish one-fourth of our criminals, forty per cent of our abandoned women, and half of the inmates of our almshouses.
>
> If every intelligent young person will follow this advice ... we may expect in the next generation to have in our State

a large body of Virginians strong in body, mind and character, capable of overcoming difficulties at home, and of influencing the Nation to push to a successful finish the reforms necessary to fit us to fill the place as leader of the nations of the world.

. . . Let the young men who read this realize that the future purity of our race is in their keeping, and that the joining of themselves to females of a lower race and fathering children who shall be a curse and a menace to our State and civilization is a crime against our society, and against the purity and integrity of their future homes and the happiness of their future loved ones and of themselves. (Plecker 1924, 8–9)

Undoubtedly, the psychological impact of this sort of eugenic literature in public schools and libraries, churches, synagogues, and civic organizations was enormous.[24] For thirty years and more, middle-class white American children and young adults were inundated with this authoritative rhetoric and the values it championed. It was their moral and patriotic duty to find a suitably eugenic mate and breed, thus to save Anglo-Saxon America from what social scientist Edward A. Ross had termed in 1901 "race suicide," an ominous phrase taken up and popularized by Theodore Roosevelt, among many others.[25]

Although a number of the activists and many of the field-workers in the eugenics movement were middle-class white women, including feminists,[26] many middle-class white women quietly refused to cooperate. They delayed marriage to go to college; some did not marry at all in order to pursue careers; and even those who did marry often defied the law and practiced birth control.[27] If the feminists didn't recruit them into spinsterhood, the lurking lesbians did. Meanwhile, the Negroes were refusing to go extinct, the Catholic dregs of Ireland and the Mediterranean lately arrived on U.S. shores were popping out squalling brats night and day, and native-born imbecilic white trash whores were screwing everything that moved and driving up the rates of feeblemindedness faster than tuberculosis and syphilis could drive it down. Something had to be done.

Phase II: Lifelong Incarceration and Sterilization for the Unfit

The movement to institutionalize the feebleminded—liberally defined so as to include virtually any person who made decisions that violated conventional notions of morality—had been underway for three decades already, as we have seen. As early as 1877, Josephine Shaw Lowell had pressed the state of New York to segregate female imbeciles to prevent them from breeding. After Goddard introduced his version of the IQ test, which was seen as an efficient way of identifying menacing imbeciles quickly, his Vineland, New Jersey, school became the national center for training young psychologists and social workers in testing methods. Over the next several years Vineland-trained social scientists were hired by local and state governments and private foundations and charities all across the country to test institutional, school, and at-large populations and to make recommendations for combating "the menace of the feebleminded" (M. Haller 1963, 100). Unsurprisingly, the verdict was unanimous in favor of institutional segregation.

The commission that the Commonwealth of Virginia established in 1914, discussed in chapter 4, was typical of these investigative panels.[28] Two of the three researchers on Virginia's commission were Vineland-trained. They followed the protocols that other, similar teams followed. They visited almshouses, reformatories, asylums, and prisons to test inmates and identify the feebleminded among them. They administered the Simon-Binet test at local schools to sample the IQ of the general population. Then they subtracted the number in institutions from their projection of the number in the general population to determine how many feebleminded people were still loose. Mark Haller describes the next step this way: "The horror of the situation could then be driven home by stories of brutal crimes and abject immorality of a few 'typical' morons and by printing pedigrees of a few degenerate families to highlight the hereditary nature of feeblemindedness" (1963, 109). The Virginia commission's report is a perfect example of this format.

The commissioners announce on page 11 that their mission is to study "the menace of the feebleminded." All of chapter 3 is devoted to a description of an elderly feebleminded woman named "Old Sal," her forty-seven filthy, wretched, disease-ridden, feebleminded progeny, and her neighbor "Peter Z" and his family, "the most vicious and immoral family in a community where virtue is not regarded as an asset." Among the other terrible things that Peter Z is guilty of—but for which he apparently was never arrested—is fathering a child by his feebleminded daughter Samantha and then burning it alive. "Peter is alleged to have said that there were too many children around the house, and so the surplus was thus eliminated" (*Mental Defectives* 1915, 18–19). This horrific story of feebleminded criminality and perversion continues for several paragraphs more until the chapter concludes with a quotation from Charles Davenport, in which he refers to feeblemindedness as "a new plague." By the end of the report, 103 pages and several prisons, reformatories, almshouses, and lunatic asylums later, it is hard to imagine any course of action other than the one the commission recommends: Lock these people away! And of course that was the recommendation from every such state commission in the country. Hereditarily defective people had to be locked up for life, not just to protect the community from their actions, which were almost unspeakably horrible in themselves, but to prevent them from burdening the tax-paying public with their worthless defective offspring and from potentially contaminating the bloodlines of the respectable people they might seduce or rape.

But lifelong institutionalization of all defective people was prohibitively expensive, despite the claim that well-managed facilities with plenty of able-bodied "defectives" could be self-supporting. In fact, no institution of this sort was ever entirely self-supporting, and those that did put inmates to work doing anything other than routine gardening, housecleaning, and care of other inmates often came under fire from labor unions and industrial competitors.

Fortunately—depending on one's perspective—technological innovations in the late nineteenth century had created a eugenic alternative: sterilization. With advances in anesthesia in the nineteenth century, it became possible to sterilize both females and males, although the first large-scale program for "a-sexualizing" women (by removing their ovaries), which was begun at Norristown Insane Asylum in Pennsylvania in 1893, had to be stopped when the fifth patient died in surgery (E. A. Carlson 2001, 204). Then, in 1897, two new procedures were introduced: vasectomy and salpingectomy.[29]

Dr. Harry Clay Sharp began performing vasectomies at Indiana's Jefferson Reformatory in 1899.[30] His stated objective was to stop masturbation and thus arrest the progress of the degeneration it allegedly initiated, but his motives certainly included eugenic ideals as well, as evidenced by his assertion that "no confirmed criminal or other degenerate ever begot a normal child" (E. A. Carlson 2001, 214). He performed more than two hundred surgeries without benefit of legal sanction, ostensibly as therapeutic procedures merely. But when the Indiana state legislature passed a eugenic sterilization law in March of 1907, Sharp began sterilizing all his inmates, whether they masturbated or not.

The new law was unsettling to many, however, and was actively opposed by the next governor, Thomas Marshall (later vice president under Woodrow Wilson). Marshall cut a deal with Sharp in 1910; he would not work aggressively to repeal the law if Sharp would simply stop performing vasectomies. Similar laws that were passed in fifteen other states over the next dozen years also faced serious challenge, and seven were struck down by state supreme courts (Bruinius 2006, 10). Eugenics activists knew they had to design a law that could withstand all possible legal objections, and then they had to push a case to the U.S. Supreme Court to clear the way for state legislatures to act.

In 1922 Dr. Albert Priddy, superintendent of the Virginia Colony for the Epileptic and Feebleminded, asked his friend Colonel Aubrey Strode, an expert in mental health legislation, to write a bill mandating nonvoluntary sterilization for the state's feebleminded. Strode realized that his bill would have to pass not just the scrutiny of Virginia's legislators and the voting public but constitutional scrutiny as well. It could not be seen as "cruel and unusual punishment," nor could it seem to pick out and mistreat a particular class of people, denying them "due process" or stripping them of "equal protection under the law." Strode studied Harry Laughlin's 1922 Model Eugenical Sterilization Law carefully and wrote a bill that not only passed the Virginia General Assembly in the 1924 session but that eventually was upheld by the U.S. Supreme Court.

Details of the story of *Buck v. Bell* are now widely available.[31] Carrie Buck was a resident of the Virginia Colony who had been declared feebleminded upon giving birth to an illegitimate child. (As a seventeen-year-old, she had been raped by the nephew of her foster parents, but the blame for immorality and thus the label of "moral defective" was placed on her.) She was committed to the colony immediately after the birth of her daughter in the spring of 1924.[32] Her mother, Emma Buck, had already been committed to the colony four years before and had been certified a moron, with a mental age of nine years on the Simon-Binet scale. Carrie's score upon admission was similar.[33] Colony doctors chose Carrie as a candidate for sterilization under Virginia's new law but then engineered a legal challenge to their decision on her behalf in order to create a test case. Aubrey

Strode, attorney for the Commonwealth, argued that Carrie Buck's condition was hereditary—as evidenced by her mother's documented feeblemindedness—and that she would pass that condition on to any children she bore, as a social worker testified that she had already done in the case of her infant daughter Vivian. The state, he asserted, had a legitimate interest in preventing the birth of such people, because they were a menace to society and a burden on the taxpayers. The U.S. Supreme Court agreed. On behalf of the eight-member majority, Chief Justice Oliver Wendell Holmes Jr. wrote: "It is better for all the world, if instead of waiting to execute degenerate offspring for crime, or to let them starve for their imbecility, society can prevent those who are manifestly unfit from continuing their kind."[34] Virginia's law having been upheld, on October 19, 1927, Dr. John Bell sterilized Carrie Buck by tubal ligation in the colony infirmary.

Buck v. Bell cleared the way for state-mandated nonvoluntary sterilization of large classes of people both inside and outside of institutions for the feebleminded. Over the next forty-five years, more than 65,000 Americans would be sterilized without their consent under state eugenics laws, 8,000 of those at the Virginia Colony alone. Tens of thousands more would be sterilized without benefit of legal procedures in states with and without laws requiring sterilization. More than half of those sterilized under state laws were female. At least a third of the state-mandated procedures were performed in California (Stern 2005, 6), where perhaps as many as three-fourths of those sterilized had been either convicted or simply "diagnosed" as "sex offenders" (M. Haller 1963, 138), a term which, in the first four decades of the twentieth century, usually meant women suspected of prostitution, although it included all the varieties of sexual predators previously discussed.[35] The largest number of legally mandated involuntary sterilizations took place in mental institutions, but eugenic sterilizations were commonplace in institutions for the mentally retarded, prisons, reformatories, hospitals, and out-patients clinics all across the country.[36]

The heyday of eugenic sterilization was the 1930s, when the vast majority of those targeted were impoverished whites like Carrie Buck.[37] In fact, at that time many institutions where sterilizations were authorized were for whites only; in many states there was little or no provision for sterilizing "defective" people of color.[38] But as the practice continued into the 1950s and a very visible and vocal black civil rights movement got underway, a growing number of the people who were forcibly sterilized were African American girls and women. Activist Fannie Lou Hamer, herself a victim of involuntarily sterilization, maintained that 60 percent of black women who passed through Sunflower City Hospital in her hometown in Mississippi were sterilized against their will and in many cases without their knowledge (Nelson 2003, 68). Hysterectomy was so common in Mississippi in the 1960s that physicians referred to it as the Mississippi Appendectomy.[39] North Carolina's Eugenics Board approved 1,620 sterilizations between 1960 and 1968. Of these, 1,023 were on black women and 56 percent on people under the age of twenty. Under North Carolina's eugenic sterilization law, a physician could declare a person permanently mentally deficient and make the decision to sterilize without a psychological examination or judicial proceeding (Nelson 2003, 72).[40] In California, where the largest number of eugenic sterilizations took place, three-fourths of those sterilized under the state eugenics law were people of color—including Latinos, Asian Americans, African Americans, and Native Americans.

State eugenics laws were not the tool most often used to sterilize girls and women in the postwar period, however. Between 100,000 and 150,000 people, mostly female, were sterilized under the auspices of federal programs. (For example, as late as 1971 the Office of Economic Development under the direction of Donald Rumsfeld recommended sterilization in cases of mental defect.) It is estimated that 90 percent of these procedures were paid for by Medicaid and that 43 percent of those sterilized were African American (Stern 2005, 201–202). Whether these federal policies were implemented for eugenic or other reasons is in most cases difficult to determine, but in at least some cases eugenic reasons played a role and eugenics laws lent support.

Federal policy took the spotlight with the case of *Relf v. Weinberger* in 1972. Twelve-year-old Minnie Lee Relf, an African American, had been sterilized as an outpatient in a Montgomery, Alabama, family planning clinic that was funded by the federal Department of Health, Education, and Welfare. Before sterilization, Relf had been given Depo-Provera shots with the consent of her mother. When Depo-Provera was discontinued because it was found to cause cancer in laboratory animals, staff at the clinic decided to sterilize Relf and her sister, whom they believed to be mentally retarded. Alabama's eugenic sterilization law did not provide for involuntary out-patient sterilization, but it did mandate involuntary sterilization of mentally defective persons upon discharge from an institution, a fact that no doubt lent weight to the idea that any at-large person whom social services deemed mentally defective should be sterilized. The clinic staff had Relf's mother, who was illiterate, place her "X" on a consent form for sterilization. Technically, then, Relf was not sterilized without consent. However, it became clear in court that consent in this and thousands of other cases was a sham. In some instances, patients or their guardians were not given correct or adequate information about the effects of the highly recommended procedure. In some instances, patients were told that they would lose their Medicaid or welfare benefits or that no doctor would treat them for any other condition if they refused the procedure. Thus "consent" was obtained either because patients were uninformed or misinformed or because they were coerced. The National Welfare Rights Organization filed suit against HEW, the Southern Poverty Law Center joined in, and in 1974 Judge Gerhard Gesell handed down a decision in *NWRO v. Weinberger,* ruling that HEW must cease funding sterilizations of minors and the mentally incompetent. Judge Gesell's ruling did not invalidate state sterilization laws, but it did withdraw federal money used to enforce many of them (Nelson 2003, 66–72).

While most sterilizations of people of color occurred after the organized American eugenics movement lost much of its public support in the late 1930s, we should not imagine that prewar eugenicists meant to target only degenerate whites. The goal was to purge America of all individuals with "bad heredity." Only thus purified would the human species—"the Race"—reach its evolutionary zenith. When Harry Laughlin talked about sterilizing ten million Americans, he meant inferior members of nonwhite races as well as inferior whites. Abnormality, deviance, weakness, defect—these were slated for elimination wherever they might be found. If it so happened that most or all nonwhites were abnormal, deviant, weak, or defective—and so it did happen, most eugenicists believed, because of the path that human evolution had already taken[41]—then obviously the agenda ultimately had to include sterilization of all or most nonwhites too, if they didn't die off on their own before the programs could be set in place.

People of color were not the primary targets of the sterilization movement between 1910 and 1940, mainly because they were the primary targets of other eugenic initiatives, such as immigration restriction and Jim Crow segregation, which was upheld as a practice by the U.S. Supreme Court in 1896, and also because powerful economic interests militated against application of some eugenic initiatives to nonwhites. For example, while eugenicists wanted to close the southern border completely to prevent any Mexicans from entering the country, Texas planters lobbied to keep the border open for migrant workers to hold down their production costs and boost their profits (Stern 2005, 74). And while some eugenicist psychiatrists wanted to build special institutions to confine and sterilize feebleminded blacks, industries that used prison labor to keep costs low and maximize profits opposed such measures because they most likely would have taken thousands of able-bodied black men off chain gangs (Larson 1995, 154). One of the reasons the United States never found the means to transport its African American population "back" to Africa in the nineteenth century as Jefferson and many others proposed was that too much money was being made off black labor, whether slave or free. The same thing was true—and true of almost all nonwhite groups—in the mid-twentieth century. As a consequence, most of the victims of forced sterilization were unemployed whites, people with disabilities, and, as the practice continued into the latter half of the century, Native Americans on reservations and women of all races subsisting on government welfare aid. Those people were not the only ones eugenicists wanted to sterilize; they were the only ones eugenicists could get away with sterilizing, the only ones who were not valuable enough to anyone with any clout to warrant protecting.

Probably too, a good many of the involuntary sterilizations performed under state eugenics laws after World War II were not really undertaken for strictly eugenic reasons. One can't help but suspect that physicians in Mississippi and North Carolina sterilized thousands of black women not so much because they believed in "bad heredity" as because they wanted to decrease the black population of their states for political reasons or because they wanted to punish individuals they saw as morally lax and they knew sterilization would inflict emotional as well as physical suffering. Eugenics laws undoubtedly became instruments of revenge in the hands of angry white physicians through the turbulent years of the civil rights movement. These suspicions are reinforced by the fact that in the 1960s and 1970s punitive sterilization bills were introduced in thirteen state legislatures—California,

Connecticut, Delaware, Georgia, Illinois, Iowa, Louisiana, Maryland, Mississippi, Ohio, South Carolina, Tennessee, and Virginia.[42]

It is undeniable that after World War II, for whatever (and perhaps varied) reasons, white middle-class citizens turned state eugenics sterilization laws against poor women of color. The point that I want to emphasize here, however, is that all these eugenic laws and practices were racist, even when they were aimed almost exclusively at white people and regardless of the motives of any individual implementers. They were racist in the same ways that virtually all efforts to manage sexuality in the late nineteenth and early twentieth centuries were racist. These laws were enacted and these practices sustained in the name of human evolution, in the name of the progress of the human race toward developmental perfection. Their explicit purpose was to eliminate defect, correct deviance, and usher the species—"the Race"—into a glorious new age of rationally managed evolutionary advancement.

As Foucault asserts, then, scientific racism was racism against the abnormal, against any individual or group that seemed out of step with the march of progress. This included all or virtually all people of color. But it also included all whites who failed to measure up to the Anglo-Saxon standard of physical, mental, and moral development—the feebleminded (the idiot, the imbecile, the moron, the moral imbecile); the mentally ill (the neurasthenic, the masturbator, the monomaniac, the sexual invert, the hysteric, the senile, the psychopath, the epileptic, the schizophrenic); the physically disabled (the deaf, the blind, the disfigured, the crippled); the ill (the consumptive, the scrofulous, the syphilitic, the cancerous); the inebriate; the chronically impoverished; the homeless; mothers of illegitimate children; prostitutes; mannish women; effeminate youths—in short, *anyone* who could not be located in the Progressive Era's picture of developmental health. These people were not merely diseased and pitiful; they were dangerous. They were enemies of the biologically conceived nation-state. They were pathogens to be eliminated, contained, or controlled in the name of the nation and its precious lives.

Phase III: The Lethal Chamber

In 1905 the Pennsylvania state legislature passed a bill giving "men of science and skill" the right to use surgical methods to help eradicate these dangers by preventing "the offspring that will be necessarily a curse to society." It would be left to the experts what method to use; the bill specified only that physicians would choose whichever procedure "shall be decided safest and most effective." When the bill, the first of its kind passed in the United States, reached the desk of Governor Samuel W. Pennypacker, he vetoed it forthwith, noting sarcastically, "It is plain that the safest and most effective method of preventing procreation would be to cut the heads off the inmates, and such authority is given by the bill to this staff of scientific experts" (Bruinius 2006, 150–51). Of course, Governor Pennypacker was right; a very effective way to prevent procreation in any class of people is a practice that Raphael Lempkin would later term "genocide."[43] In less than thirty-five years, Nazi physicians, having arrived at the same conclusion, would supplement their programs of eugenic sterilization of the mentally ill, mentally retarded, and physically disabled with programs of eugenic "euthanasia." They would begin with the mentally defective housed in state-run institutions. They would not be so crude as to cut off heads; instead, they would induce death, first by administering lethal injections, and then, in the interest of speed and efficiency, lethal doses of carbon monoxide. In 1939 they would kill 5,000 defective children. In 1940 and 1941, they would kill 70,000 defective adults. And they would move on from there.

No state in the United States ever enacted a law mandating eugenic euthanasia. But the idea was certainly discussed. When Mariann Olden took her League of Women Voters group on a tour of New Jersey's State Colony for Males at Woodbine in 1934, they were shocked at the condition of the lowest grade of idiots. "In a third building we saw truly painful spectacles, the sight of which gave the Euthanasia Society more than one new member," she wrote (Olden 1974, 7). In fact, by 1934, the idea of killing idiots and other "dysgenic" individuals had already been around for several decades. Popenoe and Johnson mentioned the possibility repeatedly in their *Applied Eugenics,* although always taking care to distance themselves from it. "To expose deformed children as the Spartans did would outrage the moral sentiments; to chloroform the incurable is a proposition that almost everyone condemns," they wrote. And: "It would be hard to find a eugenicist to-day who would propose, with Plato, that the infants with bad heredity should be put to death, but their right to grow up to the fullest enjoyment of life does not necessarily include the right to pass on their defective heredity to a long line of descendants, naturally increasing in number every generation" (Popenoe and Johnson 1926, 149, 161). Madison Grant was less demure. In his extremely popular book *The Passing of the Great Race,* he justified infanticide thus: "The laws of nature require the obliteration of the unfit, and human life is valuable only when it is of use to the community or race" (Grant 1916, 45).[44] And Goddard alluded to discussions of eugenic euthanasia in his ubiquitously cited 1912 volume, *The Kallikak Family: A Study in the Heredity of Feeble-mindedness,* wherein he noted that some had proposed "the lethal chamber" for low-grade idiots. "But," he hastened to add, "humanity is steadily tending away from the possibility of that method, and there is no probability that it will ever be practiced."[45] Not on those deemed "human" at least.

The "lethal chamber" was patented in the 1880s by British inventor Benjamin Ward Richardson. Its purpose—or at least its first use—was to euthanize stray dogs at the Battersea Dogs Home in London. It was literally a gas chamber, with death induced by carbonic acid gas (E. Black 2003, 247). As early as 1900, however, Dr. W. Duncan McKim had advocated the lethal chamber for defective human beings in his book *Heredity and Human Progress,* beginning his argument with this assertion: "It is not the mere wearing of human form which truly indicates a man. The idiot and the low-grade imbecile are not true *men,* for certain essential human elements have never entered into them, and never can; nor is the moral idiot truly a man, nor, while the sad condition lasts, the lunatic. These beings live among us as men, but if we reckon with them as human we shall fare much as if we bargained with the dead or with beasts of prey" (McKim 1901, 7–8). Lest we imagine that Dr. McKim is talking about a special class of people so different from the normal in appearance and capacity that they would be both rare and easy to recognize, he points out that most of these—and the most dangerous of them—are defective, not anatomically or even cognitively, but morally. "It appears very difficult for people generally to believe that an individual may have a fair, or even high, degree of intelligence and yet be an idiot of a special kind—a person with a brain so defective in a special realm that the corresponding function of moral sense is impossible—a moral idiot. Yet this doctrine now rests invincibly upon mental psychology and pathology" (McKim 1901, 22). Moral defectives are recognizable only by their unconventional, licentious, or antisocial behavior. But defective they are, not merely sinful or offensive or eccentric, not merely marchers to the beat of a different drum. They are defective, and therefore they are not truly human beings after all.

Furthermore, the danger that mentally defective individuals pose to society is compounded many times over by the fact that their condition is heritable and that they have a tendency toward "reckless parentage" (McKim 1901, 137). The 1890 census counted 95,571 feebleminded Americans (not including the moral idiots), and there were about 135,000 epileptics—hundreds of thousands of living threats to the normal population, that is, to actual human beings. Clearly, with a number this large and growing, institutionalization was not feasible. "The surest, the simplest, the kindest, and most humane means for preventing reproduction among those whom we deem unworthy of this high privilege, is a *gentle, painless death;* and this should be administered not as a punishment, but as an expression of enlightened pity for the victims—too defective by nature to find true happiness in life—and as a duty toward the community and toward our own offspring" (McKim 1901, 188). The best method for accomplishing this feat, according to McKim, was with administration of carbonic acid gas (1901, 193). These subhuman beings should share the fate of London's curs.

McKim's ideas were distasteful to many eugenicists, but he was not roundly condemned, and his book sold well and got some good reviews.[46] Although most people were unwilling to acknowledge the fact publicly, these conclusions really did follow logically from eugenic premises; thus it was possible to use the specter of mass killing as a means to justify and gain acceptance for comparatively less extreme regulatory procedures. Dr. William Partlow's 1936 address to the Medical Association of the State of Alabama exemplifies this strategy quite well. "Until medical science improved social, public health and sanitary conditions, nature's survival of the fittest defended the human race against the dangers of degeneracy. Now that under the present order of a humane world, the weak are preserved as well as the strong, if we are to continue as a virile, upstanding race in body and mind, eugenics demands its share of study and attention or euthanasia may become a necessity" (Partlow 1936, 12). Dr. Partlow advocated a broad expansion of Alabama's relatively narrow forcible sterilization law to include "any sexual pervert, Sadist, homosexualist, Masochist, Sodomist, or any other grave form of sexual perversion or any prisoner who has twice been convicted of rape" or imprisoned three times for any offense (Larson 1995, 140). Although he lost his bid to broaden state law, Partlow's heavy emphasis on identifying and managing sexual variation was to be the wave of the post-eugenic racist future, as we shall see in chapter 6.

The underlying message from 1900 to 1936, then, was that if we can't effectively stop these people from reproducing, we will have to start killing them. Either that, or they will kill all of us, either directly by way of violent criminal activity, or indirectly by polluting and swamping our bloodlines. People with weak minds—that is, people whose judgment seems poor to us, people who choose things we would rather have them not choose—pose a deadly biological threat to the body of the nation and to the continued evolution of the human race. In the name of the Race, therefore, such people must be eliminated. What part of that message did Adolf Hitler misunderstand?

Fascists, Fellow Travelers, and Their Critics

Had someone like Laughlin, Grant, or Partlow become *der Führer* of the United States of America, we might well have had our own Holocaust in short order. Like many Nazis, these men were true believers in racial purity and the eminent evolution of a master race. They would have done anything necessary to protect and further that biological development, no matter how radical and personally distasteful some actions might be. They would have had the courage of their convictions.[47]

And their orders would have been followed by many American physicians, psychiatrists, educators, social workers, prison wardens, police officers, and government officials at all levels, just as their German counterparts followed the orders—or in some cases merely exercised the free rein to kill, maim, enslave, and incarcerate—that Hitler's regime gave them.[48] There was widespread support for eugenic measures in the United States, even some support among groups frequently targeted, including African Americans and Jews.[49] The number of people committed to asylums for the insane and feeble-minded steadily grew, as did the number sterilized, while lethal violence against disfavored racial and ethnic groups continued virtually unchecked through the 1930s, and racial segregation was bolstered by official warnings of the biological dangers inherent in miscegenation and of the perverted and bestial sexuality endemic to black communities. Obviously a majority of Americans believed at least some of the biological claims the eugenicists made.

Many Americans went along with the eugenics program, however, just as many people in Germany did, not because of any strong commitment to race purification but because they had other interests that were served by exclusion, confinement, restriction, or elimination of certain groups of people. For people at the lower end of the economic ladder (as well as for some at the higher) reduced competition for jobs and housing could sometimes be a boon. Eugenics programs were often a boon to employers as well; institutionalized labor provided by asylums and prisons kept wages down and unions at bay, as did the near-constant availability of unemployed black workers. Even for white middle-class homemakers such as those who hired newly sterilized "parolees" from institutions like the Virginia Colony, the eugenics movement had its benefits—cheap, pre-screened, and readily available live-in domestic labor kept docile by the constant threat of re-incarceration.[50]

But labor considerations were not the only ones. As discussed above, the "helping professions," or what Foucault calls the "psy disciplines," used immigration restriction, sterilization of mental defectives, and the fear of sexual predators to enhance their professional positions, give their institutions the appearance of viability and usefulness, and make their practitioners indispensable as auxiliaries in courts of law, penal institutions, and school systems. And of course, trades-people and capitalists made money on these ventures—building contractors, pharmaceutical companies, manufacturers of all kinds of equipment for medical procedures, surveillance, restraint, record-keeping, and so forth, and publishing firms selling books like *The Rising Tide of Color, The Kallikak Family, The Fruit of the Family Tree,* and *The Passing of the Great Race.* These are just a few of the ways in which hundreds of thousands of Americans profited from the slandering, the segregation, and the sterilization of and experimentation upon hundreds of thousands of other Americans who happened, for one reason or another, to be vulnerable to classification as feeble-minded, sexually perverse, and dangerous.

It could be argued that, from the perspective of most of these "fellow travelers," what morally committed Nazis misunderstood was the degree to which profitable and productive networks of bio-power depended, not upon the successful elimination of these biological threats, but upon their managed persistence. If the experts could identify and eliminate sexual predators altogether, what need would anyone have for the experts anymore, not to mention all the workers and equipment that supported the application of their expertise? If there were no more criminals and prostitutes, what could possibly justify the continued existence of a carceral system? In a world without tuberculosis, syphilis, heart disease, kidney disease, and cancer, what would public health officials, doctors, and druggists do?[51]

Like the war on masturbation, the war on the biologically unfit was impossible to win. And that was the beauty of the thing. It could go on forever. It could even steadily escalate. And thus more and more money could be made, more and more alliances consolidated, more and more bodies colonized, manipulated, cultivated, reconfigured, and put to work in the service of systems of biopolitical expenditure and control. The possibilities were endless. But then came that crazy Hitler and his Final Solution, which threatened to jeopardize it all.

Indeed, American biologists knew—well before 1933—that many of the basic tenets of eugenics were highly questionable and probably false. Like did not always breed like, the environment did influence genetic expression, and most phenotypic traits were not Mendelian. As early as 1909, Danish geneticist Wilhelm Johannsen had argued, based on nine years of experiments with bean plants, that hereditary factors do not fully determine the phenotype, a word he coined. His work clearly implied that no one can know an individual's genetic makeup simply by visual inspection. In 1910 and 1913, Harvard geneticist Edward East, together with his colleague Rollins Emerson, published observations of maize indicating that many traits simply are not inherited according to Mendel's laws. To explain this, they advanced the "multiple gene theory," which holds that some traits are determined by the inheritance of multiple pairs of genes, making variation more common in successive generations and seriously undermining the idea that parents' traits are solid predictors of the traits of their offspring (Ludmerer 1972, 77). Furthermore, in 1917, East calculated that if feeblemindedness were a Mendelian recessive trait, as Henry Goddard claimed, one in every fourteen people would be carriers of it; thus it could not be eradicated through eugenic sterilization in three generations as so many eugenicists promised.[52] R. C. Punnett (1917, 465) took East's calculations further, estimating that it would take more than 8,000 years to reduce the number of carriers to one in 100,000.[53]

This scientific work had serious implications for, but did not directly attack, eugenic principles. By the mid-1920s, however, a few scientists did begin to publish explicit critiques. In 1925 Thomas H. Morgan, renowned for his work on the genetic complexity of fruit flies and the first recipient of the Nobel Prize for Genetics (in 1933), questioned eugenic attempts to eliminate feeblemindedness by pointing out that scientists actually knew very little about the processes by which intelligence might be inherited and that there was good reason to believe that a great deal of "feeblemindedness" was a response to demoralizing environments (Paul 1995, 115). At the Third International Congress of Eugenics in New York in 1932, Morgan's student H. J. Muller reviewed a number of recent studies from which he drew the conclusion that environment, not heredity, was largely responsible for intelligence and conduct. "The results," he declared, "show us that there is no scientific basis for the conclusion that the socially lower classes, or technically less advanced races, really have a genetically inferior intellectual equipment, since the differences between their averages are, so far as our knowledge goes, to be accounted for fully by the known effects of environment." He went on to say that if this held true for intellect, "it is even more true of temperamental traits, moral qualities, etc., since these are more responsive to conditioning than are purely intellectual characteristics" (Muller 1933, 44).

Sociologists, too, launched critiques. In 1913 Lester Ward delivered an address to the Federation for Child Study in New York in which he argued that deliberate selection—whether in the form of cattle breeding or human eugenics—is actually a form of nurture, not the facilitation of a natural evolutionary process. Thus it was no more warranted by nature than any other kind of environmental intervention, such as cleaning up slums and offering free public education. He suggested that efforts to force people of so-called good stock to breed would be a form of tyranny. And he pointed out that natural selection works to produce fitter offspring where there is spontaneous variation upon which to capitalize, implying that the abnormalities that eugenicists so distrusted could have important roles to play in evolutionary advancement (Ward 1913, 740, 748–49).

Journalist Walter Lippmann took on Lewis Terman, author of the 1916 Stanford-Binet IQ test, in the pages of the *New Republic* in 1922, carefully analyzing test results as well as test design and charging that "without offering any data on all that occurs between conception and the age of kindergarten, [Terman and his cadre of IQ testers] announce on the basis of what they have got out of a few thousand questionnaires that they are measuring the hereditary mental endowment of human beings. Obviously, this is not a conclusion obtained by research. It is a conclusion planted by the will to believe."[54] Lippmann's criticisms went to the heart of Terman's experimental design and challenged the very concept of "intelligence" as Terman and his team sought to measure it.

So there were plenty of reasons for hard-line American eugenicists to have backed off their scientific claims as well as their social policies long before the Nazis instituted their program of "euthanasia" for the "defective." But they didn't. Instead of interpreting the criticisms as reasons to change course entirely, they saw them as questions that could be answered within the eugenic framework itself. For example, R. A. Fisher argued in 1924 that Punnett's figures were misleading. While it would take many generations to breed out feeblemindedness entirely, the biggest gains would be made in the first few generations. Within three generations, it could be reduced by 17 percent, which represented a huge savings in misery and money to bequeath to our children and grandchildren (Fisher 1924, 114). In 1931, voicing a common view, Lancelot Hogben said that the fact that we cannot breed out every instance of a bad trait "is not a valid reason for neglecting to do what little can be done."[55] If tests were needed to identify carriers as well as those who expressed a trait, then tests should be developed. It was a matter of doing more in-depth research, honing theories and concepts, and developing the right kinds of tools. As to the environmental arguments, Duncan McKim had handily eliminated that objection in 1900. Environments—cities, slums, poverty, violence—were the creation of human beings and thus the expression of the same heredity directly transmitted through the germ plasm.[56]

Most of the debate over nature versus nurture really amounted to nothing more than a game of shifting the burden of proof. Just as Muller asserted that eugenicists had not sufficiently supported their claim that heredity accounted for phenotypic differences, hard-line eugenicists typically asserted that skeptics had not sufficiently supported their claim that environment accounted for those differences. Still, there was more than enough scientific evidence against the basic principles of mainline eugenics by 1933 to justify calling a halt to social policies based on them. Immigration restrictions could have been relaxed, marriage laws could have been liberalized, segregation programs could have been dismantled, and sterilization laws could have been repealed. But no scientist came forward to challenge the restrictions on immigration. No scientist campaigned against marriage restriction. And only a very few raised any questions about lifelong commitment or involuntary sterilization. Why? Perhaps many believed that traits such as insanity, feeblemindedness, criminality, alcoholism, and predisposition to disease really were inherited even though the proof wasn't in yet, and that such traits were pernicious and should be eliminated where possible.[57] Whatever their personal beliefs though, their unwillingness to bring any alternative views before the public effectively endorsed the eugenic agenda. When Georgia's state legislature took up a sterilization bill for debate in 1937, its overwhelmingly liberal supporters were unaware of any scientific critique of eugenics. "For Georgians," historian Edward Larson writes, "sterilization remained a progressive reform founded on good science" (1995, 138). The bill passed, making Georgia the thirty-second and last state to mandate involuntary sterilization for mental defectives.

The challenges to eugenics programs came not primarily from scientific sources and on scientific grounds but from people with theological and moral reservations. Catholics had resisted eugenic policies all along. Immigration restriction was in part aimed at limiting the number of Catholics coming into the country, and many Catholic Americans were immigrants or children of immigrants from eugenically suspect southern Europe and Ireland. Catholics were typically suspicious of marriage restrictions based on "fitness to reproduce" and were certainly opposed to sterilization as a form of birth control. In 1930 Pius XI issued *Conti connubii* officially denouncing sterilization, but American Catholics had been opposing it on theological grounds for two decades.[58] Some fundamentalist Protestants also opposed sterilization, although mainline Protestant denominations, even in the Deep South, accepted the practice.[59]

When Alabama considered broadening its sterilization law in 1935, moral considerations took center stage.[60] The state's 1919 sterilization law was very narrow in scope, mandating sterilizations only for those to be released from the state home for the mentally deficient. Since mentally deficient people were hardly ever released, fewer than two hundred people had been sterilized under its provisions. Medical superintendent William Partlow and state health officer J. N. Baker wanted involuntary sterilizations for patients at state mental hospitals as well as reformatories and other institutions controlled by county officials, and, as noted above, they wanted a wide range of traits to warrant the procedure, including criminality, sexual perversion, and habitual dependence on public charity.[61] In addition to these provisions, the bill their legislative allies proposed allowed no right of judicial appeal; all decisions were made by mental health officials. There followed an intense debate with a lot of press coverage. The bill was endorsed by the Medical Society of the State of Alabama and the Alabama Society for Mental Hygiene as well as by the Alabama Division of the American Association of University Women. Many newspapers with religious affiliations denounced it, as did trade unionists and the ACLU, but the major newspapers—the *Montgomery Advertiser* and the *Birmingham News*—supported the bill. When it finally came to a vote, it passed both chambers: 69–16 in the house, and 17–9 in the senate. It looked like Alabama would soon have the most draconian eugenic sterilization law in the nation.

But it was not to be. To the surprise of apparently just about everyone, Governor Bibb Graves vetoed the bill. In response, the legislature passed a second bill identical in scope but with some provision for appeals. Graves vetoed that. He explained that salpingectomy was known to result in complications and death in a limited number of cases, and he believed that it was morally wrong to expose patients to that risk for reasons having nothing to do with improving their own health.[62]

Edward Larson speculates, however, that Graves had some other reasons as well, reasons having to do with a changed political climate as the world careened toward another war. Addressing the legislature during the debate, J. N. Baker had stressed the historic importance of eugenic sterilization: "With baited breath," he proclaimed dramatically, "the entire civilized world is watching the bold experiment in mass sterilization recently launched in Germany." He projected a huge savings in tax money as a result of this "bold experiment." Baker clearly believed, as did Partlow, that the Germans had the right idea. But a number of Alabamians saw things differently. Larson reports that Governor Graves received letters suggesting that many citizens viewed the sterilization bill as, in the words of one writer, "an attempt to Hitleresque Alabama." Another constituent wrote, "In my judgment the great rank and file of the country people of

Alabama do not want this law; they do not want Alabama, as they term it, Hitlerized" (Larson 1995, 145–46). Eugenicists like Baker and Partlow were looking to Germany for inspiration in the mid-1930s, but many Americans were looking at Germany in horror.

Within two months after taking power in 1933, the Nazis had enacted a sterilization statute. It was modeled on California's law—which in turn was based on Laughlin's 1922 Model Eugenical Sterilization Law—but it was much narrower than Laughlin's model, which called for the sterilization of all "socially inadequate" persons believed likely to procreate. Laughlin defined a socially inadequate person as "one who by his or her own effort, regardless of etiology or prognosis, fails chronically in comparison with normal persons, to maintain himself or herself as a useful member of the organized social life of the state." Most socially inadequate persons fell into one or more "socially inadequate classes," which, "regardless of etiology or prognosis, are the following: (1) Feeble-minded; (2) Insane, (including the psychopathic); (3) Criminalistic (including the delinquent and the wayward); (4) Epileptic; (5) Inebriate (including drug habitués); (6) Diseased (including the tuberculous, the syphilitic, the leprous, and others with chronic, infectious and legally segregable diseases); (7) Blind (including those with seriously impaired vision); (8) Deaf (including those with seriously impaired hearing); (9) Deformed (including the crippled); (10) Dependent (including orphans, ne'er-do-wells, the homeless, tramps and paupers)" (Laughlin 1922, 447).

The new Nazi law covered only those with congenital idiocy, schizophrenia, manic depressive lunacy, congenital epilepsy, Huntington's chorea, hereditary blindness, severe hereditary malformation, and severe alcoholism.[63] Despite its comparatively narrow applicability, however, Laughlin was pleased with the law because the Germans, unlike the Americans, had enacted this as national, not state policy, and so were able to set up a national register of genetically deficient individuals and a national board of appeals. In 1934 the machinery to do this work was set in place, and by the end of the year thousands of Germans were being summoned to Hereditary Health Courts under warrants for their sterilization. By November the Nazis expanded the law to cover the feebleminded, as detected by the use of a German version of the Simon-Binet IQ test. But because officials worried that the test captured only cognitive and not moral defects, eugenics officer Dr. Ernst von Holst decreed that anyone who did not meet "German moral standards" could be sterilized. By June of 1935, the law was amended again to allow the Hereditary Health Court to order abortion in cases where a pregnant woman was found unfit for procreation (Bruinius 2006, 281).

Needless to say, some Americans found these laws frightening and tyrannical. The fact that they or ones like them could be turned against political enemies was not lost on the "rank and file of the country people of Alabama," even if it was lost on Harry Laughlin and Charles Davenport. Alabama trade unionists objected to the proposed law with precisely that argument: "There is nothing in the bill to prevent a labor man from being 'railroaded' into an institution where he could be sterilized on 'suspicion' of insanity or feeblemindedness" (quoted in Larson 1995, 141). Hitler was a dictator who was sterilizing the people he didn't like. The same thing could happen in the United States if laws passed that gave a few individuals such broad authority. Tyranny does not appeal to many people who know they will not be the ones to play the tyrant.

William Partlow did not give up. He pushed similar bills in the Alabama legislature in 1939 and 1943, but they died in committee. Laughlin and Davenport also kept the faith. But more and more Americans were becoming alarmed at Hitler's tyranny. In the fall of 1935, in the name of the purification of the race, the Nazis enacted the statutes that came to be known as the Nuremberg Laws. In September they outlawed marriage between Germans and Jews. In October they adopted a law requiring a certification of racial purity to obtain a marriage license. In November they stripped Jews of their citizenship. Some American eugenicists defended these moves. After all, marriage restriction was a cornerstone of the U.S. movement, and many states had similar licensure and anti-miscegenation laws, not to mention racial segregation and de facto if not de jure race-based disenfranchisement. Dr. Clarence Campbell, president of the Eugenics Research Association, commended the Nazis later that year at the World Population Congress in Berlin. He declared: "It is from a synthesis of the work of all such men that the leader of the German nation, Adolf Hitler, ably supported by the Minister of Interior, Dr. Frick, and guided by the nation's anthropologists, its eugenicists, and its social philosophers, has been able to construct a comprehensive racial policy of population development and improvement that promises to be epochal in racial history! . . . The difference between the

Jew and the Aryan is as unsurmountable as that between a black and white. . . . Germany has set a pattern which other nations must follow!" (quoted in Bruinius 2006, 283–84).

Of course, as attorneys for the defense at Nuremberg would argue after the war, actually it was the Americans who had set the pattern that Germany was following, as J. H. Landman had noted in 1933: "Our country has been the pioneer in this movement and is today the foremost champion and advocate of the cause in the world. In 1928 the province of Alberta in Canada, in 1929 Denmark, Finland, and the Canton of Vaud in Switzerland, in 1932 the state of Vera Cruz in Mexico, and on July 26, 1933, Germany espoused the cause" (Landman 1933, 403). The major difference was that Germany, without all those political checks and balances and pesky First Amendment liberties that plagued America, was able to carry out the program of racial purification far more swiftly and efficiently than its mentor could.

Hitler was the U.S. movement's protégé in many ways. In *Mein Kampf* in 1924, he had expressed admiration for the Johnson-Reed Immigration Restriction Act and hope that Germany would impose similar restrictions. Indeed, under that law, most of the people the Nazis found unacceptable enough to kill were denied the right to immigrate to the United States, because (thanks in part to Harry Laughlin's testimony) Americans officially found those people unacceptable too. Once in power, Hitler had solicited and received advice from Laughlin, Madison Grant, and many other Americans as he formulated his racial policies and had used Laughlin's Model Eugenical Sterilization Law as the prototype for his own. In 1934 Paul Popenoe, former editor of the *Journal of Heredity* and co-author of *Sterilization for Human Betterment*, defended Hitler from growing criticism, calling his plan a solid set of eugenic policies that "accord with the best thought of eugenists in all civilized countries" (Popenoe 1934, 257).

So what was wrong with what Hitler was doing in 1935 and 1936? What, exactly, made "Hitlerism" different from the principles that American scientists and intellectuals espoused?

Saving the Eugenic Baby by Throwing out the Nazi Bath Water

The new word that came into existence to name precisely this difference was *racism*. Hitler wasn't interested in freeing the human race of its inferior elements, his critics charged. He was interested in promoting one race, the Aryans, at the expense of others—Jews, Slavs, Africans, and so forth. And that was wrong, most American eugenicists were willing to concede, because even if on the whole Aryans were biologically superior, a given Aryan might be biologically inferior to a given Jew or Slav, or even a given Negro.[64] In such a case, a good eugenicist would relieve the public of the burden of that Aryan bloodline in favor of retaining the bloodline of the Jew or Slav or Negro. But Hitler and the Nazis were unwilling to do that. When we judge who is truly biologically inferior and who superior, we really have to look at individual traits, not racial traits; anything else is just sheer prejudice, bigotry . . . *racism*. We should judge people not by the shape of their nose or the color of their skin, but by the content of their hereditary characters. And thus we will distinguish ourselves from Hitler . . . and yet preserve our right to judge.

Racism was irrational. Morphological features like skin color, hair texture, facial angle, eye or nose shape were superficial. What really mattered was abnormality—low intellect, deficiency of inhibitions resulting in an inability to control impulses, perversion of the sexual instincts. These abnormalities were biological and hereditary, but they could exist in individuals of any morphologically identifiable race. And when they did, they had to be detected, preferably before those individuals realized their full potential to wreak havoc on the rest of society and to propagate their kind. One simply could not afford to assume that all tall, blonde, blue-eyed people were normal. (Otherwise what role would there be for experts?) There were tall, blonde, blue-eyed morons. There were tall, blonde, blue-eyed "homosexualists." Maybe Hitler's racism blinded him to those facts. But American eugenicists were rational.

In fact, of course, the Nazi sterilization program of the 1930s was aimed, first of all, at Germans, not Jews in particular—although no doubt many Jews were caught up in it because of the anti-Semitism of the physicians who screened sterilization candidates. The main point was to purge the Aryan race of its defects and decrease the state's financial outlay for long-term care. Strictly speaking, it was a program of racial purification, not racism in the 1936 sense of the term.[65] But the Nazis did have it in for Jews, and they had made no secret of that since before they came to power in 1933. The Nuremberg Laws of 1935 were clearly aimed at degrading and disenfranchising Jews as a race, and that *was* racism by 1936 standards. While there was plenty of anti-Semitism in the United States, many Americans did not accept a racist assessment of Jews. As Nazi policies developed, many became alarmed and then outraged. Some began to push for U.S. support for the Jews and the relaxation of immigration restrictions in order to offer more Jewish refugees an American sanctuary.[66]

Among American eugenicists, there were differences of opinion. Laughlin had testified before Congress that Jews as a race had criminal tendencies, and Popenoe and Johnson repeated that claim in *Applied Eugenics*—Italians tend to commit crimes of violence, Jews crimes of gain, and Slavs crimes of violence while drunk, which is why immigration from southern and eastern Europe had to be stopped (Popenoe and Johnson 1926, 304). Many Jews were smart, they acknowledged, but their moral faculties were defective; they were moral imbeciles. A few of their colleagues believed that Jews had eugenic qualities as well as dysgenic ones, however. William Ripley had asserted in 1899 that Jews were more adaptive than any other race, maintaining their racial distinction in a variety of climates. "The Jews are the most remarkable people in this respect. Montano affirms that they thrive in South America; and we know from Wallace that they are increasing, in the uttermost parts of Russia, even faster than the natives. Felkin goes even further in suggesting that a little Semitic blood is always a help in acclimatization. Although this may be doubted, the cosmopolitan adaptive aptitudes of these people has never been denied from the time of Boudin to that of Bordier" (Ripley 1913, 571). Race purifiers with imperialist ambitions could hardly fail to admire such a people, even while disparaging them.

In 1934, in response to appeals to relax immigration restrictions, the New York Chamber of Commerce established a study commission under the leadership of John Trevor. Trevor turned to Laughlin as a scientific expert. "He is beyond doubt the foremost authority in the United States today on the subject," Trevor told a reporter for the *New York Times* when the committee's report was released. Laughlin's verdict was predictable: There could be no exceptions.

> If, as a result of persecution or expulsion by any foreign country, men of real hereditary capacity, sound in physical stamina and of outstanding personal qualities, honesty, decency, common sense, altruism, patriotism and initiative, can be found,

they should, because of such qualities, and not because of persecution, win individual preference within our quotas and be welcomed as desirable human seed stock of future American citizens. If any would-be immigrant cannot meet these standards, he should, of course, be excluded. ("Relaxing Quotas," 1934, 7)

The issue was not compassion, let alone justice; it was procreation and evolution. Laughlin continued: "If those who control immigration would look upon the incoming immigrant, not essentially as offering asylum nor in securing cheap labor, but primarily as 'sons-in-laws to marry their daughters' they would be looking at it in the light of the long-time truth. Immigrants are essentially breeding stock" ("Relaxing Quotas," 1934, 7). For the same reasons, he recommended continuing the ban on persons who have no country to which they could be deported if found deficient within the five-year probationary period and those whose ancestors were not all members of the white or Caucasian race.

But by 1939, even Harry Laughlin had to concede (or at least pretend to concede) that not all Jews were bad: "The Jew ranks high in scholarship, in the learned professions, in music and in business." Still, he opined, Jews typically made poor citizens; they were "slow to assimilate to the American pattern of life" (Laughlin 1939, 20). Therefore he insisted that any Jew desiring to immigrate should "prove beyond doubt that he, when admitted and naturalized, and his children born and developed here, are in every respect Americans first and Jews second" (Laughlin 1939, 21). Then perhaps a few superior individuals might be permitted to trickle into Nordic bloodlines without slowing humanity's progress toward evolutionary perfection.

These determinations had to be made on a case-by-case basis, of course. It was the individual who must be judged, not the race. It was true that a high percentage of Jews had inherited a predisposition to steal, most had weak lungs, and the males did tend toward effeminacy, but not every one of them was a degenerate. Rational people didn't condemn all members of a race on account of the bad heredity of the vast majority.

Needless to say, a similar scenario played out in eugenic discourse regarding African Americans. In *Applied Eugenics* (published in 1918 and 1926), Paul Popenoe and Roswell Johnson found a number of reasons to conclude "not only that the Negro is *different* from the white, but that he is in the large eugenically *inferior* to the white" (1926, 285). They drew much of their evidence from the race theorists of the nineteenth century who had claimed, for example, that Africans had never created a civilization on their own, that they had failed to govern themselves effectively in the New World when they had the chance (e.g., in Haiti), and that Negroes have little or no self-control. To this they added data gathered through the methods of early twentieth-century social scientific empiricism, namely, questionnaires and IQ tests. In particular, they pointed to the work of Virginia psychologist G. O. Ferguson Jr., who studied 900 school children in Richmond, Fredericksburg, and Newport News. They summarize:

> Tests were employed which required the use of the "higher" functions, and as far as possible (mainly on the basis of skin color) the amount of white blood in the colored pupils was determined. Four classes were made: full-blood Negro, ¾ Negro, ½ Negro (mulatto) and ¼ Negro (quadroon). It was found that "the pure Negroes scored 69.2% as high as the whites; that the ¾ pure Negroes scored 73.2% as high as the whites; that the mulattoes scored 81.2% as high as the whites; and that the quadroons obtained 91.8% of the white score." This confirms the belief of many observers that the ability of a colored man is proportionate to the amount of white blood he has. (Popenoe and Johnson 1926, 288)

That these scores reflect inheritance rather than environment is shown by the fact that Negroes do poorly everywhere, not just in Virginia. Full-blood Negroes are only about 60 percent as cognitively capable as whites. And that deficiency is compounded by other inherited tendencies—for example, they are constitutionally disorganized, impulsive, and lacking in sexual inhibition. It is foolish to expect any of them ever to amount to much. And of course they never do. The few African Americans of note are of mixed ancestry, like W. E. B. DuBois, whom Popenoe and Johnson refer to as "a brilliant mulatto" (1926, 295).

Maybe there are a few unusually gifted Jews whose blood would not corrupt Nordic germ plasm, but the same cannot be said of Negroes. Negroes are utterly inassimilable: "It would be desirable to encourage amalgamation of the two races only in case the average of mulattoes is superior to the average of the whites. No one can seriously maintain that this supposition is true" (Popenoe and Johnson 1926, 293). Not only should intermarriage be banned, but states must go further and take "any legal action which can practicably be taken to make miscegenation between white and black impossible" (1926, 297). Undoubtedly this would include not only criminalizing all inter-racial sex, which Popenoe and Johnson discuss explicitly, but also reinforcing educational and social segregation. It would eventually also include—as a matter of practice, if not explicit policy—eugenic sterilization of large numbers of black girls and women, intense police surveillance of blacks in "white" space, a disproportionate rate of black institutionalization through imprisonment, and a higher fre-quency of execution for blacks convicted of crimes. Whatever it takes, no black person should ever have sexual access to any white person under any circumstances. "Justice requires that the Negro race be treated as kindly and considerately as possible, with every economic and political concession that is consistent with the continued welfare of the nation. Such social equality and intercourse as might lead to marriage are not compatible with this welfare" (1926, 297).

Negroes are good for one thing, though: cannon fodder. "In the United States are millions of negroes who are of less value than white men in organized industry but almost as valuable as the whites, when properly led, at the front. It would appear to be sound statesmanship to enlist as many Negroes as possible in the active forces, in case of war, thus releasing a corresponding number of more skilled white workers for the industrial machine on whose efficiency success in modern warfare largely rests" (Popenoe and Johnson 1926, 319).

Popenoe and Johnson leave themselves very little room for plau-sible denial of 1936-style racism in this text. Negroes as a race are stupid, violent, and sexually out of control. No full-blood Negro has ever achieved anything worthy of note. All of them are less valuable than all whites. Not one carries germ plasm that would in any way enhance Nordic bloodlines. Clearly, these two eugenicists are open to the charge of "racism," at least when it comes to Negroes, if not to Jews. But by the 1930s they, like Harry Laughlin, saw the danger of being branded with the Nazi iron; in the 1935 edition of *Applied Eugenics,* they toned down the antiblack rhetoric, and the remark about military service was removed.

Laughlin, Davenport, Popenoe, and others continued to sup-port the Nazis well into the 1930s, however, and to defend their population policies against the charge of racism. Publications of the Eugenics Record Office in 1934 proclaimed the German sterilization law fair and reasonable. "Prevention of hereditary degeneracy is the sole purpose of the new statute, which applies equally to all hereditary degenerates as specified by the law, regardless of sex, race or religion" (Larson 1995, 147). Marie Kopp, who went to Germany herself in 1936 to review the German program, came back with confirmation: "I am convinced that the law is administered in entire fairness . . . and that discrimination of class, race, creed, political, or religious belief does not enter into the matter" (in Larson 1995, 147). But this continued support was a strategic mistake. When Allied invasion and victory eventually revealed the extent of the Holocaust, the charge of racism was clearly substantiated, and the American eugenics movement was still closely enough associated with Nazism that it could not avoid the charge itself. After the Nuremberg Trials, Paul Popenoe acknowledged that the major factor in the collapse of the movement "was undoubtedly Hitlerism" (Larson 1995, 147).

The movement as a whole may have lost respect, but many individual eugenicists and several professional factions were able to distance themselves from "Hitlerism" enough to continue at least some aspects of their projects. They did this largely by buying into their critics' definition of racism and altering their rhetoric to project concern about abnormalities in individual bloodlines, not the lines of entire morphologically identifiable races. That meant they might have to accept the occasional "atypical" Jew or "brilliant mulatto" as a person worthy of consideration and be open to his or her germ line's incorporation into the Nordic race. That might prove distasteful, but it wouldn't happen often. Since they honestly believed that most of the members of those groups—like most Native Americans, Asians, Italians, and Slavs—really were genetically inferior to most Nordics, they believed they could protect and further the evolutionary advance of the race by means other than crude racial profiling. After all, when Robert Yerkes administered IQ tests to military recruits during World War I, nearly 90 percent of the Negroes tested out as feebleminded, with an average mental age of just over ten years. It wouldn't be necessary to legislate against all Negroes, perhaps, if almost 90 percent could be so easily eliminated from the breeding public through institutionalization and sterilization programs designed to address recognized social problems that transcended race. Couple that with

Negroes' hereditary tendency to die young and their disposition to sexually perverse and violent acts for which they could be locked up in sex-segregated prisons, and their numbers could be kept down to a mere handful of "brilliant mulattoes" who could have little effect on racial progress. If white people really were superior—and no doubt they were, especially given the standards typically used (by whites) to judge—nonwhite races could be targeted for discrimination, exclusion, and elimination simply by targeting various categories of people labeled "abnormal." There was no need to talk about racial differences anymore at all. In 1937, American Eugenics Society President Frederick Osborn wrote that "it would be unwise for eugenicists to impute superiorities or inferiorities of a biological nature to social classes, to regional groups, or to races as a whole." Politically unwise, that is, if one wanted to distinguish oneself from the Nazis. "Eugenics should therefore operate on the basis of individual selection" (F. Osborn 1937, 106). Henceforward, members of the AES would speak of "selective sterilization" and encourage reproduction not of the Nordic but of the "normal." Who could criticize that?

Who indeed? Who would come forward to say, "We love abnormal people. Let's encourage abnormal people to breed. Hooray for abnormality! Abnormality is the spice of life! Up with deformity, insanity, and perversion! Degenerates are just grand!" No one.

Thus the massive machinery of scientific racism, refined by thirty years of genetic research, was turned exclusively against the abnormal. This was done precisely to sidestep the charge of "racism." And yet it *was* racism. This massive network of biopolitical machinery— all its institutions for confinement and discipline, all its theoretical and practical knowledge systems, all its technologies for reconstructing human bodies and restructuring populations—had been set in place for the purpose of hastening the glorious day of Anglo-Saxon evolutionary triumph. It was all about race. It was all about white supremacy. And it was not dismantled. It was hardly even subjected to questioning. It was allowed merely to rephrase itself.

Queering Hitler

Nearly thirty years later, when John Lewis, Hosea Williams, Amelia Boynton Robinson, and nearly six hundred other civil rights marchers confronted the Dallas County sheriff and a contingent of state troopers on the Edmund Pettus Bridge on Bloody Sunday, they were thus confronting a remnant. Only in the intellectual backwaters such as Selma, Alabama, had the memo not yet been received: "We're no longer after black people per se; we're just after the 99.99 percent of them we deem *abnormal*. Let the others vote and walk the streets in peace." Either the memo hadn't traveled that far yet, or the Crackers were just too stupid to read it. Whichever, it was damned embarrassing. A federal law would have to be passed and some real troops sent to bring those imbecilic Peckerwoods in line.

Meanwhile, there were a few other loose ends to tie up. There was the question of Anglo-Saxon America's Teutonic cousins and their recent unruliness. As the magnitude of the Holocaust became inescapably apparent at war's end and the Nuremberg Trials revealed the horrifying details of the Nazis' "social programs," what were civilized people to think? Germany was a civilized country. The German people were Europeans, for God's sake, not savages. Nobody ever said to *kill* the unfit (at least, nobody *remembered* anybody ever saying it). How could something like Auschwitz happen in the homeland of Goethe and Bach?

There was only one possible answer. It was the same answer that had been given for the last sixty years whenever a child from a fine, upstanding Nordic family cut loose and ran amok. It was said in a whisper, yet with great solemnity and meaning: Something had gone wrong with their sexuality. Hitler, they whispered, was *queer*.

Homosexuality, particularly in all-male institutions, had been a national German obsession since the 1906 Eulenberg scandal at Kaiser Wilhelm II's court, and certainly since Hans Blüher published his sexual expose of the Wandervogel movement in 1912.[67] It is not at all odd that political rivals or enemies would use such a charge against Hitler's tight-knit, all-male regime, whether it was true or not, and indeed the first charges did come from German leftists seeking to discredit the Nazi Party.[68] Hitler's alleged homosexuality had become a joke in popular media in the United States long before Pearl Harbor and entry into the war.[69] In 1943, however, when the U.S. Office of Strategic Services undertook to produce a psychological profile of Hitler for use in propaganda and espionage, the accusations could not be substantiated. According to Dr. Henry Murray and his OSS associate W. H. D. Vernon, "That Hitler's attitude toward sex is pathological is already clear. . . . The best sources we have do not, however, tell us explicitly what it is that is wrong with Hitler's sex life. From the fact that his close associate, Röhm, as well as many of the early Nazis were homosexuals it has been a matter of gossip that Hitler too is affected in this way. All reliable sources, however, deny that there is any evidence whatever for such an idea" (Murray 1943, 66). Walter Langer later incorporated this material into a more detailed OSS profile, which he used as the basis of a 1972 book. Available evidence led all these OSS researchers to conclude that Hitler was effeminate and had homosexual tendencies—which made him queer by 1940s standards; however, none found any evidence of overt homosexual activity. In fact, they report many instances of heterosexual activity, although they frequently suggest deviance from "normal" vaginal intercourse.[70]

For many years Hitler did tolerate homosexuality in his inner circle, however. He knew, as did everyone else, that SA chief Ernst Röhm was homosexual, and yet he left him in charge of the military wing of the Party until late June of 1934.[71] He not only refused to discipline Röhm but seemed unperturbed by his sexuality and even at times socialized with him at parties where many attendees were lesbian or gay.

This association led many people in the 1940s to conclude that Hitler himself was homosexual. Who else could stand to be in such company? Then, when Hitler had Röhm and hundreds of his associates murdered during the Night of the Long Knives and claimed that it was a moral purge, many people concluded that Hitler himself was homosexual. Who else could be so threatened and intolerant? It seems fairly clear in retrospect, however, that the Night of the Long Knives was a preemptive strike aimed at people Hitler thought might be plotting a military coup and that his assertion that it was a purge of homosexuality was just a convenient cover.[72]

Heinrich Himmler's attitudes and goals regarding homosexuality are much clearer than Hitler's. When he became chief of German police in 1937, Himmler brought with him his intense aversion to homosexuals and his fear of a world-wide Jewish homosexual conspiracy.[73] He immediately set up a national police task force to combat homosexuality, using an expanded version of paragraph 175—Germany's anti-sodomy statute—that had been set in place in 1935. This statute reflected the new twentieth-century understanding of homosexuality as inclusive of mutual masturbation; it criminalized even acts one might commit fully clothed. Between 1937 and 1939, Himmler's police force made 90,000 arrests under paragraph 175. But that was not the extent of his antigay activity. In addition to serving as chief of German police, Himmler was also head of the SS, the elite security forces that ran the concentration camps. Upon his urging in 1941, Hitler decreed a mandatory death penalty for homosexuality within the ranks of the SS. Although this decree was apparently intended as a deterrent merely and is not known to have been invoked to justify any actual death sentence (Giles 2002, 12), Himmler took it seriously. He declared: "When someone in the Security Services, in the SS, or in the government has homosexual tendencies, he abandons the normal order of things for the perverted world of the homosexual. We can't permit such danger to the country; the homosexual must be entirely exterminated."[74]

Under paragraph 42 of the criminal code, the Law Against Habitual Criminals and Sex Offenders, an unknown number of the thousands of men that Himmler had arrested for homosexuality were castrated.[75] Many more were sent to the camps, enslaved, and murdered. Homosexual prisoners typically received especially harsh treatment. At Sachsenhausen, for example, SS guards routinely tortured homosexual men for sport. "In one case around October 1941 five homosexual prisoners were singled out and taken to the wash room. Their hands were bound behind their backs, and they were restrained by SS men while a hose was shoved down their throats and turned on full until they drowned. . . . Survivors from Sachsenhausen recalled that in the spring of 1942 homosexuals were intentionally selected at the gravel pit, and were tied to a loaded rail trolley car, with a noose around the neck of each. As the car hurtled down a slope, the victim was ordered to keep up with it, and those who failed to do so were dragged to death" (Giles 2002, 3). Some homosexual men were castrated at Buchenwald and elsewhere in the course of medical experiments.[76]

Whether Hitler knew or cared what was happening to homosexual men in the camps is unknown. He didn't seem to worry about homosexuality or homosexuals much one way or another. According to Geoffrey Giles, "His remarks were negative but infrequent" (2002, 6). Nevertheless, the idea that Hitler was obsessed with homosexuality and that his own homosexuality was a major factor in his homicidal paranoia has found its way into a number of biographical studies, most recently in the 2001 biography *The Hidden Hitler* by historian

Lothar Machtan and a 2004 Cinemax documentary based on the book, entitled *The Hidden Führer: Debating the Enigma of Hitler's Sexuality*.[77] Machtan asserts that Hitler had sexual relationships with several men and that his relationships with women, including Eva Braun, were platonic covers to prevent discovery of his secret.[78] While Machtan's book has met with skepticism from reputable historians, journalists reporting on his work have presented the public with dramatic leading headlines like "Hitler was gay—and killed to hide it, book says" (Connolly 2001). Many people apparently want to believe that Hitler was homosexual.[79]

Why? When Hitler was a ruling dictator, the accusation might have had some political value as a way to discredit him. But surely, now that the Nazis have been disgraced before the entire world, it isn't necessary to discredit Hitler any further. Hitler was a very bad fellow, sodomy or no sodomy. Yet this charge of homosexuality, substantiated or not, persists. Its purpose seems to be not so much to damn Hitler as to explain him. How homosexuality came to serve as an explanation for homicidal racism is a fascinating story, of which I can only offer a brief sketch here.

We begin with a strong motivation to set the Nazis apart from eugenics and the overwhelming majority of white middle-class Americans who favored so much of its program. The concept of *racism* was invented in the 1930s to name the difference between eugenics Hitler-style, aimed at eliminating entire races, and eugenics "proper," aimed at eliminating inferior individuals regardless of race. Racism is based on a false proposition, namely, that a person's physical appearance is a definitive indication of his or her genetic makeup and moral and social value. Scientists showed that proposition to be false way back in 1909 when Johannsen published his observations of bean plants. Robert Yerkes's military IQ tests demonstrated in 1917 that, while 89 percent of African Americans are morons and imbeciles, 11 percent are not. Given the scientific evidence, it is irrational to believe in the existence of racial (as opposed to individual) inferiority. Therefore, racist belief must be some kind of pathology or a symptom of one, a social and political expression of an underlying mental disturbance. Racists are not normal people.

Immediately after World War II, social scientists set to work to understand this sickness called racism. An enormous number of psychological studies were done, and the results tended to converge.

Prejudice, xenophobia, ethnocentrism, racism, anti-Semitism, and so forth, were symptoms of a pathological personality, sometimes called the Authoritarian Personality after Adorno's massive tome published in 1950. Individuals who develop such a personality are weak, submissive, conformist, and fearful. They take out the anger they feel toward authority figures whom they are too weak to resist on whoever seems most vulnerable, and they project the desires they have but fear to satisfy onto people they then experience as dirty and immoral. Their racism is really self-loathing, and the greater the self-loathing, the more violent and aggressive the racism.

Of course, weak, passive males are fundamentally effeminate, even if they sometimes appear to be very masculine. Their masculinity is merely a cover for their fundamental effeminacy. At the same time that they hate the powerful males who dominate them, they also identify with them and at times may even worship them. They are obsessed with virile, forceful men. They are latent homosexuals.[80]

Psychological profiles of Hitler describe exactly this sort of personality type. He was dominated by his violently erratic father and ashamed of having only one descended testicle.[81] He acted out his effeminate masochism in his sexual encounters with women.[82] But in public he assumed the role of the dominating, sadistic super-male as compensation for his effeminacy and weakness. *Voilà*, Hitler was queer.

Again and again from 1950 onward, theorists have portrayed racists as a pathological personality type marked by latent and occasionally flagrant homosexuality. "That the inordinate longing for status and power, the readiness for aggression against weaker or relatively defenseless people, and the demands for immediate recognition so common among criminals usually spring from underlying weakness, passivity, and homosexuality has often been noted" (Adorno et al., 1950, 817); indeed, the clearest example of the pathology under study in *The Authoritarian Personality* is a San Quentin inmate named Adrian, who is serving a sentence for homosexual prostitution.[83] The advent of Gay Liberation seems to have had no impact on this tendency to fuse racism with homosexuality. Joel Kovel's oft-cited neo-Freudian study *White Racism*, published in 1970, is an example. According to Kovel, dominative racists take sexual—usually homosexual—pleasure in tormenting their victims, and aversive racists are anally fixated, immature, latent homosexuals (1970, 49).

Of course, neither Kovel nor any of his antiracist colleagues would claim that all homosexual people are racist or xenophobic. But they do consistently make all people who are overtly racist or xenophobic sexually suspect. Thanks to studies like these, the link between homosexuality and irrational hatred of "out-groups" is now a standard assumption in American intellectual culture.

Thus did social scientists mark a clear separation between Nazis and normal Americans as well as between the effort to control human evolution and the plan to create a master race. Racism was carefully delineated and circumscribed as pathology, as something to be purged from an otherwise healthy and vigorous body politic. Virtually all the energy that has gone into critiquing and combating racism ever since has been aimed at this pathology rather than at the machinery of science, medicine, and government that actually generated scientific racism in the first place and perpetrated its many atrocities. That machinery remains largely in place, polished and augmented and humming away. More than forty years after Bloody Sunday, we are still fighting a rag-tag remnant, while biopolitical management projects and networks of normalization expand unchecked. Once again, sexuality—especially the fear of and the charge of homosexuality—has proven itself to be an amazingly effective instrument of biopower.

SIX

NORDICS CELEBRATE THE FAMILY

The social scientific analysis and condemnation of racism in the mid-1930s did nothing to curb enthusiasm for biopolitical interventions in reproduction and sexual behavior or for genetic management of national populations. For decades thereafter, draconian immigration restrictions remained in force. Segregation—both racial and intellectual—stood intact. Involuntary sterilization of the institutionalized, the disabled, and the poor continued and even escalated in some parts of the United States. IQ testing became big business, supplemented by standardized college admissions tests, personality inventories, and aptitude tests developed and disseminated by men who had been prominent in the prewar eugenics movement and aimed at weeding out people who were unfit for higher education, marriage and parenthood, and professional careers. Gay and lesbian people continued to be cast as psychopathic sexual predators and, with the Cold War becoming a defining fact of American life, as potential traitors and enemies of the state. And the "baby boom" began, as soldiers were demobilized and women who had been told all their lives to marry young and have at least four children left the wartime workforce and took up the task of replenishing the Nordic stock.

Many statesmen, industrialists, scholars, educators, social workers, physicians, and public health officials still dreamed of a better future—that is, a future in which Anglo-Saxon or Nordic or, at the very least, white evolutionary superiority, would translate into global economic and geopolitical supremacy—but they would no longer speak of that future in quite the same way. Their projects' origins in the theories of scientific racism would have to be forgotten if their goals were to be realized in a post-Nazi world.

For science had spoken. The morphological marks of race were not reliable indicators of genetic superiority or inferiority. There could be brilliant mulattoes. Theoretically, there could even be brilliant Negroes. (Theoretically.) Not *every* Jew was born conniving and miserly. Not every Italian had a violent temper. Not every Mexican had lice.[1] And every now and then, the sons and daughters of the whitest and best families in America turned out to be rascals or idiots or perverts. Of course, science had spoken a quarter-century before, but nobody—including most scientists—had paid much heed, so sure was everybody, even without empirical confirmation, that the morphological traits of race were inherited as units together with intelligence and the capacity for moral restraint. It took the Holocaust to amplify the voice of science enough to get most people's attention.

But before we conclude that the attempt to breed a master race was itself the final victim of Hitler's regime, we need to listen carefully to what the voice of science was actually saying: (1) Lines of genetic difference don't *exactly* follow lines of visible morphological difference. In lay terms, Strom Thurman could conceivably have more genes in common with Al Sharpton than with Jimmy Carter. (2) Variation within groups is at least as great as, and usually much greater than, variability across groups. There are tall Croats and short Croats, so there is a lot of height variation among Croats. There are also tall Zunis and short Zunis, so there is a lot of height variation among Zunis. On average, though, Croats and Zunis are probably pretty nearly the same height, so there is less height variation across those two groups than within each one. The voice of science did *not* say, however, (1) that the differences in appearance between Strom Thurman and Al Sharpton were *not* genetic or (2) that there is *no* genetically determined variation across racial populations; and, most notably, science did *not* say (3) that all human beings are equally valuable and worthy of respect. Eugenicists didn't hear the voice of science telling them to stop judging people inferior, because the voice of science never issued that command. It just politely suggested that they should judge people inferior in smaller groups. Whole morphological races are not necessarily inferior to whole other morphological races. Inferiority must be further specified.

This polite suggestion is sometimes referred to as the shift from typological thinking to population thinking, and it is often heralded as the end of scientific racism. Most eugenicists did take it seriously. Frederick Osborn, nephew of Henry Fairfield Osborn and a driving force in the transformation of eugenics through mid-century, was proclaiming these scientific tenets within the American Eugenics Society at least as early as 1937, as noted in chapter 5. He wrote in *Eugenical News* that "it would be unwise for eugenists to impute superiorities or inferiorities of a biological nature to social classes, to regional groups, or to races as a whole." He continued:

> Scientists are not at all sure that any races or social classes in this country are above or below others in biological capacity for developing socially valuable qualities. But they are sure that even if there are differences between the average bio-logical capacities of such groups, they are small compared to the much greater differences existing between individuals. Eugenics should therefore operate on a basis of individual selection. A program of selection of the best individuals and the best family stock, from every race and socio-economic class, will have wide scientific support. (F. Osborn 1937, 106)[2]

It is conceivable, if only barely, that a truly superior human race might require one or two Negro or Jewish or Asiatic genes. Osborn reiterated and enlarged upon this position in his 1940 book *Preface to Eugenics,* maintaining that eugenics is only viable in a democracy, where individuals are respected.

> The eugenics ideal recognizes that each human being is by his heredity unique. This uniqueness, which pervades every cell in his body, justifies respect for the individual. . . . Eugenics, in asserting the uniqueness of the individual, supplements the American ideal of respect for the individual. Eugenics in a democracy seeks not to breed men to a single type, but to raise the average level of human variations, reducing variations tending toward poor health, low intelligence, and anti-social character, and increasing variations at the highest levels of activity. (F. Osborn 1940, 296–97)

Eugenics is not racism, Osborn implicitly argues. Racists—like Hitler—seek to breed a single type of person; they seek conformity to one morphologic ideal. Ultimately, breeding programs of that sort are dysgenic because they do not select for the variations that really matter—strength, vitality, high intelligence, and socially valuable conduct.

But the ideological distinction that Osborn insists is decisive—
that between allegedly dysgenic type-based and allegedly eugenic
population-based breeding programs—may not actually make much
difference in practice. As Lisa Gannett points out,

> "Population thinkers" can be what we might call "statisti-
> cal racists." "Population thinking" precludes stereotyping of
> the form "person A is a certain way because *all* individuals
> belonging to that group are that way" and the differential
> treatment of entire groups. But "population thinking" is
> consistent with the stereotyping of individuals based on the
> statistical properties of the group. Such stereotyping takes
> the form: "person A is *probably/likely/may be* a certain way
> because *most/many/some* individuals belonging to that group
> are that way." "Statistical racism" is also manifested with
> respect to entire groups. "Population thinking" and its atten-
> tion to statistical differences among groups—differences in
> mean trait values or the range of values exhibited for traits—
> could be used to justify differential representation of certain
> racial/ethnic groups in various occupations or educational
> groups. . . . It is also conceivable that arguments that appeal
> to statistical differences among populations in the frequen-
> cies of genes associated with particular dispositional traits
> could be used to sanction differential social treatment—for
> example, "racial profiling" by police. "Population thinking"
> is *not* inherently anti-racist. (Gannett 2001, S490)[3]

Indeed, even many old-time—blatantly racist—eugenicists had already
acknowledged that there was significant variation within the groups
they despised. Harry Laughlin told a *New York Times* reporter, "The
Jews are no exception to races which are widely variable in family-
stock quality within their own race. There are superior Jews, and
there are inferior Jews" ("Relaxing Quotas," 1934, 7). One could find
law-abiding Italians, intelligent Irishmen, sober Indians, and chaste
Negresses; they were just very rare, so that on average, Italians were
criminals, Irishmen were imbeciles, Indians were dipsomaniacs, and
Negresses were sluts in comparison to normal ladies and gentlemen
of the Nordic race.

The lesson U.S. eugenicists learned from the Holocaust was not to
stop judging people on the basis of race, but to be more specific about
exactly what was wrong with the people so judged so that biopolitical

population management and normalization techniques would not be confused with the irrational elements of Nazism. Obviously, high IQs were better than low IQs. Obviously, law-abiding behavior was better than criminal behavior. Obviously, lucidity was better than delusion. Obviously, sobriety was better than drunkenness. Obviously, chastity was better than promiscuity. Obviously, heterosexuality was better than homosexuality. Obviously, intelligent, hard-working, sane, temperate, moral people were better than stupid, lazy, deluded, besotted, queer people. A race of people relatively full of the former and free of the latter would, on the whole, be a better race. If the black race was inferior to the white, it was not because its members were black; it was because such a high proportion of them were stupid, lazy, addicted, perverted, and so forth.[4] Just for good measure, though—because, as Osborn pointed out, theoretically there could be a few individuals of some real worth in even the lowest of races—most eugenicists dropped the talk about inferior and superior *races* altogether to speak only of superior and inferior traits in America's families. They wanted to find ways to support families likely to produce children who would be intelligent, hard-working, sane, temperate, and moral and to discourage the formation of families likely to produce children who would be retarded, mentally ill, criminal, and sexually perverse.

Who could criticize that? After all, it wasn't *racism.*

People were still a little skittish, though. The word *eugenics* tended to conjure up ugly pictures and the smell of smoke. Gradually, over the next couple of decades, eugenics organizations and periodicals dropped the word from their names. In 1954 the British *Annals of Eugenics* was renamed *Annals of Human Genetics.* In 1969 the *Eugenics Quarterly* became the *Journal of Social Biology.* In 1972 the American Eugenics Society changed its name to the Society for the Study of Social Biology. Eugenicists began to call themselves "population scientists" and "human geneticists" (Kuhl 1994, 105; Bruinius 2006, 317). As Frederick Osborn acknowledged in 1968, "Eugenic goals are most likely to be attained under a name other than eugenics" (25). Nine years later he told an interviewer: "It became evident that changes of a eugenic nature would be made for reasons other than eugenics, and . . . tying a eugenic label on them would more often hinder than help their adoption."[5] No one wanted the work of racial hygiene hampered by the memory of Hitler.

In the decades following World War II, therefore, most of the various intellectual and institutional components of scientific racism cast off their Nazi-tainted eugenic image and restyled themselves. Race purification was definitely not the goal. As California eugenicist Ezra Gosney told his staff at the Human Betterment Foundation in 1940: "We have little in this country to consider in *racial integrity.* Germany is pushing that. We should steer clear of it lest we be misunderstood" (in Kline 1997, 104). Among themselves, eugenicists like Gosney and Paul Popenoe continued to speak of "race betterment" as the aim of eugenics, but even that phrase was seldom hazarded in public. Instead, most eugenicists began to emphasize a line of thought that had been present all along but not accented during the years when immigration restriction, segregation, and sterilization were safe topics for frank public discussion. Following Frederick Osborn's lead, American eugenicists began to bill their efforts as selection of "the best family stock." As his uncle, Henry Fairfield Osborn, had said in 1921, "The monogamous family, i.e., one husband, one wife, is to be maintained and safeguarded by the state as well as by religion as a natural and hence as a patriotic institution" (313). Not in the name of The Race but in the name of The Family would eugenics carry on. In the postwar years, *family* would become the semantic substitute for *race.*

Paul Popenoe and the Birth of the Normal Family

Perhaps surprisingly, Paul Popenoe emerged as a leader in the rhetorically remodeled postwar eugenics movement. A horticulturist by training, Popenoe had become involved in the eugenics movement in the 1910s.[6] He edited the *Journal of Heredity* from 1913 to 1917 and thus worked closely with Davenport and Laughlin and was well-versed in eugenic theory and the movement's political program. During World War I he was a captain in the Army Sanitation Corps in charge of vice and liquor control around army camps; in that capacity he crusaded against prostitution and took up the banner of social hygiene. In 1918 he co-authored the immensely popular college textbook *Applied Eugenics* with Roswell Johnson. In 1929, having gone to work as the secretary of the Human Betterment Foundation, he co-authored *Sterilization for Human Betterment* with Ezra Gosney. One might imagine that this background, together with the blatantly racist and pro-Nazi comments Popenoe frequently made in print prior to World War II, would have made it difficult for him to repackage himself and his ideas. But in fact, his early work actually laid much of the groundwork for the postwar pro-family movement.

In his 1926 book *The Conservation of the Family*, Popenoe had claimed that "the" family is the oldest human institution in existence, having persisted unchanged for the last 500,000 years and that "the normal family is the only effective school for the life of the citizen" (8, 43). It is this "normal" family, of course, not just any family, that would become the focal point for a retooled eugenics after the Holocaust. Not the Nordic Race but the Normal Family must be protected from the evil forces that endanger it—for example, feminists, or, in Popenoe's terms, "oversexed and incontinent young spinsters and divorcees" and "undersexed, celibate spinsters of older age, all of whom, under the banner of individualism, are destroying the machinery of society" (1926, 136). And of course the Normal Family must be protected from the champions of birth control. "Continued limitation of offspring in the white race simply invites the black, brown, and yellow races to finish the work already begun by Birth Control, and reduce the whites to a subject race preserved mainly for the sake of its technical skill, as the Greeks were by the Romans" (1926, 144). There was only one good thing about the feminist movement, Popenoe thought: It encouraged women "lacking in normal sexual instincts, or who may even have the instincts of the opposite sex" to avoid marriage, "for should they have children they might pass on their own abnormal constitutions" (1926, 48; see also Popenoe and Johnson 1926, 379). About the birth control movement, however, he had nothing good to say. To Popenoe, protecting the family meant eradicating feminism and homosexuality altogether and keeping birth control information, devices, and procedures safely in the hands of eugenic-minded physicians and officers of the state. His basic position remained unchanged from 1926, when he published *Conservation of the Family*, through 1977, when he campaigned to curtail civil rights for homosexuals in California.[7]

Popenoe was a strong advocate of forced sterilization of the unfit from the mid-1920s onward, but when anti-Nazi sentiment made public advocacy of such eugenic practices counterproductive, he simply dropped that issue and emphasized its complement, increased fertility in normal families. The key word was *normal*. "From the biological standpoint," he had written in 1926, "the normal family may be defined briefly as one in which two adults live together happily and give birth to an appropriate number of healthy and intelligent children, whom they bring up to lives of usefulness" (6). Clearly *the* family, like *the* race, wasn't nearly the inclusive concept it might at first glance seem to be. *The* family was nuclear (with a male head), reasonably successful in a capitalist labor market (and thus not poor), fecund (but producing no offspring with mental or physical disabilities or antisocial attitudes), and of course, all of its members were heterosexual. Families that did not measure up to these requirements were not normal families, not the sort of families that had endured for 500,000 years, not the sort of families that were effective schools for people who could safely be allowed to exercise civil rights, and thus not the sort of families the state or private foundations and charities should support and encourage.

Given the political and economic realities of 1926, it was obvious that very few African American families could measure up, and that would remain true for several more decades. Financial prosperity was simply out of reach for most blacks in the 1920s. In addition to discrimination in education, union membership, and employment (which was permitted and sometimes required by law into the 1960s), blacks faced difficulties obtaining loans and life insurance policies and thus were unable to start businesses, build equity in property, and bequeath wealth to their children.[8] Because they could not depend on police or courts to protect their rights, they were sometimes cheated or bullied out of the few assets they had. As journalist Elliott Jaspin has documented, in the last two decades of the nineteenth century and the first two decades of the twentieth in many localities throughout the South and Midwest, whole communities of African Americans were driven out of their homes en masse and their property confiscated by whites.[9] As a result of these and other racist practices, a majority of black families were, to say the least, not successful in the capitalist labor market. Furthermore, many black households could not be said to have a male head—if for no other reason than that the role of breadwinner had to be shouldered by adults of both sexes.[10] And of course, severe material deprivation often resulted in birth defects and disfiguring illnesses as well as "antisocial" attitudes.

When the New Deal was struck in the early 1930s, most African Americans were left out of its provisions. Old age pensions were not extended to agricultural workers or domestic servants, largely because Southern landowners (whose representatives' support was essential for the New Deal's passage) did not want aging field hands, maids, and sharecroppers to qualify for any cash assistance that might enrich their households and thus drive up wages or finance younger relatives' exodus to lands of greater opportunity (Quadagno 1994, 20–21). Teachers, librarians, nurses, and social workers—"female" professions often pursued by middle-class black as well as white women—were also excluded from Social Security (Quadagno 1994, 157). Because the new laws allowed states to set their own standards for allocation of Unemployment Compensation and Aid to Dependent Children, state officials were free to enact policies that effectively denied blacks any sort of financial aid. And the Federal Housing Act of 1934 allowed the Federal Housing Administration to redline predominately black neighborhoods and business districts, denying African Americans loans for purchase of property in ghettos, while segregation laws and custom prohibited them from purchasing property anywhere else (Quadagno 1994, 23). The effect was to render most blacks lifelong renters with no equity in the buildings and land they inhabited and maintained. After World War II, when Veterans' Administration benefits were raising many young white men and their families out of poverty, black men were effectively denied access to educational opportunities, housing, and job training, making the GI Bill (the 1944 Serviceman's Readjustment Act) basically a set of "affirmative action programs for white males" (Sacks 1994, 90).[11] For these reasons, African American families continued to live in poverty across generations even as Americans of other races found ways out of Depression-era misery.

Thus, through the first two-thirds of the twentieth century, the Normal Family could not be black. Simply being white was not enough either, however. Popenoe's concept of The Family also made the extended kinship networks of recent immigrants and impoverished rural white communities suspect. Who really was the head of such a household? How could a young father command the respect he deserved from wife and offspring if his own parents, in-laws, aunts and uncles, or older siblings lived in the same house? And it surely goes without saying that single-parent households and same-sex couples and their children could never qualify as normal.[12] They were abnormal by definition, because to be normal a family had to have both a father and a mother who exemplified gender-appropriate behavior.

Among the most basic requirements for any set of people to be considered a real family was a formal state-issued marriage license legally binding its head to his sex partner and the children she bore. Failure to obtain a marriage license was itself proof of abnormality, indicating either moral imbecility or unfitness as defined by eugenic marriage restriction and anti-miscegenation laws. Popenoe insisted that every child's birth certificate should state the mother's marital status and should be a matter of public record. "The reason for secrecy, of course, is to prevent the innocent child from bearing a stigma," he acknowledged. "But, after all, is there any reason why the innocent child should not bear a stigma? It is inescapably stigmatized by birth, through inheritance from anti-social, probably mentally defective, and otherwise abnormal parents"—that is, parents who did not (or could not) obtain a marriage license before they had sex.[13] The requirement of state-licensed marriage—and the sorts of individuals and households it worked to exclude from the category of the "normal"—remained intact through the 1950s and 60s and, though challenged by the liberation movements and the economic dislocations of the 1970s, remains substantially in place still.[14]

By the time Paul Popenoe died in 1979, he was known nation-wide as "Mr. Marriage"; his starring role as Mr. Involuntary Sterilization of the Unfit was largely forgotten. Obituaries hailed him as "the man who saved marriages," alluding to his work as founder and director of the country's first marriage counseling center, the American Institute for Family Relations in Altadena, California, as well as his many years as editor of *Marriage and Family Living;* his two books, *Modern Marriage: A Handbook* (1925) and *Sex, Love, and Marriage* (1963); his television talk show where unhappy Los Angeles couples could air their problems and receive his advice; and, of course, his long-running column in the *Ladies' Home Journal,* "Can This Marriage Be Saved?" Popenoe's transition from scientific racism's crusader for forced sterilization to the AIFR's "Mr. Marriage" was a relatively easy one. After all, marriage counseling was not about individual happiness; it was simply a way to preserve heterosexual unions long enough for fit individuals to make what Popenoe called their "eugenic contribution" (Ladd-Taylor 2001, 300).

Popenoe traced his interest in the idea back to the 1910s: "I began to realize that if we were going to promote a sound population, we would not only have to get the right kind of people married, but we would have to keep them married." His first marriage advice book, published in 1925, was explicitly aimed at men "high enough in the evolutionary scale to let reason play an appropriate part . . . in directing their lives" (quoted in Ladd-Taylor, 2001, 300, 309), in other words, the "right kind" of men, eugenically speaking. The marriages of men lower on the evolutionary scale were never an object of Mr. Marriage's salvific ministrations. Many of his articles were aimed at educators—whom he exhorted to create more home economics courses for girls and more opportunities for heterosexual social mixing in schools—and at college-educated women—whom he alternately berated for their selfishness in delaying marriage for personal enrichment and advised on how (and where) to find suitably marriageable men.[15]

Popenoe's marriage counseling work was clearly recognized by other eugenicists as a significant part of their postwar efforts. The American Institute for Family Relations was funded by Ezra Gosney, Popenoe's coauthor in *Sterilization for Human Betterment,* through the Human Betterment Foundation. The institute made no secret of its mission. According to Molly Ladd-Taylor, "Most newspaper reports of the AIFR's opening in February 1930, quoting its press release, described the institute's purpose as to 'disseminate eugenics informa-tion and endeavor to aid persons contemplating marriage to make a success of their venture'" (2001, 311). In addition to its many pub-lications, the institute offered premarital counseling (complete with physical examinations, personality inventories, and marital aptitude tests) emphasizing hereditary fitness and compatibility, advice for couples having difficulties, and training workshops for clergy, teach-ers, and other professionals who were themselves engaged in couples counseling.

Gosney and Popenoe had pointed out in *Sterilization for Human Betterment* that arguments can be made for sterilization of the unfit, not on eugenical grounds only, but on the grounds that the practice has a positive effect on family life: "Is not the present disorganized condition of the family, with its concomitant of broken homes and sexual irregularity, largely due to the mentally unstable, and to the advice and pattern which they give to those who are on the border line between social and anti-social behavior as well as on the border line between intellectual normality and subnormality?" (1929, 106). Sterilization of the unfit prevents the formation of families that would be unstable and homes that would eventually be broken. It relieves the fears of those who know they carry a hereditary taint. It reduces the financial burden on working families whose taxes pay for the upkeep of institutionalized defectives. Involuntary sterilization is thus a pro-family measure. For some people, this is "the strongest argument that can be brought forward in its favor. They may not be used to thinking in terms of eugenics . . . but few are deaf to the humanitarian plea, and when the problem is discussed in terms of human misery, it is put in a language that they can understand" (1929, 106).[16] For similar reasons, most other eugenic measures would be translated into pro-family measures over the next several decades.

Pro-family measures, we must note, are *not* humanitarian measures. Eugenics was always deeply incompatible with humanitarianism. To relieve the suffering and prolong the lives of the unfit would be to thwart the forces of natural selection. Forget the widows and orphans, the cripples, the simpletons, the blind. People must not be encouraged to aid the needy or protect the vulnerable.[17] Sympathy and generosity must be channeled toward eugenically valuable individuals only. Thus the concept of charity as a virtue and a moral duty would gradually disappear, and the Family would emerge as the only appropriate object of public concern and support.

At the beginning of the twenty-first century, we are so used to hearing pleas for various policies or programs made in the name of the Family that we hardly give it a thought. Of course it is good to support families and bad to do anything that would undermine them! No one questions that. But we rarely notice what is not being made a matter of public concern when the Family is made paramount. If we step back and give the matter some thought, however, it seems strange that in a democratic republic established in the name of personal liberty and civic equality, public concern is not aroused by the needs of individual citizens, and programs are not justified in the name of individual aspirations. Why, for example, do we need to relieve the tax burden on working families rather than on workers? Why is it more compelling to call for police protection to ensure safe neighborhoods than it is to call for police protection to ensure safe streets? Stepping back, we may begin to wonder just who it is that the Family is crowding out of our civic consciousness, and why.

Most human beings are born into multigenerational kinship networks. Over the course of a lifetime, most also form additional relationships, some of which are incorporated into existing kinship networks. Some of these relationships are sexual and involve domestic arrangements that endure over decades. But as so many anthropologists and historians have pointed out, the organization of these relationships, networks, and domestic arrangements can vary and has varied tremendously through space and time. The Family, in Paul Popenoe's sense, is a Johnny-come-lately with a very limited range. Popenoe and others like him more or less invented the Family in the mid-twentieth century. The Family is not a naturally existing entity. It is the generative unit of Nordic supremacy. It is designed to crowd out of our civic consciousness, and therefore out of our national life, the very same individuals who were slated for restriction, segregation, and sterilization under the old plan, the ones who used to be called racial inferiors and degenerates.

Eugenically minded Nordic supremacists like Popenoe were never interested in protecting individual rights or prerogatives, not even those of individual Nordics. At bottom, they were extremely anti-democratic and antilibertarian.[18] The purpose of the state, on their view, was to protect and further the interests of the Race, and the Race transcended all individuals. Hence, not individual rights but the process of generation was what was to be safeguarded. Individuals would be cared for and protected only as long as their well-being coincided with the furtherance of racial interests—that is, only as long as they were deemed eugenically valuable and were procreating or preparing to procreate.

Among those so deemed, simple reproduction was not enough, however. To qualify as a eugenically significant contribution, a baby must be nurtured to sexual maturity and prepared for the role of mother or father to the next generation. The process of eugenic generation thus necessarily included child rearing as well as child bearing, and parenthood that did not culminate in grandparenthood was a failed project.

Eugenicists and their successors wanted to make that generative process as efficient and productive as possible. The Family was their social engineering solution, an efficient vehicle for genetic transport.[19] Structurally, it was quite compact. It did not include relatives past their reproductive years. (Rational people will plan for their retirement so as not to be a burden on the next generation, whose resources would be better spent raising as many healthy children as possible.)[20]

In fact, it did not include any adults other than husband and wife—no unmarried siblings or cousins, no friends in need of a place to stay, no lodgers, no grown children.[21] Such people might be part of the household temporarily, but they were never part of the Family. If they were eugenically valuable, they should be paired off and producing children of their own. If not, they were to be viewed with suspicion as nuisances and intruders more likely to seduce or corrupt young children than to nurture them. A family consisted of two and only two adults, one man and one woman, duly licensed by the state. And even the duly licensed couple would not be considered a real family until genes were set in motion and the process of child rearing begun.

The Confluence of Eugenics and Sexology

The bourgeois family, Foucault tells us, was and is a thoroughly sexualized institution. At its foundation lies not a tradition or a territory, as in previous versions of the concept of "family," but a single sexual relationship, the intercourse of husband and wife. By the 1920s, therefore, the work of eugenicists intersected with that of sexologists and formed mutually reinforcing networks of knowledge and normalizing disciplinary authority. That single, crucial sexual relationship not only had to be safeguarded; it also had to be good.

It had to be good in two ways. It had to be physically and emotionally satisfying to superior people who (being superior) had real alternatives. And it had to be morally acceptable, despite the fact that making it physically satisfying to both parties over the long term necessarily involved indulgence and even at times glorification of the carnal.

Sexologists had been working on making sexual pleasure morally acceptable for a long time already, although in many cases that was probably not their intent. They had done so in part by developing an idea that was already present in Buffon's work back in the eighteenth century, namely, that sexual attraction was the prototype of all human attraction and therefore the origin of human society. As noted in chapter 2, Buffon had held that Americans (by which he meant indigenous peoples) had little sexual passion (and little penises to match); consequently, they treated their women like beasts of burden and didn't love their children.[22] That was the reason that they (allegedly) had never built a thriving civilization. Jefferson had taken umbrage because Buffon's claims reflected poorly on the North American climate and, in turn, on the new nation's prospects. He had begged to differ, asserting that, on the contrary, Indians were passionate and loving and the size of their penises was wholly within the realm of the healthy.

Jefferson did not speak to the question of whether sexual attraction was essential for social cohesion, but by the end of the nineteenth century other Americans did. In 1892, for example, Dr. James Kiernan presented his theory of the evolution of human morality out of raw carnal desire:

> The phenomena of sexual selection demonstrate that a complex mental state has resulted from the evolution of the simple search for physical sexual means of satisfying protoplasmic hunger. These sexual selection phenomena show that pleasure has ceased to be dependent on simple sexual conjugation, since ideas of beauty, of attraction to the most beautiful, and of maternal love, have evolved from the sexual desire of satisfying protoplasmic hunger. Thus have been developed inhibitions on explosive sexual performances which tended to restrain egotism evident in the purely sexual propensity. Hence pleasure associated with conjugation with a given subject arose on sight of that subject, and sexual pleasure evinced itself in attempts to please the cause. These [attempts] repressed explosive manifestations of the sexual appetite[,] thus producing more intellectual and less obvious physical enjoyment of sexual society. By an ordinary law of mental association, attempts to please the cause of sexual pleasure, in themselves finally pleased without the presence of the cause. Thus developed romantic love which restrained egotism, and restraints on egotism constitute the basis of morality. (Kiernan 1892, 190).[23]

Romance is a form of moral restraint, and it gives birth to all other forms. At the origin of morality lies sexual desire. Rather than denouncing sexuality, therefore, civilized people ought to praise and cultivate it.

Cultivating it was especially important in light of the fact that eugenic marriage and child rearing required a great deal of sacrifice, especially on the part of women. Feminists had been complaining about the institution of marriage at least since Mary Wollstonecraft. Although things had changed somewhat since Wollstonecraft's time

(1759–97), women who married still gave up many of their property rights, their right to choose their domicile, and to a significant extent their right to self-defense. (A certain amount of wife-beating was a husband's prerogative well into the twentieth century.) In addition, childbearing could be mortally dangerous, and multiple pregnancies (an inevitability for most women without access to contraception) were debilitating. If there were no rewards to offset the sacrifices and risks, why would superior women, who were increasingly well educated and able to support themselves in a rising industrial economy, choose to become wives and mothers? Sexologists had the answer eugenicists sought: orgasm.

Motherhood would be praised to the heavens, but the lure that would keep those eugenically valuable females in the baby-making trenches of the marriage bed year after year after year was good sex. Sexologists like Theodore van de Velde and Helena Wright offered help. In 1928, even though in many states oral sex was a criminal act, Van de Velde recommended that men lubricate their wives' vaginas by means of the "genital kiss," that is, "by gentle and soothing caresses with lips and tongue." Wright's *The Sex Factor in Marriage* (1930) advised men to learn their wives' rhythms and lovingly attend to their clitorises.[24] In fact, marriage manuals from the 1920s into the 1940s were full of advice to men about patience, clitoral stimulation, and foreplay.[25] Very often the advice was laced with the repeated warning that the husband who failed to satisfy his wife sexually would likely lose her. Sexual competence was essential to masculine marital success. Gynecologist and eugenicist Robert Latou Dickinson opened the section on sexual relations in Morris Fishbein's 1947 anthology *Successful Marriage* with these words: "Mating belongs among those activities in which instruction can foster needed skills and forestall grievous blunders. This holds particularly for the mismanaged physical relation oftenest leading to divorce as a result of 'leaving it to nature.' Indeed, for every occupation save one, examination for fitness is the rule. That one is the most vital and worth while of all—marriage and parenthood—and for it, someday, routine preliminary examination will come to pass, through custom, into code" (Dickinson 1947, 69). Just as a man must demonstrate to authorities his skill at driving a car before he is issued a driver's license, someday a man will have to demonstrate to the authorities that he knows how to bring a woman to orgasm or he will not be granted a license to marry.[26] Dickinson's article is followed by G. Lombard Kelly's article on sexual technique, in which he warns that "the husband who does not take the necessary steps to make his relations with his wife mutually enjoyable and satisfactory may eventually ruin his marriage. If this occurs he has only himself to blame" (Kelly 1947, 94). He goes on to discuss various sexual positions, emphasizing clitoral stimulation, and then offers pointed advice about how best to "win" the female orgasm. Some authorities even turned to lesbians for help. Near the conclusion of New York's Committee for the Study of Sex Variants report, George Henry writes, "Much can be learned from study of the affectionate relations of sex variants which might contribute to the success of heterosexual unions."[27]

It may seem strange that eugenicists as far back as the 1920s would be pro-sex, especially pro-clitoral orgasm. In earlier years, they certainly were less so; some initially opposed sterilization, eventually a cornerstone of the program, because they feared it would lead to promiscuity. But as eugenicists refined their position, they came to see women's sexuality as a key component of evolutionary advance. While natural selection was compromised somewhat by modern sanitation methods, charity, government aid, and the miracles of modern medicine, sexual selection was still operative and could be made an even more important factor in evolution if women were allowed more leeway in choosing their mates. If genetically superior women were in a position to decline an offer of marriage and hold out for the best mate rather than, as so often happened, being pressed by economic considerations and social mores into marrying the first man who came along and staying with him for life, then chances were good that fewer unfit men would reproduce—or at least fewer would corrupt the bloodlines of women who were fit. Thus many eugenicists supported some feminist demands for more civil and property rights.[28] However, as women gained these rights, it was necessary to find ways to keep them from putting off marriage too long or eschewing it altogether. They had to be enticed. And they had to be kept happy once they were wed. Only so could the generative process reach its completion in the production of sexually mature, well-adjusted offspring ready to pair off and pass on those superior genes.

Sexual Predators, the Welfare State, and Gender Deviance: The Family's Enemies List

The work of child rearing was at least as important as child bearing. Parents' most important responsibilities were to protect their

children from harm and to equip them to carry on. "To carry on"
meant to reproduce not just the eugenic body but the Normal Family
as a generative structure. (Superior) children must be taught that marriage and parenthood are the ultimate sources of personal fulfillment;
their desire for heterosexual relationships must be whetted. This project carried risks, of course; once awakened, adolescent sexual desires
had to be carefully channeled and contained. Girls must not get pregnant out of state-sanctioned wedlock, and boys must not compromise
their reproductive health by consorting with inferior females. A great
deal of parental and pedagogical policing was necessary to ensure
feminine chastity and masculine prudence. But far more parental and
pedagogical effort went into molding what we might now call children's gender.

From early childhood, boys and girls must develop the qualities
associated with their future sex roles. Boys must acquire masculine
traits, and girls feminine traits. That was primarily a natural process,
spurred on by the newly discovered endocrine system, but at times it
was necessary to introduce a little artificial stimulation or even some
stern therapeutic intervention. Young people's resistance to their sexual
destiny was typically interpreted as selfishness, as lack of patriotism,
and, in especially stubborn cases, as mental illness. But it was first of
all parents who were accountable for any serious failures. The Family's
purpose was to serve as a step in an ongoing evolutionary progres-
sion. As the stewards of a precious genetic endowment, parents were
responsible for making sure that genes passed safely from their bodies
to the bodies of their grandchildren. The well-gendered body of the
child was the means through which that passage was to be secured.

Just as their predecessors had worried about menaces to the Race
from both within and without, eugenicists in the 1940s, 50s, and
60s worried about both external and internal threats to the Family.
Outside the Family lay two major kinds of threat. As before, there
was the sexual predator—the crazed black man in the bushes (now
even more agitated by mounting "racial tension"); the sexual psychopath, both male and female;[29] and the avuncular old bachelor
with bags of candy in his car. These people were obvious dangers
that had to be controlled. But they could never be completely eliminated because, paradoxically, they also served a eugenic purpose. As
so many feminist social critics have pointed out, the possibility of
sexual predation justified keeping women and children under surveil-

lance and virtual house arrest, since their venturing out alone could lead to the worst of familial tragedies. That threat—in its repetition rather than its realization—thus reinforced the Family's patriarchal structure. The second external threat to the Family was the state, the very same state that created it through marital licensure and birth certification. A state must collect taxes. To a point, those taxes were money well spent from the Family's point of view; they paid for police protection, food and drug inspection, highways, schools, and national defense. But advocates of the Family had to be ever vigilant lest the state become a dysgenic mechanism by attempting to protect or aid the weak at the expense of the worthy. Sentimental bleeding hearts were always trying to convince officials to use tax money to improve living conditions for people incapable of improving them for themselves. Where did that money come from? Out of the college funds of the brightest and best, of course. To be sure, as long as inferior people clung to life and multiplied, some money would have to be spent, if for nothing else than to segregate and imprison them. In the postwar era it was impolitic to suggest eliminating them outright—"lest we be misunderstood," to use Ezra Gosney's phrase—so the best that could be done was to minimize expenditures and hope that they would eliminate each other through unchecked contagion and crime.

Some politicians—such as New Deal heir Lyndon Johnson—courted and coddled the unfit and caved in to the troublemakers to get their votes and stay in office, dismantling racial segregation and offering expanded welfare programs to reduce the effects of poverty. It was because of such panderers that the lowest of the low—Negro women with no morals or sexual restraint—were able to live high and keep bearing their dysgenic babies throughout the 1960s and 70s. Instead of letting destitution curb their fertility, bleeding-heart liberals treated such women like royalty, forcing states to increase monthly welfare payments and food stamp allotments and to develop free lunch and head start programs for all their inferior, subnormal offspring.[30] Thus was born The Welfare Queen, an unmarried black woman who deliberately got pregnant over and over in order to collect an extra forty or fifty dollars per month per child and who raised her children to be similar parasites on the system.[31] The black urban successor to white Appalachia's Old Sal, the Welfare Queen didn't have a family; she had a brood or a litter or a warren that real families had to pay taxes to support.

As always, however, the most frightening threat was the one that came from inside the house. It was the threat of superior sexuality gone awry—or, we might say from a twenty-first-century perspective, it was the threat of gender deviance. It could take two equally monstrous forms: The Feminist or The Homosexual. Sometimes it took both at once in the truly hideous form of: The Lesbian.

The Feminist was a female of seemingly good heredity who either refused to get married at all or who got married but then artificially limited her eugenic contribution in favor of pursuing a career or political ambitions. She had made her appearance in the nineteenth century and maintained a certain prominence, usually in the form of the aspiring young college graduate, through the first three or four decades of the twentieth. Not only did she deprive the Race of her own superior genes and those of her husband too if she had one, but she also warped the few children she did deign to produce. According to William Lee Howard:

> The progeny of such human misfits are perverts, moral or psychical. Their prenatal life has been influenced by the very antithesis of what the real woman would surround her expected child with. The child born of the "new woman" is to be pitied. If it could be taken away from its environments, kept from the misguidance of an unwilling mother, nurtured, tutored, and directed along the sex line Nature has struggled to give it, often would the child be true to its latent normal instincts and grow to respected womanhood or manhood. Unfortunate it is that this development does not take place. The weak, plastic, developing cells of the brain are twisted, distorted, and a perverted psychic growth promoted by the false examples and teachings of a discontented mother. (Howard 1900, 687)

If your daughter grew up to be a feminist, your grandchildren would suffer brain damage. It was very important, therefore, to discourage female children from aspiring to postgraduate degrees, professional careers, or positions of leadership in religious or political organizations. They should be taught to content themselves with their subordinate position within the institution of patriarchal marriage and their role as mothers to the next generation of genetic transport systems. Discontent would jeopardize their chances of finding a eugenically suitable mate or, if one was found, of keeping him long enough to bear and raise the requisite four eugenically acceptable children.

Obviously the Feminist, as she was depicted by advocates of the Family, was Nordic and middle class. Women (and men) of other races and socioeconomic classes might adhere to one or another feminist ideology and might campaign for feminist reforms—in fact, a great many feminists were non-Nordic, non-bourgeois, and even non-female—but when pro-family eugenicists and their fellow travelers attacked the Feminist, they weren't interested in the actual members of any given political movement. The bogeywomen they feared were their own white, middle-class daughters who might refuse to give them grandchildren because they preferred not to subordinate themselves to husbands and devote themselves to the life of the womb.

Eugenicists of the 1920s and 30s continued to rail against the Feminist, even as real feminist movements declined in strength, and they would revive their antifeminist rhetoric quickly and easily in the early 1960s as feminism reasserted itself. (Paul Popenoe would write one of the first reviews of Betty Friedan's book *The Feminine Mystique* in 1964.)[32] But for a short time after World War II, the Feminist receded into the rhetorical background. The threatening creature who stepped into her place was the Homosexual.

Like the Feminist, the Homosexual was a sort of race traitor. He or she was a seemingly hereditarily sound individual who refused to play the proper role in the formation of a normal family and thus refused to render forth his or her eugenic contribution. Like the college-educated career woman, the Homosexual sinned against the Race by scorning the Family, that is, by selfishly pursuing his or her own individual pleasure rather than shouldering the racial duty to carry on.

Obviously the Homosexual, as he or she was depicted by advocates of the Family, was Nordic and middle-class. Individuals of other races and socioeconomic classes might engage in homosexual pleasures and might even lead lives entirely devoted to same-sex relationships.[33] But so what? When pro-family eugenicists and their fellow travelers assailed the Homosexual, they weren't interested in the sexual practices of their inferiors.[34] The bogeymen and -women they feared and railed against were their own white, middle-class sons and daughters who might refuse to give them grandchildren because, for whatever reason, they had chosen not to conform to bourgeois Anglo-Saxon gender roles. The Homosexual was a middle-class white man who refused to conform to the norms of masculinity or a middle-class white woman who refused to conform to the norms of femininity. The Homosexual was fundamentally a gender deviant.

Contemporary critics have made much of sexologists' "conflation" of gender and sexual orientation; none of these authors, so the standard criticism runs, seems able to imagine that a man could be completely masculine but sexually attracted only to other men or that a woman could be completely feminine but sexually attracted only to other women.[35] However, sexual orientation as something distinct from gender is not a transhistorical fact merely unrecognized by the impoverished imaginations of a previous generation. On the contrary, it is a product of a realignment of forces that occurred in the late 1960s and early 1970s.[36] Before that time, sexologists were not conflating two distinct categories for the simple reason that there were not two distinct categories. At least until the end of the 1960s, homosexuals just were what we now call transgendered people, and to a great extent they remain so in the popular imagination as well as in some of the clinical literature.[37]

The only salient issue in the postwar period was—anachronistically stated—gender transgression. In a racist society, gender was all about the Normal (Nordic) Family; gender was the equipment one required in order "to carry on." Sexual object choice could not be separated out, therefore, and treated as something different from, and additional to, the gendered personality. Like sexual inverts at the turn of the century, homosexual men were feminine and homosexual women were masculine by definition. If they didn't always *look* that way, well, that was because personalities can't be *seen* anymore than intelligence can be seen.[38] The only relevant questions had to do with how serious the gender inversion was (how much time had elapsed since the inversion process began and how much of the personality it had affected), whether the process could be reversed, and, if it could, how.[39] If the inversion hadn't gone too far, then with aggressive therapeutic intervention the genetic line might not be broken. But if it had gone too far to be reversed, the only answer was some form of incarceration. As public prosecutor Blaine Evans said in 1965, looking back on his role in a Boise sex scandal ten years before, "You've got to prosecute these guys because they strike at the core of society, I mean the family and the family unit. And when you get these guys crawling around the streets, you've got to prosecute to save the family" (Gerassi 1966, 25).[40] The Homosexual wasn't just a slacker who resisted familial duties; as an example to others and a seducer/recruiter, he or she was an active political threat.

Homosexuals and Marriage: Can These Nordic Genes Be Saved?

Thus the question the authorities—whether medical, psychiatric, eugenic, or forensic—asked themselves was what caused the gender inversion in the first place. Did sexual psychopathy lurk in the genes of the otherwise normal as a Mendelian recessive trait that might spring forth unexpectedly as some forms of mental deficiency did? Or was it an illness of the endocrine system that could be corrected? Or was it a psychological problem purely, one that had to do with faulty upbringing and evil influence? Throughout the twentieth century authorities as well as the general public were seriously exercised by this question of etiology—because *a lot* hung on the answer. Only by pinning down the cause of homosexuality, many believed, could a strategy for containing and managing it be developed.

On the one hand, if it turned out that homosexuality was hereditary —a throwback, as some thought, to hermaphroditic prehuman ancestors—most likely it was incurable and the families that carried it were simply inferior, despite appearances. In that case, homosexuals should not be encouraged to straighten up and marry, and if married already, whatever marital relations they might have should be terminated. Furthermore, if they were the sort likely to seduce others and bring out their latent homosexual tendencies, castration might be in order—but at the very least, they should be locked up for life. On the other hand, if homosexuality was hormonal or psychological, cure seemed much more likely, at least if it could be caught in childhood or early adolescence before it had a chance to shape a person's character. There would be a combination of therapy to change the direction of impulses and feelings, and stern discipline to force conformity to sex role norms. In that case, marriage and procreation would be the hallmarks of success.

What hung in the balance was marriage. If homosexuality was heritable, marriage should be forbidden, just as it was for epileptics, for example. If homosexuality was curable, marriage should be the goal. A mistake in either direction, however, would damage the institution of marriage and undermine the Family.[41] And that, of course, would jeopardize Civilization.

Sex researchers in the 1930s and 40s disagreed about homosexuality's symptoms and etiology. Maurice Chideckel, whose specialty was female sex perverts and whose theoretical bent was Freudian psychoanalysis, contended that there were no visually apparent anatomical differences between heterosexuals and homosexuals; the differences were entirely internal and neurological, the result of brain damage very early in life. "Unnatural deviation of the sexual instinct is a manifestation of disturbed mentality. The hunger for sex is dominated by a certain portion of the brain. Hence perverted sex cravings are morbid anomalies due to an unbalanced nervous system" (Chideckel 1935, vii). Unbalance was a result of psychic trauma, which in a little girl could be something as simple as seeing a little boy's penis and reaching the humiliating realization that she was castrated.[42] Such a jolt could destabilize the immature neurological system and even cause physical injury to the brain (1935, 69). Of course, not every girl shocked by the discovery of the phallus became homosexual, so it was still an open question whether there was some underlying and perhaps hereditary abnormality that conditioned the results of discovery in those who did. It was possible, Chideckel believed, that biological malfunction might be the deciding factor. "Nature herself often causes homosexuality by failing to transfer the seat of sensation from the clitoris to the vagina," he wrote. "And so, in the homosexuals we discussed the abnormal processes are merely the misfunctioning of a biological machine" (1935, 91, 92).

Unlike Chideckel, members of New York's Committee for the Study of Sex Variants (formed in 1935, the same year that the Eugenics Publishing Company brought out Chideckel's *Female Sex Perversion*) were not convinced that there were no anatomical differences between sex perverts and normal people. Members of the investigative team performed extensive studies of the bodies of homosexual subjects. They measured amount and distribution of body hair, size of genitals and overall body frame, and "carrying angles" (which included shoulder and hip width and torso-leg ratios). Using x-ray technology, they measured skulls, chests, and pelvises, finding "pelvic architecture" especially significant. It was difficult to get a control group for the men, although researchers believed the homosexual men's pelvises were wider than the norm. But pelvis measurements on presumably heterosexual women were readily available through Robert Latou Dickinson's gynecological practice. Dickinson found that lesbians' pelvises were narrower than those of presumably heterosexual women, a significant discovery in light of evolutionary theory. At least as far back as Havelock Ellis at the turn of the century, race theorists had seen the comparatively greater width of the white female pelvis as an indication of racial superiority (wide pelvises being necessary to accommodate the big heads of white male infants). Through the course of evolution, white women with narrow pelvises died in childbirth and so did not pass on their genes, but among races with small heads, narrow pelvises persisted. White lesbians' comparatively narrow pelvises aligned them with small-headed "primitives"; like heterosexual women of color, lesbians of all races manifested a low stage of evolutionary development.

Dickinson also conducted extensive examinations of lesbians' genitals and made wax impressions of them. Appendix VI of the committee's report contains several pages of his drawings as well as his expert summation: "The *external genitals* are large, with the special hypertrophies of various parts that accompany frequent, vigorous sexual stimulation and activity. The labia minora protrude particularly often, and the surface of the glans clitoris is long from front to rear, with three times as many large glans as is to be expected. Only autoeroticism and homosexuality produce these results" (Henry 1941, 1098). He found that black and mulatto lesbians' clitorises were even larger than those of white lesbians, an observation consonant with scientific racist claims about the relative size of the genitals of presumably heterosexual black, white, and mulatto women over the past century.

Whether these differences somehow caused homosexual behavior or were caused by it, Dickinson thought it might be possible to use these discoveries to develop guidelines for identifying lesbians through gynecological exams; knowledge of these facts could enable a physician to "*make a definite diagnosis* of homosexual practices" (Henry 1941, 1090). Having such a means of identification could be very useful, given recent legislation. In 1935 Connecticut had become the first state to require pelvic exams for marriage licensure, and by 1939 seventeen other states had enacted similar laws.[43] By the time the committee's report was published in 1941, therefore, physicians across the country had acquired an unprecedented authority to prevent women from marrying or to force them to delay marriage to undergo treatment for sexual perversion. Dickinson's drawings might enable a vigilant physician to prevent a dysgenic (and possibly fraudulent) union from taking place.

Aside from the pelvis measurements, which did seem to them to indicate congenital or physiological developmental differences between normal individuals and homosexuals, the committee's data allowed no firm conclusions as to the physical origins of homosexuality. Observed genital differences might indicate a physiological or even a genetic cause, but they also might simply be the result of long-term homosexual practice. Some lesbian subjects were thought to suffer from "innate virility" (Henry 1941, 739, 748, 787, 808, 829, 842, 855). But other causes listed include husband's lack of virility (591), adolescent groping for affection (611, 896), mother attachment (651, 711, 818, 1020), rebellion against family's hypocrisy (681), rebellion against the father (761), physical inadequacy or underdeveloped genitals (776, 798, 908), sibling rivalry (842), and emotional immaturity and lack of sex drive (878). One thing was certain, however; even if homosexuality was not genetically transmissible, these people should not raise children. "Such children are prone to psychosexual maladjustment which may become manifest in the form of sex variance, a neurosis or a psychosis."[44] One homosexual in a bloodline would corrupt the entire bloodline thereafter, either genetically or psychically or both.

Despite their inconclusive data, committee members did favor a genetic explanation for sexual inversion. "Sex variants as a group appear to have an objective constitutional make-up which is recognizably different from a 'normal' group," they wrote, although they acknowledged that "this difference is difficult to define specifically" (Henry 1941, 1065). But that objective difference in constitutional makeup, however ill-defined and unspecified, was enough to make eugenically informed predictions. "As long as sex mating continues to be irrational [a common way in the early twentieth century of designating liaisons based on emotional attachment or sexual passion rather than eugenic principles], constitutionally pre-disposed sex variants are to be expected" (Henry 1941, 1026). It would take widespread adherence to eugenic principles to rid the world of homosexuality.

For advocates of eugenic marriage—for example, Robert Latou Dickinson, who eventually became the executive director of the Human Betterment Association of America, and Lewis Terman, author of the Stanford-Binet IQ test—some method for identifying homosexuals seemed crucial. If a test could be developed, premarital counseling centers such as Popenoe's AIFR could screen for homosexuals, either active or latent, and then treat them or, if their condition proved intractable, intervene to prevent marriage.[45] Or such a test could be routinely administered to all public school students and prison inmates to facilitate early treatment or institutional segregation.

Terman became interested in developing such a test while studying gifted children in 1922. By the mid-1930s, he and his colleague Catherine Cox Miles had developed what they called the M-F test, a battery of seven pencil-and-paper tests disguised as "aptitude-interest" tests but actually designed to determine the degree to which a subject was masculine or feminine. Although they did not claim that the test was 100 percent foolproof, they did believe that homosexual men (at least those who preferred to take the "passive" role in anal intercourse or fellatio[46]) scored very differently from heterosexual men—in fact, at the masculine end of the normal female range—and that a test subject who scored similarly very likely had an inverted sexuality and might develop into a practicing homosexual if he were not one already. Based on the M-F Scale, Terman and Miles developed an "I Scale" that they thought could be used to detect sexual inversion. "Subjects at the secondary school level with high 'I' scores," they suggested, "should be followed up in order to find out what types of sexual adjustment they are likely to make. If it should turn out that young men with such scores are in fact potential homosexuals, preventive measures might be found that would direct their sexual development into normal channels" (Terman and Miles 1936, 264).

In fact, a longitudinal study of this type was done in the 1970s and 80s by Richard Green. As he reports in his 1987 volume, *The "Sissy Boy Syndrome" and the Development of Homosexuality,* Green found that a majority of boys seen as "sissies" in childhood did have a homosexual orientation as adults, a finding that affirmed clinicians' efforts to identify such boys (as well as girls who were seen as inappropriately masculine), classify them as suffering from "gender identity disorder," and enroll them in treatment programs. Green claimed repeatedly throughout his book that he did not condemn cross-gendered or homosexual behavior. He simply believed that feminine comportment in boyhood indicated that boys were acutely uncomfortable with their maleness and needed professional help coming to terms with it. In other words, transgender behavior was symptomatic of psychological distress and incipient pathology.

Thus there was plenty of reason for parents to worry and try to do something to stop it.

Most treatment programs for Gender Identity Disorder did not aim to make troubled or unhappy boys and girls more comfortable with their sexed bodies, however; instead they aimed to force conformity to gendered behavioral norms, including the expression of heterosexual orientation.[47] Parents typically sought out treatment and submitted their sons and daughters to it because they wanted them to conform to gender norms and grow up heterosexual, regardless of how the children currently felt or experienced themselves. In effect, then, treatment aimed to enforce heterosexual gender norms, the norms that enabled the Normal Family to reproduce itself. Anything that might prevent children from forming a Normal Family of their own was cause for alarm and intervention.

In Green's study, even parents who were able to accept their sons' occasionally expressed sexual interest in males could not accept their feminine comportment. For example, the mother of a sixteen-year-old boy, having confronted her son with her knowledge of his homosexual activity, reported to Dr. Green: "I told him the only thing I couldn't stand would be if he were a queen" (Green 1987, 167). The mother of an eleven-year-old boy who had been seeing Green for two years made similar comments:

> MOTHER: *I've been doing a lot of thinking about this issue. I've gotten involved in the women's movement, and of course they're taking a long hard look at roles. I've been going through a lot of turmoil about it because I don't know what I would do now, given a three-year-old boy again, how I would react if he wanted to play with the doll. The whole thing is looking very murky to me now. Women historically have been damaged a lot by the kinds of things that role-playing has done, but that also makes me take a look at boys' roles and what they are. I think I remember saying I didn't care if my son wasn't overtly a football type, but I felt strongly that I didn't want him to develop feminine characteristics. On the one hand, I'm grateful for my stand. . . . .*
>
> R[ichard] G[reen]: *What about the kinds of reactions that your son was getting from the other kids when he was showing the feminine behavior?*

MOTHER: *Well that's what makes a strong part of me glad that I took a stand. Because, you know, socially, whether the values were right or wrong, he was being ostracized, and I appreciate what I did for that reason.*

R.G.: *To my view, that is the key issue. I think it still is true today, with the new pediatric population, that kids who are grossly very feminine do get ostracized and stigmatized by the peer group. I respect the general issue that there shouldn't be sex-role stereotyping. But I'm not sure we're doing a five-year-old or seven-year-old very feminine boy a favor by saying to him, "Well, the world is really all screwed up, it's not you. Just go out there and wear a dress."*

MOTHER: *Yeah, I know. I'm very sensitive to that, and I feel relieved that I wasn't confused at that time—that I was sure what I believed in. I think I said once that it wouldn't bother me so much if my son did turn out to be bisexual. I have had sexual feelings for women from time to time. It seems almost healthy for me in a way. But a feminine man still really turns me off. I just can't help it. I'm thinking that from the very first time he picked up a doll I was horrified.* (Green 1987, 391–92)

Even with a feminist analysis of sex-roles as socially constructed and potentially damaging, and with evidence in front of her that her son did feel oppressed by the strictures of 1970s-style masculinity, this mother could not accept her child's femininity or the possibility that he might be exclusively homosexual in adulthood. Rather than take a stand for her child's right to explore and express whatever gendered comportments might free or fulfill him, she preferred to let his own peer group—other prepubescent children—dictate the confines within which his personality could unfold. And Dr. Green affirms that decision wholeheartedly. Nobody wants a little boy or a little girl whom the other children ridicule. We will accept, if we must, a certain amount of clandestine homosexual activity, but we will not accept people who openly live their lives any differently from the heterosexual norm. You can feel queer, and you can even act queer episodically and privately; but you cannot present yourself as queer, *ever.* You cannot lead a queer life. That was as true in 1975 and 1985 as it had been in 1935. Queer lives had to be prevented.

Richard Green was not really the gay-positive professional exception that he purported to be.[48] Like him, most of his psychiatrist predecessors were less interested in saving individuals from the evils of homosexuality than in salvaging the project of passing down the Family's genetic jewels to the third generation without mishap or taint (and in getting substantial material rewards for doing so). The most liberal among them agreed with D. J. West that "the man who only occasionally, and perhaps only in special circumstances, indulges in homosexual excitements, and then returns happily to his wife, is less of a social or psychiatric problem than the man who is incapable of ever enjoying a woman"; the real problem was "the hard core of complete homosexuals, represented by Kinsey's 4 percent, who eschew women all their lives" (West 1955, 15). The real problem was men and women who refused their gender roles, their roles in the Family. Such experts had little desire to help troubled people find sexual and emotional fulfillment; instead, they sought to develop the normalizing disciplinary regimes that would force a set of idealized gender roles on unwilling individuals whether it ultimately made them or their loved ones happier or not.

If the project failed and the Homosexual could not be forced into a eugenically valuable gender role, in the eyes of many professionals and the public they influenced, he or she was worse than worthless. The very presence of untreated homosexuals, regardless of how they were currently conducting themselves, posed a serious threat to society. Homosexuality in essence, according to Chideckel, was a deformity or mutilation of "the instincts that form the binding line in human relations, the instincts on which is built romantic, family, and social love." These instincts, he asserted, "are the source of human culture." They "are creative and life-giving and furnish the cohesion between the two halves of the human race, men and women." But in homosexuals, "these sublime feelings are distorted, perverted or completely absent. The impulses of the perverts are of a destructive type; they tend to disintegrate humanity instead of binding it" (Chideckel 1935, 12). Homosexuals were not simply deviants, not simply people whose sexual development had veered off the usual course. They were the very antithesis of (Nordic) heterosexuals, the nemesis of decent (Nordic) husbands and wives. Anti-Family in essence, they were destroyers of Civilization. They were devolution embodied. If left unchecked, they would conjure the savage ancestor and unravel the fabric of the world.

The Sexual Pollution of the Social Body

In 1937 FBI director J. Edgar Hoover declared "War on the Sex Criminal" (Freedman 1989, 206). At that time, in every state of the union, sex acts between males were illegal, and in many states sex acts between females were as well. Not all sex criminals were homosexual, but all homosexuals were sex criminals, a fact that was not lost on the American public. Thereafter, homosexuals came to be seen as something more than psychopathic perverts and despicable criminals—something more, even, than enemies of the Family. By the time of the Cold War, homosexuals had become America's official public enemy number one, right alongside—and often conflated with—Communists.[49]

Of course, people we would now call homosexual had been the targets of moral and medical crusades for a long time already. In the nineteenth century, before the category of sodomy was revised to accord with the modern psychiatric conception of homosexuality, not only were sodomites punished as criminals, but individuals who indulged in same-sex mutual masturbation and oral sex were, as Masturbators, subject to denunciation, aggressive surveillance, painful and humiliating physical restraints, and sometimes physical mutilation by clitorectomy or castration. By the late nineteenth century, people identified as suffering from "contrary sexual feeling" were firmly placed into the psychiatric category of the psychopath and thus subject to all the restrictions imposed on those believed to be mentally ill (which, as we have seen, were considerable). The title of Krafft-Ebing's enormously influential book, *Psychopathia Sexualis,* pretty much says it all. In 1917, American psychiatrists succeeded in having constitutional psychopathy enshrined in immigration law as a reason for denial and deportation,[50] thus effectively restricting the privilege of immigration and naturalization to heterosexuals.

Despite little empirical evidence to support the conclusion, as the rash of sexological studies undertaken in the mid-1930s implies, experts—local governmental officials, gynecologists, psychologists, social workers, educators, and many others—perceived that the "problem" was growing. FBI Director Hoover called sexual psychopaths "the most loathsome of all the vast army of crime," and the American public—in the form of angry citizens' groups across the nation—demanded that they be hunted down and eliminated.[51]

In 1940 the U.S. military began psychiatric screening of all recruits, and in 1941 the Department of Defense added homosexuality to the list of deviations that automatically disqualified a person for all branches of service (Edsall 2003, 262). Those discovered to be homosexual while in service received less than honorable discharges and no veterans' benefits.[52] Through the end of the 1940s, the military discharged on average a little over 1,000 people per year for homosexuality (D'Emilio 1998, 44).

Hoover kept up his campaign against the epic onslaught of the sexual psychopath, insisting in 1947 that "the most rapidly increasing type of crime is that perpetrated by degenerate sex offenders,"[53] a claim that enabled him to justify extending his surveillance and interrogation operations deep into the personal lives of hundreds of thousands of Americans and to put in place the domestic spying programs that he would control and exploit for his own political gain through the McCarthy era into the Nixon years.[54] By 1950, with the help of ambitious law enforcement officials like Hoover and the increasing neo-eugenic emphasis on the sanctity of the Family, the threat posed to public health by homosexuals had become, in Jennifer Terry's words, a "national obsession." As such, it was perhaps inevitable that Congress would get on the bandwagon.

According to historian John D'Emilio, the all-out persecution of homosexuals began at the national level on February 28, 1950. On that day, Secretary of State Dean Acheson testified before the Senate Appropriations Committee on his relationship with Alger Hiss, a former State Department employee and a suspected spy who had been convicted on two counts of perjury at a trial that had concluded the previous month. Acheson refused to give the Senate committee State Department personnel files, so committee members interrogated him and his undersecretary, John Peurifoy, about the reasons for dismissal of more than two hundred State Department employees since President Truman had instituted a loyalty requirement in 1947. Most of the ninety-one employees dismissed for "moral turpitude," according to Peurifoy, were fired for homosexuality.[55] D'Emilio recounts what happened next:

> In the succeeding months, the danger posed by "sexual perverts" became a staple of partisan rhetoric. Senator Joseph McCarthy, just embarking upon his career as an anticommu-

nist crusader, charged that an unnamed person in the State Department had forced the reinstatement of a homosexual despite the threat to the nation's safety. Styles Bridges, a conservative senator from New Hampshire, assailed the laxity of the executive branch in ferreting out spies and homosexuals. After the head of the District of Columbia vice squad told a Senate committee that thousands of "sexual deviates" worked for the government, the Republican floor leader, Kenneth Wherry, demanded a full-scale Senate inquiry. In May Governor Thomas Dewey of New York, who had been the party's presidential candidate in 1948, accused the administration of tolerating the employment of sex offenders. Seven thousand Republican party workers received a newsletter from their national chairman, Guy Gabrielson, alerting them to the new "homosexual angle" in Washington. "Sexual perverts . . . have infiltrated our Government in recent years," he warned, and they were "perhaps as dangerous as the actual Communists." Gabrielson implied that party loyalists had a special responsibility to arouse the country's ire over the issue, since "decency" constrained the media from "adequately presenting the facts" to the American people. Finally, in June 1950 the full Senate bowed to mounting pressure and authorized an investigation into the alleged employment of homosexuals "and other moral perverts" in government. (D'Emilio 1998, 41–42)

Over the next several months, homosexuals became the focus of a massive purge in the federal civil service. People accused of homosexuality were fired from the executive branch on an average of sixty per month. The full Senate report, entitled *Employment of Homosexuals and Other Sex Perverts in Government,* was released in December of 1950. It asserted that homosexuals lack the emotional stability of normal people and have weak moral fiber. The presence of even one homosexual in a government agency "tends to have a corrosive influence upon his fellow employees. These perverts will frequently attempt to entice normal individuals to engage in perverted practices. This is particularly true in the case of young and impressionable people who might come under the influence of a pervert. . . . One homosexual can pollute a Government office."[56] The military stepped up discharges as well, doubling its average to 2,000 per year during the early 1950s and increasing to 3,000 per year by the 1960s (D'Emilio 1998, 44–45).

Some of this was a cynical attempt to push aside individuals who stood in the way of various officials' personal ambitions, but a great deal of it was real fear of what was perceived to be a serious national security risk. Homosexuals, already known as enemies of the Family, were now also understood to be, in essence, enemies of the State.

Purges were not confined to government posts alone. In 1950 more than 12,600,000 individuals—20 percent of the U.S. labor force—were required to pass loyalty tests and/or security clearance procedures to keep their jobs. Homosexuality was a disqualifying condition in virtually all such tests. In other words, 20 percent of the jobs in the United States in the 1950s were explicitly reserved for heterosexuals. Implicitly, so were most of the rest. For homosexuals who somehow managed to gain clearance or held jobs where none was required, there was the danger that FBI or Postal Service surveillance would turn up information that government agents would pass on to private sector employers who would then initiate termination.[57] D'Emilio explains:

> The FBI sought out friendly vice squad officers who supplied arrest records on moral charges, regardless of whether convictions had ensued. Regional FBI offices gathered data on gay bars, compiled lists of other places frequented by homosexuals, and clipped press articles that provided information about the gay world. Friendship with a known homosexual or lesbian subjected anyone to investigation. The Post Office, exploiting its authority to prevent the dissemination of obscene material through the mails, joined the anti-homosexual campaign. The department established a watch on the recipients of physique magazines and other forms of gay male erotica. Postal inspectors subscribed to pen pal clubs, initiated correspondence with men whom they believed might be homosexual, and, if their suspicions were confirmed, placed tracers on victims' mail in order to locate other homosexuals. (D'Emilio 1998, 46–47)

Thousands of careers were thus destroyed and reputations ruined, sometimes regardless of the truth of the charge. To be suspected of homosexuality was as bad as being a "known" homosexual. People lost their homes, their families, custody of and visitation rights with their children. Some committed suicide.[58]

Arrests made in raids of gay bars and even private house parties were frequent in the 1950s and 60s. In Washington, D.C., on average a thousand people a year were arrested, many of them for doing nothing other than entering a space classified as "homosexual." In Philadelphia, the average number of arrests was a hundred per month. Police raided one San Francisco bar in September of 1956 and arrested 36 lesbians in one evening. In New Orleans in 1953 one raid on a lesbian bar in the French Quarter resulted in 67 arrests. In Baltimore in 1955 police arrested 162 men in one bar (D'Emilio 1998, 50). And of course for a gay man or lesbian, police custody almost always meant harassment and brutality. D'Emilio surely understates the case when he writes, "A gnawing insecurity pervaded the lives of gay men and women" (1998, 49). Some homosexuals were arrested and even incarcerated for doing nothing at all, not even so much as attending a party or having a drink in gay bar. For example, in Sioux City, Iowa, in 1959, following a kidnapping and murder of a young boy, the county attorney had twenty-nine men committed to asylums under Iowa's sexual psychopath law, which permitted commitment of homosexuals without hearing or conviction; no evidence was provided to link any of the men to the crime (D'Emilio 1998, 50–51). The widely held assumption that homosexuality was a dangerous mental illness enabled officials to disregard homosexual people's civil rights on a regular basis. Thousands were confined to mental institutions where they were held indefinitely and subjected to various forms of "therapy"—from castration and clitorectomy in the earlier years to lobotomy, hormone injections, electric shock, and aversion therapy into the 1970s.[59]

This broad campaign against homosexuality served a number of different purposes: (1) It made law enforcement, elected officials, and anti-homosexual political candidates look good to a public that wanted its neighborhoods, towns, and schools safe from sexual psychopaths. (2) It enhanced the professional positions of psychiatrists, psychologists, sociologists, social workers, educators, and others who purported to have expertise in identifying and coping with sexual deviance and justified their intrusions into the private life of anyone in any way connected with someone who might be a sexual deviant. (3) It sold all kinds of commodities from sex-typed toys, clothes, and hygiene products to standardized tests, psychotherapies, and surveillance equipment. (4) It cast into suspicion same-sex friendships and other overtly nonsexual alliances that might have supported

antiauthoritarian resistance of many sorts—in other words, it reinforced vertical, or hierarchical, relationships at the expense of hori-
zontal, or peer, relationships.[60] (5) It reinforced male control over
female sexuality and reproductive capacities (in some cases whether
males wanted that control or not). And, of course, (6) it made heterosexual marriage and parenthood the only respectable option for
everyone, at the same time informing everyone of alternatives they
might never have thought of and undermining the credibility of many
marriages by raising the suspicion that people who were in them were
actually perverts just using them as a cover—thus justifying more professional intrusion, more surveillance, and more law enforcement.

The specter of homosexuality as a looming threat has been a
crucial ingredient in the development of contemporary social institutions and norms, and it has served as a key factor in right-wing political organizing and fundraising, as in Moral Majority founder Jerry
Falwell's plea to each of his "Christian friends" to send him $25 so
that he could "keep President Clinton from hiring more homosexuals
like Roberta Achtenberg, Leonard Hirsch, and Keith Boykin—into
the federal government" (quoted in Boykin 1996, 46). If homosexuality did not exist, people like Fiorello LaGuardia and George Henry,
Joseph McCarthy and J. Edgar Hoover, Jerry Falwell and Ralph Reed
would have had to invent it.

Racism Carries On

Pro-family, anti-queer rhetoric in the mid- and late twentieth century was virtually identical to the pro-Nordic, anti-Negro rhetoric
that was current fifty years before—right down to the threats of epi-
demics of venereal disease, random assault during episodes of gay and
lesbian *furor sexualis,* and the one-drop-equals-total-corruption rule.
Irresponsible, impulsive, and dedicated to the pursuit of gratification
with no thought to future consequences, homosexuals spread social
chaos along with deadly disease. But it would be a mistake to assume
that 1936-style racism was simply replaced by homophobia. Hatred
and suspicion of, and discrimination and violence against, black people
—as well as Latinos, Native Americans, Asian Americans, and Arab
Americans, among others—was still very much alive and well.

First of all, scientific racism as an organized and self-conscious
force persisted throughout the twentieth century and is with us still.
Hardliners remained dedicated to its tenets in the postwar period and

used their influence and financial resources to fight desegregation. One well-documented example was that of Wickliffe Draper, who had supported the work of Charles Davenport back in the 1920s in a project he hoped would prove that blacks were biologically incapable of self-government (Tucker 2002, 31).[61] Heir to a New England textile fortune, Draper continued funding scientific studies aimed at undermining blacks' demand for civil equality until his death in 1972. He also funded political efforts directly. In the fight against the bill that ultimately became the Civil Rights Act of 1964, for instance, Draper provided 84 percent of the funding to the largest lobby group then on Capitol Hill, the Mississippi-based Coordinating Committee for Fundamental American Freedoms (Tucker 2002, 123–24). Draper also financed at least two court battles in an attempt to overturn *Brown v. Board of Education*. When judicial decisions ultimately went against segregation, he and his advisors undertook to create an alternative to public education for whites only. Efforts began in Mississippi in 1964 to charter schools funded through private donations and state and local government subsidies. By 1970, Jackson, Mississippi, had a complex of three educational facilities serving three thousand students, and the Mississippi state legislature had authorized money to defray tuition for children attending nonsectarian private schools (Tucker 2002, 127, 128).[62] Similar efforts were made elsewhere with some success.[63] If white people could not control the school systems, they would withdraw from them and leave public education to collapse from lack of funding and community support, which is exactly what has happened in many localities.[64]

By endowing the Pioneer Fund—an organization whose original charter outlined two goals: (1) to identify and educate white children of original colonial American stock to encourage their families to bring more children into the world, and (2) to promote the study of heredity and eugenics for race betterment (Tucker 2002, 6)—Draper created a mechanism to disperse money to scientists and scholars publishing studies that supported the tenets of eugenics and scientific racism even after his death. From its founding in 1937 throughout the remainder of the twentieth century, Pioneer Fund grants supported work that lent a cloak of academic credibility to the proposition that nonwhites are biologically inferior to whites.[65] The biggest difference is in level of intelligence, grant recipients have typically argued, although some have seen the main difference in the level of moral restraint. Michael Levin, for example, has claimed that free will correlates with race and that blacks, being on the whole deficient in free will, are driven by their biological impulses to commit crimes. Some Pioneer Fund scholars have gone on to argue that these alleged facts prove that blacks cannot be educated alongside whites without diminishing the quality of education for white children, that blacks are criminal by nature, and that racial integration results in social chaos. Testifying before Congress in 1970 on the School Emergency Aid Act, Arthur Jansen maintained that "the educational abilities and needs of the majority of white and Negro children are sufficiently different" to warrant placing them in separate classrooms (Tucker 2002, 153). Roger Pearson has claimed that an integrated society has led to "abnormal patterns of behavior ranging from homosexuality to a quest for abnormal erotic experiences including interracial sexual experimentation" (Tucker 2002, 175). At the time of this writing, psychologist J. Philippe Rushton heads the Pioneer Fund, which still actively disperses money to support such work. It also continues to pursue re-segregation through the courts: in 2002 the Pioneer Fund financed the Center for Individual Rights' lawsuit against the University of Michigan in an attempt to outlaw and dismantle what remained of affirmative action in higher education (Brace 2005, 271). In short, scientific racism perseveres to this day.

Pioneer-funded scholars and political extremists are not the only people who hold beliefs that can be traced to the scientific racism of a bygone era, however. Lucius Outlaw has argued that the basic idea that races are elements in an evolutionary hierarchy persists even outside overtly racist circles:

> Even shorn of the more crude outfittings of social Darwinism's "survival of the fittest" (those in power, or seeking power, over others being the "fittest," of course), the field of the science of "race" is still occupied by those offering orderings of human groups along an *ascending* scale with a particular group's placement on the scale being a function of the level of their supposed development (or lack thereof) toward human perfectibility: from "primitive" to "civilized" (circa the nineteenth century); from "undeveloped" or "underdeveloped" to "developed" or "advanced" (circa the twentieth century).
>
> Such arguments find fertile soil for nourishment and growth now that "evolution" (organic and superorganic [cul-

tural], often without distinction), frequently conceived as lin-
ear development along a single path which *all* "races" have
to traverse, is now a basic feature of our "common sense."
(Outlaw 2003, 68)

The framework of scientific racism, at least according to Outlaw's
analysis, still underlies much of our vocabulary and thought about
racial and international conflict, technological and economic development, and various social problems and policies. Thus it influences our
thinking whether or not we would ever consciously espouse or even
give any credence to its explicit doctrines.

Eugenics carried on through the twentieth century as well, despite
the damage done to it by its association with the Nazi regime. Even
without a highly visible international political organization, eugenicists were still capable of affecting public policy and of protecting and
even extending eugenics programs. As before the war, a major postwar goal was sterilization of people eugenicists deemed unfit, and they
pursued that goal where it was still possible to do so, mainly among
people in public institutions and on welfare. Many eugenic-minded
physicians and local officials carried out isolated programs here and
there, but there was an organized national effort as well.

After Ezra Gosney's death in 1942, the Human Betterment
Foundation's records were transferred to an organization called
Birthright, which had formerly been the New Jersey Sterilization
League.[66] Robert Latou Dickinson's New York Academy of Medicine
offices became its headquarters, and Dickinson headed the organization until his death in 1951 (Pickens 1967, 93–94). Many of its
activities were bankrolled by Clarence Gamble, wealthy heir to the
Gamble soap company, which was eventually absorbed into the mul-
tinational Proctor & Gamble conglomerate. Gamble concentrated
primarily on eugenic sterilization and birth control programs in the
South (especially in North Carolina) through the late 1940s and early
1950s.[67] He also published pro-sterilization articles in the *Journal
of the American Medical Association* and was favorably portrayed
in articles in *Newsweek* in 1947 and 1949. In his *JAMA* article in
1949, he referred to his work as "long range preventive medicine."[68]
However, moderate birth control advocacy organizations such as
Planned Parenthood, which advocated only voluntary sterilization,
were leery of Gamble's methods and would not work with Birthright.
As a result, Birthright's own moderate wing eventually reorganized,

calling itself the Human Betterment Association of America, and dropped the eugenic language in favor of the language of cost-benefit analysis.

But eugenicists did not focus solely on society's outcasts. The theories and institutions they built helped to create and perpetuate a society in which tolerance for any sort of biological or behavioral deviation was very low, a society in which ordinary individuals could be counted upon to enforce eugenic norms within their sphere of influence even without official compulsion. This was increasingly true in the area of family planning. As Lee R. Dice, director of the University of Michigan's Institute of Human Biology, put it, "If there is known to be a high probability of transmitting a serious defect, it would be an abnormal person indeed who would not refrain from having children" (1952, 2). Nobody wants a child the other children ridicule. Thus, in pursuit of eugenic social goals, was born the field that in 1947 geneticist Sheldon Reed dubbed "genetic counseling."[69]

In its early years, genetic counseling was little more than an arm of the still-active postwar eugenics movement.[70] In 1941, Charles Fremont Dight's estate conferred a substantial sum of money on the University of Minnesota which, according to his will, would "maintain a place for consultation and advice on heredity and eugenics and for rating of people, first, as to the efficiency of their bodily structure; second, as to their mentality; third, as to their fitness to marry and reproduce" (Paul 1995, 123). In early 1948, the Eugenics Record Office (which the Carnegie Institute had renamed the Genetics Record Office in 1939) transferred its records to the Dight Institute, which was also supported by money from the estate of Charles M. Goethe, a wealthy banker who devoted much of his life to eugenic work and served as president of the Eugenics Research Association in 1936, a position he had used to lavish praise upon Nazi Germany's population programs (E. Black 2003, 315). The institute ran both a marriage counseling center and a genetics counseling center. Its first director, Clarence P. Oliver, held that "a geneticist should prevail upon some persons to have at least their share of children as well as show a black picture to those with the potentiality of producing children with undesirable traits" (Paul 1995, 126). Oliver left in 1946 to take a position at the University of Texas at Austin, where he continued his work in genetics counseling (Dice 1952, 10). His successor was Sheldon Reed, who presided over Dight's acquisition of ERO materials. Reed took a less directive approach than Oliver, asserting that "the decision must be a personal one between the husband and wife, and theirs alone" (Paul 1995, 127). But like Lee Dice, his counterpart at the University of Michigan, Reed firmly believed that, provided with sound genetic information, individuals would make eugenic choices without pressure from experts. In 1952 he wrote, "If our observation is generally correct, that people of normal mentality, who thoroughly understand the genetics of their problems, will behave in the way that seems correct to society as a whole, then an important corollary follows. It could be stated as a principle that the mentally sound will voluntarily carry out a eugenics program which is acceptable to society if counseling in genetics is available to them" (Paul 1995, 128). Government need not impose eugenics programs on people conditioned from birth by normalizing disciplinary regimes. The ubiquitous pressures of modern life would steer them away from deviance and abnormality in their reproductive decisions. Nobody wants a baby the experts deem abnormal.

Dice went on to list conditions he considered serious enough to warrant deciding not to reproduce and to argue for state funding to establish clinics for the purpose of advising couples and assisting with family planning: "Defective heredity which results in the production of serious handicaps, such as idiocy, blindness, deafness, dwarfism, muscular atrophy, anemia, hemophilia, or the tendency to other serious disease is not only a calamity for the families concerned, but constitutes a serious drain on the resources of the community" (Dice 1952, 12). The state should fund physician training in genetics and establish free clinics to supply families with good information and good technologies, he argued, and then families will make the right— that is, the eugenic—decision.

Obviously, the authority of the physician or geneticist would carry a lot of weight with any couple who sought reproductive advice, and obviously, the type of training the physician or geneticist had received and the information available through research that was funded by government agencies would set the terms under which any individual or couple would be making these decisions about whether to conceive or carry a pregnancy to term.[71] Prospective parents would have to rely to a great extent on the judgment of those authorities. If the authorities believed the birth of a deaf child or a "dwarf" would be a family tragedy, no doubt many families would come to believe so as well.

Eugenicists like Lee Dice certainly knew that. Thus their claims to be leaving the decision to individuals in a free and open society were at least somewhat disingenuous.

However, by and large the eugenicists were also right. The Normal Family does not want abnormal members and will take steps—even drastic and expensive steps if there be the means—to correct anything perceived as abnormality and to prevent the birth of an abnormal child. By the mid-twentieth century, to a great extent, the eugenics movement's values had become America's values, just as the prewar eugenicists had hoped they would.[72] Forced sterilization of the poor, the mentally retarded, and the mentally ill continued for nearly thirty years after World War II; many people still advocate it today. And the new field of research and therapeutic intervention that Reed named in 1947 and Dice heralded in 1952 has expanded over the past sixty years to become a significant force in American society.[73]

Scientific racism and eugenics both carried on under their own banners. But they also gave rise to and carried on through the pro-family movement, which by the 1970s had a life of its own. Many riders on the pro-family bandwagon had little or no idea of the racist history behind their discourses or the ways in which scientific racism and eugenics informed their values. It just seemed self-evident to them that the normal nuclear family, which had existed for the past 500,000 years, was essential to the preservation and advance of civilization.[74] Anybody who thought differently was an enemy of the people who had to be neutralized. That included feminists, Communists, hippies and free love advocates, abortionists, divorce attorneys, and anybody who supported publicly funded child care. Nevertheless, the pro-family movement *was* racist, even long after it was stripped of any explicit references to racial purification or the reinforcement and spread of Anglo-Saxon domination. It was racist because it promoted The Family, a twentieth-century Nordic supremacist fabrication, to the exclusion and degradation of any alternative form of life. It refused recognition, let along respect, for families that were not nuclear, heterosexual, or patriarchal. In fact, it frequently went so far as to condemn them and pathologize their members as well as most individuals who chose not to form any kind of family at all.[75] Just as prewar eugenicists had envisioned, efforts to promote the Family favored middle- and upper-class white heterosexuals and in the process materially harmed homosexuals and non-Nordic families and individuals, African Americans in particular.

No one would dispute the claim that pro-family movements have worked against queer people. They have done so deliberately, and nowadays they announce the fact on their television and radio broadcasts and Web sites. In the name of The Family, law and policy makers have denied gay- and lesbian-headed households civil, social, and economic benefits readily available to heterosexual-headed households.[76] In the name of protecting children's ability to form their own Normal Families in the future, barriers remain, preventing gay and lesbian couples in many states from jointly adopting children or serving as foster parents.[77] Efforts have been made to prevent lesbian couples from procuring donor sperm for insemination.[78] And mothers and fathers who come out of the closet have good reason to fear loss of custody or visitation rights if ex-spouses make their sexual orientation an issue in family court.[79] As these examples suggest, many Americans believe, as George Henry did in 1941, that homosexual parents inevitably damage their children for life, despite study after study showing no evidence for such a view.[80] But slander and discrimination against same-sex life partners and the children they raise are not the chief ways in which the pro-family movement hurts and degrades queer people. Its primary point of attack is not households but individual queer people, whom it casts as biological and moral threats to those it claims to protect—innocent children, impressionable youths, young men whose virility is easily insulted, unsuspecting wives whose health may be compromised.

Pro-family groups do not proudly proclaim their animosity toward racial minorities, so it may be less obvious to some that promotion of The Family is racist. However, not only in its perhaps unconscious perpetuation of white supremacy and the project of Anglo-Saxon world domination but also in its direct material effects, it is racist. Promotion of The Family directly harms people of color—just as Paul Popenoe intended it to. We can see this harm especially clearly in the public outcry over the supposed disintegration of the Black Family.

Announced to the American mainstream in 1965 by then-Assistant Secretary of Labor Daniel Patrick Moynihan in a report entitled "The Negro Family: The Case for National Action," the disintegration of the Black Family has had a long run in U.S. history. More than forty years have passed, yet the Black Family is still reportedly disintegrating. Babies are born out of wedlock, fathers don't support their offspring, households are headed by single mothers, children are not adequately supervised or encouraged to learn in school, and so on.

Back in 1965, Moynihan held that the problem, which he believed was worsening at an alarming rate, originated during slavery, which allegedly obliterated family structure among blacks.[81] After slavery came Jim Crow—which prevented black men from earning enough money to establish dominance in the household; often denied them work entirely and thus made them dependent on women's wages; and humiliated, punished, and sometimes lynched them if they attempted to defend their wives and children against white aggression. This long history all but destroyed black male self-esteem, according to Moynihan, and then black women finished the job. Having lost respect for black men, black women took control of the purse strings as well as the household and drove their men deeper into a state of antisocial ennui. Thus arose the Black Matriarch, whose legacy includes poorly socialized black male children who cannot grow up to assume responsible adult roles; high levels of crime (especially crimes of passion and impulse); and a self-perpetuating cycle of dependency, humiliation, and antisocial behavior. Black culture, in Moynihan's words, is "a tangle of pathology" (1965, chap. 4), and the only way to untangle it is for society to prop up the historically effeminized black man so that he can be a real head of household and raise sons who know how to delay gratification, take charge, and keep women in their place.

Moynihan was a white liberal sociologist who drew on the work of black sociologists and psychologists such as E. Franklin Frazier and Kenneth Clarke. He was careful to assert that the pathology he had identified was not a racial trait. (The black middle class had managed to save themselves from it for the most part, he thought, although segregation resulted in some exposure of middle-class black children to the unhealthy climate of the ghetto.) And its cause was not black biology but an ongoing history of injustice. Moynihan warned, however, that eliminating injustice—granting blacks civil liberties, which his boss, Lyndon Johnson, was attempting to do—would not insure real equality and thus would not satisfy black expectations. The result of disappointment would be violence, the late twentieth-century equivalent of race war, which in 1965 was all too vivid a prospect.

Civil liberties could not guarantee equality, Moynihan maintained, because blacks were not psychologically prepared to take advantage of the opportunities civil liberties would bring. Only a Normal Family could provide blacks the necessary psychological preparation for competition and material success equal to that of whites in a world dominated by whites. As Paul Popenoe had pointed out nearly forty years earlier, "The normal family is the only effective school for the life of the citizen" (1926, 43). Moynihan wanted the Johnson administration to find ways to make the Black Family normal.[82]

There were liberal white critics at the time. Elizabeth Herzog, bureau chief of the Department of Health, Education, and Welfare, insisted that the problem was not a racial hangover from slavery and Jim Crow but material deprivation per se. "Among the most frequent and most challenged generalizations relating to low-income Negro families is the assumption that their present characteristics are influenced more by the legacy of slavery than by postslavery discriminations and deprivations," she wrote in 1966; evidence against that assumption includes "(1) the similarity between very poor Negro families and very poor white families, and (2) the fact that slavery ended a hundred years ago while the postslavery situation is contemporary and appalling" (Herzog 1972, 154). Black family structure was pretty much the same as white family structure if compared to whites with the same income level, Herzog maintained. Extremely poor people tend to live in female-headed, multigenerational households no matter what race they belong to, and among the desperately poor of all races there is a higher than average rate of illegitimacy and desertion. The solution is to lift all Americans out of poverty, and let family structure and self-esteem take care of itself (Herzog 1972 [1966]). But few in official circles seriously questioned the presumption that male-headed families were better than female-headed ones or that babies should be born only to married couples or that households containing more than two generations or more than two adults were somehow unhealthy.[83] The ideology of the Normal Family held sway across the political spectrum.

Moynihan and Herzog were liberals who believed they could solve social problems with governmental policy and tax money. Many other people, people who did not look forward to the coming of Johnson's Great Society, let alone King's Beloved Community, interpreted Moynihan's sociological descriptions in another way. The problem was not a history of injustice or current impoverishment. The problem was black people's failure to remain faithful to The Family as an institution fundamental to any kind of society at all. Instead, black women had become castrating bitches who produced immature, antisocial children, and black men were worthless ne'er-do-wells who impregnated women impulsively and then deserted them, thereby swelling the welfare rolls with more little bastards who would grow up to do the same. Black men were not real men, that is to say, and black women and their squalling brats were nothing more than social parasites with attitude. Moynihan's report merely reinforced the pro-family standards set by people like Paul Popenoe; the Black Family was not a real family, and the people who came out of it were sick, immoral, selfish, violent, and out of control.[84]

Thus did the old stereotypes of African Americans live on, seemingly divorced from scientific racism and the 1936-style racism it produced, nurtured in the 1960s and beyond by apparently race-neutral pro-family values and the moral condemnations they underwrote. Similar stereotypes arose of Latinos and poor immigrants from all over the globe who lived in crowded apartments and mobile homes and often traveled far from their families in search of work. Some observers see this overlap between old stereotypes and new as coincidence; others see it as proof that 1936-style racism was still present in the latter years of the twentieth century but was just camouflaging itself with disingenuous pro-family rhetoric. But in fact, a more genealogically informed explanation is that so-called family values have been racist all along. They may coincide with some of the values that most Americans espouse, and they may bolster the egos or allay the fears of a great many of the people who consider themselves white— or, if not white, at least normal. But their most consistent effect is to promote the interests of the minority of Americans who, it so happens, own most of this country and its resources and who assume they do so by biological and evolutionary right, by right of inheritance and by right of the presumed fact that they are the most intelligent, most civilized, most morally upright people who ever lived.[85]

The aims of both the revised eugenics movement and the pro-family movement of the 1950s, 60s, 70s, and beyond were biopolitical: to advance The Race—which meant, in essence, to manage human evolution by effecting biological "improvement" in the population as defined by middle-class Anglo-Saxon standards—and, often, to augment personal and professional power, prestige, and wealth while doing so. The ideals of eugenics did not die with Hitler, as so many U.S., Canadian, and European historians have recently made clear.[86] Control of evolution and the creation of a superior human race are ubiquitous twentieth-century fantasies, and by the end of the century, knowledge of the human genome, genetic engineering, and cloning technologies had brought scientists much closer to that possibility than any old-school eugenicist could ever have hoped. Much of that technology was not under the control of any nation-state, as early eugenicists and scientific racists had envisioned. Instead, it was in the hands of private transnational corporations. But the wealth, authority, knowledge, and influence to be gained and wielded were still very much the property of loyal Nordic sons.

Racism against the Abnormal Revisited

Despite occasional protestations to the contrary, both the postwar eugenics movement and its offshoot, the pro-family movement, were the direct descendants of modern scientific racism. Unlike their predecessor, the prewar eugenics movement, these new movements played down the role of the state as the enforcer of their biopolitical values, although they used state mechanisms whenever doing so suited their purposes. Instead they sought to manage family life—sexuality, reproduction, child rearing, education and vocational training, household consumption, health, aging, and even death—primarily through a variety of extra-governmental channels. Like the eugenics movement, however, these new movements served the material interests of the social scientific and medical professions and, increasingly, investors in pharmaceutical companies and health care systems, as well as the metaphysical or quasi-religious interests of true believers. And they characterized multigenerational, female-headed, and African American households as fundamentally pathological, just as the eugenics movement had, and did their best to destroy homosexual, bisexual, and transgender subcultures and individuals.

Whether we call these movements racist or not is really a matter of whether we want to hold the term to its narrow 1936 definition, which would make racism a phenomenon that arose in the very late eighteenth century and declined in the mid-twentieth, or we want to use the term to name a shifting tradition of white supremacist political strategies stretching from about 1700 to the present. If we choose the latter tack, I believe this long genealogy has shown that Foucault is right: contemporary racism, the racism that arose in the twentieth century as heir to scientific racism and racist eugenics, is racism against the abnormal.

If we take this idea seriously, racism looms much larger and goes much deeper in our national and our personal lives than even the most racially aware and sensitive among us might think. It structures all our educational institutions; it informs all our medical protocols; it shapes our self-perceptions as well as our perceptions of every person we meet. Our halls of justice reverberate with it. Our prisons and hospitals and asylums grow crowded with the consequences of it. Racism against the abnormal permeates virtually every aspect of contemporary life and is responsible for many of the disparities and injustices that mark our society.

It is easy to look back to the early years of the twentieth century, knowing what we now know about genetic inheritance, and condemn the old racist eugenicists. Their confusion of phenotype and genotype seems inexcusable. Their dismissal of entire ethnic populations as genetically inferior could only have been based (if not on rank prejudice) on a terribly simplistic understanding of the human genome, which they should have questioned and critiqued decades earlier than most of them did. In the twenty-first century, most of us—especially those of us who tend toward the left—like to congratulate ourselves on having put aside such blatantly unjust and unscientific ideas. Most people are no longer racist in that narrow 1936 sense—that is, most people don't believe that skin color is a one-hundred-percent-reliable indicator of moral worth or that all members of any one race are inferior to all members of any other.[87] Racial difference in and of itself does not equal inferiority, we assert with confidence; we are far more discriminating and sophisticated than that.

But what we do believe—a large majority of us, at least—is that abnormality *does* equal inferiority, that abnormal people are inferior to normal people, and that many abnormalities (like mental deficiency, mental illness, or sexual deviance) *are* reliable indicators of moral worth. Consider, for example, the South Carolina legislature's debate over a bill to mandate involuntary sterilization of mental defectives in 1933. Many delegates questioned the measure's wisdom. Would it really eliminate feeblemindedness and lunacy, they asked. They were skeptical. But the bill passed the house and went to the upper chamber, where freshman senator Strom Thurmond guided it through committee and to success on the full senate floor (Larson 1995, 128). We now know the skeptics had truth on their side: thirty-five years of forcible sterilization did not rid South Carolina of either idiots or crazies. But what if the proponents of sterilization had been right? Would we so glibly criticize them now? Or would we herald them as prescient heroes, as the scientifically informed progressives most of them believed themselves to be? Don't most twenty-first-century Americans agree with Strom Thurmond and the South Carolina legislature that eliminating deviance—eradicating abnormality—is a pretty good idea? Aren't our condemnations of our grandparents' generation really just condemnations of their ignorance and crude methods rather than of their ideals?[88] And if so, must we not then admit that our values and attitudes and practices—even the most progressive and scientifically informed and seemingly most antiracist of them—have not only arisen in the lineage but also bear the stamp of scientific racism? What efforts and investigations and alliances will it take to dismantle *that* racism?

SEVEN

(COUNTER) REMEMBERING RACISM

AN INSURRECTION OF
SUBJUGATED KNOWLEDGES

In casual conversations a question I always dread is this: "So, what do you do?" Most of the time, honestly, I don't really know what it is that I do. I could say, "I'm a philosopher; I philosophize." But uttered at a charity fund-raiser or a doctor's office or a bar, that kind of statement could only lead to trouble. "I teach," I say. "Teach what?" comes the next dreaded question. Soon the moment will arrive when I will have run out of red herrings and will be forced to reveal that my area of so-called expertise is one of the most esoteric, ill-defined, and seemingly useless of all possible pursuits.

But over the two years that I spent researching the eugenics movement for chapter 5, things were different. For once I had a ready answer to the dreaded question. "I'm studying the history of how poor people in Virginia were rounded up by the thousands and taken to Lynchburg and Staunton to be sterilized," I would say. And I would follow that declaration with a question of my own: "Did you know that between 1927 and 1972 state social services forcibly sterilized 8,500 people?"

Often the answer was an incredulous, yet interested, no. But now and then a new interlocutor would pause and look away for a moment. Creases would form across the brow and around the mouth and eyes. And then he or she would look back at me and say, "I remember my grandmother once told me . . ." or "I had an uncle in Craig County who . . ." or "When I was a kid, people used to whisper about. . . ." We would talk a bit, and fragments would come together. "I'll bet . . ." and "She must've been . . ." and "I remember people were angry and afraid. . . ." In Virginia, and elsewhere, the memories are still there—scattered, in pieces, dispersed into this or that individual's or family's shame and pain—but still there. The knowledge of what was done to two generations of Virginia's poor, her disabled, her nonconformists, her misfits, is a local knowledge shared by ordinary people—mostly neighbors and relatives of the officially disqualified—swirling just below the bar that marks what Foucault calls "the required level of erudition or scientificity" (2003b, 7). It is "subjugated knowledge." It is knowledge that for decades was not recognized as any kind of knowledge at all and that barely recognizes itself as such even now.

Over the past twenty years a small contingent of researchers has disinterred a lot of the buried evidence to corroborate the existence and expose the details of that official campaign against the poor, the disabled, and the vulnerable—the people Charles Davenport and Harry Laughlin so arrogantly labeled "the socially inadequate."[1] Their work has been cited repeatedly in the last two chapters of this book, which would have been impossible without them. By foregrounding historical material that hegemonic histories and official policies have de-emphasized or dismissed, they have created an erudite account of scientific racism and eugenics, and in so doing they have critiqued received views and called into question some aspects of the epistemologies that support them. This too Foucault calls subjugated knowledge, "historical contents that have been buried or masked in functional coherences or formal systematizations," material that can be brought out of the archives with the tools of scholarship and that can enable us "to see the dividing lines in the confrontations and struggles that functional arrangements or systematic organizations are designed to mask" (2003b, 7).

Foucault holds that when these two forms of subjugated knowledge come together—the buried and the disqualified, the documented and the remembered—the result is "a historical knowledge of struggles." Both types of knowledge carry within them "the memory of combats, the very memory that had until then been confined to the margins." In their merger "we have an outline of what might be called a genealogy, or of multiple genealogical investigations. We have both a meticulous rediscovery of struggles and the raw memory of fights" (2003b, 8). The result is an awareness that things are as they are, not because God or Nature so decreed, but because of the balance of power at a given time, the pressures and strains of a historical moment. And one consequence of that awareness is the recognition that today's status quo was far from inevitable and need not persist into tomorrow—even aspects of it as seemingly intractable as racism and homophobia.

In this book I have taken the erudite knowledge of investigative journalists, historians, and other scholars, as well as some of my own, and combined it with what I know from personal experience—that is, with some very raw memories of my own struggles—concerning discrimination toward, disqualification of, and violence against, queer people as well as disabled and racially marginalized people. The result is a genealogy of biopolitical normalization in the United States. I have called it a genealogy of modern racism.

Genealogical investigation is not a new empiricism, Foucault insists (2003b, 9; 2007, 3). I have not presented a story of the development of modern racism in these pages that claims to be *the* definitive, final account as over against false accounts already circulating. My goal has not been to set the record straight and lay every question to rest. Instead, I have tried to resurrect old questions and formulate a few new ones, to mess up tidy categories and definitions, to make the questions of what racism is, where it comes from, and what it allies itself with too complex and too persistent and too frightening to put down. Thus this book does not constitute a work of history so much as an act of philosophy.[2]

Genealogies, Foucault says, are insurrections "against the centralizing power-effects that are bound up with the institutionalization and workings of any scientific discourse organized in a society such as ours" (2003b, 9). The genealogy of modern racism that has taken shape in these pages is therefore not disinterested scholarship. It is *fundamentally interested scholarship*. It is an intellectual assault on the power-effects of institutionalized, entrenched, and taken-for-granted academic, clinical, moralistic, and religious discourses about racism—discourses that make racism a psychological phenomenon rather than a pervasive political condition; discourses that make racism a moral failing rather than a complex mechanism of bio-normalization; discourses that make racism separate from (and perhaps merely equal to) ethnocentrism, nationalism, sexism, heterosexism, age-ism, able-ism, and species-ism, as if racism were only about minority races in industrialized nations and not about historical and ongoing white supremacist attempts to remake the entire human race over the face of the entire planet—genetically, culturally, and economically. My goal here has been to make the question of what racism is new again—newer, in fact, than it ever was before.

This genealogy has attempted to de-subjugate and incite feminist knowledge and queer knowledge of sexuality's intimate connection with white supremacy; it has attempted to set free the shame and rage that permeate personal knowledge formed in the midst of sex, gender, and racial oppression and generations of hatred directed toward any and all lives lived in excess of licensed and certified biopolitical management systems. This genealogy has attempted to enable and equip opposition to and struggle against the coercion of unitary, formal, scientific, and theoretical discourses that tell us that racism is either a natural aspect of human evolution or just another pathology that can be handled by moral educators and social scientific and clinical experts. It is meant, in part, to show that the ways we have been taught to conceive of and talk about and fight against racism are not only not effective in eliminating it and the suffering it causes (which most of us already know, whether we admit it or not), but are, in fact, part of the racist power apparatus that produces that very suffering. And it is meant to show that the only way to fight racism successfully is to critique and displace officially recognized antiracist discourses simultaneously.

This book has argued that contemporary campaigns against sexual deviance and sexual subcultures as well as attempts to roll back civil rights and social and economic opportunities for white women, disabled people, and the world's poor are among the offspring of scientific racism and are closely allied with contemporary versions of racism directed against people of color. Scientific racism was not just an attempt on the part of some scientists, intellectually compromised by irrational prejudice, to justify the oppression of people of color. It was a set of scientific theories, disciplinary practices, and social and political institutions that projected and attempted to realize a program of human perfection in evolutionary biological terms by purging the human species—the Race—of defect, deviance, and disease.

That vision or some version of it can exert a powerful seduction on any person brought up with Enlightenment values or the promises of Messianic Christianity. To be sure, we are duly horrified at our predecessors' willingness to cage and mutilate people for bearing children out of wedlock or contracting tuberculosis. But that doesn't mean we don't share their desire for human perfection or social progress. Perhaps we just don't see "fornication" or "consumption" as serious problems or flaws; they happen not to be included on our list of imperfections to be purged. The genealogy presented here, however, aims not just to challenge particular items on scientific racists' lists of defects but to challenge the values that inform *any* such project of purification in pursuit of perfection and to place in question the rejection of the nonrational, the unmanaged, the excess, the residue that such projects necessarily entail. The most horrifying aspect of scientific racism, I contend, is not that its adherents took actions antithetical to our culture's highest ideals, but on the contrary, that scientific racism and the eugenics movement it spawned and supported embodied *precisely those ideals.*

Those of us who have been classified as the excess, the impure, the dangerous, or the eminently dispensable need to consider very carefully how to proceed. Shall we claim to be otherwise, move heaven and earth to correct the alleged misperceptions, and thus leave the ideals of purity and transcendence untouched? Or shall we find another way? Although it may not initially seem so, this question bears crucially on the controversy over the propriety of analogies between queer and black civil rights movements.

Murder and the Moral High Ground

In the late 1970s, a coalition of forces gathered from the old eugenics movement, nationalistic anticommunist movements, and movements to oppose the demands of organized labor and prevent the civic equality of people of color assembled a conglomerate of political organizations and capitalist enterprises and named itself the Religious Right. It took up the pro-family rhetoric made popular by white supremacist activists like Paul Popenoe and dressed it up in a kind of neo-Christian moralism that it dubbed "Family Values." Anyone who did not fit into the narrowly prescribed roles of the bourgeois nuclear (normal) family was said to have no moral standing to engage in social critique and no credibility as a member of that amorphous but oft-cited entity, the American People. Anyone who did not support the values that this group claimed belonged exclusively to the Normal American Family was cast as an agent of societal destruction, an enemy of civilization, a social cancer, a public pathogen. In the name of Our (normal) Children, whose precious lives had to be protected at all costs (lest we have no grandchildren), such people had to be neutralized—either managed effectively or eliminated entirely. The movement raised huge amounts of money through white fundamentalist churches and religious mass media and systematically organized to gain control of local governments as well as, eventually, some state and national governmental officials and agencies.

Within fifteen years of this political development, instead of pulling together to oppose a growing network of radical right-wing forces, African American civic and religious leaders and middle-class white representatives of movements for gay rights were hurling recriminations at each other. Despite the fact that for years there had been a great deal of support among blacks for gay rights, African American religious leaders were accusing gays and lesbians of "hijacking" the civil rights movement and endangering its successes by using its rhetoric to call for their own "special rights." And middle-class white gays and lesbians were responding by accusing African Americans of rampant homophobia, which from their perspective was the moral equivalent of racism.

Inside another decade, the head of the ultra-right-wing Christian Coalition, Ralph Reed, publicly apologized to black Christians for the racism that white Christian conservatives displayed during the 1960s and invited them to join in solidarity with his movement to make the world safe for the Family by purging society of its greatest enemy, sexual deviants.[3] Meanwhile, gay and lesbian couples begged state and municipal officials to recognize their monogamous life-commitments by issuing them marriage licenses and joint adoption papers. It was a contest for the moral high ground, with all sides pointedly indulging in a veritable orgy of familial normality.

For those of us old enough to remember when white Christian conservatives accused African Americans of setting themselves above all other citizens in their demands for "special rights" (like the right to deny white people their constitutional right of free association with only other white people) and gay and lesbian people wanted liberation from the obviously oppressive institutions of marriage and the nuclear family (as critiqued by radical feminists and gay liberationists alike), it all seemed rather carnivalesque and might even have been comic—except for the fact that it wasn't. Except for the fact that people were still getting killed.

The most publicized racist murder of recent years was that of

James Byrd, a forty-nine-year-old African American man who was offered a ride by three young white men as he was walking home from a party for his niece in the summer of 1998, just a few weeks before Matthew Shepard was killed. Once Byrd was in their custody, the three—John King, Lawrence Russel Brewer, and Shawn Berry—beat him, chained him to the back of their pickup truck, and dragged him for almost three miles along a country road. The autopsy suggested that Byrd was alive, conscious, and attempting to keep his head up through much of the dragging; he died when his body hit a culvert and his arm and head were severed. His killers dumped the pieces of his body that they could gather in a nearby black cemetery and then went off to attend a barbeque. At least two of the three assailants were members of white supremacist organizations. John King sported pro-Nazi and Aryan pride tattoos as well as a tattoo of the insignia of the Confederate Knights of America, a white supremacist prison gang to which Lawrence Brewer also belonged.

King, Brewer, and Berry were not the only Americans guilty of racist violence in recent years, however, and James Byrd was only one among a throng of victims. In 2005 alone the FBI reports that there were 4,895 racially motivated hate crimes and that 68.2 percent of the victims were African American.[4] From harassment and intimidation to robberies, beatings, and stabbings, African Americans bear the brunt of racist brutality. Here are just a few examples:

1. In June of 2005 Nicholas Minucci, a white twenty-year-old Queens, New York, man, attacked Glenn Howard, a twenty-three-year-old African American man, with a baseball bat. Minucci beat Howard apparently simply for walking with two friends through what Minucci considered a white neighborhood (Howard Beach) and for wearing Prada shoes (Kilgannon 2006).

2. In December of 2006, while on their way to a neo-Nazi rally near UCLA, Ryan White, Chad Milson, Joseph McCool, and Anthony Allen stopped off in Claremont, California, to eat a meal. Afterward, outside the restaurant, they attacked a thirty-four-year-old black man who was coming out of an adjacent liquor store, stabbing him multiple times. ("Four charged with attempted murder" 2006)

3. In July of 2006 in Manning, South Carolina, KKK member Jeremy Sweat and his friend Dustin Evans abducted a fifteen-

year-old black girl, whom they forced into a mobile home, choked, cut with a knife, and then raped. After both had raped the girl repeatedly, they pushed her into a shower stall and stabbed her until she feigned death. When they left to get trash bags to dispose of her body, she escaped and was able to attract the attention of a neighbor before going into shock from blood loss. According to the Clarendon County sheriff, Sweat and Evans chose the girl because she was black "and may have been targeting any African-American woman." Authorities linked the two to the rape of a forty-five-year-old black woman in Summerton, South Carolina, the previous month. ("Accused rapists have ties to KKK" 2006)

Blacks were certainly not the only targets of hate violence, however. After a dispute in a St. Louis restaurant, Kevin A. Johnson stood up on a table, gave a Nazi salute, and displayed his swastika tattoo before attacking another customer, whom he called "You Jew Motherfucker." Johnson chased the man across the street, where he knocked him to the ground and began to kick him and jump up and down on his head. Before bystanders could intervene, Johnson had crushed the man's skull. The victim died the next day of brain hemorrhage.[5]

And assaults on immigrants, especially those from South Asia and the Middle East, have become increasingly common since the 2001 attacks on the World Trade Center and the Pentagon. Hate crimes against people of South Asian descent rose 23 percent from 2000 to 2001 (Melwani 2003). One of the first post–9/11 incidents was in Mesa, Arizona. On September 15, 2001, Frank Roque announced in a Mesa bar that all Arabs and their children should be rounded up and executed, and that he was going to go "kill some towelheads." Roque then went on a thirty-minute shooting spree during which he fired at a Lebanese-American clerk at a Mobile gas station, an Afghani family in their home, and the Indian-American owner of a Chevron gas station. The forty-nine-year-old station owner, Balbir Singh Sodhi, died of gunshot wounds. In November of 2003, Nabeel Siddiqui, a twenty-four-year-old Pakistani student at the New Jersey Institute of Technology, died from brain damage inflicted by three white teenagers with a baseball bat when he delivered a pizza in their neighborhood. The previous July an Indian graduate student, Saurabh Bahlerao, who delivered pizzas in New Bedford, Massachusetts, was similarly attacked and beaten. On July 1, 2007, Satendar Singh, a twenty-six-year-old immigrant from Fiji, was picnicking with friends near Lake Natoma in Folsom, California, when his group was attacked; he was beaten senseless by six men shouting racist and homophobic slurs. Four days later, Singh's family removed him from life support and allowed him to die of his extensive brain injuries.[6]

While many people of Middle Eastern and South Asian descent are targeted in so-called "retaliation" for the September 11 attacks, Latinos—both persons and their property—are often attacked simply for being in the United States. Mesa, Arizona, was again the site of highly publicized killing in 2002, when white supremacists Steve Boggs and Christopher Hargrave lined up Beatriz Alvarado, Fausto Jimenez, and Kenneth Brown in a freezer at a Jack-in-the-Box restaurant and executed them with gunshots to the back. Boggs wrote a letter to police in which he stated that he wanted "to rid the world of a few needless illegals."[7] In April of 2006, one day after 50,000 people marched in a pro-immigration rally in San Diego, a Mexican restaurant in nearby Jumal was vandalized, marked with racist graffiti, and set fire. The following August in New Orleans, Mark Gautreau was charged with two counts of first-degree attempted murder after announcing that he was going to "shoot some Mexicans" and then firing on two Latino men, wounding both.[8] A number of white supremacist groups air radio shows around the country and many have Web sites. Discussion and postings in the past few years have tended to be extremely anti-immigration and to encourage violence against Latinos in particular. "They are barbarians," AllisioRex wrote in July 2005, on the neo-Nazi Web forum Stormfront: "They are our enemies, they want to destroy our civilization and we have to fight them. We need to organize better and be more open activists; otherwise, I only see race war in the future."[9]

The language of invasion and threat to civilization is not confined to the hinterlands and cyberspace; MSNBC political analyst and former presidential candidate Patrick Buchanan's 2002 book bears the title *The Death of the West: How Dying Populations and Immigrant Invasions Imperil Our Country and Civilization*. In it Buchanan asserts that the murders of James Byrd and Matthew Shepard were not hate crimes and that Shepard was really slain not because he was gay but because he propositioned one of his killers. He goes on to dismiss racist and homophobic violence along with the very concept of hate crimes by asserting: "Hate crimes are the cultural elite's way of racially profiling white males" (2002, 65, 67). Buchanan and other Religious Right-wingers with mass media platforms insist that white male Christians are under siege and have the right and even the duty to fight to take America back from those who are supposedly in the process of stealing it from them. Not only America, but Civilization— which is of course white and Christian and heterosexual—is at stake, and its defense justifies drastic action. Ralph Reed may apologize for the 1960s all he likes, and strategists on the far right see the political expediency of doing so, but clearly a great many conservative white Christians are not sorry for past discrimination against people of color and have no plans to curtail racist discrimination, injustice, and violence in the present or future. People are still getting killed.

While attacks on racial minorities persisted and hate crimes against immigrants rose, anti-queer violence continued as well. In October of 2000, some students and I put together a display for Coming Out Day. My job was to compile a list of people who had been victims of anti-LGBT hate violence in the last years of the twentieth century. Although I didn't have time to do a thorough job of scouring old headlines, the task was painfully easy.

> Jacqueline Anderson, shot to death, 1998, Portland, Oregon
>
> Barbara Gilpin, shot to death, 1998, Portland, Oregon
>
> Brian Wilmes, beaten to death, March 1998, San Francisco, California
>
> Thomas Coleman, beaten and stabbed, May 1998, Lancaster, Pennsylvania
>
> Matthew Shepard, pistol whipped to death, October 1998, Laramie, Wyoming
>
> Larry Morris, shot and burned to death, January 1999, Texas City, Texas
>
> Kevin Tryals, shot and burned to death, January 1999, Texas City, Texas
>
> Alden Judge, shot to death, February 1999, Lansing, Michigan
>
> Billy Jack Gaither, beaten, stabbed, and burned to death, February 1999, Coosa County, Alabama

Henry Edward Northington, beheaded, March 1999, Richmond, Virginia

Alex Charles, age 15, murdered, May 1999, Flat Rock, Michigan

Michael Fleming, beaten to death outside a gay bar, June 1999, Baton Rouge, Louisiana

Christopher William Jones, bludgeoned to death, June 1999, Baltimore, Maryland

John C. Lloyd, stabbed to death, July 1999, Gainesville, Florida

Gary Matson, murdered in his home, July 1999, Redding, California

Winfield Mowder, murdered in his home, July 1999, Redding, California

Pfc. Barry Winchell, bludgeoned to death, July 1999, Fort Campbell, Kentucky

Wayne Heath Johnston, severely beaten by two men outside a tavern, August 1999, Muncie, Indiana

Steen Fenrich, murdered by his step-father, September 1999, Dix Hills, New York

Neal Goodwin, beaten while riding a city bus, October 1999, San Francisco, California

Anthony McCullough, shot to death, October 1999, Center City, Pennsylvania

Muna Hawatmeh, beaten by family members, October 1999, Salt Lake City, Utah

University of Arizona undergraduate, name withheld, stabbed, February 2000, Tucson, Arizona

Two Boston high school girls, beaten and sexually assaulted at knifepoint, January 2000, Boston, Massachusetts

Jason Hair, beaten by a high school classmate, February 2000, Dedham, Massachusetts

Unnamed man, abducted, beaten, and raped, February 2000, Santa Clara County, California

Arthur "J.R." Warren, beaten and repeatedly run over with a truck until dead, July 2000, Grant Town, West Virginia

Two unnamed men, beaten, July 2000, Mahwah, New Jersey

Michael J. Hatch, beaten to death with a tire iron, July 2000, Barron, Wisconsin

Gary Massey Sr., beaten, July 2000, Dayton, Ohio

Mary Massey, beaten with a glass bottle, July 2000, Dayton, Ohio

Gary Massey Jr., beaten with a shovel, July 2000, Dayton, Ohio

Two unnamed men, assaulted with a deadly weapon, August 2000, Daly City, California

Seventeen-year-old son of Hendrick and Sharon Paterson, beaten with lead pipes by his parents, August 2000, New York, New York

Unnamed man, pistol whipped, August 2000, South Bend, Indiana

Kathy Caldwell, shot in the hand and shoulder, September 2000, Roanoke, Virginia

John Collins, shot in the abdomen, September 2000, Roanoke, Virginia

Linda Conyers, shot in the arm and hand, September 2000, Roanoke, Virginia

Danny Lee Overstreet, shot to death, September 2000, Roanoke, Virginia

Susan Smith, shot in the leg and buttocks, September 2000, Roanoke, Virginia

Joel Tucker, shot in the back, September 2000, Roanoke, Virginia

Iris Page Webb, shot in the neck, September 2000, Roanoke, Virginia

I stress that this is just a sample, not an exhaustive list, of the violent crimes committed against men, women, and children in the United States of America because somebody declared their sexual orientation unacceptable and therefore their lives and health expendable.[10] And the violence certainly did not stop in October of 2000 when my list ends. The FBI's Uniform Crime Statistics report for 2005 recorded 1,171 hate crimes motivated by "sexual-orientation bias" in that year alone, 98 percent of which were anti-queer.[11] And the National Coalition of Anti-Violence Projects—which, despite the word *national* in its name, collects reports of anti-LGBT hate crimes in only about a dozen locations around the country—reported eleven murders in

2001, ten in 2002, eighteen in 2003, twelve in 2004, ten in 2005, and eleven in 2006. Notably, NCAVP does not collect data anywhere in the mid-Atlantic or southern United States or in any part of Texas except Houston.[12]

Most anti-queer attacks aren't reported to authorities and certainly don't make the papers, especially when they are carried out by kinfolks, or when the victims or perpetrators are minors, or when the attacks are not public and the physical injuries are not catastrophic, or when the police decide that the real motive was robbery or that the assault was just a routine rape of the kind that could happen to a straight woman too if she dared to walk without a male escort at night.[13] They get lost in the sea of crime statistics or the silence of the victims' fear. But *we* hear of them. We *know*.

And we also know that there are many kinds of deaths. The brutal extinction of biological existence is only the most extreme form of oppression and assault. There are also assaults on our self-esteem, our character, our credibility, our right to raise our children or hold a job or rent an apartment. There are the leers of straight men when two lesbians enter a restaurant, the glares of neighbors when two gay men stroll outside to walk their dog—not mere prurience or disapproval but implicit threats reinforced by what we know: that so many others have already been victimized.

The last seven shootings on my list—the event that occasioned our Coming Out Day display—might have been a mass rather than a single murder but for the fact that the perpetrator had remarkably bad aim. Ronald Gay, wearing a trench coat on a warm evening and toting a handgun, asked several Roanoke pedestrians for directions to the nearest gay bar. They told him. After the shooting, he told authorities that he was angry at homosexuals for giving him—Mr. Gay—a bad name. Officials said Gay was mentally ill. No one explained why mental illness might express itself in antigay homicidal rage, much less who had really given Mr. Gay a bad name. At Danny Overstreet's funeral, several young men shouting antigay epithets assaulted mourners, including the minister, in the Roanoke Metropolitan Community Church parking lot. No one declared the young thugs mentally ill. No one even tried to explain their behavior. Was that because it was inexplicable, or just because every normal person already understood?

It is hard to know these things—to know, for example, how it feels to sit in a gay bar on a warm Virginia evening with the doors open to the sidewalk, enjoying time with friends, all the while sizing up every stranger who crosses the threshold, wondering if he or she is packing a weapon and a murderous rage—hard to know such things and not be furious at anybody who says queer people aren't subject to discrimination, oppression, dehumanization, and violence. But if memories of struggles are to coalesce into a genealogical investigation that might have political application and a positive effect in the world, we who have endured much have to draw some wisdom from what we know. Instead of fuming at people like Dennis Kuby and Jesse Jackson, we have to take a step back from the pain and the anger and the desire for immediate mass enlightenment, and ask ourselves some questions.

Why *do* LGBT people want to compare their situations to those of African Americans? And why *does* that make so many African Americans so upset? Truth be told, there are a bundle of reasons for both phenomena, some of them having (at least conceivably) nothing at all to do with racism or homophobia. Before we let our anger dictate our responses to each other and thereby jeopardize any chance for joint resistance and mutual support, we need to understand those *other* reasons. In doing so, we may find that our values and concerns don't clash as much as we sometimes think they do.

Speaking the Language of Federal Judges

First, there is a perfectly understandable strategic reason why LGBT activists have so often cited the black civil rights movement when they have tried to make a case for LGBT rights, a reason having much more to do with civil rights law and the possibilities and obstacles it presented by the 1990s than with the attitudes, positive or negative, that white gay and lesbian and transgendered people might have toward African Americans. That reason has to do with a question that goes all the way back to the founding of the United States of America, a question that wasn't originally about race or sexual orientation at all. It was this: In a democracy, how can we prevent the majority from tyrannizing over the minority?

This nation's founders were very aware of the existence of minorities and of the need to ensure that minority views were not squelched in either public discourse or lawmaking. But for Madison, Hamilton, Jay, and others, the minorities in question were simply those groups of people who held unpopular views.[14] They might be identified by

labels—Puritans, Quakers, Methodists, Unitarians—but these labels
did not indicate essential differences. Quakers, for example, were not
biologically or psychically different from their fellow citizens. It was
not until the mid-nineteenth century that Americans began to entertain the notion that there might exist a persistent and distinct class
of citizen, Negroes, who most believed were physically (and morally
and intellectually) different from non-Negroes and who might always,
therefore, have different political interests and views from the white
majority. The term *minority*, meaning both "a group having different
interests and opinions from most others" and "an oppressed or disfavored social group within a larger society," entered American political
discourse in the early twentieth century (becoming part of the official
vocabulary of modern sociology in 1928).[15] African Americans were
thus the archetype, the first "minority" in the modern sense of the
term. Regardless of what particular opinions any black person might
hold, regardless of whether he or she disagreed with the majority on
a particular issue or not, he or she was still a member of a minority.

Black Americans, then, are not only one *example* of a minority
class; they are the class that gave the modern concept of minority its
meaning. This is true historically and legally, but it is even more obviously true in popular culture, where the terms *black* and *minority* are
often interchangeable. For any group other than African Americans
to count as a minority in the popular imagination, its members have
had to resemble African Americans in some way, which usually has
meant that they had to be viewed as a physically distinct race, a group
of people presumed to share genetic similarities as well as a cultural
heritage. And that requirement very often carries over from the popular imagination into positive law.

Nowhere is this fact more evident than in debates over application of the Fourteenth Amendment, which was enacted in 1868 to
protect the rights of the emerging African American "minority" by
imposing a restraint on state governments' use of *any* kind of classification scheme. The amendment states in part: "no state shall make
or enforce any law which shall . . . deny to any person within its
jurisdiction equal protection of the laws." Whenever the law marks
out a particular set of individuals and denies them rights granted to
other citizens, the Fourteenth Amendment's Equal Protection Clause
may have been violated.

But obviously it is the government's business much of the time to divide its population into separate sets of individuals or, as constitutional lawyers put it, separate classes. For the purpose of levying income tax, most states divide residents into classes based on how much money they have earned in a given year. Most states divide their populations into classes based on age for the purposes of alcohol and tobacco sales, education, the granting of various kinds of licensure, and the right to hold state office or receive entitlements. So the Fourteenth Amendment did not take away states' right to classify populations for some purposes. The question, then, is what purposes justify such discrimination and, further, upon what bases may states discriminate? The answers to these questions are complex, but they are crucial to understanding why LGBT activists are so interested in claiming minority status under the law and why doing so requires likening their constituencies in some respects to African Americans. What follows through most of the rest of this section is an overview of relevant court decisions, which will help explain some LGBT activists' legal strategies.

Since 1942 (beginning with *Skinner v. Oklahoma*), the U.S. Supreme Court has held that if the rights denied members of a class are "fundamental rights," such as the right to vote, the state must present "compelling" reason for the classification. Only the most extreme conditions could legitimate a state's denial of fundamental rights to any class of citizens. If the right denied is not fundamental, though, the state usually only needs to show that the classification bears *some relationship* to a legitimate governmental purpose. Not since 1944, however, has the Supreme Court upheld a classification on the basis of race in any case involving limitations on rights, whether fundamental or not.[16] Every case the Court has heard wherein a governmental agency classified people by race for the purpose of awarding rights differentially has been struck down as a violation of the Equal Protection Clause. Race, the Court declared in 1944, is a "suspect class." In other words, the Court could think of few or no good reasons for states ever to divide their populations into racial classes for differential treatment.

A definitive ruling came in *Loving v. Virginia* (1967), which invalidated state laws against interracial marriage. The Court held that any law that uses race as a way of discriminating between groups of people is inherently suspect and will be subject to "strict scrutiny," no matter what rights are being limited or what goods are being distributed. Since 1967, laws that limit citizens' rights on the basis of their membership in racial groups are virtually always declared unconstitutional. It is generally held that the government has no legitimate interest in dividing its population into classes on the basis of race, no matter what. Such classification schemes are termed "invidious" or "malicious." Regardless of the government's stated purpose, the real purpose is probably to hurt a disfavored group. The same is true of classifications based on national origin and, since 1971, alienage.[17]

In the last thirty years or so, Supreme Court review in Equal Protection cases has grown more complex. Since 1976, instead of two levels of scrutiny, the Court employs at least three.[18] There are now two "quasi-suspect" classes; laws using classifications based on sex or legitimacy received heightened but not strict scrutiny, meaning proponents must show that the classifications are somehow "substantially related to an important governmental objective."[19] Governments cannot make laws that confer different rights upon men and women or upon legitimate and illegitimate children of one individual unless there is some significant goal in view and government attorneys can show that classification on the basis of sex or legitimacy will likely help to realize that goal.

In sum, then, states can classify people for the purpose of differential distribution of burdens or rights (as long as those rights are not fundamental) for any legitimate governmental purpose on any basis except race, national origin, alienage, sex, or legitimacy. Governments can classify people according to their level of income, their age, their height and weight, their educational attainments, their status as property owners, their health, their place of residence, or any imaginable characteristic other than religion, which is protected under the First Amendment and Title VII of the 1964 Civil Rights Act. All they have to do is link the differential treatment to a public good—such as containing contagion, creating safer neighborhoods, or reducing the tax burden on working families. Governmental discrimination is then considered legitimate.

Given the popular images of homosexuals as child-molesting psychopaths, Communist patsies, and carriers of degeneracy and disease, governmental discrimination against queer people historically has been readily accepted and commonplace, and nongovernmental discrimination has been widely tolerated under the law and widely practiced by employers, landlords, real estate agents, physicians, educators, and businesses and private service providers. LGBT rights advocates dispute those characterizations of queer people and want to see such differential treatment made illegal. Therefore, some assert that discrimination on the basis of sexual orientation should be construed as a violation of the Equal Protection Clause. Given more than a century of malicious and invidious characterizations of homosexuals as dangers to public health and safety, they maintain, prejudice against gay and lesbian people is prevalent; thus, sexual orientation cannot fail to be an invidious and malicious basis for classification, just as race is. Some legal experts go a step further, arguing that sexual orientation should be a suspect class and that laws invoking it must be necessary to secure some compelling governmental interest or be declared unconstitutional. If these arguments were to prevail when such laws come before the Supreme Court for review, they would receive heightened scrutiny and would probably be struck down.

Antigay groups have been working very hard to prevent LGBT activists and legal theorists from persuading judges that sexual orientation should be considered a suspect class or that cases involving queer people merit any sort of heightened scrutiny at all. Spokespeople for groups like the Traditional Values Coalition and Focus on the Family insist that government has the right to establish a classification system on the basis of sexual orientation and to discriminate against homosexuals as a group because, paradoxically, they do not constitute a true minority.[20] The legal basis of their claim is a 1938 decision in *United States v. Carolene Products Company*, which was refined in *Bowen v. Gilliard* in 1987. In *Bowen*, the Court listed three conditions that must be met in order for a person's case to warrant heightened scrutiny. The person must:

1. Have suffered a history of discrimination;
2. Exhibit obvious, immutable, or distinguishing characteristics that define him or her as a member of a discrete group; and
3. Show that the group is a minority or politically powerless, or alternatively show that the statutory classification at issue burdens a fundamental right.[21]

While it seems obvious that there has been discrimination against queer people and that people known to be homosexual or transgendered do not have easy access to the means of governance and therefore are easily construed as politically powerless, many argue that no queer person can ever meet the second criterion. Anti-LGBT activists argue that homosexuality and transgenderism are not characteristics but only intermittent behaviors. In other words, there is no such thing as a homosexual or bisexual or transsexual or transgendered person. There are only people who choose to engage in sodomy or cross-dressing. Since there are no homosexual or transgendered people—no people who have an obvious, immutable, or distinguishing identity as homosexual or transgendered—minority status cannot be accorded those who so label themselves.

It makes sense, then, that some groups defending queer lives and dignity have taken the exact opposite stance. The NAACP, for example, has offered staunch support of gay and lesbian civil rights over the past couple of decades (no doubt one reason the Christian Right has worked so hard to divide African American Christians from their "liberal" leaders),[22] but it has done so by interpreting the Fourteenth Amendment as narrowly as any of the anti-LBGT crusaders has. Julian Bond, NAACP president, published this statement in August of 2006 in protest of Virginia's proposed constitutional amendment to void all "marriage-like" contracts between same-sex couples:[23]

> "Civil rights" are positive legal prerogatives—the right to equal treatment before the law. These are rights shared by all.
>
> Gay and lesbian rights are not "special rights" in any way. It isn't "special" to be free from discrimination. It is an ordinary, universal entitlement of citizenship.
>
> The right not to be discriminated against is a commonplace claim we all expect to enjoy under our laws and our founding document, the Constitution. That many struggled and even died to gain these rights makes them even more precious.
>
> When others gain a civil right, my rights are not reduced in any way. "Civil rights" are a win/win game—the more won by others, the stronger the army defending my rights becomes.
>
> For some, comparing the African-American civil rights movement and the movement for gay and lesbian rights somehow diminishes the long black struggle for equality with all its suffering and sacrifices.
>
> People of color should be flattered, however, that our

movement has provided so much inspiration for others, and
that our tactics, methods, heroines and heroes, even our songs
have been adopted by or served as models for others.

The NAACP opposes the federal marriage amendment—
and we oppose efforts to write bigotry into Virginia's constitution, too. Sexual orientation parallels race—I was born
black and had no choice. I couldn't and wouldn't change it if
I could.

Like race, our sexuality isn't a preference—it is inborn,
and the Constitution protects us all against discrimination
based on immutable differences.

Of course, no parallel between movements for rights is
exact. People of color carry the badge of who we are on our
faces. But we are far from the only people suffering discrimination. Others too deserve the law's protections and civil
rights.

Many gays and lesbians worked side by side with me in the
'60s civil rights movement. Am I to now tell them "thanks"
for risking life and limb to help win my rights—but allow their
exclusion because of a condition of their birth? (Bond 2006)

Gay and lesbian people deserve civil rights because sexual orientation
is a biologically immutable characteristic. Homosexuals are a genetic
variety, in effect, a kind of race.

If this is true, then surely the Fourteenth Amendment applies
unproblematically; sexual orientation should be considered a suspect
class under the Constitution, and laws marking out nonheterosexu-
als for discriminatory treatment should be struck down. But what
if it isn't true? What if not everybody who engages in homosexual
or transgender practices and participates in LGBT communities is
genetically or biologically determined to be a sex variant? Or what if
procedures were developed to alter sexual orientation so that those
born gay or lesbian could become heterosexual? Bond says that even
if he could choose to be white, he would still choose to be black. Being
black means far more to him that having a certain color skin or certain facial features. It means being part of a community and a history
and a culture that he values. And shouldn't that choice be respected?
In a democracy where individual freedom is valued, shouldn't people
have the right to make that choice?

Some legal theorists have argued that "immutability" is not the
actual measure of identifiability intended in the 1938 decision or the

1987 refinement in *Bowen*. The Court was not saying that rights hinge on whether people who are members of a group could choose to be or be made to be different so that they would no longer have the identifying characteristics of their group. It was only saying that rights hinge on whether the group is established and identifiable on some recognizable basis. This argument may carry some weight. While it may be possible someday for genetic engineers to turn black skins white (and thus fulfill Benjamin Rush's dream of a cure for "Negro leprosy"), surely such an eventuality would not make it right for states to discriminate against all people who choose to remain dark-skinned. Sex changes are already possible, but the existence of such procedures does not make it right for states to discriminate against people who choose to remain female. Eric Roberts (1993, 506) points out that in *Watkins v. United States Army* (9th Cir. 1989), 498 U.S. 957 (1990) *immutability* was defined not as "absolute unalterability" but rather as "alterability only with great trauma or difficulty." Thus, the fact that women can change their sex does not make femaleness a mutable characteristic for purposes of legal review.

But many legal theorists still hold to some kind of "absolute immutability" criterion and assert that unless homosexuality is caused by something biological and is not a reversible condition, sexual orientation cannot count as a suspect class. If so, advocates of civil rights for LGBT people have very little legal leverage to do anything but promote the idea that there is some unalterable biological trait that all homosexual and transgendered people have in common, a trait that might qualify them as a true minority, as a sort of race, discrimination against which should receive heightened scrutiny. As lesbian author Mab Segrest has put it, "Any group seeking to use the Fourteenth Amendment to gain constitutional status must, by definition, compare itself to African Americans to get in the door of the Constitution" (Segrest 1999, 52). When pro-LGBT activists invoke the black civil rights movement in their pursuit of civil rights for queer people, they do so in part because they are trying to speak the language that federal judges understand.

And when anti-LGBT activists like Alveda King say homosexuality is a sinful choice rather than a fundamental characteristic that sets the terms for an individual's personality and life course, they too are trying to speak a language that federal judges understand. They know very well that they are reinforcing the legal obstacles to civil rights—not "special rights," just plain old civil rights—for LGBT people. Without legal protection, LGBT people are routinely denied the use of public accommodations, the freedom to engage in productive work for which they are qualified, the ability to attend school, the simple pleasure of living peacefully in the neighborhood of their choice, and the exercise of their first amendment rights to assembly and free speech without harassment and violence. For whatever reason, King and her allies want state governments to have the authority to curtail civil rights for LGBT people. It is hard to see this desire as reflective of anything other than either cynical manipulation of the political playing field for personal gain or just plain old hatred.

But not every person who objects to LGBT citations of the black civil rights movement is a homophobic bigot. There are objections that have nothing to do with selfishness or hatred. The main one is the one I spoke of in the introduction to this book: the situations of African Americans in the 1950s and LGBT Americans at the turn of the new century really *are* different in some significant ways, and if we lose sight of that, we erase our histories. Too often when white LGBT activists compare their concerns and their movements to those of African Americans, they do so out of profound ignorance and without any genuine desire to explore and learn about the history they invoke.[24]

The same-sex marriage movement offers an example of this ignorance. Activists' assertions to the contrary, analogies between legal bans on same-sex marriage licensure and anti-miscegenation laws do not hold. Unlike interracial couples before 1967, in all fifty states in the United States same-sex couples can hold wedding ceremonies and, at least since the *Lawrence v. Texas* decision in 2003, legally set up housekeeping—in other words, we can get married. Those marriages will not be licensed, but the couples and the clergy who perform the ceremonies will not be prosecuted, nor will conjugal domesticity result in jail or exile. The same could not be said for interracial heterosexual couples under state anti-miscegenation laws. In 1958, the famous Lovings, who were arrested, indicted, and found guilty of felonious cohabitation in violation of Virginia law, received a suspended sentence of one year in prison and were expelled from the Commonwealth (Newbeck 2005, 15).[25] Anti-miscegenation laws were not simply bans on issuing marriage licenses to interracial couples; they were bans on interracial marital relationships per se. They prohibited wedding ceremonies, cohabitation, and interracial sex, and the punishments they established for engaging in those actions either as marital partners or as clergy and witnesses were dire. So-called bans on same-sex marriage are not bans on marital relationships; they are bans on licensure alone. The people who will be punished if those laws are broken are not clergy and spouses but the civil servants who issue the licenses or record them. As such, these laws cannot be described as bans on same-sex marriage. Same-sex marriage is not punished under them—and in fact, many same-sex couples make good, very real marriages every day, just like our presumptively straight ancestors did before nineteenth-century legislatures enacted marriage licensing laws.

Real marriages. For, consider: If I fish without a license, am I not actually fishing? If I drive without a license, am I not actually driving? If I practice medicine without a license, am I not actually practicing medicine? Of course I am. Licensure laws are only necessary because people *can* fish, drive, and practice medicine without state certification. Similarly, if I marry my partner without a license, I actually am marrying her. We don't need a license to get or be married. We only need a license if we want the government's help to secure our or our children's interests when the marriage ends in divorce or death. Only in the last 140 years has the state claimed the exclusive right to determine who is and is not married to whom, and its mechanism for usurping that right from communities, families, and individuals has been the institution of the marriage license.

There are some differences between marriage licenses and many other types of licenses, to be sure. Unlike licenses for fishing, driving, and practicing medicine, a marriage license functions, not as protection against prosecution (although it used to do so in states where fornication was illegal), but rather as admission to a civil status that bestows a set of rights against one's partner and the state. A marriage license brings with it over a thousand legal rights, including the right of access to a deceased spouse's social security, pension, and insurance benefits and the right to divorce with a court-mandated and enforced custody and property settlement. These are very important rights, but surely they are not the essence of marriage in its domestic, religious, or social sense. The essence of marriage lies in ongoing marital relationships, which same-sex couples already have, not in state regulation of our separations. Anti-miscegenation laws aimed to *prevent* marital relationships between interracial couples; thus, unlike bans on same-sex marriage licensure, anti-miscegenation laws did prohibit interracial marriage in its very essence. There may be comparisons to be drawn between the same-sex marriage licensure movement and previous civil rights struggles, but anti-miscegenation laws are not the place to look for them, and asserting comparability where there is none is an act either of ignorance or of total cynicism.[26]

Most of the time, I believe, such assertions are acts of ignorance, not deliberate exploitation or willful "hijacking" (as Lou Sheldon of the Traditional Values Coalition terms them).[27] But that does not diminish their offensiveness, because so many of the people who make these assertions are educationally privileged. They have no excuse for being ignorant of the history of legalized racial oppression and the long effort to overcome it. Their ignorance must be a reflection of a judgment—made consciously or unconsciously—that the history of the struggle for African American civil rights is not important enough to study and get right. Even when the analogies they put forth *are* apt—and in many cases they *are*—most of the people voicing them do not seem to know *that* they are or *why* they are. I understand why African Americans like my Binghamton lunch companion are insulted. It is insulting to misrepresent anybody's history.

The history being misrepresented in this case, moreover, does not belong just to blacks. I was a schoolchild in Alabama during desegregation. I remember George Wallace and Bull Connor and the Knights of the Ku Klux Klan. I remember when virtually all local governments and police departments in the Deep South (and many elsewhere) were controlled by racial terrorists and anybody who even verbally challenged the color line, let alone crossed it, might be killed with impunity. I remember flaming crosses and late-night telephone harassment and death threats. And I remember the courage of the many people, black and white and every other color, who forced things to change. That is part of my history as a white Southerner and our history as Americans, and we all should want it and its many heroes and heroines remembered and honored. When every local politician who hands out a marriage license to a gay couple is called a Rosa Parks, that history is not only not honored; it is distorted and obscured.

But much more than memory and honor is at stake here. To distort or obscure a history that an oppressed group has lived through is, whether one means to or not, to exercise domination over that group. Bell hooks puts it this way:

> As subjects, people have the right to define their own reality, establish their own identities, name their history. As objects, one's reality is defined by others, one's identity created by others, one's history named only in ways that define one's relationship to those who are subject. . . . Oppressed people resist by identifying themselves as subjects, by defining their reality, shaping their new identity, naming their history, telling their story. For white women, non-white women, black people, and all individuals from various ethnic groups who are gay, there have been historical moments wherein each of our experiences were most studied, interpreted, and written about solely by white males, or solely by a group with greater power. That group became the "authority" to consult if anyone wanted to understand the experience of these powerless groups. This process was a manifestation of the politics of domination. (hooks 1989, 42–43)

When white gays and lesbians behave in ways that obscure or distort the history of the black civil rights movement, whether we intend to or not, we define that history and those who made it only in relation to ourselves. We set ourselves up as authorities over its meaning. Unless we want to participate in furthering the cause of white supremacy, we must refrain from doing that. This isn't to say that blacks are the only ones who can interpret that history or claim it. I repeat: it is *our* history as Americans of all races. But there is a wide gap between, on the one hand, acknowledging the crucial importance of a history and studying and referring to it as we analyze the world around us and, on the other hand, confiscating and claiming dominion over it. White people need to listen and learn and then *share* the task of interpreting, instead of simply assuming that a history is available for our unlimited consumption or assimilation without a thought about what our use of it does to others who also share that history crucially and intimately.

My main point here is that, while there is racism and homophobia, there is also reason on both sides of the divide. And because the latter is true, we all need to approach each other with respect. Not everybody who objects to comparisons between LGBT rights movements and black civil rights movements is a bigoted homophobe.[28] Not everybody who makes such comparisons is a racist ignoramus. That there are black homophobes and gay and lesbian racists we all must admit. But we ought not jump to conclusions about any individual's expressed concerns without careful examination. We need to listen to one another on the assumption that most people don't favor injustice and don't hope people dissimilar to themselves will suffer hurt.

But there is another thing we need to do, and it may be a more painful thing than these admissions and efforts to listen with courtesy and respect. We need to examine the fear that motivates so much of our desire to detach ourselves from each other—black and white, queer and straight.[29]

Are We Normal Yet?

Every biopolitical movement—every network of power seeking to manage human life—identifies a set of threats that it targets as pathologies; such biologized dividing practices are the hallmark of biopolitics. The postwar pro-family movement was no exception. It set three principal targets for purgation: Gays and Lesbians, Feminists, and Matriarchal Welfare Queens and their Deadbeat Baby Daddies. In fact, these figures were already quite familiar. They used to be called Sex Perverts, Feminists, and Negroes. The more things change, as they say, the more they stay the same. Old aversions are harnessed and given new life and respectability. But we should not assume the fatalistic view that this is because those aversions are natural phenomena endemic to the human psyche and therefore ineradicable. Recycling old enemies is an economic, not a biological imperative. Old images and categories reappear because shifting biopolitical interests are typically advanced with as little expenditure, and thus as little innovation, as possible.

The question is what to do in response. Given the persistence of the eugenic dream after World War II, oppressed groups apparently had only two options: convince the general (white, middle-class, heterosexual) public that your people actually are normal by their standards (despite rumors and prejudice to the contrary), or attempt to broaden the prevailing concept of normality to accommodate the differences characteristic of members of your group. Either way, a lot would depend on whether you could demonstrate a commitment to the Normal Family—meaning middle-class white masculinity and femininity as well as licensed monogamy—and a desire to conform to the dictates of a capitalist ethic of work and consumption.

The closest any oppressed group has so far come to mounting

a successful public challenge to the charge of group abnormality is surely the much-honored nonviolent black civil rights movement of the 1950s and 60s. Who could witness the events that unfolded in Montgomery in 1955 and 1956 and not recognize the organizational intelligence, the courage, the discipline, the commitment—the nobility—of the thousands of African American men, women, and children who boycotted the buses and walked mile upon mile every day to protest their civil inequality? These second-class citizens were not second-class human beings. They were not abnormal—that is, they were not primitive, undisciplined, weak-willed, or immature. They were not inferior. The judgment that had been rendered was wrong.

Had he stood alone, Martin Luther King Jr., might have been relegated to the category of "brilliant mulatto"—a fluke, a mere exception to the genetic rule—but 50,000 Negro residents of Montgomery, Alabama, could not be so easily dismissed, nor could the tens of thousands of nonviolent demonstrators marching in subsequent years through the streets of Albany, Birmingham, Meridian, and Selma. On their television sets and the front pages of their newspapers and sometimes in the streets of their own hometowns, ordinary white Americans saw ordinary black Americans taking extraordinary action exemplifying the very virtues once held to be peculiar to the biological descendents of the ancient Anglo-Saxons—heroic valor, manful self-respect, emotional control, discipline, and an overriding love of liberty. Many white people were deeply threatened, but many were also deeply moved.

The black civil rights movement of the 1950s and 60s changed laws and changed minds. It forced open doors that had been barred for centuries. Materially and emotionally, it bettered the lives of millions of people of all races.[30] In addition to giving black people opportunities for education and careers, it gave every one of us the opportunity to know and love and share the lives of people we otherwise never would have been allowed even to meet, at least as peers. Its impact was tremendous and far-reaching, and because of that it has served as an inspiration for oppressed people all over the globe. As columnist Leonard Pitts points out, "Every freedom movement from Poland's labor uprising to America's feminism to China's Tiananmen Square protests has been compared to the civil rights movement. When Czechoslovakians threw off communist rule in 1989, they sang We Shall Overcome" (Pitts 2004).

But overcome what?

There are obvious answers. People everywhere have wanted—and want—to overcome obstacles to self-fulfillment, obstacles like discriminatory laws and policies, poverty, and prejudices that result in reduction of opportunities for employment, education, housing, and use of public and private facilities and resources. People everywhere have wanted—and want—a real chance to make something of their lives. That such obstacles should be placed in the way of any set of people is blatantly unfair. Forcing removal of those obstacles is therefore an imperative of justice. The black civil rights movement was about securing African American people's civil rights and civil liberties by eliminating as many of those obstacles as possible.

At its height, though, it was much more than that. In the rousing speeches and the crowds of thousands—in which mingled white and red and brown and yellow faces along with black, in which human bodies of all descriptions breathed and swayed together in celebratory song—that movement presented the world with a vision of an American citizenry united in love of liberty and justice and respect for all individuals despite every sort of difference. It was a vision of a world without rank, one in which "the Ph.D.s marched alongside the no-Ds," as Dr. King so often said. It was a vision of a world without violence, a world where the lion would lie down with the lamb, a world in which even the least of these, the weakest and the most vulnerable, could afford to trust and venture and reach out. It was a vision antithetical to the picture of the world inherent in disciplines of normalization, management, and control. It is a vision still championed by many of its mid-century adherents, Selma veteran John Lewis among them.[31]

At its depth, however—and mostly in its aftermath—that vision was obscured. What took its place in many instances was an investment in the very practices of ranking and normalization against which its best values rebelled. What took its place was the idea that black people won their civil rights by proving to the rest of America that they were morally acceptable, that they were no threat to mainstream values, that they only wanted a chance to compete in the marketplace as ruthlessly as anybody else, that they only wanted to be examined a bit less cursorily before they were judged and ranked. What took its place was the idea that by presenting themselves as organized, peaceful, and reasonable, black people proved that they were *normal* and that being judged normal is the way to qualify for respect and the rights of citizenship.

It is clear which vision was Martin Luther King's. In his commencement speech to Lincoln University's graduating class of 1961, he addressed the issue directly:

> Every academic discipline has its technical nomenclature, and modern psychology has a word that is used, probably, more than any other. It is the word *maladjusted*. . . . But I say to you, there are certain things within our social order to which I am proud to be maladjusted and to which I call upon all men of good will to be maladjusted. . . . I never did intend to adjust myself to the evils of segregation and discrimination. I never did intend to adjust myself to religious bigotry. I never did intend to adjust myself to economic conditions that will take necessities from the many to give luxuries to the few. I never did intend to adjust myself to the madness of militarism, and the self-defeating effects of physical violence. And I call upon all men of good will to be maladjusted because it may well be that the salvation of our world lies in the hands of the maladjusted. (1986, 215–16)

The last thing King wanted was for black people to assimilate—to adjust—to the world as it was. As far as he was concerned, the movement was not about reassuring white people that black people were really just like them and thus no threat at all to prevailing values and norms. Black people didn't need to earn their civil rights by proving they were normal. They were entitled to civil rights by virtue of the fact that they were citizens of the United States of America—period. Neither moral acceptability to the moneyed white mainstream nor the labels of normality or abnormality had anything to do with the matter. In fact, both moral acceptability and normality were what had to be interrogated, because it was the socially powerful enforcers of morality and normality that had dictated a racial hierarchy in the first place.[32]

It was a rare thing in the twentieth century for anybody to reject the very notion of normality as a coherent concept or a standard of human worth. By 1961, when King spoke at Lincoln, a long and bloody history lay behind that concept, a history at which very few people cared to look. There were black activists like King who had the courage and the perspicuity such a rejection took. There were some feminists in the 1960s and 70s who set out down that difficult path. There were some gay liberationists and disabilities activists in the 1970s and 80s who insisted that it is so-called normal society, not alleged abnormality, that must submit to critique.[33] At least one historian has even suggested that all these movements can be seen, in part, as elements in a backlash against the Progressive Era's eugenics.[34]

But whenever push came to shove, most people, even members of supposedly radical political factions, have chosen to side with normality instead of questioning it. Over and over again, those who thought that maybe, just maybe, they could assimilate after all—including most white gay and lesbian activists and a great many straight black leaders—have been willing to cut loose those who could not: those who were, for example, desperately poor or seriously disabled or truly, truly queer.[35] Those people, being undeniably abnormal by virtually every standard, have just been left behind.[36] And every time that has happened, networks of normalization have gotten a little tighter and a little stronger. I believe we can gauge all those movements' failures very precisely by the degree to which their adherents blocked their ears to King's call to abandon normality as a measuring rod and a basis for discriminatory judgment. For to just that degree, they endorsed a hundred years of racist cruelty and exclusion and vicious disregard for the lives and welfare of their fellow human beings, despite what they may have proclaimed.

When any movement becomes a rush for the moral high ground, when any group of people decides it is more important to assert their normality and beg for acceptance than to assert their freedom and demand respect on their own terms, the battle for justice and equality is already lost. Indeed, the very meaning of those terms has been forgotten. But given our historical circumstances as detailed in foregoing chapters, the present situation is even worse. The only way for black people to prove they are normal is to dissociate themselves from people everybody else thinks are abnormal—"sex perverts" being at the very top of that list. The only way for white homosexuals to prove they are normal is to dissociate themselves from people everybody else thinks are abnormal—"Negro savages" having long been at the very top of that list. Given the historical circumstances, the only way either group can win the normality game is to stereotype, discredit, and beat the other group down. And in the meantime, we all had better dissociate ourselves from the mentally retarded and the mentally ill and the people with HIV and the homeless and the chronically poor. *We're* not like *them*. We're *normal*. And all we want is just this one little thing, a place at the table where the normal people sit. *Please*. We're mature enough now. We promise to not chew with our mouths open or spill our milk. We promise not to say anything that would upset anyone. Just don't make us sit on the sidelines with the cripples and drooling idiots anymore. Insofar as this controversy over whether queer people can legitimately compare themselves to black people or not is really just a contest to decide who gets to count as normal and civilized, all those involved have already lost.

All, that is, except those whose well-being depends upon the regimes of disciplinary normalization and biopolitical population management that advance themselves through our discord and disorganization. And who might that be? Who benefits when queer people and people of color fail to stand up for each others' dignity, worth, and civil rights, and when we all fail to stand up for the dignity, worth, and rights of people who live with physical and mental disabilities or with the handicaps imposed by poverty? Those are the questions we really should be asking, not the question of whether we can dissociate ourselves enough from the queens—both those on welfare and those in drag—to make ourselves acceptable to self-proclaimed standard-bearers of morality and normalcy like Pat Buchanan and Daniel Patrick Moynihan.

Shall We Overcome?

This is not a book of answers, although at times I wish as much as anybody that it could be. Instead, it is an invitation for further work and further thinking. It is intended to extend an open hand toward others who are different from me, toward people who have different experiences and different perspectives, and to provoke creative dialogue and joint struggle. I don't know exactly what to do to make our lives more livable and our communities more respectful and humane. But I do know what we must not do. I know that we must not recoil in the face of the current controversy, hunker down in our relatively insular communities and social circles, and refuse to risk the pain of engagement across real differences. I know that we must not be afraid to offer respectful criticism or to hear criticism however it is offered and examine it thoughtfully. I know that we must not close our ears to anything or anyone labeled abnormal—that is a politically motivated label wherever it occurs—and we must not tremble with anxiety over whether that label might be attached to us if we assert ourselves in opposition to the status quo. Above all, I know that we must not try to adjust to a society that oppresses us in the vain hope that the consequent lack of conscious discomfort (should we be able to achieve such a state) would be equivalent to happiness, self-affirmation, or liberty.

I also know two other things. The first is that, as important as legal opinions and governmental policies are, they alone will never give any of us freedom or equality. We who are oppressed in various ways must assert our equality—that is, we must proclaim and bear in our comportment the fact that we *deserve* the respect and consideration of our neighbors and fellow citizens. We must not ask to be granted anything. We must remind those around us as often as necessary that our moral worth is not dependent upon their assessment of us, nor is it determined by our current inferior status within institutionalized networks of power and knowledge. *And we must believe that.*

And we have to *exercise* our freedom—that is, we have to conduct ourselves as free people in ways that affirm and actualize the fact that we are free people—which means, first of all, that we have to assume responsibility for our lives and our communities and refuse to be intimidated by threats and debilitating theories even as we remain alert to the risks we run in ignoring or countering them. Biopolitical networks rely for their stability and growth upon our engagement in self-policing, upon our willingness to discipline ourselves and those around us to meet the standards of function and the direction of development that our assigned roles specify. When we know we're being watched, we're inclined to inscribe the power relation within ourselves, as Foucault puts it, to take on the work of monitoring and forcing ourselves to stay within the dictates of the prevailing norms: "He who is subjected to a field of visibility [to normalizing surveillance], and who knows it, assumes responsibility for the constraints of power; he makes them play spontaneously upon himself" (1977, 202). We may stave off punishment by responding this way. But at the same time, we do violence to ourselves; we reject fields of possibility, including alternative values, directions for development, and patterns of life. Because authorities and institutions are thus relieved of much of their policing function, the job of maintaining a normalizing hierarchy becomes much easier for them, less costly, less messy, and less overtly violent: "The external power may throw off its physical weight; it tends to the non-corporeal; and, the more it approaches this limit, the more constant, profound and permanent are its effects: it is a perpetual victory that avoids any confrontation and which is always decided in advance" (Foucault 1977, 202–203). The first step toward dismantling biopolitical—that is, racist—networks of power, therefore, is to refuse to do their work for them, to refuse to do the work of self- (and other-) policing in the name of the normal.

Refusing means, in part, that against the authorized knowl-edges that tell us that blacks are erratic and violent, that Latinos are impulsive and chauvinistic and too stubborn to learn English, that transgendered people are mentally ill, that gay men are disease-ridden boy-rapists, and that lesbians and feminists are "Darwinian blind alleys" out to destroy heterosexual hearth and home,[37] we must *know*—actively and adamantly—*what we know*. And that includes not only what we know about ourselves in opposition to what they tell us—for example, that we are unwilling to tolerate humiliation politely, that we are violently opposed to the degradation of our lives and our loved ones, that we embrace the novel and the serendipi-tous while passionately adhering to meaningful traditions, that we are able to see and think and imagine things that our detractors find too frightening to contemplate, that even when burdened with illness and threatened with ostracism we can be brave and loving, and that our sensual pleasures and the relationships they enable bring joy to our lives both individually and communally. It also includes what we know about those who would oppress us—that their allegedly rational and disinterested justifications for their actions are rooted in a desire for material gain and a drive for territorial and political hege-mony that spans four centuries of industrial development and brutal conquest, and that the allegedly objective natural and social sciences they tout were conceived and expounded in service to the racist goal of Anglo-Saxon domination.

We know these things. What we don't know is how much explo-sive power these long-dispersed, devalued, and subjugated knowledges could have if they were to coalesce, concentrate, and set themselves loose upon the world. But if we refuse to adhere to the demands and dictates of biopolitical normativity and start paying attention instead to what we know and to how what we know articulates with what others know—racial others, sexual others, the differently embodied, the differently gendered—we will certainly find out. An insurrection of our subjugated knowledges is far more likely than any executive order or legislative innovation or judicial victory to reconfigure the networks of power within which we live our lives.

The second thing I know is that an insurrection of our subjugated knowledges is only possible if we stop compartmentalizing oppression on the basis of sociological identity. Of course it is different to be a middle-class white lesbian in suburbia than it is to be a Mexican migrant worker or an Asian graduate student or an African American teenager in an urban ghetto or an Arab American store owner or a white working-class war veteran facing the rest of his life in a wheelchair. We are all different from each other. We have different histories, and we face some very different obstacles. But if we focus all our energies on our differences—that is, on our specific and distinct identities as queer or black or disabled or whatever—we will fail to perceive any aspect of the power networks that shape our lives other than the narrow face they present to our own group, and that means that we will inevitably fail to understand those power networks at all.

Modern racism, I have argued throughout this book, is a very pervasive and entrenched phenomenon, but it is also a very specific phenomenon. For all its power and extent, it is not a fundamental feature of the natural world or even of human psychology or social organization. It is neither universal nor omnipresent, as this genealogy has shown. It began at a relatively localizable place and time for fairly specifiable reasons, and it grew and shaped the world in which it unfolded through mechanisms and events that can be traced and analyzed. Just as it has identified all of us down to the tiniest measurable fractions of our deviations from its shifting norms, we can identify it. We can name it, and together we can delineate it. And in the process we can identify the gaps in it, the absences, the toeholds, the possibilities for difference that float within its myriad interstices. The first step is not to let go of our differences but to let go of our insistence that the oppression from which we and those like us suffer, whatever "ism" may currently suffice to name it, is utterly disconnected presently and historically from the oppression and suffering of those who are different from us. None of us can afford the "special right" of a unique victimization. Identity politics may well have its place, and sometimes it is important to draw boundaries around an endangered group. But we cannot let identity-based politics preclude genealogy-based politics by refusing to recognize and credit the subjugated knowledges that reveal our histories as subjugated peoples bound together across our differences through the past four hundred years. We are different, but we live in the same world. And if we can come to understand that world and how it has come to be configured so as to oppress various groups of us in various ways, we can change that configuration. We can unmake and remake what has been made.

I didn't sing "We Shall Overcome" that night. But I didn't just go back to my dark farmhouse and grieve for the dead and despair over the future for the living either. I did something: I spent the next eight years looking for ways to understand the violence and oppression so apparent in the world around me, listening to voices almost lost in an archive most Americans don't want to know exists and to voices usually discredited in our communities because they issue from the bodies of people our culture's dominant values tell us are damaged or sick or otherwise inferior. Over those eight years, I read more history than I had encountered in twenty years of formal education. I put my own childhood memories of the black civil rights movement and the turbulent 1960s in historical perspective and made important sense of feelings I have harbored since long before I could conceptualize and articulate such things. I learned to respect the knowledge of hicks and hillbillies, people I formerly feared and disdained, and to mourn for their personal and cultural losses. I learned a lot about the concerns, fears, and disagreements among African Americans, and in the process I learned to relax and play and laugh with black intellectuals as I came to trust them as peers rather than fear them as judges of my conduct and interiority. I learned to love and appreciate both the style and the courage of sissy boys and diesel dykes and transgendered people of every description even more than I did before. And through all this the lesson that impressed itself deep into my flesh is that while some people may in fact be perfect—at least for a fraction of a second in little sparks every once in a while—nobody is normal, and nobody ought to be.

So it's been a good ride, a real E Ticket, as we used to say. But unlike the rides at Disneyland, I didn't end up deposited back at the same old turnstile. Genealogy, as Foucault tells us, changes those who undergo it. In both the writing and the reading, genealogy is a transformative philosophical practice. It is also, when collectively undertaken and undergone, an incitement to further transformation, a provocation to insurrections against institutions and practices that perpetuate the arrangements of power whose investments genealogies expose.

The work in this book has given me a set of questions and interests and suspicions and values and angles of vision quite different from the ones I had eight years ago when I first embarked on this project. Much of what I thought was important then—much of what I thought I would say in this book—has simply been left behind. Nevertheless, I don't feel right closing without addressing the question I started with: Should I have sung that song?

Despite eight years of strenuous effort, it is still very hard for me to say. But I think that, as much as it hurt to refrain and to let that sad gathering fizzle out in the damp and dreary darkness, I would probably make the same choice again.

First of all, nothing would have made that awful night less awful. Grief and fear were appropriate feelings in the face of Matthew Shepard's horrible murder and the hatred that prompted it, and individuals' confrontation with injustice and their own vulnerabilities was necessary and inevitable. As much as I would have liked to make things easier for those Penn State undergraduates that night, as much as I would like to make things easier for all the members of the generations coming after me, the fact is that the world is not fair and queer people are not safe, and if we want that situation to change, every one of us has got to confront that fact and take some responsibility for addressing it. In our commercial and increasingly "virtual" culture, many of us have gotten used to being able to have the feeling of community, solidarity, strength, love, and purpose without actually having the substance. But it's the substance that makes the difference. Though it goes against my ingrained Southern feminine caretaking instinct, then, I believe it is dangerous to do anything that allows people to feel good when the situation they're in is in fact not good. And the situation of most queer people at the beginning of the twenty-first century is decidedly not good. Songs can create temporary feelings of solidarity and hope, but they can't create solidarity or sustain hope.

I do look forward to singing that song in a circle of queer people someday, however. It is a beautiful song, a beautifully simple and a beautifully carnal song—by which I mean it moves the bodies that sing it beyond their own fleshly boundaries; in its measured breaths and rhythms it breaks down physical barriers and joins together what state licensing procedures and constitutional amendments and standards of public decency would readily put asunder. I look forward to singing it with a group of people who, in the face of adversity, know their histories and the genealogies of the forces that oppress them. I look forward to singing it in reinforcement of solidarity and reassurance that I and they belong to a community that, in the face of tragedy and crisis, and even in the face of conflict and difference, pulls together and respects and supports each other. But that is a community we must build, not one that we can conjure with a song.

Second, most queer white people—frankly, most people in general, and of all races—really don't know a damn thing about the black civil rights movement or the American labor movement that preceded it and generated so many really good songs. Singing "We Shall Overcome" in most gatherings of queer white people is like singing "This Land Is Your Land, This Land Is My Land" at the Republican National Convention. It's not that black people own "We Shall Overcome" any more than working people, socialists, or anarchists own "This Land Is Your Land." It's that, without the history and the context, the meaning of the song is diminished beyond recognition. And such diminution is painful and offensive to people for whom that song does have deep, historically informed meaning.

If we need the meaning—and I believe we do—then we need the historical awareness that bears it, and such things take effort to acquire. Thus, third, we ought to study the black civil rights movement of the 1950s and 60s in depth. It is part of our history; both it and the forces that made it necessary contributed immeasurably to shaping who we are. But we ought not to take it as a blueprint of civil rights struggle. Fifty years is a very long time. Technologically, economically, and geopolitically, we don't live in the same world that Martin Luther King Jr. lived and died in. We rightly revere the efforts and sacrifices King made and those made by Jesse Jackson, Julian Bond, John Lewis, Hosea Williams, Amelia Boynton Robinson, Rosa Parks, and so many others. Those people are American heroes. But they were—and some still are—people, just like the rest of us. They took a stand. They did what the situation called upon them to do. They weren't perfect—except in little sparks from time to time—and they didn't always know whether what they were doing was right.[38]

They just did their best. The reason we revere them is that their actions resonate within our hearts; they did what we judge right in retrospect and what we hope we too would have done and would do if called upon. They show us the best in ourselves. And thus they inspire us. But they were never masters, never moral dictators to whom the rest of us had to subordinate ourselves. They just did their best. It is in that respect that we can and should do likewise.

Times have changed. Doing likewise is not necessarily doing the same. Doing likewise is taking up the challenge of inventing what to do in the absence of set models and clear precedents and of living with the uncertainties and unforeseeable consequences that invention entails. And of course doing likewise is no guarantee that we shall overcome—or that we shall be overcome as agents and conduits in an order we want to resist and dismantle. But it is, I think, the only open door, the only possibility. Go forth and do likewise—which means: Listen. Speak. Incite. Invent. And never, ever adjust.

NOTES

Introduction

1. See McCullen 1998, and Black 1998, for these and other details that came out during McKinney's preliminary hearing November 19.

2. My use of so-called identity terms throughout this book will oscillate among several different discourses, including pro-queer political discourses; queer theory, where the term *queer* functions to undermine identity; and homophobic discourses, both scientific and lay. Here I use the term *queer* as it has been used for decades as a term of derision, dismissal, and hatred. Readers should be alert, however, to the tendency of such terms to slide around throughout the book. The refusal of identity terms to mean one particular thing or to operate in one particular way is part of this book's point.

3. Every middle-aged heterosexual person has heard about a great many also, but their memories for such things are usually shorter. Typically they just have a sedimented impression, reinforced by movies like *Suddenly Last Summer, Torch Song Trilogy,* and *Brokeback Mountain,* that anti-queer violence is a fact of life.

4. See, for example, Semer 1998. Semer suggests that if Shepard had taken responsibility for his own safety, he would have avoided people who were intolerant. See also responses to Semer in the November 2, 1998, issue of the *Charlotte Observer.*

5. Most accounts say there were eight teenagers in the pickup and about a dozen already at the store, along with one or two adults. One account says there were only seven teenagers in the pickup. Yet another account says there were no other teenagers already at the store, only a few black men playing checkers. The most detailed account that I have seen of who was in the pickup lists seven people: Till; Wheeler Parker, the sixteen-year-old cousin who had accompanied Till from Chicago; Thelton Parker; Maurice and Simeon Wright (Mose and Elizabeth's sons); and Ruthie Mae and Roosevelt Crawford. Simeon Wright was the youngest at twelve; Thelton Parker, the oldest at nineteen. This list comes from an article published in the *Chicago Defender* on September 10, 1955, and is based on an interview with Wheeler Parker. It is reprinted in Metress 2002, 31. The list omits Curtis Jones, a seventeen-year-old cousin who had come down from Chicago with Parker and Till. Jones says in an interview in the PBS documentary *Eyes on the Prize: Episode 1: Awakenings (1954–1956),* 1986, that he was playing a game of checkers with an old black man on the porch when Till took the other boys' dare to go into the store. Jones says a number of people were outside the store, in addition to those who arrived in Mose Wright's pickup.

6. See Hampton et al. 1990, 3. Jones's account fits with the story that Wheeler Parker, Till's sixteen-year-old cousin, gave the *Chicago Defender* that September (Metress 2002, 31) and substantiates some of William Bradford

Huie's description of Till's behavior toward Carolyn Bryant. Huie's account depicts Till as far more forward and sexually suggestive, however, much as Carolyn Bryant herself described Till in her court testimony (Huie 1956, reprinted in Metress 2002, 203). The youngest cousin present at the store that evening, Simeon Wright (then age twelve), contradicted this account in an interview with Tavis Smiley on NPR in 2004 and in Kevin Beauchamp's documentary in 2005. Wright said he went in the store with Till, who purchased candy but said nothing to Carolyn Bryant; then, immediately after the boys exited, Bryant ran out of the store and began to fumble for something in a car. The youths quickly drove out of town, and Till whistled at Bryant as they left. I have drawn on Jones's account here rather than Wright's because it is more detailed, was given only three rather than five decades after the fact, and offers what I take to be a more plausible explanation of the behavior of all involved, including Carolyn Bryant's sudden exit from the store whose cash register she was tending, the cousins' sudden flight, and the fact that Roy Bryant and J. W. Milam were very careful to identify the "right" boy, Till, an identification that would have been impossible to make had he done nothing but whistle from a moving truck. Also, no account given at the time places any other person inside the store when the exchange between Till and Bryant took place. I have also disregarded a 1956 version of the story by Olive Arnold Adams that claims that the entire story, including Carolyn Bryant's flight from the store to her sister-in-law's car and Till's whistling at her as she went for a gun, was made up by a black man on the porch that night who told it to Roy Bryant in an effort to gain store credit. See Adams's version reprinted in Metress 2002, 221.

7. For various versions of Carolyn Bryant's testimony at the trial, see Metress 2002, 89–97. These are all contemporary accounts written by reporters who were in the courtroom. No official transcript was made of the trial.

8. Many people asserted in 1955 and subsequently that there was a woman with Milam and Bryant at the Wright house that night. Filmmaker Kevin Beauchamp told Tavis Smiley that he interviewed a number of people in Money, Mississippi, who could substantiate Moses Wright's impression that a woman was in Milam's truck the night he and Bryant came for Till, and she was the one who identified the boy. Beauchamp believes the woman to have been Carolyn Bryant. Two days before the Smiley interview, May 10, 2004, the U.S. Justice Department reopened the Till case. Beauchamp implies in that interview, and attorney Raymond Brown says in the same broadcast, that Carolyn Bryant, who was still alive in 2004 and had never been indicted on any charge relating to the events of August 1955, might eventually be indicted for the murder, a move Till's mother had been calling for since 1955 (see Smiley 2004; Beauchamp 2005). As of this writing, however, no indictment has been issued.

9. Huie 1956, reprinted in Metress 2002, 200–208. Journalist William Bradford Huie's article in *Look* magazine in 1956 and his subsequent book and movie were controversial at the time because Huie paid J. W. Milam and Roy Bryant $4,000. Some said the money was payment for the story itself and probably induced the men to exaggerate or lie, but Huie claimed he already had most of the information through other sources and payment was simply for the right to portray them on screen. For these claims, see Huie 1957, 65,

reprinted in Metress 2002, 208–13. For a detailed account of the criticism Huie faced from both white supremacists and black civil rights activists, see Huie's 1959 book, *Wolf Whistle and Other Stories,* an excerpt of which is published in Metress 2002, 235–47.

10. Huie makes a point of discussing Milam's military service in his account, suggesting that Milam had experience in the art of torture. See Huie in Metress 2002, 205 and 207.

11. A neighbor of J. W. Milam's, Mary Johnson, told filmmaker Kevin Beauchamp that she heard a beating occurring in the barn behind Milam's house that night, and she saw a fire in a barrel. This lends support to Milam's assertion to Huie that the beating took place on his property and also that he burned Till's wallet. For Johnson's statement, see Beauchamp 2005.

12. There is also at least one report of a great deal of blood being washed out of that pickup later that day. See Metress 2002, 224. Corpses don't bleed.

13. Over the past two decades, queer theorists have used the term *queer* as a tool for interrupting assumptions about sexual identities and destabilizing them. Consequently, some readers may be startled by my occasional use of the term here as the name of a recognizable group of people, as itself a sort of identity term. I want to say several things at the outset: (1) Some people do in fact recognize themselves and others as queer. I don't think, however, that such practices of recognition usually follow the same rules as practices typically associated with terms like *homosexual* or even *gay* or *lesbian.* Usually *queer* does not name or enable recognition of an homogeneous group of people. It names or enables recognition of a diverse and shifting collection of people that a dominant culture makes more or less outcast because of their divergent sexual and/or gender practices. When it does function as an identity, then, it is a transparently contingent, situational, and political identity, not an essential one. (2) Readers need not worry that my use of the term *queer* as a contingent identity category might preclude "queering" sexual identities in general. *All* racial and sexual identity terms have been harmed in the making of this text, in that none has been left uncorrupted by history and politics.

14. Harry Laughlin's several brothers attended medical school in Kirksville, and some of them practiced medicine there. Harry Laughlin himself was a teacher who for a time served as the principal of Kirksville High School.

15. Patricia Hill Collins makes a similar point, although she offers a rather different analysis than the one that I will offer here. See Collins 2005, 88.

16. Anne McClintock pointed out in 1995 that white feminists had only rarely looked at nationalism and ethnicity as phenomena worthy of sustained feminist critique. That has changed somewhat since the turn of the century, in part with McClintock's own work, but the claim is still noteworthy. See McClintock 1995, 356. McClintock goes on to show the extent to which race theorist Frantz Fanon failed to bring gender oppression into "theoretical focus" (1995, 365).

17. There are, of course, extremely important exceptions to that rule in all of these groups, and their work will be drawn upon extensively in the chapters to follow.

1. Racism, Race, Race War

1. All of this information about black civil rights activists and their work with gay and lesbian rights activists can be found in Vaid 1995, 300. For film clips of Jackson speaking to and on behalf of gays and lesbians, see *After Stonewall,* directed by John Scagliotti (First Run Features, 2005); that documentary also contains some discussion of the 1983 denunciation by D.C. representative Walter Fauntroy.

2. Kobena Mercer offers many examples of racism in the gay movement in Britain through the same time period (Mercer 1994, 11ff.). In another essay in the same collection, Mercer and coauthor Isaac Julien write, "From our point of view one of the most notable features of this political activity around sexual representation is the marked *absence* of race from the agenda of concerns—it is as if white people had colonized this agenda in cultural politics for themselves alone. While some feminists have begun to take on issues of race and racism in the women's movement, white gay men retain a deafening silence on race" (Mercer 1994, 131).

3. Boykin 1996, 186–89. Boykin repeats some of these statistics in Boykin 1999, 70.

4. For interviews with Summerville and others, see Kelly Anderson's and Tami Gold's 1996 documentary *Out at Work,* available from Frameline Films.

5. Including, apparently, the city of New York, whose municipal pension funds were in part invested in 89,000 shares of Cracker Barrel stock worth at the time about $3 million. See "Company is asked about bias in hiring," *New York Times,* March 20, 1991, B4.

6. In fact, the direct action had no discernible effect on sales. Cracker Barrel's profits soared through the next decade, with the company more than doubling in size just after the turn of the century. It did seem to jangle the nerves of some investors, however. Stock prices climbed, but stockholders were the ones whose pressure finally forced at least cosmetic changes in the company's public face.

7. The Spotsylvania, Virginia, protest also resulted in at least one arrest. Although at first the *Washington Post* reported that no arrests were made, on April 2, 1992, it published a clarification in which it noted that at least one reporter, Timothy McCarthy of Front Royal, Virginia, was expelled from the restaurant and charged with trespassing. See that day's *Post,* page A3.

8. For some discussion of Kuby's letter, see Gates 1999, 25, and B. Smith 1998, 126. For a description and discussion of the ways in which the planners of and participants in the 1993 march deliberately appropriated language and symbols of the 1963 march, see Boykin 1996, chap. 2.

9. It should be pointed out that bell hooks had addressed this issue several years earlier, noting that "in many feminist circles [it is thought that] black communities are somehow more homophobic than other communities in the United States, more opposed to gay rights." But, she goes on to say, "it is precisely the notion that there is a monolithic black community that must be challenged. . . . I have talked with black folks who were raised in southern communities where gay people were openly expressive of their sexual prefer-

ence and participated fully in the life of the community. I have also spoken with folks who say just the opposite" (hooks 1989, 121). There are many black communities, and they vary tremendously with regard to their acceptance of homosexuality.

10. Alveda King's ascent into the national spotlight began in 1996 after a chance encounter outside Atlanta's Fulton County Courthouse with Art Rocker, an African American conservative who organized Alan Keyes's presidential campaign in Georgia (Foskett 1998). Rocker helped King set up her organization "King for America," which the American Education Reform Foundation enlisted in a 1997 attempt to establish a pilot school voucher program in Washington, D.C. "The voucher initiative failed, but King's profile soared," according to *The Atlanta Journal and Constitution.* The conservative Alexis de Tocqueville Institute made her a senior fellow, she testified before a House education committee as a scholar for the Institute, and she ran for Atlanta City Council president (Foskett 1998). She came in fourth in the five-way race, pulling only six percent of the vote.

11. Although true in California, where King was speaking, this statement was false in many states of the union in 1997; in fact nobody had a right in states like Virginia, North and South Carolina, Alabama, Texas, Mississippi, Louisiana, and elsewhere to do whatever they liked in their own bedrooms, if what they liked included anal or oral intercourse with someone of the same sex. Not until 2003 did the U.S. Supreme Court (in *Lawrence v. Texas*) rule that state laws prohibiting consensual sexual relations in private between people of the same sex were unconstitutional. Even after 2003 some states did not stop enforcing so-called anti-sodomy laws.

12. Keith Boykin, former executive director of the National Black Gay and Lesbian Leadership Forum, counters this sort of claim with data from interviews he conducted with white gay and lesbian rights activists in the early 1990s. Instead, he says, the idea that gays equate themselves with blacks has been planted by white conservative groups intent on dividing oppressed groups and preventing coalition. See Boykin 1996, 48–49.

13. On the Baltimore conference, see R. Smith 1997, 20, and for more historical and political context, see Solomon 1999. The Christian Coalition promised financial aid and other forms of assistance to black churches in poor communities nationwide in exchange for black leaders' endorsement of their political activities and platform. See Argetsinger 1997.

14. Subsequently, a number of localities in Maine tried to enact ordinances banning discrimination on the basis of sexual orientation. Such ordinances were adopted in Portland, Bar Harbor, and Long Island before the end of 1998. Selectmen voted 3 to 2 not to place an ordinance on the November ballot in Kennebunk (Taylor 1998b, 12). South Portland and Falmouth were sites of bitter battles over the issue in 1998 and 1999, where the Christian Coalition mailed every resident a publication entitled "The Gay Agenda." Among other inflammatory claims, that publication asserted that homosexuals eat excrement. The *Portland Press Herald,* which had allowed the pamphlet to be distributed as an insert in its South Portland edition, later apologized for cooperating with the Christian Coalition, calling the pamphlet "offensive, inflammatory, inaccurate and vile." The Falmouth ordinance passed, but the next

year the editor of "The Gay Agenda," Mark Finks, launched the Falmouth Concerned Citizens' Ad Hoc Committee on Sexual Orientation, which worked to overthrow it by changing the town's charter (Nacelewicz 1999).

15. For a description of such an event, along with critical discussion from the perspective of a white lesbian, see Kendell 2005. At the time of her writing, the author, Kate Kendell, was the executive director of the National Center for Lesbian Rights.

16. Sample 2004. Black endorsement of Klan activities seems farfetched, but Daniels wasn't alone. Rev. James Sykes of Tampa (whom Keith Boykin calls "one of the best-known opponents of homosexuality in the black church") made headlines in the early 1990s when he told a local black reporter that he would attend an anti-gay KKK rally in nearby Largo, Florida, if the Klan was there to rally against homosexuals only. "If I knew that was the only reason that they were there, I would be there with them" (Boykin 1996, 127).

17. Coretta Scott King was a staunch supporter of LGBT rights, as was the King Center under her leadership. Statements such as this were typical: "I strongly believe that freedom and justice cannot be parceled out in pieces to suit political convenience. . . . Like Martin, I don't believe you can stand for freedom for one group of people and deny it to others" (quoted in Wright 1997, 30).

18. DePasquale 2004. This was true if we were not black, female, poor, illiterate, or convicted of a felony—and it should be remembered that in some states sodomy was a felony until 2003. Jackson was speaking in opposition specifically to the proposed state licensure of same-sex marriages, but his comments indicate that he objects to any analogy anyone might draw between the social, political, and economic condition of queer people and that of non-queer African Americans.

19. The lectures had been released in French in March of 1999 under the title *Les anormaux,* but they received little attention in North America at that time.

20. We will return to this story and examine it in more detail in chapter 4.

21. For some documentation, see Horsman 1987, esp. 43.

22. For historical accounts of the rise of degeneracy theory, see e.g., S. C. Gilman 1983, E. T. Carlson 1985, and Pick 1989.

23. Dennis 1936, 109–10. The relevant passage reads as follows: "A discussion of planning for America must assume a set of values, and explore the possibilities of their realization and the possible means to this end. If, in this discussion it be assumed that one of our values should be a type of racism which excludes certain races from citizenship, then the plan of execution should provide for the annihilation, deportation, or sterilization of the excluded races. If, on the contrary, as I devoutly hope will be the case, the scheme of values will include that of a national citizenship in which race will be no qualifying or disqualifying condition, then the plan of realization must, in so far as race relations are concerned, provide for assimilation or accommodation of race differences within the scheme of smoothly running society." Dennis clearly uses the term here to name a phenomenon very much like that of Hitler's ideology and institutionalized practices regarding Jews, Slavs, etc.

24. See Wodak and Reisigl 1999, 177, n. 4. It is possible, although uncon-

firmed, that the term appears in Roswell Johnson's dissertation filed at the University of Pittsburgh in 1934; Johnson later used the word in his theory of "overlap racism," an idea he first began to develop in his dissertation (Kuhl 1994, 74).

25. Miles writes: "The act of labeling the 'race thinking' of the nineteenth century as racism was simultaneously to label it as a scientific error" (1989, 45).

26. Benedict revised and reissued her book in 1943, and it was issued again in paperback in 1945. The whole book is an extended argument against the dogmatic assertions of her contemporary racists. See Benedict 1943, esp. chap. 1.

27. For this reason and others, Mills prefers to speak of white supremacy rather than racism, as does bell hooks (hooks 2004, 69). Were I not following out the implications of Foucault's claim, I might suggest such a choice as well. However, this is a strategic matter, and strategically it is important in this text to push the term *racism* as far as it will go.

28. See also Winant 2004, 41: "The understanding we have of racism, an understanding that was forged in the 1960s, is now severely deficient. A quarter century of sociopolitical struggle has rendered it inadequate to the demands of the present. At the same time, I would hardly wish to argue (in the manner of neoconservatives) that racism itself has been largely eliminated in the post-civil rights era. But although we are quite sure that racism continues to exist, indeed flourish, we are less than certain about what it means today."

29. His principal races were Caucasian, Mongolian, Ethiopian, and Hottentot.

30. The idea that there were several European races was a commonplace at the time. We see it also—albeit in a very different ideological and theoretical context—in W. E. B. Du Bois's early work, in particular his 1897 essay "The Conservation of Races." There he says there are eight races on the current world stage, and at least four of those he lists are European: Slavs, Teutons, English nations, and Romance nations. He also lists Semitic peoples as a race, some of whom were European as well. See Du Bois 1996, 40.

31. For a good comparative discussion of these attempts to differentiate among races, see Gossett 1997, chap. 4. For a discussion of a repetition of this crisis of definition in the Nazi regime, there, of course, regarding the criteria for determining Jewishness, see Koonz 2003, 171.

32. The debate about racial (or ancestral population) difference in cranial measures, while quiet compared to its amplification in previous times, extended through the entire twentieth century. For example, in 1990 three Israeli researchers published a study of the skull measurements of two separate Bedouin populations. See Herschkovitz, Ring, and Kobyliansky, 1990.

33. Perhaps it seems odd to see Chinese and Mexicans here treated as races. In the nineteenth century, most nineteenth-century race theorists classified the Chinese as Mongols, a racial group rather than merely a nationality; in early twentieth-century theoretical works they were usually classified as a sub-race of the "Asiatics." Their national status was indistinguishable from their racial identity—a white or a black Chinaman was unthinkable. Mexicans were typically despised, not because they were a race but because they were not—or, more specifically, because they were held to be "mongrels," products of

miscegenation between Spaniards and Indians. Whereas Africans were an inferior race, Mexicans were an abominable non-race.

34. A "Creole" was recognized in Alabama case law as a person of mixed black and white ancestry. See *Parker v. State,* 118 Ala.655, 23 So. 664 (1898). Some discussion can be found in Mangum 1940, 17.

35. This changed in the 1920s after Dr. William Plecker, the state's first director of the Bureau of Vital Statistics, went on a legal crusade to declare Native Americans "colored" and expel them from "white" public schools. By 1940 an "Indian" in Virginia was a person who had at least one Indian grandparent, no more than one Negro great-great-grandparent, and resided on a tribal reservation; relocation off the reservation, however, resulted in race reassignment to the category "colored." See Mangum 1940, 6.

36. All the foregoing discussions of varying legal rights in the late nineteenth century are taken from the first chapter of Mangum 1940. The slippage in legal categories continued well into the twentieth century. George Lipsitz reports that during World War II the 30,000 African American soldiers stationed in Hawaii learned that the Hawaiian state census classified African Americans as Puerto Rican, and therefore as Caucasian, in order to distinguish them from native and Asian Hawaiians. Thus by moving to Hawaii, blacks could become white. See Lipsitz 1998, 200. For an interesting discussion of mixed race identities and a brief discussion of multiracial siblings, see Alcoff 2006, esp. 196.

37. "In spite of the work of the geneticist and anthropologist there is still a lamentable confusion between the ideas of *race, culture* and *nation.* In this respect, anthropologists themselves have not been blameless, and therefore the deplorable amount of loose thinking on the part of writers, politicians and the general public is not surprising. In the circumstances, it is very desirable that the term *race* as applied to human groups should be dropped from the vocabulary of science. Its employment as a scientific term had a dual origin. In part, it represents merely the taking over of a popular term, in part the attempt to apply the biological concept of 'variety' or 'geographical race' to man. But the popular term is so loose that it turns out to be unworkable, and the scientific analysis of human populations shows that the variation of man has taken place on lines quite different from those characteristic of other animals. In other animals, the term *sub-species* has been substituted for 'race.' In man, migration and crossing have produced such a fluid state of affairs that no such clear-cut term, as applied to existing conditions, is permissible. What we observe is the relative isolation of groups, their migration and their crossing. In what follows the word *race* will be deliberately avoided, and the term (*ethnic*) *group* or *people* employed for all general purposes" (Huxley and Haddon 1936, 82–83).

38. For examples of race as a central category in contemporary medicine, see Saul 2005; Wheelwright 2006; and Grady 2006. For a critique of the use of racial categories in medicine, see Krieger and Bassett 1993, and Graves 2002. For some historical perspective on racialized disease categories such as sickle-cell anemia, Tay-Sachs disease, and cystic fibrosis, see Wailoo 2003.

39. It is difficult in this compressed format to emphasize sufficiently the radicalism of Foucault's position. Bodies come to be the social phenomena that they are within these power relations and disciplinary practices. In an important sense, disciplines produce our bodies.

40. For historical details about the transition to monitoring or informing, see Ariès 1962, part 2, chapter 5.

41. Foucault qualifies this analysis somewhat in the lecture series of 1978, where he contrasts discipline in relation to norms (what he there calls "normation") with management designed to alter norms within populations (what he there calls "normalization proper"). See Foucault 2007, 57–63.

42. In his 1978 lecture series, Foucault also contrasts disciplinary normalization with what he calls mechanisms or techniques of security. See Foucault 2007, esp. 45–47 and 57–63.

43. For some discussion of desertion as a counterconduct in security regimes, see Foucault 2007, 198.

44. At least what he meant by the term in 1975. He refines the term in 1978, as previously noted. See note 41 above.

45. As Jens Bartelson puts it in his 1995 book *The Genealogy of Sovereignty,* "Genealogy is strategically aimed at that which looks unproblematic and is held to be timeless; its task is to explain how these present traits, in all their vigour and truth, were formed out of that past." Genealogy's critical efficacy is found in its ability to make evident the historical emergence of "those very traits in the present which we feel are without history, and which serve as starting points for other histories and our present sense of identity: it seeks to put everything evident at present in historical motion" (Bartelson 1995, 73, 74).

46. The following discussion is based on Foucault's 1971 essay "Nietzsche, Genealogy, History" (Foucault 1998, 369–91).

47. No doubt Foucault was aware of the debate going on in the American Psychiatric Association during the early 1970s over whether to consider homosexuality a mental illness. For a fascinating history of that debate, one that deals with precisely this issue of the credibility of medical diagnosis in light of political investments, see Bayer 1981.

48. We could read the lectures of 1978, published in English in 2007 under the title *Security, Territory, Population,* as a further attempt to counteract biopower's tendency to reification. In early formulations, biopower looks like a kind of power that emerges with the rise of the nation-state, which seeks to intensify its own forces through cultivation of its vital resources. That early characterization (especially in my crude rendition of it here) makes the state into a kind of subject, wielding biopower as a kind of weapon. In *Security, Territory, Population,* Foucault raises the question of whether the state as an institution can be analyzed "from the outside," as he analyzed psychiatric and penal institutions, and thus whether "the state" can be conceived as contingent upon a field of power relations, practices and knowledges (2007, esp. lecture 5, 118–20). The series is in large part an effort to de-subjectify the state by viewing it within the domain of governmentality. From that perspective one can seriously entertain the possibility that "maybe the state is only a composite reality and a mythicized abstraction whose importance is much less than we think" (2007, 109). This move effectively resituates biopower, removing it from the "hands" of the state as a reified tool and weaving it as a loosely characterized set of events, practices, and techniques into a variegated historical field of shifting power relations.

49. Note 22 of Foucault's February 4, 1976, lecture reads as follows: "The

theory of the 'Norman yoke' (or 'Norman bondage') had been popularized in the sixteenth and seventeenth centuries by political writers (Blackwood, et cetera), by the 'Elizabethan Chroniclers' (Holinshed, Speed, Daniel, et cetera), by the Society of Antiquarians (Selden, Harrison, and Nowell), and by jurists (Coke, et cetera). Their goal was to 'glorify the pre-Norman past' that existed before the invasion and Conquest" (2003b, 113).

50. He makes a similar point in the fifth part of *The History of Sexuality, Volume 1* (1978, esp. 135–40).

51. The first extended discussion of the 1976 lectures in English is Ann Laura Stoler's 1995 monograph *Race and the Education of Desire*. Because the lectures themselves are not the subject of the present book, Stoler's interpretation will not be engaged here, but readers with an interest in Foucault's work—and especially the connections between Foucault's work and postcolonial scholarship—are strongly encouraged to consult that important volume.

2. A Genealogy of Modern Racism, Part 1

1. This assertion is commonplace in the scholarly literature. See, for example, Banton 1987, 51, and Goldberg 1993, 63.

2. Morphological differences among lineally defined races had been noted, of course, but they were not taken to be definitive. Steve Martinot says that Englishmen in the American colonies had begun to refer to themselves as white by the 1690s. I don't dispute that claim. I would suggest that this process occurred over time, probably a few decades, with a firmly recognizable public racial category emerging around 1720. But the exact date is much less important than the fact of historically localized emergence. See Martinot 2003, 66.

3. Of course, exactly what bodily characteristics this racial morphology consisted of was not specified in law or anywhere else, which led to the sometimes frantic attempts to define and classify morphological races that characterized Western science in the late eighteenth and nineteenth centuries.

4. See Jordan 1968, 87. Governor William Berkeley attempted to drive the Puritans out of Virginia. Many resettled in Maryland. See Morgan 1975, 149.

5. It is possible that one of the reasons there was a good bit of cooperation at times between English chattel bondsmen and native Americans was because English subjects who identified themselves as Saxons saw the colonization of North America as another Norman invasion and saw the natives as analogous to their own ancestors. In 1581, in his *Apologia pro regibus,* colonial apologist A. Blackwood had written, "The situation in England at the time of the Norman Conquest must in fact be understood in the same way that we now understand America's situation vis-à-vis what had yet to be called the colonial powers. The Normans acted in England as people from Europe are now acting in America." Further, when Charles V "subdued a part of the West Indies by force, he left the defeated to hold their property not by emancipation but by usufruct and subject to certain obligations. Well, what Charles V did in America—and we regard it as perfectly legitimate as we are doing the same thing—is what the Normans are doing in England, make no mistake about it. The Normans are in England by the same right that we are in America, that is, by the right of colonization" (Foucault 2003b, 102–103).

6. It would be interesting to do a systematic comparison of the two men's writings on race. Jefferson devotes most of his attention to the kind of morphological race characteristic of discussions of racial slavery. Franklin seems to work with a morphological idea of race—identifying skin color as a mark of race—but he sees skin color differences where before Europeans would have simply seen the old distinction of lineage, religion, and language. For example, he refers to the Pennsylvania Germans, whose overwhelming numbers he deplored, as a tawny race. See Jordan 1968, 254.

7. My assertion that the English ruling class would have been familiar with the concept of race prior to the establishment of the concept of the white race derives primarily from my reading of Foucault and enables me to avoid the difficulty that Martinot sees (rightly or wrongly) in accounts like Theodore Allen's. Martinot accuses Allen, among other left-leaning U.S. historians of race, of remaining "too much in the realm of class structure" and relying "too much on terms of economic relations to trace the development of the social ground on which a concept of race and white supremacy grew" (Martinot 2003, 35). According to Martinot, Allen says race emerged as a strategy for dividing the working class. But Martinot says no such strategy could have occurred to ruling class planters in the absence of any existing concept of race. My claim here is that there were concepts of race, and they were already in use in a variety of contexts as dividing strategies. The colonial innovation was to create a racial divide that mapped onto morphology. This could have occurred through both deliberate and incidental means and for a wide variety of political and economic reasons. I agree with Martinot's claim that the major reason was the enhancement of wealth rather than the control of the working class, but it is hard to separate the two goals in practice. Martinot's analysis is extremely interesting and well worth considering in detail (2003, esp. 32–51).

8. Two collections offer an interested reader a quick overview of the major writings in this area. See Eze 1997b, and Bernasconi and Lott 2000.

9. Boxill has argued that the creation of morphological race categories was originally a legitimate scientific enterprise untainted by political ambition and economic exploitation. I strongly disagree. While some individual scientific practitioners may not have stood to gain politically or economically from their theorizing, the scientific project was always, on the whole, enmeshed in the political and economic endeavors of the period. But see Boxill 2001, 5.

10. It is perhaps worth noting that these men were purchased by the Virginia Company, not by any individual. Yeardley and other officials were their supervisors, not their owners.

11. It is important to recall that the "government" of the colonies was in most cases simply a corporate board. In Virginia, for example, the Colonial Council took corporate responsibility for regulating labor just as in any modern corporation. For some discussion of this, see Martinot 2003, 41.

12. A significant number of these people, especially the children, were simply kidnapped off the streets of London and elsewhere. Often young women were purchased from their fathers. The idea that most of these people were willing immigrants, as so many of us were taught in elementary school, is simply false. See Allen 1997, 64–69.

13. Fewer and fewer European bond-laborers with any control over the

matter chose to indenture themselves to masters in Virginia after 1660 anyway, because opportunities there for land-ownership after the period of indenture were severely restricted (Parent 2003, 37). Immigrants chose other colonies with more opportunity instead. Furthermore, in England there was a declining birthrate and an outbreak of plague that resulted in higher wages, reducing motivation to immigrate at all (Parent 2003, 58).

14. That did not stop settlers from enslaving them, though. In "wars" throughout the seventeenth century, colonists took Native Americans captive and held them or sold them as slaves. This is what happened to most of the Tuscarorans (also known as Monacans) and many of the Pamunkeys.

15. I use the term "Negro" here because that is the terminology in the law. It is generally interchangeable with "African" or "person of African descent" during this time, but it identifies such people by the relative darkness of their skin. It is an important transitional term between race as lineage and race as morphology.

16. The General Assembly had already decided three years earlier, in 1667, that conversion to Christianity after enslavement did not give a person grounds for emancipation, but Virginians were still hesitant to allow Christians to be enslaved. Complications would arise, however, with the importation of Congolese slaves between 1710 and 1740. The Congolese were Christians before enslavement and transport to North America, having been converted in the early sixteenth century (Parent 2003, 160). They made up the majority of Africans enslaved by the British during this period, and a large number of them were sold in Virginia; in fact, nearly half the slaves imported to Virginia between 1727 and 1740 would be Congolese.

17. Note that the reverse is not true; it is not the case that all slaves were dark-skinned. There were those European women who insisted on marrying Negro men, for example, and their children, whose skin colors may have varied quite a bit.

18. Morgan argues that conditions were ripe for the conversion of the labor force from indentured servants to slaves by 1660. See Morgan 1975, 297.

19. There is evidence that colonial laborers were well aware of this economic fact. Georgia was founded in 1732 with the stated principle that there would be no chattel slavery there. But planters saw the prosperity of slave owners in South Carolina and began agitating for the right to emulate them. In this context, Allen quotes a Savannah citizen claiming that free laborers would be impoverished by repeal. See Allen 1997, 252–53.

20. Banton says the Virginia General Assembly actually initiated this project in the 1660s. His account agrees with Allen's: the policy was a deliberate attempt to create something that did not exist in popular culture. See Banton 1987, 49.

21. Eventually, this collection of theories would establish the scientist—and in particular the physician and the anthropologist—as the seat of the discerning gaze, the authority who could read bodily marks to determine the true racial identity of any individual presented to him. Scientific theory would not only justify racializing practices after the fact but would appropriate them as means to produce the subjectivity of Enlightenment science itself. For a lengthy discussion of the development of the "gaze" as a crucial aspect of Enlightenment medicine, see Foucault 1973, especially chapters 6 and 7.

22. The most contentious was called "An Act directing the trial of Slaves, committing capital crimes; and for the more effectual punishing conspiracies and insurrections of them; and for the better government of Negroes, Mulattos, and Indians, bond or free." See Allen 1997, 41.

23. Martinot says the bargain was sealed when the planters established slave patrols, conscripting all white settlers to act as a sort of colonial police force from 1727 forward. See Martinot 2003, 67.

24. Linnaeus named the camellia after the Jesuit botanist Georg Joseph Kamel. It is a flowering shrub or small evergreen tree originating in southern Asia. There are between 100 and 250 different varieties. Blooms vary tremendously in color, depending, at least in part, on soil conditions.

25. For the relevant excerpt from Bernier's work, see Bernasconi and Lott 2000, 1–4.

26. Over the past few years, a great deal of work has been published on Kant's understanding of race. I refer the interested reader to *The German Invention of Race* (Eigen and Larrimore 2006), a collection of essays on German theories of race in the eighteenth and early nineteenth centuries. Robert Bernasconi's work, in particular his essay "Who Invented the Concept of Race? Kant's Role in the Enlightenment Construction of Race," in Bernasconi 2001, is also quite important, as is Emmanuel Eze's work, especially "The Color of Reason: The Idea of 'Race' in Kant's Anthropology" in Eze 1997a.

27. There is some indication that at some point Kant thought whites—at least those who were brunettes—did still have the potential for variation and thus adaptation to different climates. Whites may not have yet become, or degenerated into, a race but were still very much like the original ancestors. For a discussion of this interpretation, see Larrimore 2006, 106.

28. For some discussion about his theory of hybridity and his reasons for changing his mind about which groups were distinct races, see Zammito 2006, 42. Changes are evident in Kant 1788.

29. This is also Jon Mark Mikkelsen's translation, but it is as yet unpublished. It is from Kant's essay "Defining the Concept of a Human Race" (1785), part 2.

30. Although most Americans in the late eighteenth century already thought of race as a matter of morphology, it would be several decades before British thinkers entirely abandoned the notion that race is primarily a matter of lineage. Morphological race was an Anglo-American invention, and the British were not accustomed to accepting intellectual dictates from rustic colonists. Two examples will serve to illustrate this time lag. At the beginning of the nineteenth century, the French word *race* began to shift in meaning from lineage to morphology. When Cuvier published *The Animal Kingdom* in 1817, he used the word *race* to mean morphological variety: "Quoique l'espece humaine paraisse unique, puisque tous les individus peuvent se meler indistinctement, et produire des individus feconds, on y remarque de certaines conformations hereditaires qui constituent ce qu'on nomme des races" (Banton 1987, 51). In the translation of Cuvier's work published in New York in 1831, the French word *race* is rendered by the English word *race*. But just four years earlier, when an English translation was brought out in London, Cuvier's British translator had ignored the cognate and rendered *races* as *varieties* (Banton

1987, 51). To many readers in England in the 1820s, the word *race* still meant lineage. The tide was already turning, however. In *Researches into the Physical History of Mankind,* published in 1826, British physician James Cowles Prichard complained about anthropologists who used the term *race* interchangeably with *physical type:* "Races," he wrote, "are properly successions of individuals propagated from any given stock; and the term should be used without any involved meaning that such a progeny or stock has always possessed a particular character" (quoted in Banton 1978, 30). There is no reason to assume that members of the same lineage will always look alike, nor is there reason to assume that individuals who look alike are part of the same lineage, he argued, and since the word *race* is a matter of lineage and not type, people should stop using *race* when what they really mean is *variety.* But the very fact that Prichard had to make an argument on behalf of restricting the meaning of *race* to *lineage* indicates that the shift was already well underway. He was one of the last English speakers to remember that what race a person belonged to had once had absolutely nothing to do with his or her physical appearance. Race had become morphology.

31. Smith 1965, 72, 105, 152. Of course, another explanation for the difference, if indeed Smith's observation was correct, is that more house slaves than field slaves were the children of their owner or his sons.

32. Practically all commentators mention this, but see, for example, Jordan 1974, 178, and Magnis 1999, 492.

33. Jefferson's pet plan was to emancipate slaves gradually and send them as young adults to colonize Sierra Leone. See Magnis 1999, 502.

34. That is in fact how Alexander O. Boulton reads it; see Boulton 1995, 479.

35. However, he did contend that Buffon was inconsistent on the issue of moisture, because he claimed that Dutch cattle were healthy and large because of the level of moisture in their pastures (Jefferson 1944, 75).

36. For some discussion of Buffon's (and others') notion that New World species were smaller and weaker, see Gerbi 1985, especially 3–11.

37. In fact, not only were they as large as and in some cases larger than comparable species in Europe, but Jefferson also counted more different species.

38. Jefferson's views on this issue seem to have been even stricter than his colleagues. In 1776, as a member of the Committee of Revisors in the Virginia General Assembly, Jefferson proposed a law that would punish white women who gave birth to mixed-race children by banishing them from the state within one year after the birth or, if they remained, putting them "out of the protection of the laws" (Magnis 1999, 501). Apparently, Jefferson intended to return such women to something like Locke's state of nature, subject to coercion and brutality without recourse to the commonwealth.

39. For a discussion of Jefferson's use of Saxon history, see Colbourn 1958.

40. Boulton says, "Probably no individual before Abraham Lincoln had as much practical success in setting slavery on the course of gradual extinction in the United States" (1995, 475).

41. Edmund Morgan makes this point in *American Slavery, American Freedom* (1975, 385), but he suggests that Jefferson's real fear was the creation of an underclass of impoverished people without supervision. For a discus-

sion of the debate in the 1790s about the possibility of "Negro removal," see Jordan 1974, 207–14.

42. For a quick list of relevant quotations, see Jordan 1974, 169–70.

3. A Genealogy of Modern Racism, Part 2

1. The first official use of the term occurs in Gottfried Reinhold Treviranus, *Biologie oder Philosophie der lebendigen Natur fur Naturforscher und Ärtze* (J. F. Rower, 1802). My thanks to Dr. Justin Smith for this reference.

2. In 1808 Lamarck went so far as to suggest that apes could become human beings under the right conditions.

3. See, for example, Greene 1959, 161.

4. This is Foucault (1970, 273–4) quoting Cuvier's *Lessons of Comparative Anatomy*.

5. Foucault returns to this contrast between Cuvier and Lamarck and integrates his claims about the transition from natural history to biology in his 1978 lecture series, where he analyzes the state as an effect within the field of governmentality. In the third lecture, he offers a brief but provocative rereading of *The Order of Things* to show how the concept of "population" arose (Foucault 2007, esp. 74–79).

6. For some references to literature of the period that made this connection, see McClintock 1995, 50–51.

7. His last known written endorsement was also his most extensive elaboration. It occurs in his 1824 letter to northern colonizationist Jared Sparks.

8. In fact, that is exactly what happened. Not long after Jefferson's death, Frederick Douglass was making assertions like the following: "The native land of the American Negro is America. His bones, his muscles, his sinews, are all American. His ancestors for two hundred and seventy years have lived and labored and died on American soil, and millions of his posterity have inherited Caucasian blood" (Lott 1999, 44).

9. While Jefferson held that slavery tends to corrupt the morals of slaveholders and create resentment in slaves and thus is an immoral or at least politically dangerous institution, he did not challenge its legality under the U.S. Constitution.

10. Jefferson discusses this plan in *Notes on the State of Virginia* (Jefferson 1944, 144), but much of the detail of the plan as it evolved can be found in his 1824 letter to Jared Sparks. For references and discussion of the details, see Takaki 2000, 45.

11. He did admit to Jared Sparks in 1824 that "the separation of infants from their mothers . . . would produce some scruples of humanity. But this would be straining at a gnat, and swallowing a camel" (Takaki 2000, 45).

12. He did not think the United States could do without those two million laborers, however; he suggested that immigrants from Europe could be persuaded to take their places. Interestingly, he rejected a proposal by Monroe and others that would have established a black colony in the western territories of the North American continent. He envisioned the eventual annexation of all that territory as a set of states, and he believed a black colony would be even harder to reckon with in the long run than an enslaved black population. See Onuf 1990, 38.

13. Rush's treatments including bleeding and purging, which most likely weakened patients considerably. Although yellow fever is very often fatal and most of Rush's patients probably would have died anyway, it is likely that his treatment actually killed some of them. He seriously underestimated the amount of blood in a healthy human body and often bled his patients almost to death without realizing it. For accounts of his work in the epidemic, see Powell 1949, and Binger 1966.

14. On the 152nd anniversary of his death, the American Psychiatric Association placed a bronze plaque at his grave declaring him "Father of American Psychiatry" (Binger 1966, 296).

15. For some time up until 1794, Rush did own one slave, a man named William, who served him as a physician's assistant and driver. In 1794 he emancipated William and hired him to continue in his job. William remained in Rush's household. Rush also had at least one free black assistant, called Marcus, prior to William's emancipation. William and Marcus worked with Rush, equally heroically no doubt, throughout the 1793 epidemic.

16. See Rush 1969, 19. Rush did live to see the U.S. end the slave trade in 1808.

17. He celebrated Pennsylvania's 1773 tax increase in several letters to friends and allies, and he participated in a plan to develop the maple sugar industry in Pennsylvania to reduce reliance on cane sugar produced by slave labor in the West Indies. He writes of the latter in his *Commonplace Book, 1789–1791,* reprinted in his autobiography; see Rush 1948, 177.

18. And, as Foucault suggests, the military disciplinarian Guibert did. See Foucault 1977, 155.

19. In a lecture entitled "The Progress of Medicine," he called the pulse the "nosometer" of the body (Rush 1947, 239).

20. He was castigated for his use of purging and bleeding during the yellow fever epidemic of 1793, some even charging that his treatments led to the deaths of many of his patients (and no doubt they did). The public outcry was so great over the next four years that he considered suing more than one critic, and eventually did sue William Cobbett, for libel. Rush won his case, but Cobbett never paid the full amount of damages. For a discussion of these events, see Binger 1966, 239–48.

21. This disrespect for the dead is quite remarkable and was no doubt a product of Cuvier's European as well as his scientific arrogance. But his comments do illustrate that dissection of corpses was a common practice. By the late eighteenth century, anatomists such as Cuvier were quite adept at preservation of tissues. See Foucault 1973, 125, where he writes: "Morgagni had no difficulty in the middle of the eighteenth century in carrying out his autopsies; nor did Hunter, some years later; the conflicts recounted by his biographer are of an anecdotal character and indicate no opposition on principle. From 1754 the Vienna clinic had had a dissection room; so had the clinic that Tissot had organized at Pavia; at the Hôtel Dieu in Paris, Desault was quite free 'to demonstrate on the body deprived of life the alterations that had rendered art useless.'" Many of the gruesome stories of mid-nineteenth-century grave robbers procuring bodies for dissection in England and Scotland are true, but not because dissection itself was outlawed—in fact it was required for medical licensure—but because it was difficult to get enough bodies to meet the

demand for medical training. A black market sprang up, which promoted not only grave robbing but murder at times. The supply of corpses for dissection was greater in France because French law remanded bodies of the indigent and unclaimed to the schools of anatomy. But gruesome stories are fun, and one of the best is that of anatomist-turned-race-theorist Robert Knox (Rae 1964). The story Rae recounts helps explain why Paris had gained ascendance over Edinburgh as an international center for medical education by 1830.

22. Appel 1987, 107. Gould suggests that Charles Bonnet is actually the first to put forth a recapitulation theory in 1769. Bonnet was a preformationist, so the apparent recapitulation was illusory, he thought. But Gould contends that because Bonnet argued that there is apparent progress from simple to complex, he actually did formulate a recapitulationist description of fetal development. See Gould, 1977, 22–28.

23. Gould 1977, 126. Presumably he was referring to limb-to-body ratios, as did his successors, but see below.

24. Prior to the introduction of the cotton gin (a machine that separates seeds from fibers), it was not profitable to raise thousands of acres of cotton, despite the market for cotton created by a booming textile industry in Britain and New England. Once the process of cleaning cotton was mechanized, however, the plantation economy was revitalized and slave labor was again in great demand. Eli Whitney produced a model of a cotton gin in 1793. He never made a profit on the invention, but others took it up. Gins were commonplace by the first decades of the nineteenth century, and cotton production skyrocketed from 9,000 bales in 1791 to 2 million in 1840. For figures see Du Bois 1935, 4.

25. A notable exception was Dr. Thomas Cooper, president of South Carolina College. In 1823 Cooper was already asserting that blacks were inherently inferior to whites. According to Reginald Horsman (1987, 18) he was among the first Americans to do so. His view is significant not for its immediate effects but for the fact that one of his students was Josiah Nott, who graduated from South Carolina College in 1824.

26. One reason for this preeminence was that dissection was not only legal in France but there was a well-functioning bureaucratic system for supplying cadavers on a regular basis. La Pitié was one of two hospitals where students could perform dissections under excellent supervision, which is why students from all over Europe and the United States were flocking there from the early 1820s onward.

27. Sèrres took a position at la Pitié in 1814 and was named chief physician in 1822. He remained there at least until 1839, at which time he took an appointment as chair of anatomy at the Muséum d'Histoire Naturelle, where he taught for thirty years. See Appel 1987, 122.

28. Blumenbach had written: "When the matter is thoroughly considered, you see that all do so run into one another, and that one variety of mankind does so sensibly pass into the other, that you cannot mark out the limits between them" (*On the Natural Variety of Mankind*, 98–99, quoted in Zammito 2006, 47).

29. Cuvier had made this claim as well, on the basis of fifty skulls of Egyptians that he had in his collection in Paris (Fausto-Sterling 1995, 27).

30. See Gould 1981, 54–60. Gould reanalyzed Morton's data and had

this to say: "Morton's summaries are a patchwork of fudging and finagling in the clear interest of controlling a priori convictions. Yet—and this is the most intriguing aspect of the case—I find no evidence of conscious fraud; indeed, had Morton been a conscious fudger, he would not have published his data so openly." Subsequently, John S. Michael re-checked Morton's data and Gould's analysis and argued that Morton did not make as many errors as Gould claimed. Michael more or less accuses Gould of error in the service of political goals; see Michael, 1988.

31. Calhoun put it this way: "I hold then that there never has yet existed a wealthy and civilized society in which one portion of the community did not in point of fact live on the labor of the other. . . . The devices are almost innumerable, from the brute force and gross superstition of ancient times to the subtle and artful fiscal contrivances of the modern. . . . It is useless to disguise the fact. There is and always has been in an advanced stage of wealth and civilization a conflict between labor and capital. The condition of society in the South exempts us from the disorders and dangers resulting from this conflict" (Bartlett 1993, 227).

32. See Deutsch 1944, 475; Pasmanick 1964, 6–8; and Bartlett 1993, 313–14. Deutsch actually refers to the flaws that Jarvis exposed as "one of the most amazing tissues of statistical falsehood and error ever woven together under government imprint." Jarvis looked only at the statistics for the state of Maine, but he found that census officials had counted more insane Negroes than Negroes in some towns. Congressman John Quincy Adams led the effort to have the census reviewed, but Calhoun appointed William A. Weaver to do the work, the man who had supervised the 1840 census in the first place. Not surprisingly, he failed to find any significant errors, and the false statistics continued to be cited in scholarly journals well into the 1850s. See Deutsch, 1944, 476–78.

33. Polygenism had been circulating for some time already; it had been put forth in the eighteenth century by Lord Kames, Samuel Stanhope Smith's intellectual adversary. In France it was seriously discussed in scientific circles as early as 1801 with publication of Jean Joseph Virey's *Histoire Naturel du Genre Humain*. As a biological theory, however, polygeny was not entertained in American intellectual circles until the 1830s, upon its reintroduction first by Dr. Charles Caldwell in his *Thoughts on the Original Unity of the Human Race* (1830) and then by Richard Colfax in his pamphlet *Against the Views of the Abolitionists, Consisting of Physical and Moral Proofs of the Natural Inferiority of the Negroes* (1833). Caldwell relied primarily on a religious rather than a scientific argument for his assertions, however, and Colfax's somewhat more systematic attempt was insufficiently grounded in European race theory to hold up to serious critique (see Fredrickson 1971, 73, 50). Virey's work appeared in English translation in the United States in 1837, thanks to French émigré I. H. Guenebault (Horsman 1987, 84; Fredrickson 1971, 74), giving the idea more scientific credibility. But this was not enough for Morton to stake his scientific reputation on.

34. Nott was five years younger than Morton. He was at the University of Pennsylvania during the time that Morton was in Edinburgh. Because of family obligations he was obliged to practice medicine for six years in Columbia,

South Carolina, after finishing his degree, and so did not go to Paris for further study until 1835.

35. It should be remembered that Nott is speaking during a time when there was an enormous influx of Irish into the United States. At least 1.8 million came between 1845 and 1855. They were poorer than the Irish who had come earlier, and many of them did not speak English (Ignatiev 1995, 39). From Nott's time forward for several decades, many Americans would view the new Irish immigrants with racist suspicion. Some would consider them nonwhite. Some would consider them white but not Caucasian. Some would consider them white and Caucasian but not Nordic. How they were categorized depended on the particular racial schema employed, but they were certainly considered racially inferior to Anglo-Saxons. That so many of them lived among and married African Americans (Ignatiev 1995, 41), particularly in Samuel Morton's Philadelphia, pushed them even farther down on Nott's and his colleagues' racial hierarchy.

36. I have been asked whether the term "Caucasian" is synonymous here with the term "white." The answer is that I don't know. Given Nott's disparaging assertions about Celts, it is not clear whether "Caucasian," which he and Gliddon use, following Morton (who follows Blumenbach's terminology, who follows Christoph Meiner's terminology—see Baum 2006, 59), is coextensive with the term "white." They are dealing in ideal types, not existent populations; they hold that many existing groups of people are mixtures of these ideal types. As to whether I am using the terms interchangeably, my answer is no; throughout this genealogy I employ whichever terms are current in the literature under discussion, and I make no assumptions about whether any given term translates without loss of meaning into any other. The terms in these discourses are shaping racial realities, not simply reflecting them. For a history of the term *Caucasian,* which dates back to 1785, and which for a time lost favor with many scientific racists (such as William Ripley and Madison Grant) around the turn of the twentieth century, see Baum 2006, esp. 151 and 219.

37. And size. On my bathroom scales it weighs in at five pounds. Not exactly something you would read on the trolley.

38. Madelin Joan Olds points out the monotonous recurrence of this double characterization in her review of postbellum white-authored and edited periodical literature. She quotes, for example, Thomas Dixon, Jr., author of the 1905 novel *The Clansman,* saying that adult blacks had "the intelligence of children and the instincts of savages." See Olds 1995, 184.

39. In his early years, Foucault might have seen them both as the expression of a single episteme.

40. Obviously, this requirement that people move into an institution where at least theoretically they would be subject to the discipline of a superintendent would not have appealed to any but the most desperate. Almshouses thus acted as a deterrent to needy people who might otherwise have sought help. Philip Ferguson suggests that this was part of their purpose (1994, 31).

41. I do not know whether any almshouses segregated inmates by race during this period. In the slave states, any African American asking for help at the door of an almshouse would have been immediately captured and (re-) enslaved; thus there would have been no blacks in southern almshouses. I have

no definitive information on whether inmates were supposed to be segregated by race in almshouses in "free" states before 1840. I do know that between 1840 and 1890 New York's House of Refuge was not racially segregated, and blacks did sometimes live there (Gupta 2001). As I go on to say in the body of the text, practice did not follow theory even in relation to segregation by sex, age, or infirmity, so even if some states' almshouses were supposed to be segregated by race, they probably were not, or not consistently so. I cannot begin to speak to the question of whether racial classification in almshouses affected Native Americans or Asian Americans in the first half of the nineteenth century.

42. For a detailed description of this method, see Trent 1994, 46–53.

43. He arrived with his young son Edward Constant, who later became one of the founders of American neurology.

44. Howe 1972 [1858], 2–3. For a discussion of Howe, see P. Ferguson 1994, 45–60.

45. Thomas Kirkbride, superintendent at the Pennsylvania Hospital, was particularly good at speaking to the wealthier parents of prospective pupils/inmates in morally neutral terms. See Tomes 1981, 126.

46. For discussion of this transition and some of its implications, see L. Carlson 2001, esp. 126–30.

47. Kerlin does not give his reasons for making the assertion; he seems to view it as self-evident or at least widely accepted. And in fact, from the 1870s well into the twentieth century most officials seemed to believe that sexual promiscuity was a far more serious problem among defective females than among defective males.

48. For a lengthy discussion of this equation, see Stoler, 1995, chapter 5, esp. 141–51.

49. Quoted in Gould 1977, 119. One might also compare the story of descent into savagery of the unsupervised English boys marooned on an island in William Golding's 1954 novel *Lord of the Flies*.

50. For background and figures on the Army tests as well as a detailed critique, see Gould 1981, 192–222. The interpretation of the tests that yields such a high number of feebleminded is somewhat inappropriate, according to Gould, but it was the way the test results were viewed in the popular press. Gould's critique focuses more on the tests themselves than on popular interpretations. Mark Haller, perhaps the first U.S. historian to write about the American eugenics movement, claimed in 1963 that the Army IQ test results from World War I reduced the idea of test itself to absurdity; see M. Haller 1963, 113. Certainly, there were skeptics, and psychologists realized they had to refine the tests. But there is no evidence that most psychologists—whether eugenicists or not—lost enthusiasm for intelligence testing as a consequence of these absurd numbers. Indeed, many in the present day seem to believe that IQ tests are among the most reliable of psychological inventory instruments. Furthermore, and in support of Gould's assessment of popular impact, historian Gwendolyn Mink notes that the IQ "data" had a negative influence on public support of World War I veterans: politicians and taxpayers were unwilling to bestow veterans' benefits on the returning troops commensurate with what veterans of previous wars had enjoyed, in part because they were members of a "culturally heterogeneous army, held in suspicion because of a

diversity that had been 'scientifically' correlated with a lower caliber of soldier" (Mink 1995, 22); the stinginess with which Americans greeted their returning veterans suggests that the IQ tests were taken fairly seriously by the taxpaying public and their representatives.

51. This term was popularized by Harvard anthropologist William Ripley in his book *The Races of Europe*. Emerging after Darwin's theories were generally accepted among educated Americans, the "Nordic race" was always defined in part by its alleged course of evolutionary development, unlike older categories of racial identity such as "white" (which, as we have seen, was first an extremely vague legal and popular category referring ambiguously to both European lineage and light-colored skin) or Caucasian (which began life as a pre-Darwinian anthropological classification referring to geographical origin and climate-induced features as are supposedly typical of the population of present-day Chechnya, Dagestan, and parts of Georgia, Azerbaijan, and Armenia). For a discussion of the alleged geographical locus of the Caucasian race, see Baum 2006, 221.

52. Catholicism was not a racial category in and of itself, but insofar as it was viewed as a symptom of feeble volition—because it entailed subordination of one's will to the pope rather than to one's own conscience—it was often taken to be a religion of inferior races. Mariann Olden goes so far as to suggest that the reason the Catholic Church resisted state-imposed sterilization of the defective was that it was attempting to protect its own membership from decimation: "Since the Catholic Church guards so jealously the reproductive power of our socially inadequate classes, it is pertinent to discover to what extent it is guarding the reproductivity of its own members, whom it is prone to remind us are voters. Such an inquiry was completed in 1935 in New Jersey. . . . Catholics were 25% of New Jersey's population in 1930. In 1935 they constituted 37% of the resident population in the five institutions for the mentally deficient and epileptic; 52% of the patients in the three mental hospitals; 47% of the delinquents in eight correctional institutions, and 53% of the dependent children under the Board of Children's Guardians and in the School for the Deaf. The Church of Rome cannot be absolved from selfishness in opposing intelligent control of procreation" (Olden 1974, 30–31). Unlike Catholics, Jews were sometimes considered a race unto themselves. But not always. It really depended on the political agenda of the moment. Whether Jewish or not, however, Slavs were generally considered to be stupid, lazy, violent, sickly, promiscuous, and alcoholic.

53. Comparisons between so-called "lower" races and mental defectives were commonplace at the turn of the twentieth century. John Down made the comparison official with his claim that certain forms of mental defect in white children—mental development arrested at a certain stage—effectively render them members of "lower" races. This idea still survives in the colloquial use of the term "Mongoloid" for persons with what is now more commonly called "Down Syndrome." Down actually identified a full range of racial types among white defectives, with the Mongoloid being the highest. For a relatively sympathetic contemporary appraisal of that system of classification, see Barr 1913, 82. Barr himself repeatedly refers to Negroes as mentally defective as a race, asserting that they are in a condition of "unquestionable backwardness"

(1913, 207). He believes it is possible to prevent some backward individuals from sliding into imbecility, but it requires education and possibly institutionalization. Charles McCord drew the comparison between criminals and African Americans explicitly in 1914. He asserted that, like Lombroso's criminals, Negroes typically have long arms, prognathism, low brain weight and cranial capacity, high cheekbones, flat feet and low instep, prehensile big toe, wooly hair, infrequent gray hair (in men), thick hair but thin beard, rare baldness, gynecomasty (over-development of breasts), narrow pelvis, protruding frontal eminences, better eye sight, especially at a distance, low respiratory capacity, frequent structural abnormalities, and insensitivity to pain (McCord 1914, 28–31).

4. Scientific Racism and the Threat of Sexual Predation

1. For a detailed description of the events of Bloody Sunday, see Lewis 1998, chap. 16.

2. Jackson and his mother and grandfather had taken part in a public protest over the county's refusal to register black voters. State troopers chased him and his family into a nearby café. They shot Jackson when he attempted to defend his mother and grandfather from attack. He died eight days later from infection.

3. The governor was not unaware of the events in Selma; in fact, he had ordered state troopers to the scene on Bloody Sunday. The governor was George C. Wallace, as unlikely a sympathetic ear as could be found in Alabama at the time. The actual purpose of the march was to focus media attention on the issues, of course, not to visit Governor Wallace.

4. A number of genetic diseases had been identified by 1910, most of which are in fact inherited as Mendelian traits. In 1900, Karl Landsteiner discovered blood types, and by 1910 these were shown to be inherited according to Mendelian laws (Ludmerer 1972, 46; Stepan 1985, 139). This led to lots of scientific speculation over the possibility of Mendelian inheritance of other traits, including feeblemindedness, criminality, insanity, epilepsy, alcoholism, and even pauperism, nomadism, shyness, and a predisposition to cancer.

5. Actually, a great many people still had not fully accepted natural selection as the sole or primary cause of variation at the turn of the twentieth century. Some, including some biological scientists, still held to versions of Lamarckian inheritance of acquired characteristics. But the scientific trend was already very clear, and within a decade Lamarckianism was pretty much laid to rest. For a fairly comprehensive, albeit popularized and eugenically oriented account of the state of biological science in the 1910s, see Popenoe and Johnson 1926 (originally published in 1918).

6. The idea that humanity rose up from savagery to civilization was a relatively new one in the late eighteenth and early nineteenth centuries. Previously, most Westerners had held that humanity was created civilized and then, after the fall from grace and expulsion from the Garden of Eden, degenerated into varying states of savagery.

7. Madison Grant tells the story in much this way in his introduction to Lothrop Stoddard's 1920 book *The Rising Tide of Color Against White*

World-Supremacy. Most of evolution occurred in Europe, Grant tells us: "In other words those groups of mankind which at an earlier period found refuge in the Americas, in Australia, in Ethiopia, on the islands of the sea, represent to a large extent stages in man's physical and cultural development, from which the more energized inhabitants of Eurasia have long since emerged" (Stoddard 1925, xii). Consequently, he fears, "If this great race, with its capacity for leadership and fighting, should ultimately pass, with it would pass that which we call civilization" (xxix).

8. For some discussion of this debate over white viability in the tropics and Ripley's contribution to it, see Stepan 1985, 102–104.

9. Ripley means, of course, the balance of power within Europe. Any European nation who could possess those lands as colonies would quickly become more powerful than all the rest. For interesting discussions of the history of this idea of the balance of European powers, see Foucault 2007, chap. 11, and Bartelson 1995, 226.

10. Gorgas based his views on the work of Dr. Ronald Ross, who had proven in 1897 that mosquitoes carried malaria, and Drs. Carlos J. Finlay and Walter Reed, who had proven in 1900 that mosquitoes carried yellow fever. Gorgas had already applied the principle in his work in 1902 in Havana with some success, but opposition to his measures was still quite strong. This, despite the fact that the idea that an insect was the vector of the disease was not new; it had been proposed several decades earlier. Dr. Josiah Nott, for one, had suggested the possibility in 1854. He had traced the spread of a major yellow fever outbreak in Mobile on maps of the region and had noted the similarity between that spread and the spread of boll weevil destruction through cotton fields. Undoubtedly, Nott shared his speculations with members of Gorgas's family. Gorgas himself was born near the end of that terrible outbreak, in October of 1854, and Nott was the attending physician at his delivery. Gorgas's uncle, William Crawford, was for a time Nott's partner in his medical practice (Horsman 1987, 169).

11. Alexandra Minna Stern suggests that the construction of the canal was a turning point in white self-conception and a spur to white imperialistic ambitions for just these reasons (Stern 2005, chap. 1).

12. Hoffman 1892, 531. Hoffman's statistical theories were widely known at the time. W. E. B. Du Bois refers to them in his 1940 essay "The Concept of Race," where he notes that he lived to see all of Hoffman's claims invalidated. See Du Bois 1996, 78.

13. For a long list of these studies, see J. Haller 1970, 154, n. 2.

14. For some discussion of this phenomenon, see S. Gilman 1985, chap. 5.

15. Charles Bacon, for one, worried that the economy could not easily withstand the loss of labor power that black extinction would entail. "Leaving ethical considerations out of the question, 3,000,000 workers form too valuable an economic factor to be eliminated unless the race problem is too dangerous to the state and there is no possibility of solving it in any other way" (Bacon 1903, 342).

16. John Haller, writing about the medical profession, said: "Physicians were generally agreed on the condition of the Negro in the late nineteenth century. Arguments to the contrary were simply not to be found in the transactions

and journals of the medical societies. Expressing the quiet intimacy of a consulting-room conversation, doctors exhausted all possible arguments in their commentaries on the Negro and his health. They vehemently dismissed the possibility for race improvement and, with a minimum expenditure of rhetoric, they offered a prophetic warning for the race's future" (J. Haller 1971, 68).

17. I have only had access to Beard's 1881 and 1888 editions of his two books, but both Charles Rosenberg and Eric Carlson state that Beard's work on neurasthenia first began to appear in 1869. See Rosenberg 1962, 248, and E. Carlson 1985, 130.

18. This observation is a commonplace in the medical and anthropological literature of the period. Isaac Kerlin made the same claim one year later, the reader will recall from chapter 3; see Kerlin 1889, 37. Kerlin was referring to the moral sense specifically, but contemporaries believed this to be true of all the faculties and traits they deemed "higher."

19. Among those to be diagnosed with neurasthenia was German philosopher Martin Heidegger, who on that basis was exempt from military service in 1914 (Koonz 2003, 50). Among the critics of the diagnostic category was psychiatrist Edward Spitzka; for discussion, see Rosenberg 1962, 258.

20. August Morel had argued back in the 1850s that all these factors, plus tobacco, arsenic, and several others, initiated organic degeneration. For a detailed evaluation of the evidence for and against these so-called "racial poisons" in the early twentieth century, see Popenoe and Johnson 1926, chap. 2. As ardent anti-Lamarckian eugenicists, Popenoe and Johnson are eager to rule out most environmental causes of change in the germ line, so they discount almost all these factors. But the evidence brought forth is of historical interest nonetheless, and their treatment of it suggests that many people still held to Morel's view as late as 1918, when their book was originally published, and even as late as 1926, when it was brought out a second time without alteration to that section.

21. By the turn of the century, the idea that women were more like children than adult men had been completely absorbed into scientific discourse. It appears, for example, in Iwan Block's sexological work *The Sexual Life of Our Time*, published in 1907. Block writes, "Woman remains more akin to the child than to the man" (Bland and Doan 1998, 32). But perhaps Caesar Lombroso summed it up best when he wrote in 1895, "What terrific criminals would children be if they had strong passions, muscular strength, and sufficient intelligence; and if, moreover, their evil tendencies were exasperated by a morbid psychical activity! And women are big children; their evil tendencies are more numerous and more varied than men's, but generally remain latent. When they are awakened and excited they produce results proportionately greater" (Lombroso and Ferrero 1958, 151).

22. As Howard himself puts it, "According to the general law, to which this is no exception, the genital organs of the male are in proper proportion, as regards size, to the dimensions of the female organ" (1903, 425). There was a long history of anatomical study of black women's reproductive and sexual organs by this time, stretching back into the eighteenth century. Howard was no doubt familiar with the medical literature on African American female genital anatomy, including articles such as Howard Turnipseed's "Some Facts in

Regard to the Anatomical Differences between the Negro and White Races" in which he reported on eight cases in which he had observed that "the hymen of the negro woman is not at the entrance of the vagina, as in the white woman, but from one and a half to two inches from its entrance in the interior, with an opening below for the passage of the menses" (Turnipseed 1877, 32). Turnipseed was trying to establish a basis for viewing blacks and whites as distinct species, a pursuit somewhat out of vogue by Howard's time, but empirical "evidence" presented in this body of literature very often outlasted its political and theoretical context.

23. See, for example, Robert Latou Dickinson's Appendix VI in Henry 1941, 1085–115. For a discussion of this long-term scientific interest in the size of female genitalia, especially in lesbians and women of minority races, see Gilman 1985, chap. 3.

24. This is quoted in J. Haller 1970, 162. Haller's article is full of quotations like this from prominent physicians all over the United States. Anyone who thinks Howard and Lydston were on the medical or scientific fringe should take a look at this collection and the articles Haller cites. Unfortunately, I have been unable to obtain a copy of the original article by Mcguire and Lydston. Haller's citation is as follows: Hunter Mcguire and G. Frank Lydston, "Sexual crimes among the southern Negroes; scientifically considered," *Virginia M. Monthly,* 1893, vol. 20:110. I suspect, however, that the passage Haller attributes to Lydston and Hunter is actually a quotation they lift out of a work by Kiernan. Lydston repeats this claim and attributes it to Kiernan in his 1904 monograph, *The Diseases of Society.* See Lydston 1904, 397. There he writes: "Kiernan has asserted that *furor sexualis* in the negro resembles similar sexual attacks in the bull and elephant, and the running amok of the Malay. He further notes the sadism manifested by the negro in the torture or murder of his ravished victim. This is distinctly atavistic and occurs occasionally in whites." Unfortunately, Lydston offers no citation from Kiernan's body of work.

25. Patricia Hill Collins says the myth of the Jezebel originated under slavery and served then as a justification for white men's sexual assaults on black women (Collins 1991, 76). I don't contest that historical claim. I only mean to suggest here that as the figure of the Jezebel was absorbed into the discourse of biology and social Darwinism in the late nineteenth century, it became part of the general complex of the myth of the sexual predator threatening to disrupt evolutionary advance. In more recent work, Collins has carefully linked the sexual assault of black women and the lynching of black men in one systemic analysis, concluding that "lynching and rape as forms of state-sanctioned violence are not now and never were as gender-specific as once thought" (Collins 2005, 218).

26. Note that this way of framing the phenomenon makes it very easy to blame the lynching of black men on white women, as many people have done over the years. Psychoanalyst Helene Deutsch, for example, claimed that lynching was spurred on by white women's rape fantasies and their subsequent false reports of rape. For a discussion of this and related issues, see Giddings 1984, 207.

27. According to Patterson, most of these acts were "noncriminal and protopolitical; Afro-Americans were defending either themselves or the honor

of their wives and members of their families, or they had simply had enough of the outrages against them and had exploded in psychologically healthy rage against their torturers and persecutors." Patterson goes on to ask why lynching has not been interpreted as retaliation against black men for their assaults on white men. He believes that a major reason is that some did not want to acknowledge that black men actually were guilty of anything, and others did not want to acknowledge that black men were formidable opponents of white men. Some African Americans in the 1890s did see things in the way that Patterson describes. Novelist Pauline Hopkins is a case in point: "Lynching was instituted to crush the manhood of the enfranchised black. Rape is a crime which appeals most strongly to the heart of the home life. . . . No; it is not rape. If the Negro votes, he is shot; if he marries a white woman, he is shot . . . or lynched—he is a pariah whom the National Government cannot defend. But if he defends himself and his home, then is heard the tread of marching feet as the Federal troops move southward to quell a 'race riot.'" This passage comes from Hopkins' *Contending Forces: A Romance Illustrative of Negro Life North and South,* published in 1900; I have taken it from Carby 1985, 275. Even Booker T. Washington pointed up the fact that lynchings often had nothing to do with accusations of rape. See his 1904 letter to the editor of the Birmingham *Age-Herald,* "A Protest Against Lynching" and his 1908 statement in the aftermath of the Springfield, Illinois, race riots, both reprinted in Wintz 1996, 52–53 and 66–68.

28. Wells, quoted in McMurry, 1998, 143. For more discussion of Wells's position, see Carby 1985, 268–70. Patricia Hill Collins agrees with Wells's assessment of lynching, but she critiques Wells's relative silence on rape, which Collins views as part of the same apparatus of oppression. See Collins 2005, 223.

29. For some discussion of economic versus political accounts of lynchings' motivations, see Lott 1999, chapter 3, "Frederick Douglass on the Myth of the Black Rapist," reprinted in *Frederick Douglass: A Critical Reader,* ed. Bill E. Lawson and Frank M. Kirkland (Oxford: Blackwell, 1999): 313–38. See also A. Philip Randolph's 1919 article in *The Messenger,* "Lynching: Capitalism Its Cause; Socialism Its Cure," reprinted in Wintz 1996, 253–59.

30. George Lipsitz recounts the 1944 lynching of Isaac Simmons in Amite County, Mississippi. Simmons owned a 295-acre farm beneath which, it was rumored, lay an oil field. Whites attempted to force Simmons to sell them the property, but he refused and engaged an attorney. Six white vigilantes then attacked the 66-year-old Simmons and his son Eldridge. They forced Eldridge Simmons to watch as they shot his father to death and mutilated his body. They knocked out all Simmons' teeth with a baseball bat and cut out his tongue for being what they called a "smart nigger." See Lipsitz 1998, 163.

31. Still, money and property did play a huge role not only in the practice of lynching but also in what Elliott Jaspin terms "racial cleansings" in the same period. Jaspin has studied twelve U.S. counties in which entire black populations were simply driven out and all or most of their land and possessions simply confiscated by whites. In some cases these actions followed upon a charge of rape, but often they did not. They were systematic and calculated. "An attack on a white woman might be a convenient rallying cry, but more

often than not what separated a single lynching from a mass expulsion was economic rivalry" (Jaspin 2007, 215). Compare Jaspin's assertions about the systematic and lucrative nature of the American racial cleansings with Koonz's claims about German citizens' complicity in Jewish expulsions and "relocations" in the 1930s: "Between 1933 and 1938, the combination of SA vigilantes and SS racial detectives appeared to function effectively. About 40 percent of the 562,000 citizens defined as Jewish left Germany. In 1938 over half of the 183,000 Jews living in Austria emigrated" (Koonz 2003, 246). After 1935, Nazis confiscated "between 75,000 and 80,000 businesses owned by Jews" (2003, 191). Property and possessions were seized in raids and sold. Non-Jews "'purchased' Jews' property for as little as 10 percent of its market value" (2003, 271). Compare also what George Lipsitz has to say about Californians' attempt in the 1990s to undercut the political power of undocumented Mexican workers in order to make them more vulnerable to economic exploitation (Lipsitz 1998, 48–49).

32. Historian Grace Hale notes that Matthew Williams was not only murdered by a mob in 1931, but his skin was tanned and made into shoes (Hale 1998, 229). Hale argues that lynching was a modern ritual of consumer society, combining expression of fears about the homogenization of races in consumer culture and producing commercialized mass spectacles for white-only consumption.

33. Robyn Wiegman makes a similar point, as does Patricia Hill Collins. See Wiegman 2001, 350, 354, and Collins 2005, 218.

34. Compare sociologist Gail Mason's comment about anti-homosexual assault: "The collective legacy of homophobia-related violence is found, not only in the harm and injury it inflicts on many individuals, nor in the personal and social veiling of a 'wayward' or 'unruly' population, but, moreover, in the capacity to incite this population to manage the equivocal and contested nexus between homosexuality and visibility, when the very troubled nature of that nexus is itself the source of much uncertainty and tension" (Mason 2002, 95). Violence directed against any socially defined group over time disciplines group members' behavior and results in self-policing.

35. As Hazel Carby has put it, "Emancipation meant that white men lost their vested interests in the body of the Negro and . . . lynching and the rape of black women were attempts to regain control" (Carby 1985, 269).

36. Of the 4,951 people that Walter White reports were lynched in the United States between 1882 and 1927, 1,438 were not African American. Many of them were white (or at least people we would now consider white), but quite a number were foreign nationals. Lynching became a real embarrassment for the United States, as countries around the world demanded indemnity payments from the federal government for their citizens who were lynched on U.S. soil. White reports that between 1887 and 1903 the U.S. government had to pay $480,499.90 to foreign governments, including China, Italy, Great Britain, and Mexico (1969, 207).

37. Hazel Carby writes: "The North conceded to the South's argument that rape was the cause of lynching; the concession to lynching for a specific crime in turn conceded the right to lynch any black male for any crime: the charge of rape became the excuse for murder. The press acted as accomplices in the

ideological work that disguised the lesson of political and economic subordination which the black community was being taught" (1985, 269).

38. Some officials, such as Charles Henry Smith, went so far as to call for complete disenfranchisement and a separate penal code for blacks, whose criminal behavior he claimed was the obvious reason for lynching (Fredrickson 1971, 273).

39. Daniel 1893, 291. Daniel discusses Lydston's views at length. He also cites William Hammond and Orpheus Everts as advocates of castration for sex offenders and notes that castration to cure epilepsy and insanity are already done on an experimental basis in many asylums. Daniel waffles on the question of whether to castrate (or de-sex) female sex offenders, but he suggests it as a possibility.

40. Both of these laws were rescinded within five years after going into effect. Sterilizations continued across the country but happened far more often in lunatic asylums and colonies for the epileptic and feebleminded than in prisons and thus were not considered punishment (Brunius 2006, 211, 218).

41. In a discussion of recidivism—not limited to black offenders or to sex offenders—Duncan McKim writes, "Is it surprising that the common people resort to lynching murderers when the law is incapable of dealing with such terrors to the community as this?" (1901, 273–74). Lynching was frequently characterized as a rational response to a failure of law enforcement, thus justifying calls for more law enforcement.

42. Consider this passage from Patricia Hill Collins: "African American men's experiences with the criminal justice system may signal a convergence of institutionalized rape and institutionalized murder (lynching) as state-sanctioned forms of sexual violence. Since 1980, a growing prison-industrial complex has incarcerated large numbers of African American men. Whatever measures are used—rates of arrest, conviction, jail time, parole, or types of crime—the record seems clear that African American men are more likely than White American men to encounter the criminal justice system. For example, in 1990, the nonprofit Washington, D.C.–based Sentencing Project released a survey result suggesting that, on an average day in the United States, one in every four African American men aged 20 to 29 was either in prison, in jail, or on probation/parole. Practices such as unprovoked police brutality against Black male citizens, many of whom die in police custody, and the disproportionate application of the death penalty to African American men certainly suggest that the state itself has assumed the functions of lynching" (Collins 2005, 233).

43. Not only does that ubiquitous image hurt black men's chances of gaining employment and social status and of beating false accusations of crime, but it also does serious harm to black families and couples. For a discussion of the damage done to intimate relationships between black men and black women by the image of black men as sexual predators, see Collins 2005, 162.

44. Tommy Lott insists on analyzing campaigns against black male and black female sexuality together for this reason (Lott 1999, 33–35).

45. For a discussion of studies of cretins and their link to the history of sexuality, see S. Gilman 1985, 192–3.

46. Quoted in S. Gilman 1985, 193. By the early twentieth century cretinism was recognized as a physical condition. In 1913 Martin Barr notes that

studies indicate some sort of thyroid problem as the likely cause, and injection of thyroid extracts as a promising treatment (Barr 1913, chap. 8).

47. Martin Barr asserts that in all idiots and imbeciles the penis and prepuce are always large, although ovaries are generally undersized (1913, 126).

48. For a discussion of the writings of Isaac Newton Kerlin on the menace of the moral imbecile, see Trent 1994, 84–88.

49. Similar events were occurring in England, where progressive thinkers such as sexologist Havelock Ellis were calling for eugenic measures against the feebleminded and warning of their predatory proclivities. In a pamphlet first issued in 1911 and reprinted many times, Ellis wrote, "But it is not only in themselves that the feebleminded are a burden on the present generation and a menace to future generations. They are seen to be even a more serious danger when we realize that in large measure they form the reservoir from which the predatory classes are recruited" (Ellis 1926, 28).

50. That is, as distinct from crime or impoverishment; in other words, they should not be put in almshouses or jails. Optimally, they should be put in "colonies," institutional farms where they would live under constant surveillance for the rest of their lives. Weak-minded individuals who committed misdemeanors were to be placed in special "misdemeanant" colonies apart from other prisoners, and they were to remain there indefinitely, regardless of the nature of their crime.

51. Quoted in Kline 1997, 40. Kline points out that Terman was concerned primarily with female sexuality, as evidenced by the fact that he does not say people should be locked up for life. In fact, many women were institutionalized for thirty or forty years and then simply expelled at menopause to face an unfamiliar world without family, friends, or financial support.

52. Kline (1997, 44) offers an extended discussion of Terman and Lucas's 1918 book *Surveys in Mental Deviation*. She also points out that once a test for syphilis (the Wasserman Test) became available in 1910, routine admissions tests in Terman's own institution, the Sonoma State Hospital for the Feeble-Minded, revealed that only 4 percent of the women admitted were infected. But as in the anti-lynching crusade, empirical evidence that their hypotheses were wrong seemed to make no difference to the officials and scientists making the claims.

53. This is Harry Laughlin's estimate, but the idea that 10 percent of the white population was defective is commonplace in eugenics literature. See Kuhl 1994, 18.

54. With a grant from the men's fellowship of Saint Paul's Episcopal Church, they also tested Richmond prostitutes on the street and found similar rates of feeblemindedness. One wonders what prompted the men of Saint Paul's to finance this study.

55. In fact, however, to the extent that incarceration was seen as "charity" or "care," blacks were typically excluded. Most institutions were racially segregated, with wards for blacks and other nonwhites usually smaller and less well equipped. In the Deep South many institutions simply did not admit blacks, and many states had no separate facilities for them. So it seems unlikely that these reformers actually believed their full plan would ever be realized. Some historians have argued that the incarceration movement of the early twentieth

century was really just a front for the incipient sterilization movement. The idea was to convince the general public that there was a problem—sexual excess—and to propose institutionalization as a remedy. But institutionalization was bound to fail because of the high cost of lifelong maintenance, so sterilization and parole would be the compromise. In fact, of course, it was. Whether or not most advocates of incarceration entered into this negotiation with sterilization and parole as their real goal is open to debate. But they surely must have realized that what they were proposing would at the very least have created a tremendous redistribution of the labor force, bringing the vast majority of unskilled laborers under the direct control of the state and unavailable for private employment except with the state as an intermediary. Perhaps it should be noted here that this movement to institutionalize a huge percentage of the U.S. manual labor force coincides with aggressive federal, state, and corporate attempts to break up labor unions.

56. Paula Giddings notes that lynching decreased in the 1940s for economic reasons also. She quotes Jessie Daniel Ames: "We have managed to reduce lynchings not because we've grown more law-abiding or respectable but because lynchings became such bad advertising. The South is going after big industry at the moment, and a lawless, lynch-mob population isn't going to attract very much outside capital" (Giddings 1984, 239). Local officials somehow found the resources and wherewithal to suppress lynching when their financial investments were at stake. Much the same scenario would play out in Birmingham in the 1960s when local financial stakeholders such as real estate executive Sidney Smyer realized they could not attract foreign business interests to the city as long as the city resisted integration (Eskew 1997, 170).

57. Although he does not give the kind of analysis I offer here, Robert L. Zangrando notes that the NAACP began rethinking its definition of lynching in the 1930s (1980, 132). Lynchings were not such public spectacles anymore; they had begun to resemble gang murders and thus were harder to distinguish from violence that was not apparently racially motivated. However, the distinction between lynching and other forms of murder was always contested, and it shifted several times over the history of the anti-lynching crusade. See Waldrep 2000.

58. See, for example, Foucault 1978, 149. This prioritization of sexuality over race is one that Brady Heiner has also noted and for which he has criticized Foucault: "The *1976 Lectures* also disclose two historical facts that it is important to point out. First, they demonstrate that Foucault initially developed his theory of biopolitics in the context of an analysis of 'the discourse of race struggle' and a critique of State racism—discussions which themselves arose within the horizon of a self-reflexive critique of genealogical discourse. Secondly, given that the final lecture of the *1976 Lectures* (delivered in March 1976) served as the basis from which Foucault produced the first published version of his account of biopolitics (published October 1976), the former allows us to see that in the latter Foucault erases every reference to race and racism, replacing them instead with the concepts of sex and the so-called 'deployment of sexuality'" (Heiner 2007, 336).

59. For the 1700 date, see, e.g., Engelhardt 1974, 235; for the 1710 date, see, e.g., Fishman 1982, 282, n. 16, and Mosse 1985, 12; for the 1715 date,

see Stengers and Van Neck, 2001, 37. Laqueur 2003, 13, says "in or around 1712" but acknowledges that no one knows for sure and so his choice of dates is just splitting the difference between different sources (179).

60. Tissot asserted that the author was a clergyman named Bekker. Most sources say the author is unknown. But Laqueur claims to have discovered the real author and presents evidence for its having been one John Marten, a sometime pornographer and surgeon known to have dispensed what Laqueur refers to as "quack" medicines (Laqueur 2003, 32).

61. The word *onanism* as a synonym for masturbation appears only in 1719 (Stengers and Van Neck, 2001, 53).

62. This is a condition in which the foreskin becomes so tight that it cannot slide back to allow the penis to become erect. Presumably, that would be painful.

63. Slow, painful urination.

64. According to Laqueur 2003, 15, this is a "white vaginal flux."

65. See Hare 1962, 2. For details about the content of the advertisement and some quotations from it, see Stengers and Van Neck 2001, 41, and Laqueur 2003, esp. 26–32.

66. Laqueur (2003, 26) says that twelve shillings was more than two weeks' wages for the average footman; curing the ills caused by masturbation became a very lucrative business.

67. One reason for all the reprinting was the fact that each new edition contained new letters from customers and replies to them, so that the publication began to resemble a magazine full of prurient details about both illness and sexual practices. No doubt many people bought every edition to read the latest correspondence. See Stengers and Van Neck 2001, 46; also Laqueur 2003, 27.

68. Here I rely on the scholarship of E.H. Hare, 1962, 2.

69. For detailed documentation of his influence, see Stengers and Van Neck 2001, chap. 6, "Tissot's Triumph."

70. This shift was occurring at the same time in European countries as well. An editorial in the British medical journal *The Lancet* makes the point very succinctly: "We are responsible for the employment of our peculiar authority in promoting the purification and well-being of human society" (quoted in Mosse 1982, 226).

71. The YMCA was founded in the 1850s by Protestant evangelicals, among them Anthony Comstock, the Connecticut moral purity crusader after whom the infamous Comstock Law against pornography was named. YMCA leaders did not become interested in physical fitness until the early 1880s, when they began to see it as an antidote to all forms of degeneracy (Edsall 2003, 144).

72. According to Elof Carlson, castration was used to treat masturbation for the first time in the United States by Dr. Joseph Crosby of New Hampshire in 1843 (E. A. Carlson, 2001, 30). Clitoridectomy was used from about 1858, Carlson writes, and in 1894 Dr. A. J. Bloch performed the surgery on a two-and-a-half-year-old girl, as he reports in the *Transactions of the Louisiana Medical Society* (2001, 31).

73. Hare notes that potassium bromide, which causes impotence, was often

prescribed to stop masturbation in epileptics, masturbation being believed to be the cause of their seizures. The drug did, in fact, reduce the number and severity of seizures in many patients, which was taken as further evidence for the idea that masturbation was their epilepsy's cause (Hare 1962, 18).

74. In an article in the journal *Technology and Culture,* Vern Bullough lists twenty U.S. patents for devices to prevent masturbation (Bullough 1987, 832, and yes, there are pictures). Presumably Bullough was counting patents on devices for preventing masturbation in human beings. One Web site asserts that between 1856 and 1919 the U.S. Patent Office issued a total of 49 patents for anti-masturbation devices, thirty-five of which were designed to prevent masturbation in horses, an equinian tidbit that raises many more questions than it answers. I very much wanted clarification, but given the Bush administration's broad citizen surveillance program and what turned up on my first Internet search, prudence dictated that I not venture far in that direction. There is a brief description of a stallion masturbating in Rosse 1892, 799, which suggests that one might not want one's horse to masturbate because it could prevent him (or her?) from winning races. Stengers and Van Neck (2001) discuss some devices for sale in Europe and provide a few pictures.

75. Stoler suggests that this was particularly important in colonies where European children had more contact with nonwhite servants than with other Europeans and that the discourse really focused more on women servants and native mothers than on children (Stoler 1995, 18). However, it is easy to see in U.S. medical literature that physicians and other officials were at least as concerned about policing American servants and mothers as they were about controlling childhood sexuality. One could say, conceivably, that the United States still was in many respects a colonial settlement in the nineteenth century, but I think perhaps Stoler simply underplays the degree to which regulating masturbation and childhood sexuality was always about regulating the behavior of mothers and other caretakers. After all, Foucault says very clearly that the war on masturbation enabled authorities to make inroads into the family and household. Diderot warns French parents to watch their domestics, lest they teach children to masturbate (Stengers and Van Neck 2001, 81). Freud himself warns of European caretakers masturbating their charges (1931, 232–33). Given the fact that before the seventeenth century it was commonplace for servants and parents to fondle their children's naked genitals openly, no doubt many people not yet fully initiated into the new fear of masturbation did still use this strategy to amuse or quiet children in their care. For example, see Ariès 1962, 100–101. We might speculate that those who lagged behind in the new mores were likely to be members of the lower social classes, classes from which were drawn many servants.

76. Howe is adamant about this. He suggests not only talking to children openly but also giving them books on the subject. He exhorts parents not to be squeamish where so much is at stake. See Howe 1972 [1848], 31–33.

77. Even contemporaries noted that their strategies did have the opposite effect. See Stengers and Van Neck 2001, 99.

78. For a discussion of Tissot's account of the humors, see Stengers and Van Neck 2001, 69–74.

79. In fact, virtually all the physicians who wrote about these issues spoke often and uncritically of intercourse outside marriage. They seemed to expect

healthy young men to seek out prostitutes and to have sexual relations with numerous female partners.

80. Beard 1972b [1898], 123. For an assessment of Beard's influence in the history of psychiatry, see Rosenberg 1962.

81. Tissot believed that some of the loss was offset in coition by the absorption of the partner's perspiration. A century later, the benefit was not through perspiration but through the exchange of magnetic current thought to occur through two bodies at orgasm (Stengers and Van Neck 2001, 109). In women, masturbation was also dangerous because it did not allow for the prophylactic effect of semen; some physicians believed semen deposited in the vagina helped protect women from various diseases that could be caused by sexual excitement (Gibson 1997, 117).

82. Hence the widespread belief that avid readers developed weak eyes, or Dr. William Hammond's claims that too much study led to imbecility or insanity and that hard physical labor made children puny and feeble (Hammond 1974 [1887], 94).

83. Foucault argues convincingly that this became its primary task. Those whose status, wealth, and political clout depended on maintaining and enlarging the powerful positions that the war on masturbation gave them were not about to acknowledge its futility or irrelevance and to declare an end to hostilities; their interests lay not in achieving the goal, and certainly not in abandoning it, but in making sure it was continually reinvoked and yet forever unobtainable. A similar pattern is evident in the FBI's war on sex criminals and communists in the twentieth century (which gave J. Edgar Hoover far-reaching authority to manipulate the lives of Americans across the political and socioeconomic spectrum) and in George Bush's and Dick Cheney's war on terrorism in the twenty-first (which has enabled them to effect a massive redistribution of wealth through noncompetitive war contracts with private corporations, many of which they and their associates profit from directly, and to raise the value of the oil they own worldwide).

84. Pedagogue C. G. Salzmann advised, "As far as is possible never let the children under your care work or play without being watched" (quoted in Laqueur 2003, 229). This advice is typical, but it represents a huge change in child rearing practices from previous centuries.

85. As is so often the case, Dr. William Lee Howard of Baltimore says it most forcefully: "The female who prefers the laboratory to the nursery; the mother quick with child who spends her mornings at the club, discussing 'social statics,' visiting the saloons and tenements in the afternoon, distributing, with an innocence in strange contrast to her assumptions, political tracts asking the denizens to vote her ticket, is a sad form of degeneracy. Such females are true degenerates, because they are unphysiological in their physical incompleteness. The progeny of such human misfits are perverts, moral or psychical. Their prenatal life has been influenced by the very antithesis of what the real woman would surround her expected child with" (Howard 1900, 687). Howard goes on and on in this vein. He labels these women "androids" and "hysterics" and suggests that their blasphemies radiate from the "portals of their money-making mosques," thus apparently de-Christianizing them and aligning them with an imagined form of materialistic Islam.

86. Too often the nuances of Victorian thinking about feminine sexuality

go unheeded. Krafft-Ebing, for example, writes, "Woman, however, if physically and mentally normal, and properly educated, has but little sensual desire" (Krafft-Ebing 1965, 8). Note that this low level of sensual desire is very qualified and is not presumed to be entirely natural.

87. Thus was nymphomania an ever-present threat to feminine health and propriety. For a feminist analysis of the medical concept of nymphomania, see Groneman 1995.

88. According to anatomist George Ludwig Kobelt, if an unawakened woman's clitoris became erect, she would not connect her physical state with anything sexual. She would only have "a dim premonition"; "an external stimulating effect" would be necessary for her to take conscious notice of this physiological state of excitation, because "simple arterial congestion cannot bring about the required intensity of internal blood pressure on the nerve content of the *glans clitoridis*." And a good thing, too, Kobelt adds. "In the interest of the individual and species life, [simple congestion] would not be allowed to bring it about" (Kobelt 1841, in Lowery 1978, 37). One is left to wonder what horrible things would happen to the woman and to the human species if she could recognize and focus her own sexual arousal without the aid of an external stimulating effect! Putting that issue aside, however, it is important to note that Kobelt held the clitoris and the system of tissues connected to it to be an organ whose purpose was nothing other than "the sensation of sexual pleasure" (Lowery 1978, 38). How "Victorian" is that?

89. Quoted in Lindsay 1998, 547. This view was still quite current thirty years later when physician William Robinson wrote: "Sexual impotence is not hereditary, but impotence in the male either so complete that he cannot perform the act or consisting only in premature ejaculations (relative impotence or sexual insufficiency) should constitute a bar to marriage. This impotence may not interfere with impregnation; the wife may have children and the children will not be in any way defective, but the wife herself, unless she is completely frigid, will suffer great tortures, and may quickly become a sexual neurasthenic, a nervous wreck, or she may develop a mental disorder. Any man suffering with impotence should have himself treated before marriage until he is cured; if his impotence is incurable, then for his own sake and for the sake of the girl or woman he is supposed to love he should give up the idea of marriage. The only permissible exception is in cases in which the prospective wife knows the nature of her prospective husband's trouble, and claims that she does not care for gross sexual relations and therefore does not mind the impotence. In case the wife is absolutely *frigid,* the marriage may turn out satisfactory. But I would always have my misgivings, and should the wife's apparently absent but in reality only dormant libido suddenly awaken there would be trouble for both husband and wife. It is therefore necessary to emphasize: in all cases of impotence—caution!" (Robinson 1917, 197–98).

90. Nineteenth-century commentators almost invariably assumed that women became prostitutes as a result of lust. Prostitution was closely associated with nymphomania. But nymphomania, like masturbation, both enervated people and left them even more lustful than before, so they had to seek out ever more exotic forms of stimulation. Hence, prostitutes often became lesbians.

91. References to the dangers of the treadle sewing machine—which had

to be peddled to make operate and thus supposedly stimulated the genitals of the operator—abound in the literature, along with discussion of working-class female sexuality in general. See, for example, Krafft-Ebing 1965, 407. For a brief discussion of the subject, see Gibson 1997, 120.

92. Although some physicians preferred infibulation, which is burying the clitoris under the labia by suturing the latter together. Paul Broca recommended this procedure in 1864 after performing it on a five-year-old girl. But his colleagues debated the efficacy, some averring that means would still be found to stimulate the organ if it were not excised entirely. For some of this debate, see Stengers and Van Neck 2001, 111–14.

93. Both of these cases and many others just as entertaining can be found in Hammond 1974 [1887]. The engineer's case is in chapter 1, and the minister's case is in chapter 2.

94. For a history of this change, see Hare 1962, 8–9.

95. Sander L. Gilman points out that George Beard's list of the symptoms of neurasthenia parallels Voltaire's list of the results of masturbation. He writes, "Masturbatory insanity, insanity *ex onania,* has evolved into neurasthenia" (Gilman, 1985, 200).

96. In this claim, Beard echoed his German predecessors, Johann Ludwig Casper, who wrote about the dangers of masturbation and its homosexual consequences in the 1850s, and before him, Heinrich Kaan in the 1840s. The difference is that Beard's work in the 1880s is concurrent with the rise of the homosexual as what Foucault calls "a personage." For a discussion of Casper and Kaan, see Hekma 1994, 215–17.

97. Men and women who cross-dressed habitually and/or passed as members of the "opposite" sex were usually diagnosed as insane and often committed to lunatic asylums on no other grounds. Kiernan reported on several such cases of women (Kiernan 1884). His favorite case seems to be that of "Joe," who is treated at length in 1884, shows up in other articles by Kiernan over the years, and can also be found cited repeatedly in the writings of other sexologists of the period. Joe was a woman in Pennsylvania who passed as a man and married another woman. Joe was classified as a nymphomaniac and committed to an asylum.

98. Although instead of emphasizing the masculinity of the females, commentators usually emphasized the effeminacy of the males. (See Magubane 2003, 108–10, and McClintock 1995, 52–55, but scattered throughout, for discussions of the feminization of African males in colonial literature and anthropology.) Either way, though, the effect was less difference between the sexes than existed among middle- and upper-class white Europeans and North Americans. For an extended discussion of the allegation of effeminacy among German Jews, see Mosse 1985, 143–46.

99. Kiernan 1888, 129. Kiernan repeats his argument from 1888 and elaborates on it to explain hermaphroditism as well as sexual inversion in 1892 (Kiernan 1892, 194–95). Krafft-Ebing reiterates this principle as late as the 12th edition of *Psychopathia Sexualis,* published in 1903: "This differentiation of the sexes and the development of sexual types is evidently the result of an infinite succession of intermediary stages of evolution. The primary stage was undoubtedly bi-sexuality, such as still exists in the lowest classes of animal

life and also during the first months of foetal existence in man" (Krafft-Ebing, 1965, 28).

100. Belief that homosexuality is the result of over-stimulation of the sexual imagination, if not the sexual organs, persists. In a 2004 article in *Essence* magazine, Taigi Smith explains the supposed increase in homosexuality among African American men at the turn of the twenty-first century as a result of overexposure to sex:

> Why *now* does it seem that so many more Black men are secretly choosing to have sex with other men? Part of the answer has to do with the oversexualization of American culture in general. Today any child old enough to reach for the remote can be bombarded with sexual images of video girls shaking their booties, showing us their boobs or otherwise displaying sex set to music. . . . By the time a boy reaches 18, he is already desensitized to both the sexual act and the feelings of women. It's no wonder that as our men become sexually desensitized, it takes more to stimulate them physically. (How many times can you watch a thrusting pelvis before it stops having any meaning?) They start to crave sex that may be a bit more risky and a lot more lewd as the ante is upped on what will satisfy them. (T. Smith 2004, 150)

As Keith Boykin has pointed out, there is no reason to assume that there *is* more homosexuality among black men than ever before; there is just increased attention to black male bisexuality as the media try to account for apparently increasing rates of HIV among black women (Boykin 2005). In fact, he casts doubt not only on the idea that increases in black female HIV infection rates are the result of sex with bisexual black men but even on the idea that there really is a significant increase in the HIV infection rate among black women who are not intravenous drug users. He goes on to argue for increased acceptance of homosexuality in black communities and more openness about sexual behavior in general and for increased attention to HIV/AIDS among black gay men, prison inmates, and drug users. But regardless of any change in the frequency of homosexuality among black men in recent years, Smith's etiology is as old as the concept of homosexuality itself.

101. Although oddly reminiscent of early 1970s warnings that smoking marijuana drives people to inject themselves with heroine.

102. Stengers and Van Neck do not mention oral sex, but one of the first examples they give of the debilitating effects of masturbation is a peasant woman who has lost her nose and most of her lips and mouth from the foul practice. I would speculate that contemporaries would have assumed she was engaging in oral sex (Stengers and Van Neck 2001, 7). G. Stanley Hall tells a similar story in his autobiography. He says his father once warned him against masturbation by describing a young man who abused himself and went with prostitutes and as a result lost his nose and became an idiot (Moran 2000, 3).

103. Not those engaging in mutual masturbation or oral sex with opposite-sex partners, of course. But it is clear in the medical literature that everyone assumed that most people who engaged in masturbation with others did so with others of the same sex—personal servants, other children in same-sex school settings, for example. It is unusual to see any discussion of "hetero-

sexual" mutual masturbation or oral sex until the marriage manuals of the 1920s—in other words, *after* masturbation's definition has been narrowed.

104. This argument has been revived by biologist Simon LeVay (1993).

105. For a discussion of lesbian brains, see Gibson 1998. One dissenter was Charles Ford, who in 1929 argued that many lesbians were feebleminded. As Gibson notes, Ford was obviously arguing against the received view.

106. This example comes from Gibson 1998, who cites the work of Douglas McMurtrie. Writing in 1914, McMurtrie compared a lesbian who murdered her husband to a Chinese man.

107. The meanings of these two terms are somewhat unstable over the course of the nineteenth and twentieth centuries. *Erotomania* was first described by Etienne Esquirol in 1838: "It is a chronic cerebral affection, characterized by an excessive love, be it for a known object or an imaginary one. In this disorder, only the imagination is damaged: the understanding is at fault. It is a mental illness in which amorous ideas are fixed and dominant." According to Bridget Aldaraca, Esquirol characterized erotomania as a purely mental illness in contrast to nymphomania, or *furor uterinus,* a behavioral disorder attributable to lesions on the reproductive organs (Aldaraca 1995, 208). Later on, Freud claimed that erotomania was a defense against repressed and latent lesbianism, while Emil Kraepelin held it to be a specifically female type of paranoid delusion of grandeur (Aldaraca 1995, 209). Erotomania was revived as a diagnostic category in the DSM-III-R in 1987, just in time to be used to discredit the testimony of Anita Hill against Supreme Court nominee Clarence Thomas in 1992 (Aldaraca 1995, 210–15).

Although never a diagnostic category in the DSM series, *nymphomania* had a long career as an explanation of everything from prostitution to lesbianism through the late nineteenth and early twentieth centuries. Women who were driven to seek more and more sexual stimulation by the demands of a presumably diseased uterus or ovaries eventually would also seek more and more unusual forms of stimulation. James Kiernan quite matter-of-factly states that he treats lesbianism as nymphomania (Kiernan 1884, 484). For a discussion of the frequent connection drawn between prostitution and lesbianism from 1840 to 1940, see H. L. Miller 2000.

108. Merl Storr points out that in this passage Krafft-Ebing basically undercuts his own distinction between congenital and acquired inversion. His analysis provides no way to tell the difference in most women (Storr 1998, 20).

109. Again, I refer the reader to Gibson's study of the history of appraisals of lesbian brains and to Douglas McMurtrie's 1914 case study of a lesbian murderer. Gibson writes: "Instead of simply constructing a lesbian brain that was similar to a male brain, doctors depicted a lesbian brain with characteristics similar to a nonwhite, or lower-class masculine brain." She then quotes McMurtrie's case study as follows: "She [the invert] also had male physiognomical traits, her face being long, with a strong jaw, the upper lip thin and greenish. She had high cheek bones, a high but retreating forehead (stenocrotaphia); taken altogether, a face which reminded one of a Chinese" (Gibson 1998, 5).

110. There was apparently some suggestion of lynching her; see Katz 1983, 226.

111. Tramps were a constant preoccupation for many American sexologists,

probably in great part because of John Addington Symmonds's "partici-
pant observer" report on homosexuality among tramps that Havelock Ellis
published as Appendix B in *Sexual Inversion* in 1897 (Ellis and Symmonds
1975, 252–57). Symmonds lived as a tramp for eight months. He estimated
that about 10 percent practiced "unnatural intercourse," usually by seducing
impoverished boys away from their homes. Queer tramps, then, also recruit,
and they recruit boys into both homosexuality and the life of the tramp, a
double whammy.

112. Boag 2003, 181, 198. In that same year there was a scandal in
Philadelphia's most affluent Episcopal parish, St. Mary's, where the rector,
Alfred Garnett Mortimer, was dismissed and defrocked, as were several of his
curates in the first weeks of 1913. According to Loughery (1998, 13), "The
bishop refused to discuss the case, despite a public outcry for information, but
rumors about a homosexual ring at St. Mary's were widespread."

113. Terry 1999, 270. See also John Loughery, who discusses both the New
York crackdown and similar measures taken in Atlantic City, San Francisco,
and Los Angeles (1998, 58–61).

114. These names come from Terry 1995, 138. Terman had already made
a name for himself as an advocate of sterilization and a foe of the imbecilic
whore. Earnest Hooten is notable as one of the Harvard professors who participated in Harvard's "secret court," which expelled or drove to suicide several
homosexual members of the Harvard classes of 1920 and 1921 (W. Wright
2005). I thank Ivan Round for bringing this book to my attention.

115. He also describes them verbally: "The *external genitals* are large, with
the special hypertrophies of various parts that accompany frequent, vigorous sexual stimulation and activity. The labia minora protrude particularly
often, and the surface of the glans clitoris is long from front to rear, with three
times as many large glans as in general groups. The prepuce is considerably
hypertrophied, two or three times as often as is to be expected. Only autoeroticism and homosexuality produce these results" (Dickinson, Appendix VI, in
Henry 1941, 1098). This description is very similar to earlier anthropological
descriptions of the genitals of African women and of European prostitutes. But
nothing can convey the tenor of this work better than the pages and pages of
pictures. This is a book you have to see to believe. And even then. . . .

116. John Loughery discusses a number of these sensationalized sex crimes
in the 1930s (1998, 108–110).

117. This is from *Newsweek*'s October 10, 1949, issue, in an article entitled
"Queer People." The article, which is actually a review of J. Paul de River's
book *The Sexual Criminal,* appeared in the Medicine section of the magazine.

5. Managing Evolution

1. This tenet was commonly cited in medical literature as a reason for
studying sexuality and as a justification for treating sexual perversion. For
example, Dr. William Lee Howard writes, "Every physician should understand
the sexual side of life, for it is sexual activity that governs life, permits the continuation of the species and promotes crime and its causes. It is the basis of all
society, whether it be that of the Australian Kurnai, or that of the Anglo-Saxon
home" (Howard 1904, 14).

2. Of course, as Foucault points out in *"Society Must Be Defended,"* the French had to do some fancy story-telling of their own to make this idea seem plausible. In 1899 William Ripley claimed that the French state comprised at least three distinct, if ideal, racial types: the Mediterranean, the Alpine, and the Teutonic. But certainly nowhere was homogeneity of a population less in evidence than it was in the United States.

3. At the Second International Congress of Eugenics, Henry Fairfield Osborn asserted that nearly half of the Nordic race was to be found in the United States by 1921 (Osborn 1921, 312). Such declarations make it sound as though the migration of the peoples of northwest Europe to North America and their conquest of the indigenous peoples was a biological process like growth and maturation, which is exactly what twentieth-century eugenicists thought it was.

4. Foucault discusses both of these levels in contrast to one another in *Security, Territory, Population* (2007, chap. 3).

5. In *The Journal of Mental and Nervous Disease,* Dr. Irving Rosse offers a long list of personal observations of sexual perversity among "lower races," beginning with incidents of bestiality among the French, the Chinese, and American Negroes, and continuing with descriptions of Negro homosexuals in Washington, D.C. Of the latter he adds, "The same race, a few years ago, had one or more gangs that practiced a kind of phallic worship. An informant, who has made a study of scatological rites among lower races, described to me how a big buck, with turgescent penis, decorated with gaily colored ribbon, stood and allowed his comrades to caress and even osculate the member" (Rosse 1892, 802). Havelock Ellis maintains that lesbian sexual activity was quite common among "negroes and mulattos of the French Creole countries" (quoted in Gibson 1997, 121) and asserts that "among lower races homosexual practices are regarded with considerable indifference. . . . Even in Europe today a considerable lack of repugnance to homosexual practices may be found among the lower classes" (Ellis and Symmonds 1975 [1897], 5). William Hammond had already identified homosexuality among the Zuni in 1887 (Hammond 1974 [1887], 163–64). James Kiernan discusses Hammond's work and notes that homosexuality was common among the Aryan, Shemite, and Cushite peoples of long ago but that we find only repugnance to the practice among the ancient Teutonic tribes (Kiernan 1892, 185–86). In 1914 Charles McCord asserted that "sodomy is very rare [among black males] except within prison walls or in isolated camps." But among black females homosexual acts were common (McCord 1914, 217–18). Discrepancies in these reports seem to have little to do with observation and plenty to do with whether the "expert" in question believed homosexuality to be a form of degeneration (in which case it could only be found among the higher races) or a form of atavism (in which case it would be found more often among the lower races).

6. *White* was the most inclusive term (and usually overlapped referentially with *Caucasian,* a term that sprang from late eighteenth-century anthropology and implied a certain—highly questionable—geographical origin). So for all scientific race theorists of the turn of the twentieth century, an all-white human race would be better than what then obtained. However, depending on the situation or self-identification of each given writer, "better still" might have meant a more Nordic human race or a more Anglo-Saxon human race or, in Germany,

for example, a more Aryan human race. These terms were not coextensive with *white* or *Caucasian* but were much more exclusive. Most North American writers would have considered Slavs and Italians white, for example, but would not have considered them members of the most superior race, the Anglo-Saxon. When it came to cultivating the human race to achieve its full potential, scientific race theorists were not going to settle for a race of Slavs or Italians any more than for a race of Jews or Chinese or Negroes. Contemporary debates over whether Italians or Irishmen or Jews were once considered nonwhite in the United States and then became white assume that the term *white* had a great deal more stability (and a great deal more political importance) around 1900 than it actually did. To be deemed eugenically valuable, one needed not just to be white, but to be, say, Nordic. Most theorists classified the Irish, for example, as Celtic in opposition to Anglo-Saxon, and as Alpine in opposition to Nordic. Thus they were inferior, even though white or Caucasian.

7. According to historian Mark Haller, in the mid-1890s the campaigns against the socially unfit and the racially unfit had not yet merged. It was the eugenics movement that would bring these together (Haller 1963, 40).

8. This is Kenneth Ludmerer's list (1972, 95).

9. I say *apparently* race-based because the Chinese apparently were considered (and objected to as) a distinct race and not simply a group with a distinct national origin. The restriction did not bar other Asians—for example, Japanese—although eventually most Asian immigration would be brought to a halt.

10. This was asserted by the eugenicists themselves. See, for example, Popenoe and Johnson 1926, 312–13: "What are the grounds, then, for forbidding the yellow races, or the races of British India, to enter the United States? The considerations urged in the past have been (1) Political: it is said that they are unable to acquire the spirit of American institutions. This is an objection which concerns eugenics only indirectly. (2) Medical: it is said that they introduce diseases, such as the oriental liver, lung and intestinal flukes, which are serious, against which Americans have never been selected, and for which no cure is known. (3) Economic: it is argued that the Oriental's lower standard of living makes it impossible for the white man to compete with him. The objection is well founded, and is indirectly of concern to eugenics, as was pointed out in a preceding section of this chapter. As eugenicists we feel justified in objecting to the immigration of large bodies of unskilled Oriental labor, on the ground that they rear larger families than our stock on the same small incomes."

11. William Williams, appointed by President Theodore Roosevelt to serve as commissioner for immigration for the port of New York and its depot Ellis Island from 1902–1905 and 1909–1914, held that "the greatest number of illiterates come to-day from Southern Italy and from Austria, Poland, and Russia." Thus a literacy test "would certainly bar out a large number, perhaps 150,000 to 175,000" (Dowbiggen 1997, 197).

12. See Duster 1990, 12–13. This figure was certainly in accord with Charles Davenport's assessment in his 1911 book *Heredity in Relation to Eugenics.* Davenport held that Jews were the worst possible immigrants because they differed most from the original American stock, by which he

meant people like his own New England Puritan ancestors. Jews were particularly likely to engage in thievery and "offenses against chastity." Thus they, like all feebleminded people, were sexual menaces (Bruinius 2006, 167). Only 40 percent might score low on a test of cognitive endowment, but if morality could be measured, no doubt the Jews would be found to be an entire race of weak-minded people; they were moral imbeciles even if they had high IQs.

13. Laughlin served Congress in this capacity for a full ten years (M. Haller 1963, 155). He had not had a doctorate when he took over the Eugenics Record Office. He had been a high school history teacher in the Midwest. During World War I, when work at the ERO slowed down, Laughlin had moved to Princeton and earned a Ph.D. with a dissertation on growth in onion plants.

14. Laughlin 1939, 47. The Johnson-Reed Act also established the Mexican border patrol. The eugenicists were unable to prevent migration across the Mexican border because Texas planters wanted seasonal labor. The border patrol was a compromise measure. It began with a budget of $1,000,000 and 472 men. Within in five years it employed 875. The border patrol was deemed the first line of defense against an army of aliens (Stern 2005, 74).

15. This remark has been widely quoted; see, e.g., Gossett 1997, 407, and Gould 1981, 232. For a detailed discussion of the congressional debates over the Johnson-Reed Act, see Ludmerer 1972, 103–13.

16. Rosen 2004, 53. Walter Sumner was also very active in the sex education movement in Chicago. He headed the commission that designed the first sex education curriculum for Chicago city schools in 1913 (Moran 2000, 51).

17. This did not always translate into real regulation. Many doctors wrote certificates without doing exams. Ralph Kirwinio got certified and married a woman in the state of Wisconsin after the requirement went into effect despite the fact that he was female (Rosen 2004, 72).

18. Comstock laws—which banned the dissemination of obscene materials—were used to prevent wide dissemination of birth control information well into the twentieth century. Bans on the sale of birth control devices were in force in many states until the 1960s. With the introduction of the mass-produced birth control pill in 1961, pressure mounted to eliminate impediments to this extremely lucrative enterprise. Health problems associated with use of the pill and the fact that no comparable preventative existed for use by men conspired to make voluntary sterilization the most popular method of fertility control among white men and women by the early 1970s. However, many white women were denied sterilization when they requested it. Many physicians would not sterilize white women until the number of children they had borne multiplied by their age equaled 120 (so, for example, a thirty-year-old woman would have to have borne four children to qualify for voluntarily sterilization). In some states, legal bans on voluntary sterilization for middle-class white women were not repealed until the 1970s (Nelson 2003, 74–75).

19. Selden 1999, 9, 32–34. Typically, seven to ten of these contests were held per year (Bruinius 2006, 237). Readers can see photographs of the contest winners on the Web site of the American Philosophical Society at www.amphilsoc.org/library/mole/a/aes.htm.

20. Davenport had advocated these numbers in his famous 1914 address to the Second National Conference on Race Betterment in San Francisco in 1915, entitled "Eugenics as a Religion." For excerpts of the text, see Bruinius 2006, 222. We see them again, for example, Popenoe and Roswell's 1918 college science text, *Applied Eugenics* (1926, 382).

21. Italicized words are the keywords that give answers to the quiz at the end of the chapter in which this statement occurs (Selden 1999, 76). This quotation, given in Selden, is from Hunter 1941, 767.

22. Jordan was a particularly ardent supporter of eugenics. As early as 1898 in his book *Footnotes to Evolution,* he wrote, "The pauper is a victim of heredity, but neither Nature nor Society recognizes that as an excuse for his existence" (E. A. Carlson 2001, 188).

23. In 1926 the prize went to Rev. Phillips Endecott Osgood, rector of St. Mark's in Minneapolis (Rosen 2004, 120–24).

24. For more on Plecker's crusades, see E. Black 2003, 160–82, and Fiske 2004, 14, 17–19. For an analysis of Virginia's Racial Integrity Acts, see Dorr 1999.

25. This phrase was coined in 1901 by Edward A. Ross in his annual address before the American Academy of Political and Social Science in Philadelphia. Said Ross: "For a case like this I can find no words so apt as 'race suicide.' There is no bloodshed, no violence, no assault of the race that waxes upon the race that wanes. The higher race quietly and unmurmuringly eliminates itself rather than endure individually the bitter competition it has failed to ward off by collective action" (Ward 1913, 751).

26. For some discussion of this, see Larson 1995, chap. 4. As one example among many, see Olden 1974.

27. Wendy Kline notes that by 1900 one in five urban women lived on her own, and by 1920 women were nearly 50 percent of the university population. Roosevelt blamed the falling white birth rate on these women and called them race criminals (Kline 1997, 10–11). Paul Popenoe was still furious about the issue in 1926, when he wrote, "If charity begins at home, Birth Control should begin abroad. Continued limitation of offspring in the white race simply invites the black, brown, and yellow races to finish the work already begun by Birth Control, and reduce the whites to a subject race preserved mainly for the sake of its technical skill, as the Greeks were by the Romans" (Popenoe 1926, 144). More on this in chapter 6.

28. Larson (1995, 60) discusses similar commissions in the Deep South— Florida, Georgia, South Carolina, Alabama, Mississippi, and Louisiana—all between 1914 and 1916. Popenoe and Johnson (1926, 167–69) discuss and quote at length from the Pennsylvania report, using it to lend weight to their argument in *Applied Eugenics* for life-long eugenic confinement for this "plague." They conclude their discussion of the Pennsylvania example with these words: "Those who see in improvement of the environment the cure for all such plague spots as these tribes inhabit, overlook the fact that man largely creates his own environment. The story of the tenement-dwellers who were supplied with bath tubs but refused to use them for any other purpose than to store coal, exemplifies a wide range of facts."

29. Mark Haller (1963, 49) says vasectomy was first performed in the

United States in 1899, but Dowbiggin (1997, 77) says the first case report in the United States came from A. J. Ochsner of Chicago in 1897. According to Dowbiggin, although Ochsner actually performed the surgery on two men suffering from prostate trouble, he suggests it be used "to eliminate all habitual criminals from the possibility of having children" and asserts that the operation "could be reasonably suggested for chronic inebriates, imbeciles, perverts, and paupers" (Dowbiggin 1997, 77). Salpingectomy, now more commonly called tubal ligation, was developed by Ochsner at the same time.

30. See Paul 1995, 82, and E. Black 2003, 64. For various benchmark figures of the number of sterilizations he performed, see Black 2003, 65–66.

31. In great part this is thanks to Dr. Paul Lombardo, a University of Virginia bioethicist who researched the case carefully and published his work in the *NYU Law Review* in 1985. For a book-length narrative of the case, see Smith and Nelson 1989.

32. Neither pregnant women nor children under the age of eight were admitted to the colony. Otherwise her foster parents would have had her committed several months earlier.

33. For a description of how this test was administered and details of Emma's and Carrie's responses and scores, see Bruinius 2006, chap. 3.

34. Quoted in Bruinius 2006, 71–72. The ruling was handed down on May 2, 1927. Justice Pierce Butler was the lone dissenter (E. A. Carlson, 2001 254).

35. Wendy Kline reports that at California's Sonoma State Hospital for the Feebleminded, where thousands of sterilizations were performed over a forty-year period, women were a slight majority and were usually sterilized for sexual promiscuity. Very few of these had actually been convicted of any crime. Many were simply described as "passionate." By comparison, Kline notes that of the one hundred case files of men sterilized between 1922 and 1925, only thirty-seven mention sexual tendencies—16 were masturbators, one had exposed himself in public, and ten were passive sodomites; see Kline 1997, 55. Still, 37 percent is a large number. If it is consistent over the history of Sonoma's sterilization program, close to 70 percent of all sterilizations were apparently performed for reasons of so-called sexual deviance. Smith and Nelson (1989, 234) cite G. B. Arnold's 1938 study of the first thousand legal eugenic sterilizations at the Virginia Colony (Carrie Buck being the first), wherein Arnold reported that of the females, 404 were "guilty" of "sexual immorality." How many of the thousand were female is not given, unfortunately, and there are no statistics given on the number of males sterilized after being deemed sexually deviant.

36. Kline (1997, 107) reports that by 1936 seven states mandated sterilization of mental defectives who were not institutionalized: Delaware, Idaho, Iowa, South Dakota, Michigan, North Carolina, and Vermont.

37. Poor whites were not the only whites sterilized, however. Eugenic sterilization laws were occasionally used even against wealthy white women. In 1936, for example, Ann Cooper Hewitt, an heiress, sued her mother and two surgeons for sterilizing her without her knowledge. Experts testified that Ann, who was never institutionalized, was a high-grade moron passing for normal, and her mother testified that she was sexually out of control, prompting the

decision to have her sterilized. It came to light during the series of hearings that there was also a family dispute over the estate of Ann's recently deceased father, a dispute that any future child of Ann's would have figured into in a prominent way. Once in place, it would seem, eugenic sterilization laws could be used in a variety of ways against a variety of "enemies." For details of this case see Kline 1997, chap. 4.

38. Nor, of course, was there any state-funded provision for caring for them.

39. Hysterectomy rather than tubal ligation apparently because Medicaid paid doctors much more money to do the more complicated surgery. According to Dorothy Roberts, "In 1975, a hysterectomy cost $800 compared to $250 for tubal ligation, giving surgeons, who were reimbursed by Medicaid, a financial incentive to perform the more extensive operation—despite its twenty times greater risk of killing the patient" (D. Roberts 1997, 90).

40. Despite the ease with which a North Carolina physician could perform sterilization lawfully, many operations apparently were performed without authorization. When investigative journalists at the *Winston-Salem Journal* examined Wake Forest University's role in the eugenics movement, they found that Dr. C. Nash Herndon, head of the Department of Medical Genetics from 1943 through 1948 (and simultaneously president of the Human Betterment League) reported that thirty sterilizations were performed at the university's hospital during academic year 1943–44, although the state board had not approved nearly that number (Deaver 2003).

41. See, for example, Popenoe and Johnson 1926, chap 14. They conclude their review of various studies with this statement: "From the foregoing different kinds of evidence, we feel justified in concluding that the Negro race differs greatly from the white race, mentally as well as physically, and that in many respects it may be said to be inferior, when tested by the requirements of modern civilization and progress, with particular reference to North America" (291–92).

42. The South Carolina example is typical. In 1971, Republican representative Lucius Porth introduced a bill that would force a woman on welfare with more than two children to submit to sterilization or lose her aid (Nelson 2003, 68–69, and D. Roberts 1997, 214).

43. In fact, Lempkin's classic definition of genocide includes not only direct but also indirect murder through deprivation and prevention of procreation, so the sterilization program itself might be construed as an act of genocide (Lempkin 1946).

44. Thomas Gossett has called Grant "one of the most powerful racists this country has ever produced" (Gossett 1997, 353). He was wealthy, from a very wealthy family, politically influential on a national level, and very popular. For a discussion of the reviews his book received, many of them quite enthusiastic, see Gossett 1997, 362–63.

45. Secondary sources that cite the 1912 edition put this on page 102. My edition is the reprint from 1927, and apparently the pagination is slightly different; see Goddard 1927, 101. Dr. William Robinson, chief of the Department of Genito-Urinary Disease and Dermatology at the Bronx Hospital and Dispensary, held a view similar to Goddard's. In *Eugenics, Marriage and Birth*

Control he writes, "From the point of view of abstract justice, and of the greatest good not only to the greatest but to the whole number, the best thing would be to gently chloroform these children or to give them a dose of potassium cyanide, but in our humane and civilized age such measures are not looked upon with favor. So the State is taking care of them" (Robinson 1917, 74).

46. For example, it was favorably reviewed in *The Nation* on November 1, 1900 (see "Heredity and Human Progress," 349–50). It was mildly lampooned by Ambrose Bierce, but what wasn't? (Bierce 2006 [1909]). Bierce's satire makes it clear that at least among a circle of Bierce's readers, McKim's name and ideas were well known.

47. It is no exaggeration to call these "convictions." For those who believed fervently in the tenets of eugenics, disregard for the dignity and autonomy and even the lives of their "inferiors" was a moral imperative. Claudia Koonz argues persuasively that Nazis saw their conduct, including their attempt at genocide, as the height of morality (Koonz 2003).

48. According to Elof Carlson, no German law ever actually *required* any physician to kill a patient. Hitler wrote a personal letter, dated September 1, 1939, in which he charged Reichsleiter Philip Bouhler and Dr. Karl Brandt with "enlarging the authority of certain physicians" to *allow* them to accord incurable patients a merciful death. Many German physicians were apparently quite willing to take on this responsibility (E. A. Carlson 2001, 325).

49. Kelly Miller discussed eugenics in relation to African Americans with some interest in a 1917 article in *The Scientific Monthly*. The possibility of using eugenics measures for "racial uplift" among African Americans was actively advocated in the NAACP journal *Crisis* in 1924 in an article by Albert Beckham called "Applied Eugenics." For details of this discussion in the black press, see Hasian 1996, chap. 3. A number of Jewish intellectuals participated in the eugenics movement, including several rabbis who held membership in the American Eugenics Society in the 1920s. For details on Jewish involvement, see Rosen 2004, 18–19. Some of this discussion may have been stimulated by leaders of the movement such as Henry Fairfield Osborn, who suggested in his 1921 address of welcome to the Second International Congress of Eugenics that different races have different strengths to cultivate (Osborn 1921, 312). Perhaps the extent of eugenics' acceptance among middle-class whites can be gauged by a 1937 *Fortune* magazine poll indicating that two out of every three of its readers supported eugenic sterilization for mental defectives, 63 percent supported sterilization for criminals, and only 15 percent opposed both (Paul 1995, 83). Jewish support for eugenics persists in some quarters even today. John Glad and Seymore Itzkoff contend that the Nazis were not practicing true eugenics but rather "aristocide," because they feared the superior class of people they were incarcerating and executing. A true eugenics would breed a humanity of intelligent, strong, altruistic people. See Glad, 2006.

50. Smith and Nelson note that Carrie Buck was paid $5 per month to act as live-in domestic help after her parole from the Virginia Colony and that her parole was extended, despite her pleas for complete release. Thus she was prevented for a time from courting and marrying William Eagle, her eventual husband, and instead persisted in servitude (Smith and Nelson 1989, 188–96).

51. Moran gives a particularly clear example of this concern to protect

the status of professionals in his discussion of the American Social Hygiene Association's hesitation to accept penicillin as a cure for syphilis and gonorrhea in the late 1940s (Moran 2000, 123–24).

52. For a quick list of these promises, see Paul 1995, 67–68. She quotes Goddard claiming that two-thirds of the feebleminded could be eliminated in one generation; Laughlin making similar sweeping claims; Herbert Eugene Walter arguing that sterilization would eliminate nine-tenths of crime, insanity, and sickness in four generations; Florence Mateer saying the burden of state support would be eliminated in one generation; and Charles Davenport asserting that segregation during the reproductive years would reduce the number of defectives to practically nothing in one generation. These arguments were used not only to rally support for eugenic measures but to convince state and local governments to undertake the financial burden of institutionalization and other programs in the belief that the outlay was temporary.

53. For a discussion of this debate and some explanation of the Hardy-Weinberg Principle that lies behind it, see Paul 1998, chap. 7.

54. Lippmann 1976, 26. The anthology from which I have taken this passage contains six of Lippmann's articles on the subject, followed by a response from Terman entitled "The Great Conspiracy" and a rejoinder from Lippmann entitled "The Great Confusion," which are in turn followed by one letter each from Lippmann and Terman to the editor of the *New Republic*. The debate between the two men stretched into January of 1923.

55. This statement is quoted in Paul 1995, 69. For a discussion of eugenics and the political left in the United States and Britain, see Paul 1998, chap. 2.

56. This is evident from a footnote to page 76, where McKim writes, "By the term heredity the author is always to be understood in the broadest sense, as meaning the sum of ancestral influences directly transmitted from parents to offspring, whether as specific tendency or deficient vitality." See also McKim 1901, 80.

57. Julian Huxley is often cited as a critic of scientific racism. But consider this passage: "I regard it as wholly probable that true negroes have a somewhat lower average intelligence than whites or yellows. But neither this nor any other eugenically significant point of racial difference has yet been scientifically established" (1936, 19).

58. Larson (1995, 115) argues that Catholics were responsible for the fact that the state of Louisiana never passed a eugenic sterilization law. Certainly eugenics activists perceived the Catholic Church as a major opponent. See, for example, Olden 1974, esp. 27.

59. See Larson 1995, 167. For a specific reference to Methodist endorsement in New Jersey, see Olden 1974, 81.

60. This example in all its detail comes from Larson 1995, 135–47.

61. The state home was an all-white facility, in contrast to the state institutions for the mentally ill. If Partlow had gotten his wish, for the first time blacks would have been sterilized under Alabama law.

62. Although there were not many published reports of death during or after salpingectomy, there were a few. In 1938 Dr. G. B. Arnold of the Virginia Colony presented a paper to the American Association on Mental Deficiency reviewing the first thousand legal eugenic sterilizations there. He noted two deaths, including one fifteen-year-old girl (Smith and Nelson 1989, 231). This

paper was given after the 1935 Alabama debate, but the deaths themselves and published reports of them may have occurred earlier. And Gosney and Popenoe's assessment of the California eugenic sterilization program had already been published. In their review of the first 6,255 legal eugenic sterilizations in that state, Gosney and Popenoe acknowledged a total of four deaths (sex of inmates unspecified) (1929, xiv).

63. For this list of what the Nazi law covered, see Bruinius 2006, 279. Diane Paul notes that the Nazis, like most of the more moderate eugenicists in the United States, were mostly concerned about mentality and behavioral traits, not physical disabilities. She reports that only about 10 percent of the sterilizations carried out under the 1933 law were justified by the presence of a physical disorder (Paul 1998, 144).

64. Many U.S. race theorists were also skeptical of the category "Aryan," which they contended was a linguistic rather than a properly racial group. But this did not mean that they thought the practical effects of the Nazi purge were not valuable.

65. Thus many Americans considered it "scientific" rather than "racist." See, for example, Mariann Olden's attempt to defend the German sterilization program while at the same time apparently very genuinely denouncing Nazi anti-Semitism in Olden 1974, chap. 5.

66. Among them, as Paula Giddings notes, were Mary McLeod Bethune and the National Council of Negro Women. At a 1938 meeting, Mary Jackson McCrorey sponsored a motion to "let our President [Roosevelt] know that we heartily recommend the action of our government toward the rehabilitation of the suffering Jews of the world, assuring him at the same time that our approach is one more sympathetic than could come from any other group in this country because of our experience in this country." The councilwoman who seconded the motion suggested the NCNW include the statement that "we can sympathize because Hitler is endeavoring to reduce the status of Jews in Germany to that of the Negro in New York" (Giddings 1984, 228).

67. For a long discussion of both these events, see Edsall 2003, 149, 164. For a discussion of early twentieth-century German attitudes toward manliness and homosexuality—and the ambiguous relations between the two—see Mosse 1985, esp. 56–58.

68. There is evidence that some people thought Hitler had homosexual tendencies even in his young manhood, especially during his military service, but there is no clear record of his ever having been disciplined for any kind of homosexual activity. Bromberg and Small (1983) allude to a reprimand for pederasty during World War I, as does Vernon (Murray 1943). But it is not at all clear what counted as pederasty under military rules (Edsall 2003, chap. 15).

69. For examples, including Walter Winchell's lampoon of "Adele Hitler," see Loughery 1998, 106–107.

70. W. H. D. Vernon speaks of Hitler's physical effeminacy, especially his hands, and asserts that his physique bespeaks a certain type of personality. See pages 73 and 74 of the OSS report.

71. Mosse offers some discussion of Hitler's decisions regarding Röhm. He claims Hitler was guided throughout his relationship with Röhm by tactical concerns (Mosse 1985, chap. 8, esp. 158).

72. For a discussion of this, see Plant 1986, chap. 2.

73. See Giles 2002, 10, and also Mosse 1985, 164–70.

74. Quoted in Plant 1986, 99. See also excerpts from Himmler's Tölz Bad speech of 1937 in Mosse 1985, 166–70. Among his other comments, Himmler states that homosexuals should not only be killed, but their lives entirely effaced; he aims for "the snuffing out of life as if it had never existed."

75. According to Koonz (2003, 247), Jewish men who had sex with non-Jewish women were also castrated.

76. See Plant 1986, 104, 175–78. Himmler also turned to castration as a condition of "parole," much as his American counterparts did. As the tide of war turned against Germany in 1943, Himmler began offering homosexual men the chance to leave the camps and work in defense industries if they would submit to castration. Richard Plant interviewed one man who had agreed to castration under those circumstances (1986, 191, 202).

77. For a review of the Cinemax film, see Gilbert 2004, F1. Machtan is fairly straightforward: "Hitler's determination to destroy anything that might have provided an insight into his private life is well documented. He got rid of anything he could, and his arm was long, even before 1933. Those privy to his secrets were bribed, sworn to secrecy, blackmailed or killed. Such conduct makes it clear that Hitler was anxious to avoid being compromised at any price, that the real threat to his reputation—as he must have perceived it—lay in revelations about his private life. It is unlikely that he was afraid of being thought a 'loser' because of the adverse circumstances surrounding the first half of his life. Despite his questionable past and his rantingly demagogic manner, from the mid-1920s on he was regarded as a semirespectable professional politician who was well known to have come from a humble background. Hitler's great secret, I will argue, was his homosexuality and his homoerotic relationships. This was the stigma from his past that threatened at any time to rear its head as he rose politically. Hitler had to live a lie in order to conceal his proclivity, and he defended that secret by all available means" (Machtan 2001, 20–21).

78. Suggesting that Hitler's relationship with Braun was asexual and that Braun herself might have been a lesbian, Machtan writes, "As long as Eva kept up appearances and played the role of his mistress, what she did in other respects mattered little to him. And so she led a double existence: on the one hand, she lived with Hitler, who not only marginalized her but pampered her with gifts of all kinds—jewelry, nice clothes, Ferragamo shoes; on the other, he left her free to enjoy herself as she pleased—although not with other men, for that would have humiliated him" (Machtan 2001, 171). Machtan also suggests that Hitler hated Jews because the Jewish journalist Maximilian Harden was the one who pressed the issue of Philipp, Prinz zu Eulenberg's influence over Wilhelm II and exposed his homosexuality (Machtan 2001, 47–50).

79. Richard Plant offers a pained discussion of this phenomenon and its history (1986, 15–16).

80. When I was a child, there was a toy on the market called a "Slip 'n' Slide," which was basically a carpet of plastic sheeting connected to a garden hose. When I read the foregoing paragraph, I feel that, conceptually and rhetorically, I am *there*. Nevertheless, I promise that the paragraph does not exaggerate.

81. The number of Hitler's testicles remains unconfirmed. His body was

badly burned before it was recovered, and no medical reports exist. But OSS psychiatrists as well as numerous other experts have held to this theory for eighty years.

82. Bromberg and Small (1983, 173) report that their evidence suggests he was unable to reach orgasm unless he was allowed close visual scrutiny of the female genitals, urination, and defecation. Context indicates that at times he had women urinate or defecate on him.

83. See especially Adorno 1950, 416 and 862. Machtan suggests that Hitler worked as a prostitute in Vienna in 1912 (Machtan 2001, 55).

6. Nordics Celebrate the Family

1. Although it sounds silly, body lice as an indication of racial identity actually has a scientific history. In 1861 British entomologist Andrew Murray collected lice from residents of a number of different countries. He conducted experiments, reporting that the lice not only varied in color and structure but that lice from some races of human beings could not live on members of other races. Charles Darwin took Murray's work seriously. He thought it was possible that lice could be used to distinguish different races in cases where other indices were inconclusive (Gossett 1997, 81).

2. Osborn knew whereof he spoke. The preface to Osborn's 1968 book *The Future of Human Heredity* was written by Theodosius Dobzhansky, one of the greatest geneticists of the twentieth century. There Dobzhansky acknowledged that "zealous proponents" had hindered the acceptance of eugenics as a practice. "And yet," he maintained, "eugenics has a sound core. The real problem which mankind will not be able to evade indefinitely is where the evolutionary process is taking man, and where man himself wishes to go. Mr. Osborn has for several decades been the clear-sighted leader of the eugenical movement in America, who strove to make the substance of eugenics scientific and its name respectable again" (in F. Osborn 1968, vi).

3. For an example of what appears to be population thinking in support of racial profiling by police, see Levin 2003, esp. 152–54. Levin writes, "Race is an information-bearing trait. Knowledge of race redistributes probabilities about past and potential commission of crimes. So, unless countervailing considerations can be brought [and he thinks they cannot], the state is entitled to use race in screening. The New Jersey Highway Patrol, for instance, reportedly stops young black males in expensive new cars for drug searches" (152). At least some of Levin's research is supported by grants from the Pioneer Fund, which historically has supported scholarship that promoted white supremacy. For discussions of the Pioneer Fund, see the penultimate section of this chapter as well as Tucker 2002, and Lombardo 2002.

4. There was really no reason for racists to fear that individual eugenic selection would not turn out the same way that race-based selection would. As Frederick Osborn pointed out in 1939, "If it were actually the case that any particular group of people contained an unusual proportion of valuable individuals, the result of an effective system of individual selection would be to favor the increase of an unusually large proportion of individuals in that group, but not in any sense of group discrimination" (1939, 34).

5. This latter statement is quoted in Paul 1995, 125. In another essay,

Paul cites a statement Osborn made in a 1968 interview: "Birth control and abortion are turning out to be great eugenic advances of our time. If they had been advanced for eugenic reasons, it would have retarded or stopped their acceptance" (Paul 1998, 142). Clearly these name changes were deliberate, designed to disguise what Osborn saw as important eugenic work.

6. Much of this background information can be found in Ladd-Taylor 2001, 303.

7. See Ladd-Taylor 2001, 320.

8. For a long list of systematic economic policies and practices that severely disadvantaged racial minorities in the United States, see Lipsitz 1998, esp. chap. 1.

9. Analyzing census data, local tax records, and oral histories, Jaspin (2007) documents these events of racial cleansing in twelve counties stretching from North Carolina to Missouri. His data suggest that many more incidents like these occurred and may not have been confined to the regions he investigated. For some estimates of the value of land left behind in north Georgia, see Jaspin 2007, 135–38 and 241–43.

10. Roderick Ferguson writes, "The heteronormative household was practically a 'material impossibility' for people of color in the U.S. 'Family wage' in the early twentieth century defined the American home as white, heterosexual, and American, and thereby excluded people of color on the grounds that they were incapable of, or uninterested in, constituting heteronormative families and adopting their regulatory demands" (2004, 104). This quotation comes from Ferguson's chapter on Gunnar Myrdal's *An American Dilemma,* which Ferguson claims "was inspired by heteronormative anxieties that constructed African Americans as figures of nonheteronormativity who could potentially throw the American social order into chaos" (2004, 88).

11. Returning white servicemen went to college in unprecedented numbers with the assistance of the GI Bill. They also bought homes and received training for skilled jobs, which they then got in the booming industries of the postwar period. Things were different for women and black men returning from war. Women of all races were ineligible for benefits under the GI Bill because their units were not approved for combat. Black men who had seen combat were technically eligible for benefits, but they could not take advantage of them. Black colleges were overcrowded, yet blacks were denied admission to many white colleges. As already mentioned, Federal Housing Administration rules together with de facto and de jure neighborhood segregation made it difficult for any black person to secure a loan to buy property; the Veteran's Administration followed the same rules. And racial discrimination in job training programs and career counseling referrals worked against black men. Discrimination is also evident in the military itself. Between August and November of 1946, 21 percent of white soldiers were dishonorably discharged, but 39 percent of black soldiers were. A dishonorable discharge automatically canceled a soldier's veterans' benefits.

12. But they did exist. We know this not just because we have to imagine that some people with children would form same-sex unions and households but also because there is an interview with at least one lesbian couple raising a child they adopted in George Henry's *Sex Variants* (1941, 839). A number of

the other lesbians interviewed were also raising children, but it is not always clear in the text whether they were doing so with a life-partner or alone.

13. Dorothy Allison fans will recognize that people like Paul Popenoe had a tremendous and negative impact on the lives of many individuals whose birth certificates, by law, carried the notation "illegitimate" in many states, including Allison's home state of North Carolina. See Allison's *Bastard Out of Carolina,* 1992.

14. It is oftentimes embraced by members of the very same groups it was designed to stigmatize. Cheryl Clarke points this out in her essay "The Failure to Transform: Homophobia in the Black Community," where she writes: "Because the insular, privatized nuclear family is upheld as the model of Western family stability, all other forms—for example, the extended family, the female-headed family, the lesbian family—are devalued. Many black people, especially middle-class black people, have accepted the male-dominated nuclear family model, though we have had to modify it because black women usually must work outside the home" (Clarke 1983, 200).

15. For an example of his addresses to educators, see his "Education and Eugenics" (1935a). For an example of his advice to college-educated women, see his "Where Are the Marriageable Men?" (1935b). He suggests that eugenically valuable women move to the Pacific Northwest, because the ratio of men to women is greater there. Note that both of these articles predate World War II.

16. It was an argument that obviously made a great deal of sense to later involuntary sterilization activists like Mariann Olden, who founded the Sterilization League of New Jersey in 1937. "Sterilization holds families together, as the fear of pregnancy begets antagonism toward the husband, and the husband often deserts when the family gets too large" (Olden 1974, 25). In 1943 Olden went on to found the first national involuntary sterilization organization, Birthright, whose motto, printed on its letterhead, was: "There should be no child in America that has not the complete Birthright of a sound mind in a sound body, and that has not been born under proper conditions" (1974, 93).

17. British sexologist and eugenicist Havelock Ellis suggested in 1911 that charitable impulses should enrich eugenics foundations and initiatives rather than help people in need. Giving money to eugenics rather than to relief is real charity "in accordance with the whole Christian conception and tradition of charity," he wrote. "But it would be charity according to knowledge, charity applied at the right spot, and not merely allowed to run to waste, or, worse, to turn to poison" (Ellis 1926, 28).

18. A number of historians have suggested that the United States has always been what Pierre van den Berghe in 1981 called a *Herrenvolk Democracy,* a nation in which democracy was deemed the appropriate form of government for one race, class, or ethnic group, while the rest should be left in servitude. I don't disagree with this thesis. However, I do think that the extremists in the eugenics movement were not *Herrenvolk* democrats. They were, in fact, totalitarians. For interesting discussions of the United States as a *Herrenvolk* Democracy, see Mills 1998, 139–66, and Fredrickson 1971, 61–91.

19. For an early discussion of the continuity between the eugenics movement and the marriage counseling and pro-family movement, see Pickens 1967.

20. Those who failed to plan were clearly not rational and had probably

bequeathed their mental deficiency to their offspring, so it was just as well that they go ahead and be an inhibiting burden. In no case should tax money pay for the upkeep of elderly citizens, because taxation took resources away from Nordic families.

21. Lodgers seemed to pose an especially big threat in the minds of many in the 1940s, according to Roderick Ferguson, who points out that Gunnar Myrdal "identifies lodgers as a factor that contributes to African American family disorganization. Almost 30 percent of African Americans in the North reported that they were lodging people not part of the immediate nuclear family in their homes. This figure Myrdal compares to 10 percent among northern whites. In the South, 20 percent of black families in urban areas report having lodgers, compared to 11 percent for whites. Common law marriage, out-of-wedlock births, lodgers, single-headed families, and unattached individuals are all indicators of African American disorganization defined in terms of its distance from heterosexual and nuclear intimate arrangements that are rationalized through American law and cultural norms that valorize heterosexual monogamy and patriarchal domesticity" (Ferguson 2004, 93).

22. Charles McCord makes exactly this claim about Negroes in 1914. The only family feeling Negroes have, he asserts, is between mother and son, and that is very weak (1914, 38).

23. Strangely enough, at least one recent account of the evolution of sex suggests something very like this, at least in that it claims sex evolved out of microbial cannibalism. See Margulis and Sagan 1991, esp. 187–200.

24. Excerpts from both these works can be found in Bland and Doan 1998, 125–33. The quotation from Van de Velde's 1928 book, *Ideal Marriage,* is on page 128.

25. For an overview, see Neuhaus 2000.

26. I know my paragraph continues, but just pause here for a moment and think about that last sentence. It is hearty food for the healthy imagination.

27. Henry 1941, 1026. Henry does not hesitate to supply details. This is by far the most sexually explicit government report I have ever seen. Indeed, it is hard to imagine how a report could be more so. Jennifer Terry has pointed to this book as a perfect example of what Foucault calls "the perverse implantation," a veritable "how-to" book of lesbian carnality (Terry 1999, 263). Every library should own a copy.

28. See, for example, William Robinson's eugenic argument for legalization of birth control and women's reproductive autonomy (1917, esp. 34), or even more to the point, Whiting 1925, who writes: "It may take a revolution to put in control of human affairs those who are interested in salvaging humanity from the unbridled breeding of morons. It may take another to put woman in such a position economically that she is mistress of those functions which most rightfully belong to her, namely the functions of reproduction. In our present world, the majority of women must choose between the devil and the deep blue sea. Either they must become more or less economically dependent upon some husband to whom they presumably did not propose, or they must resign themselves to spinsterhood. Rare indeed is the woman wealthy enough to support a man of her own choosing; but if any selection of the fathers of the next generation is to be done, it must be done by the women" (167). Whiting goes on to

argue for a socialist revolution to make women economically equal to men and child care publicly funded.

29. For discussion of sexual psychopathy and homosexuality, see Freedman 1989; for discussion specifically of lesbian sex offenders, see Freedman 1996.

30. Roderick Ferguson writes, "Displacing the contradictions of capital onto African American female-headed households established the moral grammar and the political practices of the very neoconservative formations that would roll back the gains of civil rights in the 1980s and 1990s and undermine the well-being of black poor and working-class families. Hence the Moynihan Report and the pathologizing of black mothers as nonheteronormative provided the discursive origins for the dismantling of welfare as part of the fulfillment of global capital by the millennium's end. . . . The pathological image of nonheteronormative formations like the female-headed household played a key role in this conservative resurgence. Neoconservatives explicitly based their objections to public spending on the discourse of black matriarchy, arguing that black 'welfare queens' were getting fat off liberal social policies and producing destructive urban environments in which young blacks had no regard for competition and honest work" (Ferguson 2004, 124, 125).

31. In the mid-1990s, according to Dorothy Roberts, AFDC payments for an additional child would have been about $64 per month. The exact amount varied from state to state. See Roberts 1997, 213.

32. Predictably, he did not like it. See Stern 2005, 194.

33. Homosexual activity among both working class and poor whites and members of nonwhite races had been documented for decades in anthropological and medical literature. See, for example, Rosse 1892, 802–806; Hammond 1974, 161–64 (orig. 1887); Kiernan 1892, 185–88; Ellis and Symmonds 1975, 5 (orig. 1897). There was also a fairly long tradition of attributing it to foreigners. Albert Moll, for example, claims it originated in Armenia and then spread to the Orient (Moll 1931, 20). He cites evidence of pederasty amid the ancient Teutons, Gauls, and Osques in Italy (36). And he offers proof that pederasty is not rare among "primitives," having been found by Mantegazza in Panama (46). He of course cites Hammond, whose investigations of homosexual activity among the Native Americans of the Southwest was by that time legendary.

34. This is not to say they were not interested in the sexual practices of their alleged inferiors at all. They certainly were. But whether they practiced anal or oral sex among themselves in same-sex pairs or groups was of less interest than many of the other degenerate and dangerous sexual things they supposedly did.

35. Jennifer Terry, whose work is otherwise extraordinarily valuable, holds this position (Terry 1999, 181).

36. Unfortunately, there is no room here to explore that avenue, but I would argue that it was the tenuous result of a confluence of medical research on transsexualism and a growing gay rights movement that emphasized the California "clone" look—that is, as John Loughery describes it, "the de rigueur jeans or army fatigues, leather jacket, moustache, muscular build, and handkerchief codes that assigned pastels, limp wrists, and aunties to the netherworld" (Loughery 1998, 392–93). Foucault is describing precisely this style, with both sympathy and amusement, in an interview in *Christopher Street* in October of

1981: "You're always with men, you have mustaches and leather jackets, you wear boots" (Foucault 1994, 161). But the idea that homosexuality is gender deviation hung on in most parts of the United States despite these and other changes in style among gay and lesbian people. Keith Boykin notes that growing up in St. Louis in the 1970s, he was unable to identify himself as gay in great part because he thought homosexuality was a matter of gender comportment rather than sexual behavior or desire (Boykin 1996, 12).

37. This is of course the primary reason why gay and lesbian activists over the past two or three decades have been so reluctant to ally themselves with groups who embrace and celebrate their own cross-gender comportment. Only by denying any connection with transgendered people could they deny *being* transgendered people. For an account of some of this hostility, see Wilchins 2004, 24.

38. Both Chideckel (1935) and Terman and Miles (1936) call attention to the fact that homosexuals often don't look cross-gendered and so can't be detected by laypeople, although Terman and Miles did find some large group correlations between male homosexuality and certain physical characteristics such as a lighter beard, less body hair, and shorter stature. See Chideckel 1935, 12, and Terman and Miles 1936, esp. 250–54.

39. Albert Moll is the only sexologist I have come across who suggests there is an ethical question in treatment. He says that since curing a sexual invert means not only changing his or her sexual orientation but also his or her gender (although he does not use those terms), the attempt will unbalance the entire personality. Do we have that right? Moll asks in his chapter on treatment. He also worries that if treatment successfully changes the personality and allows the individual to marry and procreate, the abnormal constitution will be passed on to the children. Nevertheless, he says, the duty of the doctor is to cure his patients. So despite the risk of completely unbalancing people and of tainting future generations, he presses on for a cure (Moll 1931, 188–89).

40. Evans certainly did his part. In Boise's 1955 sex scandal, he sent quite a few men to the state penitentiary. Many of them received sentences of up to fifteen years, and one, Ralph Cooper, was sentenced to life. These punishments were for consensual acts between adults in private. Apparently the Family is too delicate to withstand even such subtle "assaults."

41. Havelock Ellis had already discussed this concern in 1897. We must be careful with alleged cures, he asserted in *Sexual Inversion*, because they don't work well, and if they lead to marriage, they can just make things worse. "Nor is it possible to view with satisfaction the prospects of inverts begetting or bearing children. Often, no doubt, the children turn out fairly well, but for the most part they bear witness that they belong to a 'neurotic' and failing stock. Sometimes, indeed, the tendency to sexual inversion in eccentric and neurotic families seems merely to be Nature's merciful method of winding up a concern which, from her point of view, has ceased to be profitable." He continues: "We can seldom, therefore, safely congratulate ourselves on the success of any 'cure' of inversion. The success is unlikely to be either permanent or complete, in the case of a decided invert; and in the most successful cases we have simply put into the invert's hands a power of reproduction which it is undesirable he should possess" (Ellis and Symmonds 1975 [1897], 145–46).

42. Other initiating traumas mentioned by Chideckel include witnessing

heterosexual coitus and being punished for masturbating. His patient Babette's heterosexuality was destroyed, for example, when her mother tied her hands and feet to the bed posts to prevent her from touching her genitals (Chideckel 1935, 56).

43. By 1964 the number had increased from 17 to 37. Lewis goes on to say that by 1950 physicians had moved from merely screening women to providing consultation about "sexual adjustment" in marriage, including breaking or stretching the hymen or simulating intromission to allay virginal fears of intercourse. A 1954 article in the *Journal of the American Medical Association* offering advice to physicians on how to conduct these examinations goes into some detail. See C. Lewis 2005, 94, 98.

44. Henry 1941, 1024. It is not clear how the team arrived at this conclusion, since only one of the sex variant subjects interviewed had a homosexual parent; quite a number of the lesbian subjects had children, but no study of them was undertaken.

45. Because homosexuality was considered a mental illness until 1973, state laws prohibiting the marriage of mental defectives could be construed to prohibit the marriage of those with homosexual tendencies.

46. In case it isn't obvious (and it isn't), the passive role in fellatio consists of taking a penis into one's mouth and manipulating it with tongue and lips until it ejaculates, while the active role consists in lying, standing, or sitting still while these manipulations are performed on one's penis.

47. For a first-person account of going through such treatment in the 1980s, see Scholinski 1997.

48. He did strongly support removing homosexuality from the list of mental illnesses in the early 1970s while many of his colleagues were stubbornly hanging onto it, but he very much wanted to classify cross-gender comportment as a symptom of impending if not present mental illness, just as so many of his predecessors and contemporaries did. See Bayer 1981, 177.

49. For a contemporary observation of this phenomenon, see Gerassi 1966, 49. He notes that Boise, Idaho, in 1955 was in the midst of its own homosexual McCarthy era. "In the early 1950s, thousands of people were calling the *Statesman* [the local newspaper] or the police or the local FBI office to denounce an acquaintance, a neighbor, an enemy, even a friend, as a Communist. In 1955, they were denouncing homosexuals." It was an easy slide to make, and Boise is not the only place where it occurred.

50. For a history of this, see Dowbiggin 1997, esp. 224.

51. Politicians made political hay out of the situation. In Chicago in 1937, State's Attorney Thomas Courtney established a central "Sex Bureau" to keep records on pedophiles, according to *Time* magazine. Not to be outdone, New York's mayor Fiorello LaGuardia did likewise and moved to keep men guilty of sex crimes locked up: "Roared the impetuous little mayor: 'There are many legal loopholes through which these offenders can now escape full punishment for their crimes. But, God help the judge who turns one of these men loose if anything happens afterward.' To the citizens of the community, he gave this advice: Keep children away from lonely places; teach them to avoid strangers and never to accept any gifts from strangers; teach them to report all cases of molestation; and see that the man is arrested" ("Pedophilia" 1937, 42).

52. Discharge for homosexuality, at least by the early 1950s, was known

as an "Undesirable Discharge" and was even more stigmatized than a dishonorable discharge. For a reproduction of such a discharge paper, see Weiss and Schiller 1988, 45.

53. This information comes from Freedman 1989, 206.

54. This was a process that had begun during World War I, when the Justice Department expanded its Bureau of Investigation. Although some believed the expansion would be reversed with the end of the war, officials within the Justice Department argued that because the United States did not sign the Treaty of Versailles, hostilities were not officially at an end in 1918, and in fact did not come to an official close until 1921. During that time, which included the "Red Scare" of 1919, officials continued expanding the Bureau and in 1919 established a General Intelligence Division to track down radicals that might be associated with a series of anarchist bombings. J. Edgar Hoover, then a young Justice Department attorney, was put in charge of the new division (Kornweibel 1998, 5–6). Throughout the 1920s Hoover would use his extensive powers to harass, intimate, manipulate, and whenever possible eliminate anyone he considered to be a threat to American values, including, as Kornweibel so carefully shows, not only anarchists, socialists, and communists, but also labor unionists, black nationalists, anti-lynching crusaders, and African American journalists who denounced racist laws and policies. "The belief that black militancy posed a serious threat to the racial status quo and that socialists, communists, and anarchists were eager to subvert the race had become embedded in Hoover's thinking and the anti-radical crusade" (1998, 66). In other words, at the federal level, protection of white supremacy was part and parcel of protection of the American way of life.

55. White 1950, 2. For a discussion, see D'Emilio 1998, 41.

56. This passage is quoted in D'Emilio 1998, 42. The entire text of the report is available in Cory 1975, 270–77.

57. The Postal Service had long been involved in domestic espionage as well as political censorship, as Kornweibel documents. "Of all the agencies involved in the political intelligence system during and after World War I, the Post Office Department was the only one with a preexistent nationwide structure that needed no fundamental alterations to meet the national emergency. It efficiently handled 'many thousands of communications of confidential character' for its partners in domestic counter-espionage, registered enemy aliens, and censored the mail. A staff of dollar-a-year volunteers, known variously as the Translation Bureau or Bureau M-1, monitored black, socialist, and anti-war publications as well as nearly 300 foreign-language newspapers, the latter task done by a translation force of over 400 college professors. President Wilson urged Postmaster General Albert Sidney Burleson to 'act with the utmost caution and liberality' in placing restrictions on printed matter, but Burleson took advantage of the president's laissez-faire leadership and cracked down hard on the dissenting and foreign-language press. Many offenders lost their second-class mailing permits—forcing them to pay much higher first-class postage rates—or went out of business rather than knuckle under to government pressure" (Kornweibel 1998, 13–14).

58. For detailed accounts of some of these events, see Loughery 1998, chap. 13.

59. Many accounts of these procedures exist. Here is one excerpt from Ordover 2003, 112: "Even as hormone injections were being administered by some physicians, others were subjecting their gay patients to LSD-25, hypnosis, and variations on Max's aversion therapy. Ralph Blair related a 1953 study in which the twenty-five gay male subjects drank coffee or tea with emetine (an antibacterial, rarely used anymore due to its toxicity). Ten minutes later they were given an injection of emetine, ephedrine (a bronchodilator, used to treat asthma, which increases heart rate), pilocarpine (used in the treatment of glaucoma and causing pulmonary edema, a drop in blood pressure, sweating, vomiting, twitching, and a slowing of heart action), and apomorphine (a respiration-depressing narcotic that also causes nausea and vomiting). As nausea and then vomiting set in, the subjects were shown slides of males in various stages of undress. Later, while feeling the effects of a 50 mg dose of testosterone, they were shown 'provocative' films of women. This cycle was repeated ten times, with little of the impact the researchers were so desperately seeking. Other mutations of aversion therapy were also tried. In one instance, the patient was given brandy along with his apomorphine injection to increase its effect and made to listen to a tape of his own case history. This is not to suggest that inducing nausea replaced electric shock treatment. The latter continued, sometimes, as reported in the *British Medical Journal,* by court order."

60. During the Boise, Idaho, sex scandal in 1955, John Gerassi reports, every bachelor got nervous. Men, both single and married, stopped going to bars without female escorts. One regular weekly poker game was halted until a woman friend could be found who was willing to hang around the house during the game as a witness that no homosexual activity was taking place (Gerassi 1966, 48). All male-male friendships, and even casual interactions, were suspect during the surveillance operation that turned up names of 500 alleged homosexuals.

61. This project involved sending a research team to Jamaica to study both blacks and mulattoes to determine whether mulattoes were less capable than the parent stocks of developing proper social organization. Details of this study can be found in Tucker 2002, 31–32, and in E. Black 2003, 288–94.

62. Legislative authorization of funding had come in 1966. The buildings and resources in these schools far exceeded those available in most Mississippi public schools. Not only admissions, but also curricula, were privately decided and were outside public control.

63. Three states abolished their public education systems to circumnavigate *Brown:* Mississippi, Georgia, and South Carolina. A number of localities in Virginia did so as well, and intense efforts were made to do so at the state level. There is evidence that Draper funded some, if not all, of these projects as well.

64. The right-wing politician and author Patrick Buchanan advocates what he calls "secession" from America's "polluted" culture in every possible way, especially by withdrawing children from public schools. "In the 1980s," he notes, "Evangelical and Fundamentalist Christians began to create an alternative culture and parallel institutions—Christian schools, TV shows, magazines, radio stations, networks, bookstores, and publishing houses. Millions of children attend Catholic and Christian schools; over a million are homeschooled" (Buchanan 2002, 249). Buchanan is careful not to tie this movement to

white flight in the face of desegregation, but it is in fact continuous with the establishment of whites-only Christian schools all over the South as public schools integrated in the 1970s, and in context it is clear that Buchanan thinks America's "cultural pollution" is closely tied to the ongoing process of integration of people of color and their art, music, linguistic forms, and other cultural productions into the mainstream of what most people now call American culture. The fact that Buchanan's discourse is continuous with scientific racism is obvious when, for example, he describes reactions to a speech by President Bill Clinton: "At that Portland State commencement where Mr. Clinton said that in fifty years there would be 'no majority race left in America,' students broke into spontaneous applause. Surely, it is a rarity in history that a people would cheer news that they and their children would soon be dispossessed of their inheritance as the majority in the nation their ancestors built" (Buchanan 2002, 209). The assumption that whites (or Nordics or Anglo-Saxons) built the United States and possess it by right of inheritance comes right out of the work of Lothrop Stoddard, as does the subtitle of Buchanan's book.

65. Including, for example, the work of Carleton Putnam (author of *Race and Reason,* a defense of segregation in public schools); Henry Garrett (professor of education, author of *IQ and Racial Differences,* and pamphleteer for White Citizens Councils; see Brace 2005, 242); R. Travis Osborne (psychologist and author of *Twins Black and White* who testified in court against school desegregation); and William Shockley (co-inventor of the transistor, staunch advocate of sterilization for people with IQs below 100, and proud donor of "genius sperm" to the Repository for Germinal Choice, a sperm bank established in 1978 in California by Robert K. Graham, a racist who wanted to freeze the sperm of white Nobel laureates and encourage women to have themselves inseminated with it. Over its 21-year existence the bank produced two hundred successful pregnancies. Shockley was the only Nobel laureate to acknowledge that he had donated. See Agar 2004, 4). The Fund also supported Garrett Hardin (ecologist and author of "The Tragedy of the Commons"); Roger Pearson (anthropologist and editor of *Mankind Quarterly*), Arthur Jansen (author of *The g Factor: The Science of Mental Ability,* notorious among other reasons for his 1992 claim that at least 25% of African Americans are mentally retarded; see Brace 2005, 246); Thomas Bouchard (psychologist and director of the Minnesota Center for Twin and Adoption Research, famous for his study of identical twins reared apart); Michael Levin (philosopher, author of *Why Race Matters,* and advocate of the use of torture in the war on terror); and J. Philippe Rushton (author of *Race, Evolution, and Behavior*). Several of these men's articles are available online at the Pioneer Fund Web site, www.pioneerfund.org. In addition, the site gives a long bibliography of articles by grantees. Several more of their articles are available at www.eugenics.net.

66. The founder of this organization, Margaret Olden, produced an account of its history in the mid-1970s. See Olden 1974.

67. Wickliffe Draper also funded some of North Carolina's sterilization efforts through the Wake Forest University School of Medicine in Winston-Salem. Draper donated at least $140,000 between 1951 and 1953. The Medical School, under the leadership of C. Nash Herndon, conducted involun-

tary sterilizations and offered genetic counseling to prospective parents (Deaver 2003). For an uncritical account of North Carolina's sterilization program, see Woodside 1950. Moya Woodside was a psychiatric social worker from England who studied the program in 1949. Her work was published in 1950 with a foreword by Robert Latou Dickinson.

68. See Reilly 1991, 126. I must note that Pickens' and Reilly's account of the history of Birthright—particularly its succession of name changes—are not in complete agreement. I have tried to navigate through the inconsistencies here without choosing between them. Olden's account is not much help because of its obvious personal animosity toward the organization's eventual espousal of voluntary sterilization only, a change that brought about her ouster.

69. Paul 1995, 123. Elsewhere Paul discusses the complexity of Reed's position on genetic counseling. He believed those who sought counseling were generally of higher intellectual quality than average, so despite physical disabilities he often encouraged reproduction, even though he realized that in some respects the long-term results would be "dysgenic." Until fetal screening tests were developed and abortion was legalized, reproduction was an all-or-nothing proposition. Reed preferred to run the risk of a physically disabled child rather than the risk of removing eugenically valuable talents and intelligence from the gene pool (Paul 1998, chap. 8).

70. Paul (1998, 133) suggests that this focus was common among practitioners into the 1960s.

71. By 1972 many eugenicists considered abortion of defective fetuses a "therapeutic" option open to physicians, even though individual women did not yet have the right to obtain an abortion for reasons of their own except in the state of New York (Fraser 1972).

72. That happened in part because eugenicists deliberately marketed those ideas as of a piece with the values upon which the United States was founded. Frederick Osborn, who was one of the founders of the Pioneer Fund in 1937 (along with Draper, Harry Laughlin, Malcolm Donald, and John Marshall Harlan) and its president from 1941 to 1958, realized that eugenics was most likely to succeed if the movement moderated its approach, shedding the rhetoric and even many of the tenets of the scientific racism that had fueled it in through the 1920s and emphasizing individual uniqueness and choice. In 1954, the American Eugenics Society, which had received funding directly from Wickliffe Draper for several years, rejected his grant and sought other financial resources. The society, under Osborn's presidency, was unwilling to accede to Draper's request that the organization publicly espouse the position that blacks were biologically inferior to whites (Tucker 2002, 58). Much of what was left of the organized eugenics movement devoted itself thereafter to the promotion of eugenic marriage, as already noted, although often it used non-eugenic language to appeal to the public. But it also continued to work for sterilization and birth control among those it deemed unfit—including record numbers of black, Latina, and Native American women.

73. Paul (1998, 147ff.) notes that the field changed markedly during the 1970s when Sarah Lawrence College opened the first master's degree program in genetics counseling. Most of the first wave of graduates were women, were not trained as geneticists, and were deeply influenced by "client-centered"

counseling approaches. For a discussion of "nondirectiveness" as an ideal in contemporary genetic counseling, see Patterson and Satz 2002.

74. This way of thinking still surfaces in contemporary public discourse. Consider 2000 presidential candidate Pat Buchanan's comments in *The Death of the West:* "By freeing husbands, wives, and children of family responsibilities, European socialists have eliminated the need for families. Consequently, families have begun to disappear. When they are gone, Europe goes with them" (2002, 13). In part Buchanan is talking about a reduction in the white population of Europe. He really means that when the white birthrate falls, Europe's population will no longer be white. But if that was all he meant, the statement would be practically tautological. Beyond that, he is attributing European culture to a certain form of kinship system; even if white people continued to reproduce but did so outside of The Family, he claims, Europe as a culture would collapse. It is odd for a Roman Catholic make such claims, even indirectly—after all, for centuries most of European culture was produced and preserved in same-sex celibate communities administered by the Catholic Church, an institution that for many years would not even allow marriage ceremonies—rituals endorsing essentially carnal relationships—to be performed inside its walls (Ariès 1962, 357). But his view is widely shared.

75. This pathologization includes priests and nuns. The eugenic and sterilization literature is vehemently anti-Catholic, and as the pro-family movement took the place of those movements, the anti-Catholicism quickly took the form of suspicion of the sexuality of people who choose religious celibacy as a way of life.

76. In Virginia, through the mid-1990s, same-sex partners and their dependents were prohibited from bringing cases to Domestic Relations Court and from qualifying for home loans through the Virginia Housing Association, for example. Now, under Virginia's new constitutional amendment outlawing same-sex marriage, it is not clear whether various kinds of civil contracts between same-sex life partners, including financial and child-custody agreements, will hold up in court. This is in addition to the prohibitions enacted "in defense of marriage" at the federal level in the 1990s.

77. New Jersey became the first state officially to allow same-sex joint adoption in 1998, after a lawsuit brought against the state by Michael Galluccio and Jon Holden, who wanted to adopt the child they had foster-parented for two years (Clark 1998, 1). Second-parent adoption is now possible by statute in at least eight other states and the District of Columbia. Additionally, in fifteen states some trial judges in some counties have allowed second-parent adoptions. Four states—Colorado, Nebraska, Ohio, and Wisconsin—forbid second-parent adoptions by statute. In three states even single queer people cannot adopt children: Florida, Utah, and Mississippi. This information is available on the Web site of the National Center for Lesbian Rights.

78. Before the mid-1980s, most sperm banks refused services to lesbians (Taylor 1998a, 5). Many physicians will not perform, and some insurers will not cover, artificial insemination for lesbians (D. Roberts 1997, 248, and Wikler and Wikler 1991, 30).

79. A number of bizarre custody and visitation cases around the country over the last decade have taken children away from lesbian and gay parents,

sometimes putting them in clearly unsuitable and even dangerous situations—as in a 1998 Alabama case in which custody of two young children was taken from their lesbian mother and given to a father who had a history of physically abusing them ("Alabama prefers abusive father" 1998, 23). In Virginia non-heterosexual parents can lose custody not only to their children's other biological parent but also to other of the children's blood relatives. The precedent was set in 1993 when Sharon Bottoms lost custody of her son to her mother, the boy's grandmother. Bottoms tried for years to regain custody and, failing that, to liberalize visitation restrictions, but even today she is not allowed to host the boy in the home she shares with her life partner. At the time of this writing the boy is seventeen years old; see "Judge again rules against Lesbian mom" 1998, 14.

80. The most recent study, released in March of 2006 from the Evan B. Donaldson Adoption Institute, is entitled "Expanding Resources for Children: Is Adoption by Gays and Lesbians Part of the Answer for Boys and Girls Who Need Homes?" and is available online at the Institute's Web site. The American Psychological Association, the American Academy of Pediatrics, the National Association of Social Workers, and the Child Welfare League of America have all issued statements in support of lifting bans on same-sex couple adoption and foster parenting. Statements and references are posted on the Web site of the National Center for Lesbian Rights.

81. Whether slavery did or did not obliterate black families is much debated. In a review of a number of histories of slavery, Angela Davis (1981) has suggested that it did not. Hortense Spillers, however, has argued that by denying any parental rights to enslaved women, the institution effectively abolished black maternity (Spillers 1987, 79). These two views can be reconciled semantically, at least somewhat, but some of the views discussed in these two articles cannot be.

82. For an extended commentary on this point, see Ferguson 2004, chapter 4, where he writes, "The Moynihan Report attempted to transform a presumably 'pathological' culture into one that was suitable for gender and sexual conformity and compliant with heteropatriarchal regulation" (2004, 122).

83. Herzog does hint at some of these criticisms, however, foreshadowing feminist critiques to come. She does wonder, momentarily, whether the presence of a male should be the sole measure of family stability, and she does say in conclusion that The Black Family is a fiction and that there are many kinds of families (Herzog 1972, 147 and 157).

84. This was, of course, a predominantly white view, but there were black people who took up these stereotypes as at least partially true, particularly the idea that black women emasculated black men. Black feminists have tried to debunk this idea since it was first put forth. See, for example, Bond and Peery 1970, 141–48. Patricia Hill Collins addresses this issue at length in Collins 2005, especially Part II.

85. This is not arrogance or selfishness, self-styled "paleoconservative" Patrick Buchanan insists, "but a new moral certitude and self-confidence on the part of those to whom the truth has been given" (2002, 246).

86. See Duster 1990; McLaren 1990; Hasian 1996; Kline 1997. See also Rafter 1997, 212, and Dowbiggen 1997, 240.

87. For the past fifty years, sociological studies have tended to show a

decline in racist beliefs about blacks among whites. For a recent appraisal of that phenomenon, including a discussion of the various ways in which it has been interpreted, see Bonilla-Silva 2003, 4–8.

88. In 1969, Paul Popenoe asserted that "the fundamental proposition" of eugenics was "that important human traits are inherited, and that survival of a nation is possible only if a majority of births are in families that can produce children who are mentally and physically sound rather than defective" (quoted in Ladd-Taylor 2001, 302). I suspect that a majority of people in the industrialized world believe that proposition still. And even those who don't believe in the inheritance of behavioral traits probably believe in state and private intervention to eradicate and prevent behavioral abnormalities by regulating sexuality and family life. We suffer from the effects of biopower because so many of us buy into it.

7. (Counter) Remembering Racism

1. Laughlin pressured the Census Bureau for years to adopt this term to cover the categories of people that they called "defectives" (primarily the insane), "dependents" (the elderly and infirm), and "delinquents" (prisoners) since 1880. The Census Bureau finally prevailed in 1919, but Laughlin continued to press for the use of this phrase in other government agencies, and as the reports to various state legislatures in those years demonstrate, he often succeeded. See E. Black 2003, 159–60.

2. It is true, as an anonymous reader of this manuscript pointed out, that Foucault's work blurs disciplinary boundaries, particularly the boundary between philosophy and history, so my insistence here on the philosophical as opposed to the historical nature of my project may seem a little odd. However, when it came to genealogical work, Foucault himself was very adamant on this particular point: "The analysis of these power relations may, of course, open out onto or initiate something like the overall analysis of a society. The analysis of mechanisms of power may also join up with the history of economic transformations, for example, But what I am doing . . . is not history, sociology, or economics. . . . [W]hat I am doing is something that concerns philosophy, that is to say, the politics of truth, for I do not see many other definitions of the word 'philosophy' apart from this. So, insofar as what is involved in this analysis of mechanisms of power is the politics of truth, and not sociology, history, or economics, I see its role as that of showing the knowledge effects produced by the struggles, confrontations, and battles that take place within our society, and by the tactics of power that are the elements of this struggle" (2007, 2–3).

3. This occurred in Baltimore at the Christian Coalition's Racial Reconciliation Congress on May 10, 1997. According to the *Washington Post,* "Ralph Reed acknowledged the Christian right's past support of segregation and asked the audience of about 300 black churchgoers for 'absolution'" (Argetsinger 1997). In exchange for absolution and black support, Reed unveiled the Christian Coalition's Samaritan Project, designed to channel money to inner-city black churches' social programs. There are those who have suggested that this effort was an insincere attempt to undermine black leaders, contending that they are out of touch with their constituencies. One might note

the name of the conference, which conjures up two major civil-rights-era organizations, the Fellowship of Reconciliation and the Congress of Racial Equality. Writing in *Newsweek* in 1993, Farai Chideya charged that the Christian Right, in particular the Traditional Values Coalition, was deliberately driving a wedge between black leaders and conservative black Christians by producing a video entitled "Gay Rights/Special Rights," which they sent to 50,000 churches and Christian bookstores in black communities. In the video, TVC founder Rev. Lou Sheldon declares, "The freedom train to Selma has been hijacked." And Mississippi Senator Trent Lott and former Attorney General Edwin Meese both make appearances in support of black civil rights and in denunciation of gay and lesbian activists' allusions to the mid-century movement. See Chideya 1993, 73. Former Clinton staffer and executive director of the National Black Gay and Lesbian Leadership Forum Keith Boykin has made a similar charge. Boykin writes, "In an effort to confuse and anger African Americans, the religious right has embarked on a campaign to convince blacks that homosexuals are claiming to be exactly like they are," the purpose of which is "to divide two oppressed minorities from each other, outwardly to weaken the homosexual movement but actually to splinter all those with whom the right disagrees" (Boykin 1996, 48–49).

4. Whites made up 19.9 percent, with 975 victims; Asian/Pacific Islanders made up 4.9 percent, with 240 victims; Native Americans and Alaskan Natives made up 2 percent, with 97 victims; and in 4.9 percent of the cases, the victims or groups of victims were of mixed race. See these statistics at www.fbi.gov/ucr/hc2005/incidentsoffenses.htm. No doubt most or all of these categories are underreported. For evidence that attacks against South Asians are underreported, see Melwani 2003.

5. This information, which does not include the victim's name, comes from the Missouri Court of Appeals decision in case number ED85588, handed down December 20, 2005. The appeals court upheld the lower court's conviction of second degree murder. See www.courts.mo.gov/courts/pubopinions.nsf.

6. For details of the crime, see Richie and Minugh 2007, and Richie 2007.

7. See Kiefer 2005. It is particularly ironic that one of the three victims, twenty-seven-year-old Kenneth Brown, was Native American.

8. For details on the San Diego arson case, see "Schwarzenegger Condemns Attack" 2006. For details on the New Orleans shooting, see Scallan 2006.

9. The Anti-Defamation League monitors many of these sites. This quotation comes from their report. See Anti-Defamation League 2006.

10. I compiled the list from newspaper articles in my possession, which I had collected over the past several years. No doubt many other violent crimes were reported in newspapers I simply did not have access to. And of course many hate crimes against queer people are not reported in newspapers. In May of 2007, *New York Times* reporter Ian Urbina cited studies by the National Gay and Lesbian Task Force and the Coalition for the Homeless indicating that at least 20 percent of homeless youths under the age of 21 are homosexual, bisexual, or transgendered and have left home because they suffered violence at the hands of relatives. Many also suffer violence in homeless shelters and so often don't seek services that are available (Urbina 2007). This is merely an

indication that violence against people because of their sexual orientation is far more extensive than the incidents that make headlines.

11. Yes, that means 2 percent were anti-heterosexual hate crimes. It does happen, just as 19.9 percent of racially motivated hate crimes recorded by the FBI that year were anti-white. See these statistics at www.fbi.gov/ucr/hc2005/incidentsoffenses.htm.

12. All of the NCAVP annual reports can be found at www.avp.org/publications/reports/reports.htm.

13. As if we should accept the routine rape of straight women as a simple fact of life.

14. The classic text is, of course, James Madison's Federalist Number 10, in Madison, Hamilton, and Jay's *The Federalist Papers,* published in 1787. There Madison explains that the evils of democracy, which include the tyranny of what might be a misguided majority faction over an enlightened minority, can be offset by a representative republican form of government and a large population with a relatively large deliberative body. See Madison et al. 1937, 53–62.

15. M. G. Smith offers an interesting history of the evolution of the term *minority* in sociology through 1978. Smith (1987, 341) cites L. Mair, *The Protection of Minorities* (1928) as the first use of the term in its modern sense. He then goes on to suggest that the first systematic usages of the term should really be dated as 1945, with the publication of L. Wirth's "The Problem of Minority Groups," in *The Science of Man in the World Crisis,* ed. R. Linton (New York: Columbia University Press).

16. The last case where race was allowed as a means of classification was *Korematsu v. U.S.,* 323 U.S. 214 (1944) in a six to three decision.

17. See *Graham v. Richardson,* 1971. The word *alienage* simply means the state of being an alien or a noncitizen.

18. This first occurred in *Craig v. Boren,* 429 U.S. 190 (1976), a sex discrimination case. Oklahoma had set the age at which males can purchase 3.2% beer at 21, while for females the age was 18. They had also set the age for criminal responsibility at 18 for females and 16 for males. Substantial statistical information was provided to the Court to demonstrate that the behavior of males and females differed and thus differential treatment was appropriate for the legitimate governmental purpose of reducing the incidence of drunk driving. However, the Court held that differential treatment on the basis of sex in this case invidiously discriminated against males.

19. Paul Popenoe and many other old-style eugenicists would have argued that the government does have a real interest in discriminating against people on the basis of illegitimacy, because such people are inevitably biologically inferior to legitimate persons. By the mid-1970s such eugenic language was out of fashion, of course, but promotion of the Family was considered a paramount concern of government. Lawyers for the state of Illinois argued in *Trimble v. Gordon* 430 U.S. 762 (1977) that prohibiting illegitimate children from inheriting from their father's estate if he died intestate was a way of promoting legitimate family bonds. A majority of the U.S. Supreme Court (5–4) was not convinced by their argument. "No one disputes the appropriateness of Illinois'

concern with the family unit, perhaps the most fundamental social institution of our society," said Justice Powell, writing for the majority. "The flaw in the analysis lies elsewhere." In previous opinions, which Powell cited, the Court had opposed state measures that attempted to control the behavior of adults by taking steps directed against their children. "The Equal Protection Clause requires more than the mere incantation of a proper state purpose," he said; it would require a clear causal argument that would show efficacy and balance the interests of the child and the interests of the state. Illinois failed to do that, so the Court held that the Illinois Probate Act was in violation of the Fourteenth Amendment. Thus legitimacy became a quasi-suspect class along with sex, a trigger for heightened but not strict scrutiny.

20. Boykin cites a press release from the Traditional Values Coalition dated July 29, 1994, which proclaims: "There is no comparison: Homosexuals are not the same as racial minorities." See Boykin 1996, 48.

21. Cited in E. Roberts 1993, 497.

22. For some background on systematic efforts to do this by using the issue of homosexuality as a wedge, see Solomon 1999, esp. 64. In 1993 the right-wing organization Citizens United for the Preservation of Civil Rights produced a video entitled *Gay Rights/Special Rights: Inside the Homosexual Agenda* especially for black Christian audiences. They mailed free copies to black churches across the country and urged ministers to play the video for their congregations to warn them of the ways in which the "gay agenda" would damage blacks' civil status.

23. The amendment passed in November of 2006 and enshrined in the state constitution a law that had been enacted in 2004 voiding all contracts between same-sex couples that were intended to give them any rights that might be granted automatically to couples who obtain marriage licenses. The law and the amendment are vague, so at present it is not known whether same-sex couples in Virginia who have a variety of contracts concerning property, child custody, medical decision making, and so forth will be able to count on the courts' honoring those agreements should there be a dispute.

24. Kate Kendell suggests that it is also a sign, sometimes, that queer people have little confidence that our concerns and issues can stand on their own. She writes, "I think the reason for these comparisons may have been a failure to appreciate our own history as queer people in this country, or perhaps a fear that our own history would not resonate enough with the rest of America" (Kendell 2005, 135).

25. The Lovings had a marriage license issued in Washington, D.C., where they had gone to be married on June 2, 1958. They framed it and hung it on the wall of their bedroom. The sheriff, acting in accordance with Virginia state law, simply refused to recognize its validity when he sent three police officers to burst into their room in the dead of night on June 11 (Newbeck 2005, 11).

26. As previous chapters in this book have suggested, there *are* similarities between the effort to prevent same-sex coupling and the effort to prevent interracial coupling. But they are not as simple as a parallel between two sets of laws. A better place to look is in the rhetoric attorneys have used to defend the respective laws. As Boykin points out, Virginia's arguments in support of its

anti-miscegenation laws in *Loving v. Virginia* in 1967 do look like some of the arguments Washington state attorneys used to defend denying licenses to same-sex couples in *Singer v. Hara* (Boykin 1996, 250–51).

27. He uses this term in the Traditional Values Coalition video *Gay Rights/ Special Rights*. See Chideya 1993, 73.

28. In fact, some of them, at times, are black gay and lesbian activists like author Barbara Smith, who objected to New York Lesbian Avengers' use of the term "freedom ride" for a political action they took in October of 1993 (1998, 128).

29. This is a question that African American *Washington Post* columnist William Raspberry was already asking in relation to same-sex marriage in 1997: "What are we afraid of?" I don't know what answers Raspberry would offer to his own question, so I can't know whether they would agree with the ones I offer below, but perhaps some of them would. Here is an excerpt from his January 31 column: "I confess that the idea of going against widely held beliefs makes me uneasy. Sometimes what we see as mere prejudices turn out to be the hard-earned collective wisdom of society. But sometimes (as used to be the case for transracial marriage) they *are* mere prejudices—no matter what social or scientific or religious evidence we offer in their defense. I could, if I put my mind to it, come up with a fair load of evidence against same-sex marriage. What keeps me from doing so is experience. I've known enough committed gay and lesbian couples to lose my fear that they are somehow dangerous. Many of these couples have seemed as loving and as devoted to one another as my wife and I. And if they want to mark that commitment by invoking the religious and civil forms used for the purpose, why isn't that a good thing? What are we afraid of?" (Raspberry 1997).

30. Of course it is important not to overstate the gains made. The movement failed in many respects. It did not eliminate racism, and it did not even better the economic situations or improve the prospects of many African Americans.

31. In response to the effort to outlaw same-sex marriage licensure through amendments to the U.S. Constitution, Lewis, now a Congressman representing Georgia's Fifth District, posted this statement on his Congressional Web site in June of 2006: "I have fought too long and too hard to abolish legalized discrimination in America to be silent when the President of the United States advocates writing it into the U.S. Constitution." In his 1998 memoir, *Walking with the Wind,* Lewis wrote:

> The gay community, women—my connection with them and their
> issues sprang from that same affinity I felt with Jewish people,
> the understanding of what it means to be treated unequally, to
> be treated as less than, simply because you are different from
> the long-entrenched white Anglo-Saxon Protestant standard that
> defined and controlled our society for its first two hundred years.
>
> We have come a long way in recent decades in terms of our
> treatment of blacks and women and gays in America—and
> Hispanics, and Native Americans, and the poor. But we still
> have a good way to go. And we must not tolerate the kind of

backlash that has gathered in recent years against each of these movements—the attempts to repeal affirmative action, the hard-heartedness of wholesale welfare reform, the rising complaints of that newly emerging "oppressed" class of Americans, white males. Those complaints might well be, to a certain extent, justified. But there is a difference between fixing something and throwing it out. We must never lose sight of the distance we have traveled in recent decades in pursuit of a just, fair and inclusive Beloved Community, and we must not let the kinks in the programs we have created along the way blind us to the worthiness of what those programs aim to achieve. (Lewis 1998, 468)

32. Charles Mills's essay "White Right: The Idea of a *Herrenvolk* Ethics" examines this issue in some philosophical depth. The dominant morality, Mills argues, is a morality that valorizes and privileges whites, even while maintaining a veneer of racial neutrality (1998, 139–66). Compare also bell hooks 2004, 70: "Assimilation is . . . a strategy deeply rooted in the ideology of white supremacy and its advocates urge black people to negate blackness, to imitate racist white people so as to better absorb their values, their way of life."

33. One of the best-known critiques at the end of the century was queer theorist Michael Warner's *The Trouble with Normal* (1999). Warner is particularly critical of the same-sex marriage movement. This book is required reading for anyone interested in that issue.

34. See Stern 2005, 10: "The protest movements of the 1960s and 1970s —ranging from feminism to gay liberation—arose in part as an assault on the decades-long effects of eugenics-based policies and rationales. Certainly, the 1960s should not be reduced to a revolt against eugenics, but this tumultuous era cannot be comprehended outside of the troubled history of hereditarianism in the United States."

35. This has occurred whenever gay and lesbian groups have refused to work with and support rights for transgendered people, whenever LGBT groups have purposely projected the idea that most of us are middle class despite the obvious fact that persecution prevents many of us from finishing our educations and discrimination prevents us from getting decent jobs, whenever LGBT antiviolence groups have neglected to analyze the fact that a high percentage of reported anti-queer violence is perpetrated against queer people of color, whenever any of us has refused to see HIV as anything but a gay disease and therefore unimportant in the lives of people of color, and whenever straight African Americans have ostracized or injured queer African Americans on the grounds that such people are traitors to the black race or not really black. I could cite reams of examples of all these things. They happen all the time. We have turned the weaponry of normality on our own groups over and over again, and many of us die of friendly fire.

36. Keith Boykin, former executive director of the National Black Gay and Lesbian Leadership Forum, points out that to the extent that the black civil rights movement of the 1950s and 60s did promote acceptance of black people as more or less like the white mainstream—by carefully managing demonstrations such as the 1963 March on Washington, for example—it failed to

transform society. He writes, "It became acceptable to be black and prosperous and well-educated, but poor, undereducated blacks were still despised" (Boykin 1996, 66).

37. Pat Buchanan attributes this phrase to Katarina Runske, who (according to Buchanan) has studied the 2000 census figures and determined that because so many women are refusing to marry or stay married, (white) America's population is dwindling. Buchanan concludes, "In short, the rise of feminism spells the death of the nation and the end of the West" (2002, 42).

38. Examples include the debate over whether to take the risk of staging the Freedom Rides in 1961 to protest segregation in interstate travel, whether to allow the Children's March in Birmingham in 1963, and whether to resume the 1965 Selma march immediately after Bloody Sunday without waiting for a court ruling.

WORKS CITED

"Accused rapists have ties to KKK, investigators say." 2006. WIStv.com Columbia, S.C. (July 10).

Adorno, T. W., Else Frankel-Brunswik, Daniel J. Levinson, and R. Nevitt Sanford. 1950. *The Authoritarian Personality.* New York: Harper and Brothers.

Agar, Nicholas. 2004. *Liberal Eugenics: In Defence of Human Enhancement.* Oxford: Blackwell.

"Alabama prefers abusive father." 1998. *Washington Blade,* May 15:23.

Alcoff, Linda. 2006. *Visible Identities: Race, Gender, and the Self.* Oxford: Oxford University Press.

Aldaraca, Bridget A. 1995. "On the Use of Medical Diagnosis as Name-Calling: Anita F. Hill and the Rediscovery of 'Erotomania.'" In *Black Women in America,* ed. Kim Maria Vaz, 206–21. London: Sage Publications.

Allen, Theodore W. 1997. *The Invention of the White Race: The Origin of Racial Oppression in Anglo-America.* London: Verso.

Allison, Dorothy. 1992. *Bastard Out of Carolina.* New York: Penguin Books.

Allport, Gordon W. 1954. *The Nature of Prejudice.* Reading, Mass.: Addison-Wesley.

Anti-Defamation League. 2006. "Extremists Declare 'Open Season' on Immigrants; Hispanics Target of Incitement and Violence." www.anti-defamationleague.us/hispanics_target_of_incitement_and_violence.htm. Washington, D.C. (April 24).

Appel, Toby A. 1987. *The Cuvier-Geoffroy Debate: French Biology in the Decades Before Darwin.* New York: Oxford University Press.

Ariès, Philippe. 1962. *Centuries of Childhood: A Social History of Family Life.* Trans. Robert Baldick, New York: Vintage.

Argetsinger, Amy. 1997. "Christian Coalition Courts Black Churches; Group Promises Aid to Inner City In Return for Political Support." *Washington Post.* May 11:A18.

Bacon, Charles S. 1903. "The race problem." *Medicine* 9:338–43.

Banton, Michael. 1987. "The Classification of races in Europe and North America: 1700–1850." *International Social Science Journal* 39 (Feb. 1987): 45–60.

Barr, Martin W. 1913. *Mental Defectives: Their History, Treatment and Training.* Philadelphia: P. Blakiston's Son and Co.

Bartelson, Jens. 1995. *A Genealogy of Sovereignty.* Cambridge: Cambridge University Press.

Bartlett, Irving H. 1993. *John C. Calhoun: A Biography.* New York: W.W. Norton.

Baum, Bruce. 2006. *The Rise and Fall of the Caucasian Race: A Political History of Racial Identity.* New York: New York University Press.

Bayer, Ronald. 1981. *Homosexuality and American Psychiatry: The Politics of Diagnosis.* New York: Basic Books.

Beard, George M. 1972a [1881]. *American Nervousness: Its Causes and Consequences.* New York: Arno Press.

———. 1972b [1898]. *Sexual Neurasthenia: Its Hygiene, Causes, Symptoms and Treatment,* 5th ed. New York: Arno Press.

Beauchamp, Kevin. 2005. *The Untold Story of Emmett Louis Till.* THINKFilms LLC.

Benedict, Ruth. 1943. *Race: Science and Politics.* New York: Viking Press.

Bernasconi, Robert, ed. 2001. *Race.* Oxford: Blackwell.

Bernasconi, Robert, and Tommy Lott, eds. 2000. *The Idea of Race.* Indianapolis: Hackett.

Bierce, Ambrose. 2006. "Crime and its Correctives." www.olympus.net/personal/gspencer/bierce07.html. This essay is from *The Shadow on the Dial and Other Essays,* published originally in 1909.

Binger, Carl. 1966. *Revolutionary Doctor: Benjamin Rush, 1746–1813.* New York: W.W. Norton.

Black, Edwin. 2003. *War Against the Weak: Eugenics and America's Campaign to Create a Master Race.* New York: Four Walls Eight Windows.

Black, Robert W. 1998. "Shepard Murder Hearing Under Way." Associated Press, November 19.

Bland, Lucy, and Laura Doan, eds. 1998. *Sexology Uncensored: The Documents of Sexual Science.* Chicago: University of Chicago Press.

Blaustein, Albert P., and Robert L. Zangrando, eds. 1991. *Civil Rights and African Americans.* Evanston, Ill.: Northwestern University Press.

Block, Iwan. 1907. *The Sexual Life of Our Time.* Excerpted in *Sexology Uncensored: The Documents of Sexual Science,* ed. Lucy Bland and Laura Doan. Chicago: University of Chicago Press, 1998.

Boag, Peter. 2003. *Same-Sex Affairs: Constructing and Controlling Homosexuality in the Pacific Northwest.* Berkeley: University of California Press.

Bond, Jean Carey, and Patricia Peery. 1970. "Is the Black Male Castrated?" In *The Black Woman: An Anthology,* ed. Toni Cade Bambara. New York: Washington Square Press.

Bond, Julian. 2006. "Virginia is against loving—again." *Richmond Free Press,* August 24–26: A1, A6.

Bonilla-Silva, Eduardo. 2003. *Racism Without Racists; Color-Blind Racism and the Persistence of Racial Inequality in the United States.* Lanham, Md.: Rowman and Littlefield.

Booher, Kary. 2004a. "In the footsteps of civil rights? Local pair fights for gay marriage recognition." *Jackson Sun* (March 14).

———. 2004b. "Comparing gay marriage, civil rights movements: Family with history of local civil rights fights has differing opinions." *Jackson Sun* (March 14).

Boulton, Alexander O. 1995. "The American Paradox: Jeffersonian Equality and Racial Science." *American Quarterly* 47, no. 3 (September): 467–92.

Boxill, Bernard. 2001. "Introduction." In *Race and Racism,* ed. Bernard Boxill, 1–42. Oxford: Oxford University Press.

Boykin, Keith. 1996. *One More River to Cross: Black and Gay in America.* New York: Anchor Books.

———. 1999. "Blacks and Gays in Conflict: An Interview with United States Representative Barney Frank." In *Dangerous Liaisons: Blacks, Gays, and the Struggle for Equality,* 70–79. New York: New Press.

———. 2005. *Beyond the Down Low: Sex, Lies, and Denial in Black America.* New York: Carroll and Graf.

Brace, C. Loring. 2005. *"Race" Is a Four-Letter Word: The Genesis of the Concept.* New York: Oxford University Press.

Brandt, Eric, ed. 1999. *Dangerous Liaisons: Blacks, Gays, and the Struggle for Equality.* New York: New Press.

Bromberg, Norbert, and Verna Volz Small. 1983. *Hitler's Psychopathology.* New York: International Universities Press.

Bruinius, Harry. 2006. *Better for all the World: The Secret History of Forced Sterilization and America's Quest for Racial Purity.* New York: Alfred A. Knopf.

Buchanan, Patrick J. 2002. *The Death of the West: How Dying Populations and Immigrant Invasions Imperil Our Country and Civilization.* New York: Thomas Dunne Books.

Bullough, Vern L. 1987. "Technology for the Prevention of 'Les Maladies Produite par la Masturbation." *Technology and Culture* 28, no. 4 (October): 828–32.

Carby, Hazel. 1985. "'On the Threshold of Women's Era': Lynching, Empire, and Sexuality in Black Feminist Theory." *Critical Inquiry* 12, no. 1 (Autumn): 262–77.

Carlson, Elof Axel. 2001. *The Unfit: A History of a Bad Idea.* Cold Spring Harbor, N.Y.: Cold Spring Harbor Laboratory Press.

Carlson, Eric T. 1985. "Medicine and Degeneration: Theory and Praxis." In *Degeneration: The Dark Side of Progress,* ed. J. Edward Chamberlin and Sander L. Gilman. New York: Columbia University Press.

Carlson, Licia. 2001. "Cognitive Ableism and Disability Studies: Feminist Reflections on the History of Mental Retardation." *Hypatia* 16, no. 4 (Fall): 124–46.

Carmichael, Stokely, and Charles V. Hamilton. 1967. *Black Power: The Politics of Liberation in America.* New York: Vintage.

Carter, Julian. 1997. "Normality, Whiteness, Authorship: Evolutionary Sexology and the Primitive Pervert." In *Science and Homosexualities,* ed. Vernon Rosario, 155–76. New York: Routledge.

Chideckel, Maurice. 1935. *Female Sex Perversion.* New York: Eugenics Publishing Co.

Chideya, Farai. 1993. "How the Right Stirs Black Homophobia." *Newsweek* (October 18): 73.

Clark, Keith. 1998. "New Jersey extends equal adoption status." *Our Own.* (Richmond, Va.) Vol. 22, no. 3 (January): 1.

Clarke, Cheryl. 1983. "The Failure to Transform: Homophobia in the Black Community." *Home Girls: A Black Feminist Anthology,* ed. Barbara Smith. New York: Kitchen Table: Women of Color Press.

Colbourn, H. Trevor. 1958. "Thomas Jefferson's Use of the Past." In *William and Mary Quarterly*, 3rd Series, vol. 15, no. 1 (January): 56–70.

Collins, Patricia Hill. 1991. *Black Feminist Thought: Knowledge, Consciousness, and the Politics of Empowerment.* New York: Routledge.

———. 2005. *Black Sexual Politics: African Americans, Gender, and the New Racism.* New York: Routledge.

Connelly, Kate. 2001. "Hitler was gay—and killed to hide it, book says." *The Observer* (October 7). http://observer.guardian.co.uk/international/story/0,6903,564899,00.html.

Cory, Donald Webster. 1975. *The Homosexual in America: A Subjective Approach.* New York: Arno Press.

Daniel, F. E. 1893. "Should Insane Criminals, or Sexual Perverts, be Allowed to Procreate?" *Medico-Legal Journal* 11, no. 3 (December): 275–92.

Davis, Angela. 1981. *Women, Race, and Class.* New York: Vintage.

Deaver, Danielle. 2003. "WFU medical school apologizes again for role." *Winston-Salem Journal.* http://againsttheirwill.journalnow.com.

Deggans, Eric. 2004. "Gay rights/civil rights." *St. Petersburg Times* (January 18).

D'Emilio, John. 1998. *Sexual Politics, Sexual Communities: The Making of a Homosexual Minority in the United States, 1940–1970,* 2nd ed. Chicago: University of Chicago Press.

———. 1989. "The Homosexual Menace: The Politics of Sexuality in Cold War America." In *Passion and Power: Sexuality in History,* ed. Kathy Peiss and Christina Simmons, 226–40. Philadelphia: Temple University Press.

Dennis, Lawrence. 1936. *The Coming American Fascism.* New York: Harper and Bros.

DePasquale, Ron. 2004. "Gay debate splits black community." *Chicago Tribune,* March 14.

Deutsch, Albert. 1944. "The First US Census of the Insane (1840) and Its Use as Pro-slavery Propaganda." *Bulletin of the History of Medicine* 15 (May): 469–82.

Dice, Lee R. 1952. "Heredity Clinics: Their Value for Public Service and for Research." *American Journal of Human Genetics* 4, no. 1:1–13. This article is reproduced in *Eugenics Then and Now,* ed. Carl Jay Bajema, 336–48. Stroudburg, Pa.: Dowden, Hutchinson, and Ross, 1976.

Dickinson, Robert L. 1947. "Anatomy and Physiology of the Sex Organs." In *Successful Marriage: An Authoritative Guide to Problems Related to Marriage from the Beginning of Sexual Attraction to Matrimony and the Successful Rearing of a Family,* ed. Morris Fishbein, 69–91. Garden City, N.Y.: Doubleday.

Dorr, Linda Lindquist. 1999. "Arm in Arm: Gender, Eugenics, and Virginia's Racial Integrity Acts of the 1920s." *Journal of Women's History* 11, no. 1 (Spring): 143–67.

Dowbiggin, Ian Robert. 1997. *Keeping America Sane: Psychiatry and Eugenics in the United States and Canada, 1880–1940.* Ithaca, N.Y.: Cornell University Press.

Du Bois, W.E.B. 1935. *Black Reconstruction in America, 1860–1880.* New York: Simon & Schuster.

———. 1996. *The Oxford W.E.B. Du Bois Reader,* ed. Eric J. Sundquist. New York: Oxford University Press.

Duffy, John. 2003. "Clitoridectomy: A Nineteenth Century Answer to Masturbation." The Female Genital Cutting Education and Networking Project, www.fgmnetwork.org/articles/duffy.htm.

Duster, Troy. 1990. *Back Door to Eugenics.* New York: Routledge.

Edlin, Gordon. 1990. "Reducing Racial and Ethnic Prejudice by Presenting a Few Facts of Genetics." *American Biology Teacher* 52, no. 8 (Nov./Dec.): 504–6.

Edsall, Nicholas C. 2003. *Toward Stonewall: Homosexual and Society in the Modern Western World.* Charlottesville: University of Virginia Press.

Eigen, Sara, and Mark Larrimore, eds. 2006. *The German Invention of Race.* Albany: State University of New York Press.

Ellis, Havelock. 1926. *The Problem of Race Re-generation.* New York: Privately Printed by Douglas C. McMurtrie. This pamphlet was originally printed in 1911 as the first of "New Tracts for the Times" published for the National Council for Public Morals by Cassell and Co., Ltd., London.

Ellis, Havelock, and John Addington Symmonds. 1975. *Sexual Inversion.* New York: Arno Press. Originally London: Wilson and Macmillan, 1897.

Engelhardt, H. Tristram, Jr. 1974. "The Disease of Masturbation: Values and the Concept of Disease." *Bulletin of the History of Medicine:* 234–48.

Eskew, Glenn T. 1997. *But For Birmingham: The Local and National Movements in the Civil Rights Struggle.* Chapel Hill: University of North Carolina Press.

Eyes on the Prize: Episode 1: Awakenings (1954–1956). 1986. Boston: Blackside. Distributed by PBS Video.

Eze, Emmanuel Chukwudi, ed. 1997a. *Postcolonial African Philosophy: A Critical Reader.* Oxford: Blackwell.

———, ed. 1997b. *Race and the Enlightenment: A Reader.* Oxford: Blackwell.

Fausto-Sterling, Anne. 1995. "Gender, Race, and Nation: The Comparative Anatomy of 'Hottentot' Women in Europe, 1815–1817." In *Deviant Bodies,* ed. Jennifer Terry and Jacqueline Urla, 19–48. Bloomington: Indiana University Press.

Ferguson, Philip M. 1994. *Abandoned to Their Fate: Social Policy and Practice toward Severely Retarded People in America, 1820–1920.* Philadelphia: Temple University Press.

Ferguson, Roderick A. 2004. *Aberrations in Black: Toward a Queer of Color Critique.* Minneapolis: University of Minnesota Press.

Fisher, R. A. 1924. "The Elimination of Mental Defect." *Eugenics Review* 16: 114–16.

Fishman, Sterling. 1982. "The History of Childhood Sexuality." *Journal of Contemporary History* 17:269–83.

Fiske, Warren. 2004. "The Black and White World of Walter Plecker." *Style Weekly* (Richmond, VA) 22, no. 38 (September 22): 14, 17–19.

Foskett, Ken. 1998. "The conservative King; critics say she twists the legacy of her slain uncle; supporters say she saves it." *Atlanta Journal and Constitution,* January 18:1C.

Foucault, Michel. 1970. *The Order of Things: An Archeology of the Human Sciences*. New York: Vintage Books.

———. 1973. *The Birth of the Clinic: An Archeology of Medical Perception*. Trans. A. M. Sheridan Smith. New York: Vintage.

———. 1977. *Discipline and Punish: The Birth of the Prison*. Trans. Alan Sheridan. New York: Vintage Books.

———. 1978. *The History of Sexuality, Volume One: An Introduction*. Trans. Robert Hurley. New York: Vintage Books.

———. 1994. "The Social Triumph of the Sexual Will." In *Ethics, Subjectivity, and Truth: The Essential Works of Michel Foucault, 1954–1984*, Vol. 1. Ed. Paul Rabinow, 157–62. New York: Free Press.

———. 1998. "Nietzsche, Genealogy, History." In *Aesthetics, Method, and Epistemology: The Essential Works of Michel Foucault, 1954–1984*, Vol. 2. Ed. James D. Faubion, 369–91. New York: Free Press.

———. 2003a. *Abnormal: Lectures at the College de France 1974–1975*. Trans. Graham Burchell. New York: Picador.

———. 2003b. *"Society Must Be Defended": Lectures at the College de France, 1975–1976*. Trans. David Macey. New York: Picador.

———. 2006. *Psychiatric Power: Lectures at the College de France, 1973–1974*. Trans. Graham Burchell. New York: Palgrave.

———. 2007. *Security, Territory, Population: Lectures at the Collège de France, 1977–1978*. Trans. Graham Burchell. New York: Palgrave.

"Four charged with attempted murder, felony hate crimes." 2006. *Claremont Courier* (December 16). www.claremont-courier.com/pages/Topstory1216.2.html.

Fraser, G. R. 1972. "The Implications of Prevention and Treatment of Inherited Disease for the Genetic Future of Mankind." *Journal de Genetique Humaine* 201, no. 3:185–205.

Fredrickson, George M. 1971. *The Black Image in the White Mind: The Debate on Afro-American Character and Destiny, 1817–1914*. New York: Harper and Row.

Freedman, Estelle. 1989. "'Uncontrolled Desires': The Response to the Sexual Psychopath, 1920–1960." In *Passion and Power: Sexuality in History*, ed. Kathy Peiss and Christina Simmons. Philadelphia: Temple University Press.

———. 1996. "The Prison Lesbian: Race, Class, and the Construction of the Aggressive Female Homosexual, 1915–1965." *Feminist Studies* 22, no. 1 (Summer): 397–423.

Freud, Sigmund. 1931. "Female Sexuality." *Standard Edition*, vol. 21.

Gannett, Lisa. 2001. "Racism and Human Genome Diversity Research: The Ethical Limits of 'Population Thinking.'" *Philosophy of Science* 68, no. 3 (Proceedings Supplement): S479–S492.

Gates, Henry Louis, Jr. 1999. "Backlash?" In *Dangerous Liaisons: Blacks, Gays, and the Struggle for Equality*, 25–30. New York: New Press.

Gerassi, John. 1966. *The Boys of Boise: Furor, Vice, and Folly in an American City*. New York: Macmillan.

Gerbi, Antonello. 1985. *Nature in the New World: From Christopher Columbus to Gonzalo Fernández de Oviedo*. Trans. Jeremy Moyle. Pittsburgh: University of Pittsburgh Press.

Gibson, Margaret. 1997. "Clitoral Corruption: Body Metaphors and American Doctors' Construction of Female Homosexuality, 1870–1900." In *Science and Homosexualities,* ed. Vernon Rosario, 108–32. New York: Routledge.

———. 1998. "The Masculine Degenerate: American Doctors' Portrayals of the Lesbian Intellect, 1880–1949." *Journal of Women's History* 9, no. 4 (Winter): 78–104.

Giddings, Paula. 1984. *When and Where I Enter: The Impact of Black Women on Race and Sex in America.* New York: Harper Collins.

Gilbert, Matthew. 2004. "Was Hitler in Closet: And If So, So What?" *Boston Globe.* April 20: F1.

Giles, Geoffrey. 2002. "Why Bother About Homosexuals? Homophobia and Sexual Politics in Nazi Germany." Washington, DC: United States Holocaust Memorial Museum Center for Advanced Holocaust Studies.

Gilman, Sander L. 1985. *Difference and Pathology: Stereotypes of Sexuality, Race, and Madness.* Ithaca, N.Y.: Cornell University Press.

Gilman, Stuart C. 1983. "Degeneracy and Race in the Nineteenth Century: The Impact of Clinical Medicine." *Journal of Ethnic Studies* 10, no. 4:27–50.

Glad, John. 2006. *Future Human Evolution: Eugenics in the Twenty-first Century.* Schuylkill Haven, Pa.: Hermitage Publishers.

Goddard, Henry Herbert. 1927 [1912]. *The Kallikak Family: A Study in the Heredity of Feeble-Mindedness.* New York: Macmillan.

Goldberg, David Theo. 1993. *Racist Culture: Philosophy and the Politics of Meaning.* Oxford: Blackwell.

Gosney, E. S., and Paul Popenoe. 1929. *Sterilization for Human Betterment: A Summary of the Results of 6,000 Operations in California, 1909–1929.* New York: Macmillan.

Gossett, Thomas F. 1997. *Race: The History of an Idea in America.* New ed. New York: Oxford University Press.

Gould, Stephen Jay. 1977. *Ontogeny and Phylogeny.* Cambridge, Mass.: Harvard University Press.

———. 1981. *The Mismeasure of Man.* New York: W.W. Norton.

Grady, Denise. 2006. "Racial Component Is Found in Lethal Breast Cancer." *New York Times,* June 7.

Grant, Madison. 1916. *The Passing of the Great Race, Or the Racial Basis of European History.* New York: Charles Scribner's Sons.

Graves, Joseph L., Jr. 2002. "Scylla and Charybdis: Adaptationism, Reductionism, and the Fallacy of Equating Race with Disease." In *Mutating Concepts, Evolving Disciplines: Genetics, Medicine and Society,* ed. L. S. Parker and R. A. Ankeny, 127–41. Dordrecht: Kluwer Academic Publishers.

Green, Richard. 1987. *The "Sissy Boy Syndrome" and the Development of Homosexuality.* New Haven, Conn.: Yale University Press.

Greene, John C. 1959. *The Death of Adam: Evolution and Its Impact on Western Thought.* Ames: Iowa State University Press.

Groneman, Carol. 1995. "Nymphomania: The Historical Construction of Female Sexuality." In *Deviant Bodies,* ed. Jennifer Terry and Jacqueline Urla. Bloomington: Indiana University Press.

Gupta, Gunja San. 2001. "Black and 'Dangerous'? African American Working

Poor Perspectives on Juvenile Reform and Welfare in Victorian New York, 1840–1890." *Journal of Negro History* 86, no. 2 (Spring): 99–131.

Hale, Grace Elizabeth. 1998. *Making Whiteness: The Culture of Segregation in the South, 1890–1940.* New York: Pantheon Books.

Haller, John S., Jr. 1970. "The Physician Versus the Negro: Medical and Anthropological Concepts of Race in the Late Nineteenth Century." *Bulletin of the History of Medicine,* 44 (March/April): 154–67.

———. 1971. *Outcasts from Evolution: Scientific Attitudes of Racial Inferiority, 1859–1900.* Urbana and Chicago: University of Illinois Press.

Haller, Mark. 1963. *Eugenics: Hereditarian Attitudes in American Thought.* New Brunswick, N.J.: Rutgers University Press.

Hammond, William A. 1974 [1887]. *Sexual Impotence in the Male and Female.* New York: Arno Press.

Hampton, Henry, Steve Fayer, and Sarah Flynn, eds. 1990. *Voices of Freedom: An Oral History of the Civil Rights Movement from the 1950s through the 1980s.* New York: Bantam Books.

Hare, E. H. 1962. "Masturbatory Insanity: The History of an Idea." *Journal of Mental Science* 108, no. 452 (January): 1–25.

Hasian, Marouf Arif, Jr. 1996. *The Rhetoric of Eugenics in Anglo-American Thought.* Athens: University of Georgia Press.

Heiner, Brady Thomas. 2007. "Foucault and the Black Panthers." *City* 11, no. 3 (December): 313–56.

Hekma, Gert. 1994. "'A Female Soul in a Male Body': Sexual Inversion as Gender Inversion in Nineteenth-Century Sexology." In *Third Sex, Third Gender: Beyond Sexual Dimorphism in Culture and History,* ed. Gilbert Herdt, 213–39. New York: Zone Books.

Henry, George W. 1941. *Sex Variants: A Study of Homosexual Patterns,* Vol. 2. New York: Paul B. Hoeber.

Herder, Johann Gottfried von. 2000. "Ideas on the Philosophy of the History of Humankind." In *The Idea of Race,* ed. Robert Bernasconi and Tommy Lott, 23–26. Indianapolis: Hackett Publishing Co.

"Heredity and Human Progress." 1900. *The Nation* (November 1): 349–50.

Herschkovitz, I., B. Ring, and E. Kobyliansky. 1990. "Efficiency of Cranial Bilateral Measurements in Separating Human Populations." *American Journal of Physical Anthropology* Vol. 33:307–19.

Herzog, Elizabeth. 1972. "Is There a 'Breakdown' of the Negro Family?" In *The Black Ghetto: Promised Land or Colony?* ed. Richard J. Meister, 147–58. Lexington, Mass.: D.C. Heath and Co. Originally published in *Social Work* 2, no. 1 (January 1966): 3–10.

Hinmon, Derrick. 1991. "18 arrested at restaurant over protest of gay firings." *Atlanta Journal and Constitution.* June 10:C2.

Hoffman, Frederick L. 1892. "Vital Statistics of the Negro." *The Arena,* 29 (April): 529–42.

hooks, bell. 1989. *Talking Back: Thinking Feminist, Thinking Black.* Boston: South End Press.

———. 2004. "Overcoming White Supremacy: A Comment." In *Oppression, Privilege, and Resistance: Theoretical Perspectives on Racism, Sexism, and Heterosexism,* ed. Lisa Heldke and Peg O'Connor. Boston: McGraw Hill.

Horsman, Reginald. 1987. *Josiah Nott of Mobile: Southerner, Physician, and Racial Theorist.* Baton Rouge: Louisiana State University Press.

Howard, William Lee. 1900. "Effeminate Men and Masculine Women." *New York Medical Journal* 71: 686–87.

————. 1903. "The Negro as a Distinct Ethnic Factor in Civilization." *Medicine* 60 (May): 423–26.

————. 1904. "Sexual Perversion in America." *American Journal of Dermatology and Genito-Urinary Diseases* 8:9–14.

Howe, Samuel Gridley. 1972 [1848]. *On the Causes of Idiocy: Being the Supplement to a Report by Dr. S.G. Howe and the Other Commissioners Appointed by the Governor of Massachusetts to Inquire into the Condition of the Idiots of the Commonwealth, Dated February 26, 1848.* New York: Arno Press.

Hughes, John S. 1992. "Labeling and Treating Black Mental Illness in Alabama, 1861–1910." *Journal of Southern History* 58, no. 3 (August): 435–60.

Huie, William Bradford. 1956. "The shocking story of approved killing in Mississippi." *Look* (January 24). www.pbs.org/wgbh/amex/till/sfeature/sf_look_confession.html.

————. 1957. "What happened to the Emmett Till killers?" *Look* (January 22): 63–66.

Hunter, George William. 1941. *Life Science: A Social Biology.* New York: American Book Company.

Huxley, Julian. 1936. "Eugenics and Society." *Eugenics Review* 28, no. 1:11–31.

Huxley, Julian S., and A. C. Haddon. 1936. *We Europeans: A Survey of "Racial" Problems.* New York: Harper Bros.

Ignatiev, Noel. 1995. *How the Irish Became White.* New York: Routledge.

Jaspin, Elliott. 2007. *Buried in the Bitter Waters: The Hidden History of Racial Cleansing in America.* New York: Basic Books.

Jefferson, Thomas. 1944. *Basic Writings of Thomas Jefferson,* ed. Philip S. Foner. New York: Willey Book Co.

Johnson, Wendy. 1997. "MLK's niece criticizes Gays at conference." *Washington Blade.* September 19:16.

Jordan, Winthrop. 1968. *White Over Black: American Attitudes Toward the Negro 1550–1812.* Chapel Hill: University of North Carolina Press.

————. 1974. *The White Man's Burden: Historical Origins of Racism in the United States.* London: Oxford University Press.

"Judge again rules against Lesbian mom." 1998. *Washington Blade,* March 13:14.

Kant, Immanuel. 2001 [1788]. "On the Use of Teleological Principles in Philosophy." Trans. Jon Mark Mikkelsen, in *Race,* ed. Robert Bernasconi, 37–56. Oxford: Blackwell.

————. 2000. "Of the Different Human Races." Trans. Jon Mark Mikkelsen. In *The Idea of Race,* ed. Robert Bernasconi and Tommy Lott, 8–22. Indianapolis: Hackett.

Katz, Jonathan Ned. 1983. *Gay/Lesbian Almanac.* New York: Carroll and Graf.

Kelly, G. Lombard. 1947. "Technic of Marriage Relations." In *Successful*

Marriage: An Authoritative Guide to Problems Related to Marriage from the Beginning of Sexual Attraction to Matrimony and the Successful Rearing of a Family, ed. Morris Fishbein, 92–101. Garden City, N.Y.: Doubleday.

Kendell, Kate. 2005. "Race, Same-Sex Marriage, and White Privilege: The Problem with Civil Rights Analogies." *Yale Journal of Law and Feminism* 17, no. 1:133–37.

Kerlin, Isaac. 1858. *The Mind Unveiled: or, A Brief History of Twenty-Two Imbecile Children*. Philadelphia: U. Hunt and Son.

Kiefer, Michael. 2005. "Murderer of three in Mesa eatery to be executed." *Arizona Republic* (May 13).

Kiernan, James G. 1884. "Insanity: Lecture XXVI, Sexual Perversion." *Detroit Lancet* 7, no. 11 (May): 481–84.

———. 1888. "Sexual Perversion and the Whitechapel Murders." *Medical Standard* 4: 129–30, 170–72.

———. 1892. "Responsibility in Sexual Perversion." *Chicago Medical Recorder* 3 (May): 185–210.

Kilborn, Peter T. 1992. "Gay Rights Groups Take Aim at Restaurant Chain That's Hot on Wall Street." *New York Times*, April 9:A12.

Kilgannon, Corey. 2006. "Queens Jury Returns Guilty Verdict in Hate Crime Case." *New York Times* (June 9). www.nytimes.com/2006/06/09/nyregion/09cnd-howard.html.

King, Martin Luther, Jr. 1986. *A Testament of Hope: The Essential Writings and Speeches of Martin Luther King, Jr.*, ed. James M. Washington. San Francisco: Harper Collins.

Kline, Wendy. 1997. *Building a Better Race: Gender, Sexuality, and Eugenics from the Turn of the Century to the Baby Boom*. Berkeley: University of California Press.

Koonz, Claudia. 2003. *The Nazi Conscience*. Cambridge, Mass.: Belknap Press of Harvard University Press.

Kornweibel, Theodore, Jr. 1998. *"Seeing Red": Federal Campaigns Against Black Militancy, 1919–1925*. Bloomington: Indiana University Press.

Kovel, Joel. 1970. *White Racism: A Psychohistory*. New York: Pantheon.

Krafft-Ebing, Richard von. 1965. *Psychopathia Sexualis, with Especial Reference to the Antipathic Sexual Instinct: A Medico-Forensic Study*, 12th ed. Trans. Franklin S. Klaf. New York: Bell Publishing Co. This edition was originally published in German in 1903 and was the last one Krafft-Ebing edited himself.

Krieger, Nancy, and Mary Bassett. 1993. "The Health of Black Folk: Disease, Class, and Ideology in Science." In *The "Racial" Economy of Science: Toward a Democratic Future*, ed. Sandra Harding, 161–69. Bloomington: Indiana University Press.

Kuby, Dennis. 1993. "Sex Survey May Say Most About Society's Attitudes to Gays; Different Set of Rights." *New York Times*, April 25:16.

Kuhl, Stefan. 1994. *The Nazi Connection: Eugenics, American Racism, and German National Socialism*. New York: Oxford University Press.

Ladd-Taylor, Molly. 2001. "Eugenics, Sterilization and Modern Marriage in the USA: The Strange Career of Paul Popenoe." *Gender and History* 13, no. 2 (August): 298–327.

Landman, J. H. 1933. "The Human Sterilization Movement." *Journal of Criminal Law and Criminology (1931–1951)* 24, no. 2 (July–August): 400–408.

Langer, Walter. 1972. *The Mind of Adolf Hitler: The Secret Wartime Project.* New York: Basic Books.

Laqueur, Thomas W. 2003. *Solitary Sex: A Cultural History of Masturbation.* New York: Zone Books.

Larrimore, Mark. 2006. "Race, Freedom and the Fall in Steffens and Kant." In *The German Invention of Race,* ed. Sara Eigen and Mark Larrimore, 91–120. Albany: State University of New York Press.

Larson, Edward J. 1995. *Sex, Race, and Science: Eugenics in the Deep South.* Baltimore: Johns Hopkins University Press.

Laughlin, Harry H. 1922. "Model Eugenical Sterilization Law." *Eugenical Sterilization in the United States, A Report of the Psychopathic Laboratory of the Municipal Court of Chicago,* Municipal Court of Chicago: 446–52, 454–61. This is reprinted as it appears in the original report in *Eugenics Then and Now,* ed. Carl Jay Bajema, 138–52. Stroudsburg, Pa.: Dowden, Hutchinson & Ross, Inc., 1976.

———. 1939. *Immigration and Conquest.* New York: Special Committee on Immigration and Naturalization of the Chamber of Commerce of the State of New York.

Lempkin, Raphael. 1946. "Genocide." *American Scholar* 15, no. 2 (April): 227–30.

LeVay, Simon. 1993. *The Sexual Brain.* Cambridge, Mass.: MIT Press.

Levin, Michael. 2003. "Responses to Race Differences in Crime." In *Race and Racism,* ed. Bernard Boxill, 145–79. Oxford: Oxford University Press.

Lewis, Carolyn Herbst. 2005. "Waking Sleeping Beauty: The Premarital Pelvic Exam and Heterosexuality During the Cold War." *Journal of Women's History* 17, no. 4 (Winter): 86–112.

Lewis, John, with Michael D'Orso. 1998. *Walking with the Wind: A Memoir of the Movement.* New York: Harcourt Brace.

———. 2006. "Marriage Amendment Is Political Pandering of the Worst Kind." (June 9). www.johnlewis.house.gov.

Lewontin, Richard, Steven Rose, and Leon J. Kamin. 1984. *Not in Our Genes: Biology, Ideology, and Human Nature.* New York: Pantheon.

Lindsay, Matthew. 1998. "Reproducing a Fit Citizenry: Dependency, Eugenics, and the Law of Marriage in the United States, 1860–1920." *Law and Social Inquiry* 23, no. 3 (Summer): 541–85.

Lippmann, Walter. 1976. "A Future for the Tests." In *The IQ Controversy: Critical Readings,* ed. N. J. Block and Gerald Dworkin, 26–29. New York: Pantheon Books.

Lipsitz, George. 1998. *The Possessive Investment in Whiteness: How White People Profit from Identity Politics.* Philadelphia: Temple University Press.

Livingstone, Frank B. 1993. "On the Nonexistence of Human Races." In *The "Racial" Economy of Science: Toward a Democratic Future,* ed. Sandra Harding. Bloomington: Indiana University Press.

Lombardo, Paul A. 1985. "Three Generations, No Imbeciles: New Light on

Buck v. Bell." *New York University Law Review* 60, no. 30 (April): 30–62.

———. 2002. "'The American Breed': Nazi Eugenics and the Origins of the Pioneer Fund." *Albany Law Review* 65, no. 3:743–830.

Lombroso, Caesar, and William Ferrero. 1958 [1895]. *The Female Offender.* New York: Philosophical Library.

Lott, Tommy L. 1999. *The Invention of Race: Black Culture and the Politics of Representation.* Oxford: Blackwell.

Loughery, John. 1998. *The Other Side of Silence: Men's Lives and Gay Identities: A Twentieth-Century History.* New York: Henry Holt and Co.

Lowell, Josephine Shaw. 1879. "One Means of Preventing Pauperism." NCCC *Proceedings, 1879:* 189–200.

Lowery, Thomas Power, ed. 1978. *The Classic Clitoris: Historic Contributions to Scientific Sexuality.* Chicago: Nelson and Hall.

Ludmerer, Kenneth M. 1972. *Genetics and American Society: A Historical Appraisal.* Baltimore: Johns Hopkins University Press.

Ly, Phuong, and Hamil R. Harris. 2004. "Blacks, Gays in Struggle of Values." *Washington Post,* March 15.

Lydston, G. Frank. 1904. *The Diseases of Society (The Vice and Crime Problem).* Philadelphia: J.P. Lippincott.

Machtan, Lothar. 2001. *The Hidden Hitler.* Trans. John Brownjohn. New York: Basic Books.

Madison, James, Alexander Hamilton, and John Jay. 1937. *The Federalist Papers: A Commentary on the Constitution of the United States.* New York: Random House.

Magnis, Nicholas E. 1999. "Thomas Jefferson and Slavery: An Analysis of His Racist Thinking as Revealed by His Writings and Political Behavior." In *Journal of Black Studies* 29, no. 4 (March): 491–509.

Magubane, Zine. 2003. "Simians, Savages, Skulls, and Sex: Science and Colonial Militarism in 19th Century South Africa." In *Race, Nature, and the Politics of Difference,* ed. Donald S. Moore, Jake Kosek, and Anand Pandian, 99–121. Durham, N.C.: Duke University Press.

Mangum, Charles. 1940. *The Legal Status of the Negro.* Chapel Hill: University of North Carolina Press.

Mann, Edward C. 1893. "Medico-Legal and Psychological Aspect of the Trial of Josephine Mallison Smith: Tried for Murder, in Philadelphia, Penn., November 29th, 30th, 31st and December 1st, 1892." *Alienist and Neurologist* 14:467–77.

Margulis, Lynn, and Dorion Sagan. 1991. *Mystery Dance: On the Evolution of Human Sexuality.* New York: Summit Books.

Martinot, Steve. 2003. *The Rule of Racialization: Class, Identity, Governance.* Philadelphia: Temple University Press.

Mason, Gail. 2002. *The Spectacle of Violence: Homophobia, Gender and Knowledge.* London: Routledge.

McAdam, Doug. 1988. *Freedom Summer.* New York: Oxford University Press.

McClintock, Anne. 1995. *Imperial Leather: Race, Gender, and Sexuality in the Colonial Contest.* New York: Routledge.

McCord, Charles H. 1914. *The American Negro as a Dependent, Defective and Delinquent.* Nashville, Tenn.: Benson Printing Co.

McCullen, Kevin. 1998. "Suspect describes how he beat gay Wyoming man, watched as pal left him bound to fence." *Rocky Mountain News* (November 20).

McKim, W. Duncan. 1901. *Heredity and Human Progress.* New York: G.P. Putnam and Sons.

McLaren, Angus. 1990. *Our Own Master Race: Eugenics in Canada, 1885–1945.* Toronto: McCelland and Stewart.

McMurry, Linda O. 1998. *To Keep the Waters Troubled: The Life of Ida B. Wells.* New York: Oxford University Press.

Megary, Mik. 2004. "Don't equate black, gay struggles." *Baltimore Sun,* March 20.

Melwani, Lavina. 2003. "Hate Crimes Against Indians." *Little India* (November 5). www.littleindia.com.

Mendieta, Eduardo. 2000. "The Race of Modernity and the Modernity of Race: On Foucault's Genealogy of Racism." Unpublished paper delivered at the meetings of the Society for Phenomenology and Existential Philosophy at Penn State University.

———. 2002. "'To Make Live and Let Die': Foucault on Racism." Available on Mendieta's Web site: www.sunysb.edu/philosophy/faculty/emendieta/.

Mental Defectives in Virginia: A Special Report of the Board of Charities and Corrections to the General Assembly of 1916, on Weak-Mindedness in the State of Virginia, 1915. Richmond, Va.: David Bottoms, Superintendent of Public Printing.

Mercer, Kobena. 1994. *Welcome to the Jungle: New Positions in Black Cultural Studies.* New York: Routledge.

Metress, Christopher, ed. 2002. *The Lynching of Emmett Till: A Documentary Narrative.* Charlottesville: University of Virginia Press.

Michael, John S. 1988. "A New Look at Morton's Craniological Research." *Current Anthropology* 29, no. 2 (April): 349–50.

Miles, Robert. 1989. *Racism.* London: Routledge.

Miller, Heather Lee. 2000. "Sexologists examine lesbians and prostitutes in the United States, 1840–1940." *NWSA Journal* 12, no. 3 (Fall): 67–83.

Miller, J. F. 1896. "The Effects of Emancipation Upon the Mental and Physical Health of the Negro in the South." *North Carolina Medical Journal* 38, no. 10 (November 20): 285–94.

Miller, Kelly. 1917. "Eugenics of the Negro Race." *Scientific Monthly* 5, no. 1 (July): 57–59.

Mills, Charles W. 1997. *The Racial Contract.* Ithaca, N.Y.: Cornell University Press.

———. 1998. *Blackness Visible: Essays on Philosophy and Race.* Ithaca, NY: Cornell University Press.

Mink, Gwendolyn. 1995. *The Wages of Motherhood: Inequality in the Welfare State, 1917–1942.* Ithaca, N.Y.: Cornell University Press.

Moll, Albert. 1931. *Perversions of the Sex Instinct: A Study of Sexual Inversion Based on Clinical Data and Official Documents.* Trans. Maurice Popkin. Newark, N.J.: Julian Press.

Montagu, Ashley. 2000. "The Concept of Race in the Human Species in the Light of Genetics." In *The Idea of Race,* ed. Robert Bernasconi and Tommy L. Lott. Indianapolis: Hackett.

Moran, Jeffrey P. 2000. *Teaching Sex: The Shaping of Adolescence in the 20th Century.* Cambridge, Mass.: Harvard University Press.

Morgan, Edmund S. 1975. *American Slavery, American Freedom: The Ordeal of Colonial Virginia.* New York: W.W. Norton.

Morris, Holly. 1991. "Gay-rights group targets restaurants; They'll press issue of Cracker Barrel firings." *Atlanta Journal and Constitution,* June 9: D-10.

Mosse, George L. 1982. "Nationalism and Respectability: Normal and Abnormal Sexuality in the Nineteenth Century." *Journal of Contemporary History* 17, no. 2 (April): 221–46.

———. 1985. *Nationalism and Sexuality: Respectability and Abnormal Sexuality in Modern Europe.* New York: Howard Fertig.

Moynihan, Daniel Patrick. 1965. "The Negro Family: The Case for National Action." Office of Policy Planning and Research, U.S. Department of Labor. Washington, D.C. Available online at www.blackpast.org.

Muller, H. J. 1933. "The Dominance of Economics over Eugenics." *Scientific Monthly* 37, no. 1 (July): 40–47.

Murray, Henry A. 1943. "ANALYSIS OF THE PERSONALITY OF ADOLF HITLER with predictions of his future behavior and suggestions for dealing with him now and after Germany's surrender." U.S. Office of Strategic Services. Available online at www.lawschool.cornell.edu/library/donovan/hitler/.

Nacelewicz, Tess. 1999. "Falmouth choosing sides over gay rights." *Portland Press Herald* (October 12). www.portland.com/news/news.shtml.

Nelson, Jennifer. 2003. *Women of Color and the Reproductive Rights Movement.* New York: New York University Press.

Neuhaus, Jessamyn. 2000. "The Importance of Being Orgasmic: Sexuality, Gender, and Marital Sex Manuals in the United States, 1920–1963." *Journal of the History of Sexuality* 9, no. 4 (October): 447–73.

Newbeck, Phyl. 2005. *Virginia Hasn't Always Been For Lovers: Interracial Marriage Bans and the Case of Richard and Mildred Loving.* Carbondale: Southern Illinois University Press.

Niesse, Mark. 2004. "Black Pastors Rally Against Gay Marriage." Associated Press, March 22.

Nott, Josiah. 1843. "The Mulatto a Hybrid—probable extermination of the two races if the Whites and Blacks are allowed to intermarry." *American Journal of the Medical Sciences* (1843): 252–56.

Nott, Josiah, and George Gliddon. 1854. *Types of Mankind: or, Ethnological Researches.* London: Trübner and Co.

Nye, Robert A. 1985. "Sociology and Degeneration: The Irony of Progress." In *Degeneration: The Dark Side of Progress,* ed. J. Edward Chamberlin and Sander L. Gilman, 49–71. New York: Columbia University Press.

Olden, Mariann S. 1974. *History of the Development of the First National Organization for Sterilization.* This volume was privately printed. No publishing information is included. The copy at the Boatwright Memorial Library of the University of Richmond bears a plate inside the front cover that reads: "Gift of Mariann S. Olden."

Olds, Madelin Joan. 1995. "The Rape Complex in the Postbellum South." In

Black Women in America, ed. Kim Marie Vaz, 179–205. London: Sage Publications.

Omi, Michael, and Howard Winant. 1994. *Racial Formation in the United States From the 1960s to the 1990s.* New York: Routledge.

"One in Every Family: Martin Luther King's Niece Speaks Up for Intolerance." 1997. *Pittsburgh Post-Gazette,* August 24: B-2.

Onuf, Peter S. 1990. "'To Declare Them as Free and Independent People': Race, Slavery, and National Identity in Jefferson's Thought." *Journal of the Early Republic* 18, no. 1 (Spring): 1–46.

Ordover, Nancy. 2003. *American Eugenics: Race, Queer Anatomy, and the Science of Nationalism.* Minneapolis: University of Minnesota Press.

Osborn, Frederick. 1937. "Implications of the New Studies in Population and Psychology for the Development of Eugenic Philosophy." *Eugenical News* 22, no. 6:104–107.

———. 1939. "The Comprehensive Program of Eugenics and Its Social Implications." *Living* 1, no. 2/3 (Spring/Summer): 33–38.

———. 1940. *Preface to Eugenics.* New York: Harper and Sons.

———. 1968. *The Future of Human Heredity: An Introduction to Eugenics in Modern Society.* New York: Weybright and Talley.

Osborn, Henry Fairfield. 1921. "The Second International Congress of Eugenics Address of Welcome." *Science.* New Series, 54, no. 1397 (October): 311–13.

Osunsami, Steve. 2004. "Are Gay Rights Civil Rights?" ABC News (March 13). http://abcnews.go.com/sections/WNT/US/same_sex_marriage_movement_040312–1.html.

Outlaw, Lucius. 2003. "Toward a Critical Theory of 'Race.'" In *Race and Racism,* ed. Bernard Boxill, 58–82. Oxford: Oxford University Press.

Parent, Anthony. 2003. *Foul Means: The Formation of a Slave Society in Virginia, 1660–1740.* Chapel Hill: University of North Carolina Press.

Partlow, William. 1936. "A Debt the World Owes Medical Science." *Journal of Medical Association of the State of Alabama* 6, no. 1 (July): 6–12.

Pasmanick, Benjamin. 1964. "Myths Regarding the Prevalence of Mental Disease in the American Negro." *Journal of the National Medical Association* 56, no. 1:6–17.

Patterson, Annette, and Martha Satz. 2002. "Genetic Counseling and the Disabled: Feminism Examines the Stance of Those Who Stand at the Gate." *Hypatia* 17, no. 3 (Summer): 118–42.

Patterson, Orlando. 1998. *Rituals of Blood: Consequences of Slavery in Two American Centuries.* Washington, D.C.: Civitas/Counterpoint.

Paul, Diane B. 1995. *Controlling Human Heredity: 1865 to the Present.* Atlantic Highlands, N.J.: Humanities Press.

———. 1998. *The Politics of Heredity: Essays on Eugenics, Biomedicine, and the Nature-Nurture Debate.* Albany: State University of New York Press.

"Pedophilia." 1937. *Time,* August 23: 42, 44.

Pick, Daniel. 1989. *Faces of Degeneration: A European Disorder, c. 1848–c. 1918.* New York: Cambridge University Press.

Pickens, Donald K. 1967. "The Sterilization Movement: The Search for Purity in Mind and State." *Phylon* 28, no. 1 (1st Qtr.): 78–94.

Pitts, Leonard, Jr. 2004. "Blacks should be supportive of gays' struggle." *Miami Herald,* March 12. www.miami.com/mld/miamiherald/living/columnists/leonard_pitts/8164391.htm.

Plant, Richard. 1986. *The Pink Triangle: The Nazi War Against Homosexuals.* New York: Henry Holt.

Plecker, W. A. 1924. *Eugenics in Relation to The New Family and the Law on Racial Integrity.* Bureau of Vital Statistics, State Board of Health. Richmond, Va.

Poole, Shelia M. 1999. "Plaintiffs seek to expand Cracker Barrel wage suit." *Atlanta Journal and Constitution,* October 16:C3.

Popenoe, Paul. 1926. *The Conservation of the Family.* Baltimore: Williams and Wilkins Co.

———. 1934. "The German Sterilization Law." *Journal of Heredity* 25, no. 7 (July): 257–60.

———. 1935a. "Education and Eugenics." *Journal of Educational Sociology* 8, no. 8, Education and the Family (April): 451–58.

———. 1935b. "Where Are the Marriageable Men?" *Social Forces* 14, no. 2 (December): 257–62.

Popenoe, Paul, and Roswell Hill Johnson. 1926 [1918]. *Applied Eugenics.* New York: Macmillan.

Powell, J. H. 1949. *Bring Out Your Dead: The Great Plague of Yellow Fever in Philadelphia in 1793.* Philadelphia: University of Pennsylvania Press.

Punnett, R. C. 1917. "Eliminating Feeblemindedness." *Journal of Heredity* 8: 464–65.

Quadagno, Jill. 1994. *The Color of Welfare: How Racism Undermined the War on Poverty.* New York: Oxford University Press.

Rae, Isobel. 1964. *Knox: The Anatomist.* Edinburgh: Oliver and Boyd.

Rafter, Nicole Hahn. 1997. *Creating Born Criminals.* Urbana and Chicago: University of Illinois Press.

Raspberry, William. 1997. "Raw Prejudice Impedes Same-Sex Marriage." *Richmond Times-Dispatch,* January 31: A15.

Reilly, Philip. 1991. *The Surgical Solution: A History of Involuntary Sterilization in the United States.* Baltimore: Johns Hopkins University Press.

"Relaxing Quotas for Exiles Fought." 1934. *New York Times,* May 4:7.

Richie, David. 2007. "Man injured in attack at lake dies." *Sacramento Bee,* July 6. http://saldef.org/anm/anmviewer.asp?a=1726&print=yes.

Richie, David, and Kim Minugh. 2007. "Deputies cite reports by witnesses that racism, homophobia fueled lake melee." *Sacramento Bee,* July 4. http://saldef.org/anm/anmviewer.asp?a=1720&print=yes.

Ripley, William Z. 1913 [1899]. *The Races of Europe: A Sociological Study.* London: Kegan Paul, Trench, Trubner and Co.

Roberts, Dorothy. 1997. *Killing the Black Body: Race, Reproduction, and the Meaning of Liberty.* New York: Pantheon.

Roberts, Eric. 1993. "Heightened Scrutiny Under the Equal Protection Clause: A Remedy to Discrimination Based on Sexual Orientation." *Drake Law Review* 42:485–510.

Robinson, William J. 1917. *Eugenics, Marriage and Birth Control [Practical Eugenics].* New York: Critic and Guide Co.

Rosen, Christine. 2004. *Preaching Eugenics: Religious Leaders and the American Eugenics Movement*. Oxford: Oxford University Press.

Rosenberg, Charles E. 1962. "The Place of George M. Beard in Nineteenth Century Psychiatry." *Bulletin of the History of Medicine* 36:245–59.

Rosse, Irving C. 1892. "Sexual Hypochondriasis and Perversion of the Genesic Instinct." *Journal of Mental and Nervous Disease* 17, no. 11 (November): 795–811.

Rothman, David J. 1971. *The Discovery of the Asylum: Social Order and Disorder in the New Republic*. Boston: Little, Brown and Co.

Rush, Benjamin. 1799. "Observations intended to Favour a supposition that the black Color (as it is called) of the Negroes is derived from the LEPROSY. Read at a Special meeting July 14, 1797." *Transactions of the American Philosophical Society* 4 (1799): 289–97.

———. 1947. *The Selected Writings of Benjamin Rush*, ed. Dagobert D. Runes. New York: Philosophical Library.

———. 1948. *The Autobiography of Benjamin Rush, His "Travels Through Life" together with his Commonplace Book for 1789–1791*, ed. George W. Corner. American Philosophical Society. Princeton University Press.

———. 1951. *Letters of Benjamin Rush: Volume II: 1793–1813*, ed. L. H. Butterfield. American Philosophical Society. Princeton University Press.

———. 1969. *The Anti-Slavery Crusade in America*. New York: Arno Press.

Sacks, Karen Brodkin. 1994. "How Did Jews Become White Folks?" In *Race*, ed. Steven Gregory and Roger Sanjek, 75–102. New York: Routledge.

Sample, Herbert A. 2004. "For many blacks, gay fight isn't theirs. Civil rights analogy is widely discounted." *Sacramento Bee*, March 16.

Saul, Stephanie. 2005. "U.S. to Review Heart Drug Intended for One Race." *New York Times*, June 13.

Scallon, Matt. 2006. "Bond set for Gonzales man accused of hate crime in St. Charles Parish," *New Orleans Times-Picayune*, August 22. www.NOLA.com.

Scholinski, Daphne, with Jane Meredith Adams. 1997. *The Last Time I Wore a Dress*. New York: Riverhead Books.

"Schwartzenegger Condemns Attack on Jamul Restaurant." 2006. NBCSanDiego.com (April 24).

Segrest, Mab. 1999. "Race and the Invisible Dyke." In *Dangerous Liaisons: Blacks, Gays, and the Struggle for Equality*, ed. Eric Brandt, 46–56. New York: New Press.

Selden, Steven. 1999. *Inheriting Shame: The Story of Eugenics and Racism in America*. New York: Teachers College Press, Columbia University Press.

Semer, Melinda Ashton. 1998. "Shepard paid high price for his carelessness." *Charlotte Observer*, October 26.

Shepard, Beverly. 1992a. "Restaurant protesters want charges dismissed; Cracker Barrel case awaits ruling." *Atlanta Journal and Constitution*, January 4:B6.

———. 1992b. "Frank joins restaurant protesters in Lithonia." *Atlanta Journal and Constitution*, January 20:B2.

———. 1992c. "'A very big shock.'" *Atlanta Journal and Constitution*, March 29:D7.

Smiley, Tavis. 2004. "Feds to Re-Open Case of 1955 Murder of Emmett Till."
    The Tavis Smiley Show. National Public Radio (May 12). Available
    online at NPR.org.
Smith, Barbara. 1998. *The Truth that Never Hurts: Writings on Race, Gender,
    and Freedom.* New Brunswick, N.J.: Rutgers University Press.
Smith, J. David, and K. Ray Nelson. 1989. *The Sterilization of Carrie Buck.*
    Far Hills, N.J.: New Horizons Press.
Smith, M. G. 1987. "Some problems with minority concepts and a solution."
    Ethnic and Racial Studies 10, no. 4 (October): 341–62.
Smith, Rhonda. 1997. "Civil rights leaders swiftly condemn anti-Gay
    remarks." *Washington Blade,* August 29:1 and 20.
Smith, Samuel Stanhope. 1965 [1880]. *An Essay on the Causes of the Variety
    of Complexion and Figure in the Human Species,* ed. Winthrop D.
    Jordan. Cambridge, Mass.: Harvard University Press.
Smith, Taigi. 2004. "Deadly Deception." *Essence* 35, no. 4 (August): 148–51.
Solomon, Alisa. 1999. "Nothing Special: The Specious Attack on Civil Rights."
    In *Dangerous Liaisons: Blacks, Gays, and the Struggle for Equality,* ed.
    Eric Brandt, 59–69. New York: New Press.
Spillers, Hortense, 1987. "Mama's Baby, Papa's Maybe: An American
    Grammar Book." *Diacritics* 17, no. 2 (Summer): 64–81.
Stengers, Jean, and Anne Van Neck. 2001. *Masturbation: The History of a
    Great Terror.* Trans. Kathryn Hoffmann. New York: Palgrave.
Stepan, Nancy. 1985. "Biological Degeneration: Races and Proper Places." In
    Degeneration: The Dark Side of Progress, ed. J. Edward Chamberlin and
    Sander L. Gilman, 97–120. New York: Columbia University Press.
Stern, Alexandra Minna. 2005. *Eugenic Nation: Faults and Frontiers of Better
    Breeding in Modern America.* Berkeley: University of California Press.
Stocking, George. 1968. *Race, Culture, and Evolution: Essays in the History of
    Anthropology.* New York: Free Press.
Stoddard, Lothrop. 1925. *The Rising Tide of Color Against White World-
    Supremacy.* New York: Charles Scribner's Sons.
Stoler, Ann Laura. 1995. *Race and the Education of Desire: Foucault's* History
    of Sexuality *and the Colonial Order of Things.* Durham, N.C.: Duke
    University Press.
Storr, Merl. 1998. "Transformations: Subjects, Categories and Cures in Krafft-
    Ebing's Sexology." In *Sexology in Culture,* ed. Lucy Bland and Laura
    Doan, 11–25. Chicago: University of Chicago Press.
Takaki, Ronald. 2000. *Iron Cages: Race and Culture in Nineteenth Century
    America.* Rev. ed. New York: Oxford University Press.
Taylor, M. Jane. 1998a. "'Lesbian mom boom' still underway: Most Lesbian
    mothers practice a version of 'planned parenthood.'" *Washington Blade,*
    January 16:5, 10.
———. 1998b. "Lawmakers nix ballot proposal in Maine town." *Washington
    Blade,* September 4:12.
Terman, Lewis, and Catherine Cox Miles. 1936. *Sex and Personality: Studies
    in Masculinity and Femininity.* New York: McGraw Hill.
Terry, Jennifer. 1995. "Anxious Slippages Between 'Us' and 'Them': A Brief
    History of the Scientific Search for Homosexual Bodies." In *Deviant*

Bodies: Critical Perspectives on Difference in Science and Popular Culture, ed. Jennifer Terry and Jacqueline Urla. Bloomington: Indiana University Press.

———. 1999. *An American Obsession: Science, Medicine, and Homosexuality in Modern Society.* Chicago: University of Chicago Press.

Tomes, Nancy J. 1981. "A Generous Confidence: Thomas Story Kirkbride's Philosophy of Asylum Construction and Management." *Madhouses, Mad-Doctors, and Madmen: The Social History of Psychiatry in the Victorian Era,* ed. Andrew Scull. Philadelphia: University of Pennsylvania Press.

Trent, James W., Jr. 1994. *Inventing the Feeble Mind: A History of Mental Retardation in the United States.* Berkeley: University of California Press.

Tucker, William H. 2002. *The Funding of Scientific Racism: Wickliffe Draper and the Pioneer Fund.* Urbana and Chicago: University of Illinois Press.

Turnipseed, Edward. 1877. "Some Facts in Regard to the Anatomical Differences Between the Negro and White Races." *American Journal of Obstetrics and Diseases of Women and Children* 10:32–33.

Urbina, Ian. 2007. "Gay Youths Find Place to Call Home in Specialty Shelters." *New York Times,* May 17.

Vaid, Urvashi. 1995. *Virtual Equality: The Mainstreaming of Gay and Lesbian Liberation.* New York: Anchor Books.

Wagner, Norma. 1991. "Gay activists target Norcross Cracker Barrel." *Atlanta Journal and Constitution,* March 4:D2.

Wailoo, Keith. 2003. "Inventing the Heterozygote: Molecular Biology, Racial Identity, and the Narratives of Sickle Cell Disease, Tay-Sachs, and Cystic Fibrosis." In *Race, Nature, and the Politics of Difference,* ed. Donald S. Moore, Jake Kosek, and Anand Pandian, 235–53. Durham, N.C.: Duke University Press.

Waldrep, Christopher. 2000. "War of Words: The Controversy over the Definition of Lynching, 1899–1940." *Journal of Southern History* 66, no. 1 (February): 75–100.

Ward, Lester F. 1913. "Eugenics, Euthenics, and Eudemics." *American Journal of Sociology* 18, no. 6 (May): 737–54.

Warner, Michael. 1999. *The Trouble with Normal: Sex, Politics, and the Ethics of Queer Life.* New York: Free Press.

Weiss, Andrea, and Greta Schiller. 1988. *Before Stonewall: The Making of a Gay and Lesbian Community.* Tallahassee, Fla.: Naiad Press.

Wells, Ida B. 2002. *On Lynchings.* Amherst, N.Y.: Humanity Books.

West, D. J. 1955. *Homosexuality.* London: Gerald Duckworth and Co.

Wheelwright, Jeff. 2005. "Human, Study Thyself: Genes, Races, and Medicine." *Discover* 26, no. 3 (March): 38–45.

White, Walter. 1969 [1928]. *Rope and Faggot: A Biography of Judge Lynch.* New York: Arno Press.

White, William S. 1950. "Never Condoned Disloyalty, Says Acheson of Hiss Stand." *New York Times* (March 1): 1, 2.

Whiting, P. W. 1925. "Selection, the Only Way of Eugenics." *Birth Control Review* 9, no. 6 (June): 165–67.

Wiegman, Robyn. 2001. "The Anatomy of Lynching." In *A Question of*

Manhood: A Reader in U.S. Black Men's History and Masculinity, Vol. 2: *The 19th Century: From Emancipation to Jim Crow,* ed. Earnestine Jenkins and Darlene Clark Hine, 349–69. Bloomington: Indiana University Press.

Wikler, Daniel, and Norma J. Wikler. 1991. "Turkey Baster Babies: The Demedicalization of Artificial Insemination." *Milbank Quarterly* 69, no. 1:5–40.

Wilchins, Riki. 2004. *Queer Theory, Gender Theory: An Instant Primer.* Los Angeles: Alyson Books.

Williams, Eric. 1944. *Capitalism and Slavery.* New York: Russell and Russell.

Winant, Howard. 2004. *The New Politics of Race: Globalism, Difference, Justice.* Minneapolis: University of Minnesota Press.

Wintz, Cary D., ed. 1996. *African American Political Thought, 1890–1930: Washington, Du Bois, Garvey, and Randolph.* Armonk, N.Y.: M. E. Sharpe.

Wodak, R., and M. Reisigl. 1999. "Discourse and Racism: European Perspectives." *Annual Review of Anthropology* 28:175–99.

Woodside, Moya. 1950. *Sterilization in North Carolina: A Sociological and Psychological Study.* Foreword by Robert Latou Dickinson. Chapel Hill: University of North Carolina Press.

Wright, Kai. 1997. "Activist helps King 'change people's hearts': Lynn Cothren assists Coretta Scott King in fighting for 'unity and inclusion.'" *Washington Blade,* September 19:30.

Wright, William. 2005. *Harvard's Secret Court: The Savage 1920 Purge of Campus Homosexuals.* New York: St. Martin's Press.

Zammito, John H. 2006. "Policing Polygeneticism in Germany, 1775: (Kames,) Kant, and Blumenbach." In *The German Invention of Race,* ed. Sara Eigen and Mark Larrimore, 35–54. Albany: State University of New York Press.

Zangrando, Robert L. 1980. *The NAACP Crusade Against Lynching, 1909–1950.* Philadelphia: Temple University Press.

INDEX

Abnormal, 28–32, 34, 45, 52, 96, 338n19
abortion, 114, 122, 133, 230, 286, 381n5, 391n71
affirmative action, 253, 282, 399n31
Allen, Theodore, 62, 64, 68, 72–75, 343n7
almshouses, 125–128, 167, 209, 212, 351nn40–41, 361n50
American Breeders Association, 205, 208
American Eugenics Society, 209, 238, 247, 249, 377n49, 391n72
American Genetics Association, 208
American Institute for Family Relations, 254, 255, 271
Anglo-Saxon, 64, 119, 122, 137, 138, 144, 145, 150, 164, 194, 198, 199, 201–202, 203, 204, 210, 218, 238, 239, 243, 245, 265, 290, 320, 370n1, 371n6, 390n64, 398n31; and world domination, 144, 164, 199, 286, 287, 326. *See also* Caucasian, Nordic, Saxon, white race, white supremacy
anti-Semitism, 34, 36, 37, 232–233, 243, 379n65. *See also* Jew, Nazi
Anti-Violence Projects, 3, 305–306, 396n12
arrest of development, 96, 113–114, 116, 123, 124, 129, 131, 135, 136, 137, 161, 194
Aryan, 231, 232, 300, 341nn5,6, 371n6, 379n64
atavism, 135, 153, 157, 162, 186, 189, 190, 194

Barr, Martin, 166, 353n53, 360n46, 361n47
Beard, George, 150–151, 154, 177, 182, 183, 184, 356n17, 365n80, 367nn95–96

biology, discipline of, 46, 61, 62, 78, 81, 99–102, 110, 116, 129, 139–140, 199, 202, 297, 347n1, 354n5, 357n25
biopower, 13, 15, 53, 58, 101, 104, 140, 197, 223, 244, 341n48, 394n88
birth control, 210, 227, 251, 260, 283, 373n18, 374n27, 376n45, 381n5, 382n5, 384n28, 391n72
Birthright, 283–284, 383n16, 391n68
bisexuality, 183, 273, 291, 312, 367n99, 368n100, 395n10. *See also* sexual difference
Bloody Sunday, 141–143, 238, 244, 354n3, 400n38
Blumenbach, Johann Friedrich, 66, 112, 117, 349n28
Boise sex scandal, 266, 386n40, 387n49, 389n60
Bond, Julian, 312–313, 330
Bowen v. Gilliard, 311, 314
Boykin, Keith, 280, 337n12, 338n16, 368n100, 386n36, 395n3, 397n26, 399n36
Brown v. Board of Education, 26, 27, 281, 389n63
Buchanan, Patrick, 302–303, 389n64, 392n74, 393n85, 400n37
Buck, Carrie, 213–214, 375nn33,35, 377n50
Buck v. Bell, 213–214
Buffon, Comte de (Georges Louis Leclerc), 66, 88–90, 121, 258–259, 346n35
Byrd, James, 300, 302

Calhoun, John C., 118–121, 148, 350n31
carceral, 55, 161, 194, 224
castration, 241, 267, 268, 275, 279, 360n39, 380nn75,76; female, 268, 360n39, 363n72, 367n92;

LADELLE McWHORTER is the James Thomas Professor of Philosophy and Professor of the Women's, Gender, and Sexualities Studies Program at the University of Richmond. She is author of *Bodies and Pleasures: Foucault and the Politics of Sexual Normalization* (Indiana University Press, 1999).

Milton Keynes UK
Ingram Content Group UK Ltd.
UKHW020945110724
445408UK00005B/201